The Blackwell

# Aesthetics

MW00487960

# —— Blackwell Philosophy Guides ——

Series Editor: Steven M. Cahn, City University of New York Graduate School

Written by an international assembly of distinguished philosophers, the *Blackwell Philosophy Guides* create a groundbreaking student resource – a complete critical survey of the central themes and issues of philosophy today. Focusing and advancing key arguments throughout, each essay incorporates essential background material serving to clarify the history and logic of the relevant topic. Accordingly, these volumes will be a valuable resource for a broad range of students and readers, including professional philosophers.

# The Blackwell Guide to
# Aesthetics

*Edited by*

*Peter Kivy*

350 Main Street, Malden, MA 02148-5020, USA
108 Cowley Road, Oxford OX4 1JF, UK
550 Swanston Street, Carlton, Victoria 3053, Australia

First published 2004 by Blackwell Publishing Ltd

*Library of Congress Cataloging-in-Publication Data*

The Blackwell guide to aesthetics / edited by Peter Kivy.
p.   cm. — (Blackwell philosophy guides)
Includes bibliographical references and index.
ISBN 0-631-22130-1 (alk. paper) — ISBN 0-631-22131-X (pbk.: alk. paper)
1. Aesthetics.   I. Kivy, Peter.   II. Series.

BH39.B556 2004
111′.85—dc21
2003010096

A catalogue record for this title is available from the British Library.

Set in 10 on 13 pt Galliard
by SNP Best-set Typesetter Ltd., Hong Kong

For further information on
Blackwell Publishing, visit our website:
http://www.blackwellpublishing.com

*In this new soil a new growth of aesthetic theory has sprung up; rich in quantity and on the whole high in quality. It is too soon to write the history of this movement, but not too late to contribute to it.*

R. G. Collingwood

# Notes on Contributors

**Philip Alperson** is director of the Temple Society of Fellows in the Humanities and professor of philosophy at Temple University. He is the editor of several books, including *The Philosophy of the Visual Arts* (1992), *What is Music?: An Introduction to the Philosophy of Music* (1994), *Musical Worlds: New Directions in the Philosophy of Music* (1998), and *Diversity and Community: An Interdisciplinary Reader* (2002). He was the editor of the *Journal of Aesthetics and Art Criticism* from 1993 to 2003.

**Noël Carroll** is Monroe C. Beardsley professor of philosophy at the University of Wisconsin–Madison, and a past president of the American Society for Aesthetics. He is widely published in the fields of aesthetics and philosophy of art, as well as in film theory. His latest book is *Beyond Aesthetics*.

**Ted Cohen** is professor of philosophy at the University of Chicago. He is the author of various essays in aesthetics, an essay about his grandfather, one essay on baseball that won a Pushcart Prize, and the book *Jokes*. He is a past president of the American Society for Aesthetics.

**Donald W. Crawford** is professor of philosophy at the University of California, Santa Barbara. He has published articles on the aesthetics of nature and Kant's aesthetics and is the author of *Kant's Aesthetic Theory* (1974). He is a past editor of the *Journal of Aesthetics and Art Criticism*.

**George Dickie** is professor emeritus of philosophy from the University of Illinois, Chicago. He is the author of *Art and Value* (2001), *Introduction to Aesthetics* (1997), *The Century of Taste* (1996), *Evaluating Art* (1988), *The Art Circle* (1984), *Art and the Aesthetic* (1974), and other works in aesthetics.

**Marcia Muelder Eaton** is professor of philosophy at the University of Minnesota. She is the author of several books on aesthetics and the philosophy of art. She has taught and lectured internationally and is a former president of the American Society for Aesthetics.

**Susan Feagin** is editor of the *Journal of Aesthetics and Art Criticism* and research professor of philosophy at Temple University. She is the author of *Reading With Feeling: The Aesthetics of Appreciation* (1996), co-editor (with Patrick Maynard) of *Aesthetics* (1997), and author of numerous articles on interpretation and appreciation, especially in relation to the visual arts and literature.

**Berys Gaut** is a senior lecturer in the Department of Moral Philosophy at the University of St Andrews, Scotland. He has written extensively on aesthetics, philosophy of film, and moral philosophy. He is a co-editor of *The Routledge Companion to Aesthetics* (2001) and of *The Creation of Art* (2003). He is currently completing a book entitled *Art, Emotion, and Ethics*.

**Alan Goldman** is the William R. Kenan, Jr, professor of humanities at the College of William and Mary. He is the author of six books on aesthetics, ethics, and epistemology, including *Aesthetic Value* (1995) and *Practical Rules: When We Need Them and When We Don't* (2002).

**Paul Guyer** is the Florence R. C. Murray professor in the humanities in the Department of Philosophy of the University of Pennsylvania. He has written widely on Kant, the history of philosophy, and the history of aesthetics. His works on Kant's aesthetics include *Kant and the Claims of Taste* (1979, 1997), *Kant and the Experience of Freedom* (1993), a new translation of the *Critique of the Power of Judgment* (2000, with Eric Matthews), and two anthologies, *Essays in Kant's Aesthetics* (1982) and *Kant's Critique of the Power of Judgment: Critical Essays* (2003). He is currently preparing to write a history of modern aesthetics.

**Peter Kivy** is Board of Governors professor of philosophy at Rutgers University and a past president of the American Society for Aesthetics. He has published numerous articles and books in aesthetics and the philosophy of art. His most recent books are *The Possessor and the Possessed: Handel, Mozart, Beethoven, and the Idea of Musical Genius* (2001), *New Essays on Musical Understanding* (2001), and *Introduction to a Philosophy of Music* (2002).

**Peter Lamarque** is professor of philosophy and head of department at the University of York. He has published widely on fictionality, philosophy of literature, and aesthetics, including *Truth, Fiction, and Literature* (1994, with Stein Haugom Olsen) and *Fictional Points of View* (1996). He is editor of the *British Journal of Aesthetics* and was also philosophy subject editor for the 10-volume *Encyclopedia of Language and Linguistics*.

**Joseph Margolis** is Laura Carnell professor of philosophy at Temple University, and a past president of the American Society for Aesthetics. He has written books and articles on virtually every field of philosophy, including substantial contributions to the philosophy of art.

**Mary Mothersill** is professor emeritus at Barnard College and senior scholar at Columbia University. She is the author of *Beauty Restored* (1984) and has written on various topics in philosophical aesthetics and moral psychology.

**Stein Haugom Olsen** is chair professor of humanities and head of the Department of Philosophy at Lingnan University, Hong Kong. He is the author of *The Structure of Literary Understanding* (1978), *The End of Literary Theory* (1987), and (with Peter Lamarque) *Truth, Fiction, and Literature: A Philosophical Perspective* (1994), as well as of a number of articles on literary theory, literary criticism, and aesthetics. He is an elected fellow of the Norwegian Academy of Science and Letters.

**Jenefer Robinson** is professor of philosophy at the University of Cincinnati. She is the author of many essays in aesthetics and emotion theory and the editor of *Music and Meaning* (1997). Her book *Passionate Encounters: How Emotions Function in Literature, Music, and the Other Arts* will be published shortly.

**Francis Sparshott** taught philosophy at the University of Toronto from 1950 to 1991. His general works on aesthetics include *The Structure of Aesthetics* (1963) and *The Theory of the Arts* (1982), and he has written two fat books on the philosophy of dance, *Off the Ground* (1988) on dance generally and *A Measured Pace* (1995) on dance as an art, though he would rather be known as author of eleven slim volumes of poetry.

**Laurent Stern** is professor emeritus of philosophy at Rutgers University in New Brunswick, New Jersey. He has published articles on interpreting and translating, and he is working on a book on these topics.

**Amie L. Thomasson** is associate professor of philosophy at the University of Miami. She is the author of *Fiction and Metaphysics* (1999) and of many articles on metaphysics, philosophy of mind, phenomenology, and philosophy of art. She is currently working on a book entitled *Ordinary Objects* and co-editing (with David W. Smith) a volume of essays on phenomenology and philosophy of mind.

**Nicholas Wolterstorff** is Noah Porter professor emeritus of philosophical theology at Yale University. He has written widely, not only on aesthetics but on epistemology, metaphysics, history of philosophy, and philosophy of religion. In addition to many essays on aesthetics, his two books in the field are *Works and Worlds of Art* (1980) and *Art in Action* (1980). He is a past president of the American Philosophical Association, and has delivered the Gifford Lectures at St Andrews University and the Wilde Lectures at Oxford University.

# Contents

# Introduction: Aesthetics Today

In the second edition of the *Critique of Pure Reason* (1787), Immanuel Kant passed a severe judgment upon the nascent philosophical discipline that his own countrymen had dubbed "aesthetics." He wrote, in part,

> The Germans are the only people who currently make use of the word "aesthetic" in order to signify what others call the critique of taste. This usage originated in the abortive attempt made by [Alexander] Baumgarten, that admirable analytic thinker, to bring the critical treatment of the beautiful under rational principles, and so to raise its rules to the rank of a science. But such endeavours are fruitless. The said rules or criteria are, as regards their chief sources, merely empirical, and consequently can never serve as determinate *a priori* laws by which our judgment of taste must be directed. (Kant 1950: 66n)

The background against which Kant projected this pessimistic verdict on aesthetics as a viable philosophical discipline was two-fold. On the one hand, as the above quotation makes explicit, if obliquely, Kant thought that Baumgarten and the rationalist German tradition in aesthetics had one thing right: if aesthetics was to be a philosophical discipline, it must be free of the empirical. But as Kant saw things in 1787, an a priori critique of taste was impossible, Baumgarten's failed attempt to "rationalize" aesthetics an egregious case in point.

On the other hand, the British tradition, both in aesthetics and in moral theory, inaugurated by Francis Hutcheson, was, Kant thought, on the wrong track entirely, right from the start, much as Kant admired some of its practitioners; for, unlike the German rationalists, it placed the "philosophy" of the beautiful and the good, taste and moral judgment, squarely in the empirical realm of moral and aesthetic "psychology." Which is to say, it was not a failed philosophy, like Baumgarten's, but no philosophy at all. As Kant puts this point, in one of the pre-critical *Reflexionen* (1769–70): "The principle of Hutcheson [that is, the moral sense] is unphilosophical, because it introduces a new feeling as a basis for explanation; secondly, because it sees in the laws of the senses objective grounds" (quoted in Schilpp

1960: 11). And again, in the *Grundlengung*: "Here [moral] philosophy must show its purity as the absolute sustainer of its laws, and not as the herald of those which an implanted sense or who knows what tutelary nature whispers to it . . . These fundamental principles must originate entirely a priori and thereby obtain their commanding authority" (Kant 1959: 43–4). Kant has written here of Hutcheson's moral theory; but it applies, *pari passu*, to his aesthetic theory as well.

The upshot is, then, that as late as 1787, Kant apparently was dismissing the possibility of a philosophy of taste and beauty. It was not susceptible of an a priori critique, as Baumgarten's attempt had shown, and in the hands of Hutcheson and his followers, it did not even attain the status of bad philosophy, although it may have been good psychology, which is all one might hope for as an account of beauty and taste. In short, the greatest philosopher of his age declared philosophical aesthetics to be a non-subject.

In the mid-twentieth century we found ourselves in a position with regard to aesthetics and the philosophy of art not unlike the one these disciplines faced in the wake of Kant's condemnation of 1787. At the end of World War II, logical positivism was still flourishing, and was no friend to the philosophical study of art, beauty, and taste, since aesthetic "judgments" had been relegated by its followers to the category of emotive grunts and groans, much as Hutcheson had relegated them to an internal "sense," a move in which Kant, as we have seen, more or less acquiesced until very late in the day.

Nor was the newly emerging school of linguistic analysis, in its various forms, the savior of aesthetics. To the contrary, if anything, it passed an even harsher judgment on the discipline than did the positivists. For whereas the positivists were more or less content to give it a dismissive shrug in the direction of the "emotive," the language analysts took special pains to exclude aesthetics, not with a whimper but with a bang.

The major source for the linguistic analysts' rejection of aesthetics as a philosophical discipline was a collection of essays which appeared in 1959 with the title *Aesthetics and Language*, edited by William Elton. There had been a spate of such collections, since the end of the war, with "Language" as the second term of a conjunction: *Logic and Language, Ethics and Language,* and so on. So the appearance of a volume with the title *Aesthetics and Language* suggested that linguistic philosophy had a place for the discipline, even though logical positivism had not. Alas, our hopes were dashed; for although there were some very suggestive essays in the collection, the two most influential of them cast a pall over the entire enterprise. The essay by John Passmore (1959), "The Dreariness of Aesthetics," pretty much told all in its title, and discouraged many a prospective aesthetician from even giving the subject a try, or, for that matter, reading Passmore's essay: the title was enough.

In a far more philosophically substantial piece called "Logic and Appreciation," Stuart Hampshire (1959) too pretty much closed the door on aesthetics as a philosophical enterprise. He began with the obviously rhetorical statement, "It seems that there *ought* to be a subject called 'aesthetics,'" obviously suggesting that there *isn't* one, and, appearances to the contrary notwithstanding, *shouldn't* be one, which is to say, there is no subject matter for such a discipline to engage. As Hampshire continued his thought:

> There is moral philosophy – the study of the nature of the problems of conduct – in every library and in every syllabus; there ought to be a philosophical study of Art and Beauty – if there are such problems; and this is the question that comes first. That there are problems of conduct cannot be doubted; . . . one can discuss the nature of these problems and the form of arguments used in the solution of them; and this is moral philosophy. But what is the subject-matter of aesthetics? Whose problems and whose methods of solution? Perhaps there is no subject-matter; this would fully explain the poverty and weakness of the books. (Hampshire 1959: 161)

Of course the placing of aesthetics together with moral theory was a natural and obvious move; it had been a long-standing tradition in the academy to categorize both as two branches of "value theory." But it had the unfortunate and unjustified result of damning aesthetics for not having the credentials of moral theory. Thus Hampshire: "I conclude that everyone needs a morality to make exclusions in conduct; but neither an artist nor a critical spectator unavoidably needs an aesthetic" (1959: 169). One might well ask, in a similar vein, who *needs* a metaphysics, an epistemology, or a philosophy of science. Aesthetics was obviously being chastised for not performing a function that neither it nor other bona fide philosophical practices were ever meant to perform. (If a painter doesn't need a philosophy of art, does a physicist need a philosophy of science?)

It is indeed the case that Hampshire never says, outright, that there cannot be aesthetics or philosophy of art. His conclusion simply is that there cannot be such a thing functioning in the same manner as ethics or moral philosophy. But in presenting no alternative model, for aesthetics and philosophy of art, to the moral or ethical one, and pushing to an extreme the claim that no generalizations about art and the aesthetic are possible, he surely passes an even more negative judgment on it than Passmore's charge of "dreariness." A dreary discipline, after all, is, at least, a *discipline*.

In any event, the parallel between the state of aesthetics as the analytic philosophers saw it in the 1950s, and as Kant saw it in the 1780s, is a close one. For Kant, as for the analysts, aesthetics failed to qualify as a philosophical discipline. And to put it in Kantian terminology, the failure, in both cases, was seen to be the same: aesthetics was not susceptible of a philosophical "critique." What a philosophical critique amounted to was, of course, a very different thing for Kant from what it was for Anglo-American philosophy: a "transcendental" critique for Kant, a "linguistic" or "conceptual" critique for the analysts. But the moral of the story was much the same. Questions concerning art, beauty, taste, and criticism were empirical questions for psychology or anthropology, sociology or art history to deal with: questions of who liked what, and why; and questions for art critics to answer in their own distinctive ways, untainted by philosophy. They were not "conceptually deep."

The parallel does not, however, end here. For, as is well known, Kant radically altered his skeptical view of aesthetics as a philosophical discipline, and published, in 1790, as part of his *Critique of Judgment,* the very transcendental Critique of Aesthetic Judgment that, as late as 1787, he was still maintaining was impossible. And the change in philosophical climate, vis-à-vis aesthetics and philosophy of art, was almost as abrupt, between the time Passmore, Hampshire, et al. passed their skeptical ukase against the disciplines, in the 1950s, and their current philosophical health and vigor. For by 1968, when the late Nelson Goodman's epoch-making book, *Languages of Art,* first appeared, aesthetics and philosophy of art had undergone a sea change that had made them occupations of some of the leading philosophers of the day, of whom Goodman, of course, was one of the most illustrious. And as I write, if there are any branches of philosophy that deserve the epithet "dreary," neither aesthetics nor philosophy of art is one of that number. Both flourish as never before.

The reader of this volume, indeed, should require no further evidence for the philosophical health of aesthetics than the volume itself. For had a series of Guides to Philosophy been contemplated by any publisher in (say) 1959, a guide to aesthetics would not, I am certain, have been part of the project. And today, no such project could be contemplated without one.

But more direct evidence for the health of aesthetics will be discovered by the reader who peruses the essays of which this volume is composed. In them will be found a wide array of topics broached that not only touch on the major issues in aesthetics, but have connections with numerous philosophical concerns, in metaphysics, epistemology, philosophy of mind, philosophy of language, ethics, and a host of other core philosophical areas. It is an additional sign of conceptual health in a philosophical discipline that it makes and sustains such connections, as the present essays do.

## The Essays

The division of this volume into a part on what I have called "The Core Issues" and another on "The Arts and Other Matters" reflects the state of the discipline today. For it has become clear in aesthetics, as in other philosophical disciplines, that although theory and analysis at the highest level of generality and abstractness are still very much a part of the practice, the time is long past when philosophers could do their work in sublime ignorance of the subject matters their philosophies were philosophies *of,* or without the inevitable specialization that that change implies. As Bertrand Russell perceived, early in the twentieth century, "What is feasible [for philosophy] is the understanding of general forms, and the division of traditional problems into a number of separate and less baffling questions. 'Divide and conquer' is the maxim of success here as elsewhere" (Russell 1951: 113).

Of course other editors would have sliced the pie differently from the way this editor has done. And, no doubt, there will be subjects included here that another editor would have excluded in favor of subjects this editor has excluded. Such disagreements are to be expected, and are neither here nor there. What is agreed now, on all hands, is that this division, or one like it, is a fact of philosophical life. "'Divide and conquer' is the maxim of success here as elsewhere."

When a philosophical discipline is flourishing, and at speed, as aesthetics is today, it is natural for it to seek its historical roots. For philosophy lives in its history, although the reasons for this are not altogether clear; and it is no less true for aesthetics than for any other branch of the subject.

It is altogether appropriate, therefore, to begin this volume with an essay on the origins of modern aesthetic theory. And philosophers are in general agreement that these origins lie in early modern philosophy, and, in particular, in the eighteenth century, even though Plato and Aristotle did so much to influence our thinking about what *we*, not they, think of as "the fine arts," or, as Paul O. Kristeller called them, in a seminal essay on the subject, "The Modern System of the Arts" (1992).

It was Kristeller's view, and it has stood up pretty well to scrutiny since he stated it in 1951–2, that the discipline of aesthetics, as we now know it, was made possible and established by the Enlightenment philosophers and critics, who gave it its subject matter by gathering together the arts that we recognize as the fine arts into a group which, they were convinced, belonged together because of a common essence or nature. In the inaugural chapter of this volume, "The Origin of Modern Aesthetics: 1711–35," Paul Guyer by no means departs from Kristeller's general view. But he breaks new ground in his claim that "the central idea to emerge in eighteenth-century aesthetics is that of the freedom of the imagination, and it was the attraction of this idea that provided much of the impetus behind the explosion of aesthetic theory in the period" (p. 16).

But if the eighteenth-century philosophers and critical theorists were the first to gather all of the fine arts, as they knew them, into a "definable" group, then the major question they bequeathed to us is the question of what that definition might be. George Dickie takes up this question, perhaps the dominant one in philosophical aesthetics since the beginning of the twentieth century, in chapter 2. Dickie has been the most prominent defender of what is called the institutional theory of art, according to which what all artworks have in common as their defining "property" is a certain relation to what has come to be known as the artworld. In his chapter, Dickie pushes the definition in the direction of what might be called the "human sciences," and concludes: "There is an intimate cultural connection between 'work of art' and the nature of a work of art that our cultural anthropologists can discover such that that nature can be converted into a definition of 'work of art.' I hope it will be discovered that the definition is my institutional one" (p. 61).

As the eighteenth century bequeathed to us the philosophical task of defining the work of art, so too it bequeathed the task of defining the "aesthetic," which may or may not be co-extensive with the "artistic." (Indeed, the eighteenth century coined the word.) In the third chapter, Marcia Eaton takes on the job of examining the concept of the aesthetic and its relation to the artistic. Of the class of aesthetic objects, and the class of artistic objects, Eaton writes: "They might be equivalent . . . Or they might be totally separate. Or one class might be included in . . . the other. The most common view – and the one I share – is that the last possibility holds: the class of artistic objects is included in the class of aesthetic objects, but the latter class includes more than just artistic objects" (p. 63).

Amie Thomasson takes on, in chapter 4, one of the most vexed and deeply philosophical questions in contemporary aesthetic theory: the ontological status of the various arts. In simple terms, it arises from the commonsensical observation that you can put the *Mona Lisa* in the trunk of your car, but not Beethoven's Fifth Symphony. What sort of "object" then is the musical work; and is the painting the kind of "object" it might seem to be on the face of it, which is to say, a "physical object"? In her ground-breaking essay, Thomasson points out that "the central criterion of success for theories about the ontology of art is their coherence with the ordinary beliefs and practices that determine the kinds of entities works of art are." And she observes that "although different philosophers have tried placing works of art in just about all of the categories laid out by standard metaphysical systems . . . none of these," it has turned out, "fits completely with common-sense beliefs and practices regarding works of art" (p. 88). These considerations push her to the conclusion that "if, rather than trying to make works of art fit the off-the-rack categories of familiar metaphysical systems, one attempts to determine the categories that would really be suitable for works of art as we know them through ordinary beliefs and practices, the payoff may lie not just in a better ontology of art, but in a better metaphysics" (p. 90).

Moving on from the highly abstract questions of ontology to ground more familiar to the ordinary "consumer" of artworks, Alan Goldman, in chapter 5, investigates the question that surely has occurred to anyone who has ever discussed a movie or book or play with another who has experienced the same work of art: can we agree whether it is good or bad; and if so, how? As Goldman says at the outset: "Evaluations of artworks pervade descriptions and discussions of them" (p. 93). That being the case, "It remains to be seen whether different works from different genres affect us in some similar way by these very different means, and whether this similarity, if it exists, constitutes a criterion of evaluation for particular works." The general consensus is negative. But Goldman, defying the consensus, suggests that "there is some initial evidence for a positive answer" (p. 95).

Closely related to the general practice of evaluating works of art is the practice of interpreting them. For, clearly, what value we place on a work is contingent upon what we take the work to be: what it means, if meaning is relevant; and what "makes it tick": how it functions as an aesthetic and artistic object. These are the provinces of artistic interpretation; and the central question for artistic interpretation, in our times, has been the role (or lack thereof) of the artist's intentions. As Laurent Stern puts the point, in chapter 6: "Any disagreement about the artist's unrealized intentions is a disagreement about the artist, and not about his creation. The question arises: is there a disagreement that requires reference to the artist's intentions?" (p. 112). His own conclusion is a modest one: "While I happen to favor the anti-intentionalist side of the debate, . . . the prospect of a continuing debate on these matters is more important than converting opponents to the side where I have been led by what lawyers call the preponderance of the evidence" (pp. 123–4).

There is no question, perhaps, more closely associated with the concepts of evaluation and interpretation in the arts than the question of moral relevance, which is to say, the questions of whether artworks have moral "content," and, if they do, whether that content is relevant to their evaluation: whether, that is, "immoral" content should count against the value of the artwork, morally praiseworthy content in favor of it. Arguing in a more or less "commonsensical" vein, Noël Carroll opts, in chapter 7, for what might be termed a "moderate" stand. He observes that "so much art traffics in moral matters and presents moral viewpoints that when moral considerations are raised with respect to the relevant artworks, nothing seems amiss – at least to the plain reader, viewer, or listener" (p. 127). And although he acknowledges (and examines) some of the formidable philosophical arguments against moral relevance, Carroll reaches the moderate conclusion that "Art and morality have been linked together for so long and in so many ways that it appears commonsensical for plain readers, viewers, and listeners to assume that it is natural – at least some of the time – to . . . suppose that sometimes the moral evaluation of an artwork may be relevant to its aesthetic evaluation" (pp. 146–7).

Finally, no canvass of the concepts surrounding the evaluation of artworks could possibly be thought complete without considering perhaps the most venerable aesthetic concept of them all, the concept of beauty, which is, at the same time, the concept that, since time out of mind, has been thought to characterize the fine arts and to constitute their peculiar value to us. This concept is taken up by Mary Mothersill in chapter 8. Mothersill points out that since the founding of modern aesthetic theory, in the eighteenth century, the term "beautiful" has more or less dropped out of critical discourse, in favor of the technical phrase "aesthetic value." It is her view that this is not a welcome change; that we should, indeed, "go back to the tradition, say that aesthetics explores the concept of beauty, and just wait and see how far such exploration gets you in understanding the arts." For, as she puts it, "Beauty is a distinctive and a timeless concept" (p. 157), as basic to us, in fact, as the concept of truth.

With the issues of evaluation, interpretation, and beauty behind us, it seems reasonable to go on to the closely related question of "taste." For since the eighteenth century, artistic "taste" has not just been an innocent metaphor drawn from the pleasures of the table, but a name for the human faculty that sums up, both in the expert and in the lay person, the ability to understand, value, criticize, and appreciate the fine arts and, in general, the aesthetic dimensions of human life. In chapter 9, Ted Cohen begins with the assumption that "It seems plausible to suppose that . . . the person of better taste prefers A to B, while others do not, and he does this because he is aware of elements of *A* and *B* not recognized by others" (p. 167). And he concludes with a question he thinks "unsuspected but extremely interesting," to wit: "if there is a difference between better and worse taste, why should anyone wish to have better taste?" (p. 170). In responding to this question he comes to the seemingly paradoxical conclusion that "in matters of taste there is a gap between a recognition of 'accurate' taste and the desire to have accurate taste. This somehow sounds wrong, but I think it might well be right" (p. 173).

Part I concludes with a discussion, by Jenefer Robinson, of the relation between the arts and the emotions. A unique and intimate relationship is supposed by most of us to obtain between art and emotion. The supposition is controversial and venerable with age. As Robinson avers, at the beginning of chapter 10: "Beginning with the early treatises on the arts by Plato and Aristotle, thinkers in the western tradition have often commented on the close connection between the arts and the emotions" (p. 174). After carefully and cautiously examining the ins and outs of the supposed connection, Robinson comes to the safe, and (in my view) correct conclusion: "it is appropriate to end this chapter on the emotions in art by reminding you that there is much good art that is really not very interested in the emotions . . . The emotions have been important in art over the centuries, but they are not a sine qua non for artistic achievement" (p. 190).

It seemed to me appropriate to begin part II, which might well have been called "Philosophies of Arts," with a chapter on the philosophy of literature. For even though there has certainly been a drastic decline in the consumption of read and seen literature, in the wake of television and the movies, literature remains "everyone's art" in a way that even television and the movies are not. If you are literate, one way or another you are a consumer of literary fiction. It is ubiquitous. Its philosophy is the oldest philosophy of art we have, as is recognized, tacitly, by Peter Lamarque and Stein Olsen, in chapter 11, which begins with Plato's "famous reference to the ancient quarrel between poetry and philosophy" (p. 195). Plato, as Lamarque and Olsen point out, issued "an invitation to defend literature in terms of its usefulness" (p. 195). But in acquainting us with the many responses to this Platonic invitation that have been proffered, they ask us to remember that, in the last analysis, "Those with knowledge of literature and a feel for the literary seek a special kind of pleasure from the works they read; . . . and a pleasure that is not instrumental or utilitarian but a pleasure in the literary for its own sake" (p. 211).

The visual arts, next to literature, have probably received the most philosophical attention in recent years, in what might well be called the aesthetic renaissance. The major issue has been pictorial representation; and it is that issue that Joseph Margolis takes up in chapter 12. Focusing on the much-discussed question of pictorial "realism," arguably the central question of pictorial perception, Margolis argues that "there is no way to explain the perception *of* a painting without bothering to explain what *kind* of 'thing' a painting is; and there is no way to explain *that* without bothering to explain whether paintings *and* their perception are (or are not) inherently subject to historical (or historicized) change." The latter he characterizes as the "dread question nearly all fashionable philosophies of art wish to evade" (p. 227).

It seems natural to pass on from pictures to "moving pictures" in the philosophies of arts. And it is the order I have followed here, even though Margolis concentrates on pictorial seeing, and Berys Gaut, in chapter 13, concentrates rather on the issue of cinematic narrative, which, not surprisingly, looms large in motion pictures, arguably the most influential fine art of the twentieth century, and principally consumed in its story-telling capacity. This is not to say that pictorial seeing is not a serious problem for the movies, as it has been for still photography, with a long history of speculation. But it is the nature of filmic narrative that has been the central concern in recent years among philosophers of film, and, in particular, the role of the filmic "narrator." In his carefully argued chapter, Gaut comes to "two conclusions. First, there is more reason to believe in implicit narrators in novels than in films; and second, this difference is to be traced to media-specific differences – to the nature of an auditory-visual medium as opposed to a lexical medium" (p. 248).

Perhaps the two most philosophically neglected of the major art forms, during the twentieth century, are music and the dance. The reasons for this neglect are unclear, given how deeply these two artistic practices penetrate our lives, and have done since the earliest emergence of the human animal. But both have now been brought under philosophical scrutiny, and in chapter 14, Philip Alperson surveys some of the recent work in philosophy of music. Focusing principally on music without words, "absolute music," as it came to be called in the nineteenth century, Alperson moves on a trajectory from formalism, the view that such music is to be understood in terms of pure musical structure alone, to what he calls "enhanced formalism," which allows "pure structure" an "expressive" component, to the conclusion that we may have to go beyond *both* to gain a full understanding of the musical experience. As Alperson puts it,

> These considerations suggest a rather more radical estimation of the western fine art tradition of composed music in which modern musical formalism arose. It may be that a robust philosophical understanding of music must set the theoretical understanding of the practice of music in the fine art tradition alongside the plurality of functions that music serves. (p. 272)

As strange as it might sound to the academic philosopher to talk of a "philosophy of dance," there is now such a thing, and we owe the birth or rebirth of this endeavor largely to Francis Sparshott. In chapter 15, Sparshott begins by remarking that "The scandal or paradox of dance aesthetics is that this topic is persistently ignored by students of aesthetics and their journals." It is this very neglect of dance as a subject of philosophical inquiry, in spite of the fact that "dancing is traditionally held to be among the major forms of artistic activity," that he identifies as perhaps the major issue a philosophy of dance must address. As Sparshott puts it, "the reasons for its near absence from the everyday concerns of academic aesthetics remain a central topic for the philosophy of dance itself," and suggests, "it may be that there is something in dance that resists the preferred methods of aesthetics and of philosophy generally. If so," he urges, "the philosophy of art needs to consider what that might be" (p. 276). This is the central theme of Sparshott's discussion.

That the literary genre of tragedy is singled out as the sole artistic genre to be given a separate hearing on these pages should surprise no one, given its venerable age, the fact that it is the art form most discussed by the ancient founders of our subject, and the respect it has always commanded as perhaps the "pinnacle" of "serious" artistic achievement in the West, not least because of its perceived moral import. Furthermore, it raises in particularly acute form an issue that has permeated the philosophy of art since Aristotle. As Susan Feagin says, in chapter 16, "Recurrent themes are the relevance of both pleasure and pain in response to tragedy, and the myriad ways of accounting for the apparently paradoxical pleasures that humans experience in response to what is unpleasant or painful" (p. 291). In a welcome departure from tradition, Feagin chooses to concentrate on works from the contemporary art of cinema rather than such traditional examples as the tragic works of the Greeks, or Shakespeare, or the German tragedians. In response to the claim, by many twentieth-century theorists, that the concept of tragedy was "sufficiently alien to the beliefs and concerns of modern life that attempts to adapt it to them no longer made sense," Feagin has opted to "discuss three twentieth-century American films, two of which," she argues, "have plots that qualify as tragic in the full-blooded Aristotelian sense, and the third of which, a late twentieth-century comedy, demonstrates the relevance of the tragic to contemporary life by showing how one can maintain one's happiness and therein avoid tragedy" (p. 291).

*The Blackwell Guide to Aesthetics* concludes with two chapters on what might seem to the reader, for different reasons, to be peripheral issues: the aesthetics of "nature" and the religious dimensions of art. But both were central to the enterprise throughout most of its early history. And the former is now undergoing a long overdue revival. That the latter too deserves serious consideration I will suggest in my conclusion to this introduction.

Donald Crawford, in chapter 17, concentrates on two crucial questions in the aesthetics of nature and the environment. The first question is, quite simply, "What is it about nature and natural objects that we find aesthetically interesting or pleasing?" – a question that involves, among other things, the subsidiary question, of long standing, of how the aesthetics of nature may be related to the aesthetics of fine art: "Do we find nature beautiful because it resembles art, or is art beautiful because it resembles nature?" (p. 306). But of equal or perhaps greater significance is the question of what precisely the "nature" is that we are supposed to be studying the aesthetic character *of.* As Crawford puts it: "the concept of *pure nature* does not allow for any human alteration of nature, however slight, to occur without the object ceasing to be natural, while *unrestricted nature* countenances any and all such changes. Pure nature is too scarce, and unrestricted nature is too abundant" (p. 318).

Finally, it surely will come as a surprise to most readers, in this secular age, to find an anthology of contemporary aesthetic theory concluding with a chapter on the religious dimensions of art and the aesthetic. But it would be prudent for the secularist to consider what would be left of western art if its religious artworks were subtracted from the sum, and to consider as well the multitude of those for whom the experience of these artworks has been inextricably bound up with their religious content and purpose. The secularist, furthermore, might want to think on the suggestion that the closest he or she is likely to come to the phenomenon of the "religious experience," however it might be construed, is the experience of the great artworks of the canon. As Nicholas Wolterstorff urges, in the concluding chapter of this anthology, "According to the modern grand narrative of art, . . . art in the eighteenth century finally freed itself from service to religion. What strikes anyone who follows out the various tellings of the narrative, however, is how often this liberated art is described in religious terms, and how often religious hopes and expectations are lodged in it." In a word, "veneration has by no means disappeared from our engagement with works of art" (p. 337). If that is so, then the aesthetic secularists, of which I count myself one, have a lot to learn from the religious experience, as described by those who have had it. And if for us secularists art has taken on something like the place of religion in our lives, it is no wonder that artists have become our high priests, and philosophy of art the interpreter of their sometimes dark and impenetrable sayings.

Peter Kivy

# References

Hampshire, Stuart (1959). "Logic and Appreciation." In William Elton (ed.), *Aesthetics and Language*. Oxford: Blackwell: 161–9.

Kant, Immanuel (1950). *Critique of Pure Reason*, trans. Norman Kemp Smith. New York: Humanities Press.

——(1959). *Foundations of the Metaphysics of Morals*, trans. Lewis White Beck. Indianapolis, New York, Kansas City: Bobbs-Merrill.

Kristeller, Paul Oskar (1992). "The Modern System of the Arts: A Study in the History of Aesthetics," Parts I and II. Reprinted in Peter Kivy (ed.), *Essays on the History of Aesthetics*. Rochester: University of Rochester Press: 3–64.

Passmore, J. A. (1959). "The Dreariness of Aesthetics." In William Elton (ed.), *Aesthetics and Language*. Oxford: Blackwell: 36–55.

Russell, Bertrand (1951). "On Scientific Method in Philosophy." In Russell, *Mysticism and Logic and Other Essays*. London: George Allen and Unwin: 97–124.

Schilpp, Paul Arthur (1960). *Kant's Pre-Critical Ethics*. 2nd edn. Evanston: Northwestern University Press.

.

# Part I

# The Core Issues

# Chapter 1

# The Origins of Modern Aesthetics: 1711–35

## *Paul Guyer*

It is well known that aesthetics, as a recognized and customary subject within the academic practice of philosophy, received its name in 1735. In that year, in his dissertation *Meditationes philosophicae de nonnullis ad poema pertinentibus* ("Philosophical considerations of some matters pertaining to the poem"), the 21-year-old Alexander Gottlieb Baumgarten introduced the term to mean "a science of how things are to be known by means of the senses" (*scientiam sensitive quid cognoscendi*) (1735, §§cxv–cxvi). (Four years later, in his *Metaphysica*, Baumgarten would expand this definition to include the "logic of the lower cognitive faculty, the philosophy of the graces and the muses, lower gnoseology, the art of thinking beautifully, the art of the analog of reason"; and another decade later, in his monumental fragment *Aesthetica*, the first treatise to bear the title of the new subject, he would combine his two previous definitions to form his final definition of the subject: "Aesthetics (the theory of the liberal arts, lower gnoseology, the art of thinking beautifully, the art of the analog of reason) is the science of sensitive cognition" (1739, §533; 1750, §1).) It is equally well known that although Baumgarten was the first to name the new subject and perhaps the first German philosophy professor to give it a regular place in his lectures and treatises, he by no means invented the subject itself. Of course, philosophers since antiquity had at least occasionally argued about the nature of beauty and the value of what we now group together as the fine arts, such as literature, visual arts such as painting and sculpture, and music. But around the beginning of the eighteenth century, there began a torrent of writing about the character and value of beauty and other properties, notably the sublime, both in art and in nature itself, a flood to which professional philosophers as well as other men of letters (of course the writers were without exception male) contributed and which has since hardly abated. In particular, the second and third decades of the eighteenth century have a real claim to be the moment of the origin of modern aesthetics. This moment was marked by the appearance in the second decade of the *Characteristics of Men, Manners, Opinions, Times* by Anthony Ashley Cooper, third earl of Shaftesbury, in 1711, of Joseph Addison's eleven essays "On the Pleasures of the Imagination" in the *Spectator* in June and July, 1712, and finally of the 1719 *Critical Reflections on Poetry, Painting and Music* by the abbé Jean-Baptiste Du Bos, a work that went through at least five editions in French in the next two decades and was widely circulated in Britain long before its translation into English in 1748. The moment was marked in the third decade by the first treatise of Francis Hutcheson's *Inquiry into the Original of our Ideas of Beauty and Virtue* in 1725. None of these writers except Hutcheson was a professor of philosophy. But the issues they raised and the positions they took in these books prepared the way for the more professional philosophical work of much of the rest of the century, and beyond, and so modern aesthetics should be conceived of not as if it sprang full-grown from the brow of Baumgarten in 1735, but rather as having developed much of its eventual programs and positions in the years from 1711 to 1735. It is thus this period that will be the focus of the present chapter.

Is there a common idea that marks this foundational epoch of modern aesthetics? Some have argued that it was this period which first saw the invention of the idea that what we now almost unwittingly lump together as the "arts" or the "fine arts," for example the "poetry, painting and music" of Du Bos' title, constitute some sort of system, an assumption that was necessary to supply a subject for the discipline of aesthetics as the philosophy of art (Kristeller 1951). Others have focused on the addition of the idea of the sublime to the traditional idea of beauty,[1] or on the emergence of the idea of artistic genius as a special form of human mentality (Abrams 1953). More recently, it has been argued that it was in the eighteenth-century writings on aesthetics that modern ideas of subjectivity and individuality first came to the fore,[2] while yet others have argued that it was in the aesthetics of this period that the modern practice of ideology, masking the claims of a single class to domination of society behind a sham claim to universal validity, first emerged (Eagleton 1990). But without rejecting any of these claims outright (although I think the last one tells us more about the preoccupations of the late twentieth century than of the eighteenth), I will pursue a different tack. As I see it, the central idea to emerge in eighteenth-century aesthetics is that of the freedom of the imagination, and it was the attraction of this idea that provided much of the impetus behind the explosion of aesthetic theory in the period.

However, the idea of freedom, whether of the imagination or anything else, is notoriously vague and ambiguous. Later in the eighteenth century, Kant was to make famous a distinction between negative and positive conceptions of freedom, that is, a conception of freedom as consisting simply in the absence of determination or control of some specified type as contrasted to a conception of freedom as consisting precisely in the determination or control of action by one specified kind of agent or agency rather than another. Kant introduced this distinction, of course, in his practical philosophy, where he described a negative conception of freedom as the independence of the will from determination by causes alien to the true self, especially determination by merely sensory impulses or inclinations, and the positive conception of freedom as the determination of the will by the legislation of pure reason (Kant 1785: IV, 446). A central theme of Kant's moral philosophy is then that the freedom exercised in and valued by human morality is never simply freedom negatively conceived, but positive freedom, the freedom to conduct ourselves autonomously by a law legislated by pure reason, which is the most distinctive feature of our selves and whose law is thus the purest expression of our own autonomy. But we may also understand Kant's aesthetic theory as dominated by an apparent tension between negative and positive conceptions of freedom of the imagination and the effort to resolve this tension.

In the initial phase of his analysis of what he calls the aesthetic judgment of the beautiful, or more properly the reflective rather than merely sensitive aesthetic judgment, Kant begins with the purported disinterestedness of the judgment of taste, its independence from any merely sensory agreeableness of an object on the one hand and from any recognition of it as good in light of its classification under a determinate concept on the other. This is, of course, a purely negative conception of the nature of aesthetic response and judgment in the straightforward sense that it tells us what it is not, not what it is. Kant goes on to give a more informative characterization of aesthetic response as based on a harmony or free play between the cognitive faculties of imagination and understanding, in which the subjective conditions of cognition are satisfied apart from the satisfaction of what is ordinarily the objective condition of cognition, namely, the subsumption of an object under a determinate concept (for example, the recognition of a three-sided, closed plane figure as a triangle or a four-footed mammal with a certain pattern of dentition as a dog). But this may still be regarded as a negative conception of the freedom of imagination in aesthetic response, for it emphasizes that the imagination satisfies our general objective in all cognition without being determined or constrained by any particular concept – where Kant takes the concept of a concept itself quite broadly, to include representational content and intended purpose as well as classification, as in ordinary concepts like *triangle* or *dog*.

Just as in his moral theory, however, Kant is not content with a negative conception of the freedom of the human will, but argues that human freedom can only be fully understood as the positive expression of a self-legislated law of reason, so in his aesthetic theory he moves from a negative conception of the basis of aesthetic response and pleasure, the free play of imagination and understanding, to one or indeed several positive conceptions of the basis of our pleasure in both natural and artistic beauty – to a conception of art as the expression of aesthetic ideas, and of the experience of beauty itself as a symbol of morality, thus as both the manifestation of the freedom of the imagination and the representation of freedom more broadly understood by means of the works of imagination. And just as the trick in Kant's moral theory is to show that the negative and positive conceptions of freedom are not in fact two competing conceptions of human freedom, but rather two sides of the same coin – for freedom from domination by mere inclination can in fact be achieved only by self-governance in accord with the law of pure reason instead[3] – so the key to Kant's aesthetics is his reconciliation of his negative and positive conceptions of the freedom of the imagination –

his theory that it is precisely in virtue of the freedom of the imagination in aesthetic response from determination by ordinary concepts of the understanding that this response is itself suited to serve as a symbol of morality, because it can thereby represent the freedom that is the essence of morality, yet which is not otherwise made palpable to us in the world of our senses.[4]

Just as in his moral philosophy and for that matter in his critique of pure reason in general Kant found a way to put together what previous philosophers had held apart – Kant's most general argument in philosophy, of course, was that intuition and concept, sensory input and intellectual classification, on which previous thinkers had erected two competing schools of philosophy, could only provide human knowledge when firmly yoked together – so in aesthetics Kant found a way to tie together what for many (although, as we will see, not all) earlier writers had been alternative and competing conceptions of the freedom of the imagination in the experience of art and beauty. At the outset of the eighteenth century, we find thinkers excited by a new sense of the freedom of the imagination, but in many cases torn between competing conceptions of this freedom. On the one hand, we find a conception of aesthetic judgment as disinterested, as independent from any of our other practical and cognitive concerns and instead linked most closely to the sheer perceptual form of objects. It was Shaftesbury who introduced the idea of disinterestedness into aesthetic discourse, but it was not in fact he who introduced a truly negative conception of the nature of aesthetic response; this was left to Francis Hutcheson in the following decade, who borrowed the idea of disinterestedness from Shaftesbury but used it to ground a very different theory from that of his supposed master. On the other hand, we find a conception of the imagination as taking a very positive delight in the symbolization of important ideas, a train of thought epitomized by Addison's claim that we enjoy images of grandeur because the imagination delights in symbols of human freedom. And we find complicated cases like that of Du Bos, whose theory looks as if it begins with a purely negative conception of aesthetic response, as a mere release from tedium and *ennui*, but who transforms that into a positive account of the pleasure that we take in the engagement of our emotions. But, although both Addison and Baumgarten were to anticipate him, not until Kant do we find within professional philosophy a fully achieved synthesis of the negative and positive conceptions of the freedom of the imagination in aesthetic experience, but especially in the experience of art – a synthesis that was to prove quite fragile, and largely came apart again in the nineteenth century, as witnessed by a contrast like that between Schopenhauer's conception of aesthetic contemplation as offering a release from the pain of quotidian existence, on the one hand, and Ruskin's conception of Gothic architecture as an image of the freedom of everyone involved in its production, on another. But that would be a story for another occasion; here, my attention will be confined to the first two decades of modern aesthetics, the period from 1711 to 1719 already mentioned, and the ensuing years from 1725 to 1735, which will bring us to the first works of Hutcheson and Baumgarten. What I will argue is that in this period we find evidence of the competing conceptions of the freedom of the imagination that I have described, which would eventually be reconciled by means of Kant's appropriation of Baumgarten's conception of the character of specifically artistic representation, although Baumgarten himself, while clearly recognizing the complexity of aesthetic objects and our response to them, had not used this recognition to reconcile the two conceptions of the freedom of the imagination developed by his immediate predecessors.

## 1.1   Shaftesbury and Hutcheson

Anthony Ashley Cooper, third earl of Shaftesbury (1677–1713), grandson of the leader of the Whigs in their struggle against the ascension of James II and tutee of John Locke, his grandfather's physician, secretary, and political operative, is widely credited with having introduced disinterestedness as the criterion of aesthetic response and judgment (Stolnitz 1961; Kneller 1998). Shaftesbury did not actually use the terms "interest" or "disinterestedness" in connection with what we now call aesthetic phenomena, but Francis Hutcheson (1694–1746), who invoked the name of Shaftesbury in the preface to his 1725 *Inquiry into the Original of our Ideas of Beauty and Virtue*, did when he wrote:

> The Ideas of Beauty and harmony, like other sensible Ideas, are *necessarily* pleasant to us, as well as immediately so; neither can any Resolution of our own, nor any *Prospect* of Advantage or Disadvantage, vary the Beauty or Deformity of an Object: . . . in the external Sensations, no View of *Interest* will make an Object grateful, nor View of *Detriment*, distinct from immediate *Pain* in the Perception, make it disagreeable to the Sense. (Hutcheson 1725, 1738: sec. I, §xiii, 11)

Hutcheson's statement seems a natural extension of passages in Shaftesbury where the earlier writer argues that our pleasure in something beautiful is distinct and independent from all thoughts of *control* and *use* of the object and of the *possession* on which our ability to control and use an object might depend. Thus, in the dialogue *The Moralists, a Philosophical Rhapsody*, which together with the earlier *Inquiry Concerning Virtue or Merit* constitutes the heart of his *Characteristics*, Shaftesbury's spokesman Theocles argues to his interlocutor Philocles:

> "Imagine then, good Philocles, if being taken with the beauty of the ocean, which you see yonder at a distance, it should come into your head to seek how to command it and, like some mighty admiral, ride master of the seas. Would not the fancy be a little absurd?" . . .

> "Let who will call it theirs," [continued] Theocles, "you will own the enjoyment of this kind to be very different from that which should naturally follow from the contemplation of the ocean's beauty . . .

> But to come nearer home and make the question still more familiar. Suppose, my Philocles, that, viewing such a tract of country as this delicious vale we see beneath

us, you should, for the enjoyment of the prospect, require the property or possession of the land."

"The covetous fancy," replied [Philocles], "would be as absurd altogether as that other ambitious one."

"O Philocles!," said he, "may I bring this yet a little nearer and will you follow me once more? Suppose that, being charmed as you seem to be with the beauty of those trees under whose shade we rest, you should long for nothing so much as to taste some delicious fruit of theirs and, having obtained of nature some certain relish by which these acorns or berries of the wood became as palatable as the figs or peaches of the garden, you should afterwards, as oft as you revisited these groves, seek hence the enjoyment of them by satiating yourself in these new delights."

"The fancy of this kind," replied [Philocles], "would be as sordidly luxurious and as absurd, in my opinion, as either of the former." (Shaftesbury 1711: 318–19)

So Shaftesbury certainly proposes that our pleasure in the beauty of objects, here natural objects or views thereof, is independent of any expectation of the use or consumption of those objects that might in turn be dependent upon the possession of the objects. But it would be a mistake to suppose that he means to restrict himself to a negative characterization of the nature of aesthetic response, let alone to a negative characterization of the free play of the imagination as the foundation of aesthetic response, and thus that he means to separate the sources of aesthetic response from other fundamental forms of human thought and action. On the contrary, he means his insistence upon the independence of aesthetic response from promises of personal use or advantage to associate or even identify our response to beauty with our response to other forms of value, above all with the response to goodness which constitutes the moral sense. Shaftesbury discusses the sense of beauty in order to introduce his account of the moral sense, but his view is not at all what Hutcheson's was to be, namely that there is a sufficient analogy between the sense of beauty and the moral sense to make the evident immediacy and necessity of the former a good argument for the immediacy and necessity of the latter. Shaftesbury's view is rather that our sense of beauty is an instance of the very same sensitivity to the wonderful order of the universe that is also manifested by the moral sense. As Philocles observes, "beauty . . . and good with you, Theocles, I perceive, are still one and the same" (Shaftesbury 1711: 320), or as Theocles says, with Shaftesbury's own italics, "with us, Philocles, it is better settled, since for our parts we have already decreed that *beauty and good are still the same*" (Shaftesbury 1711: 327).

Shaftesbury's introduction of the criterion of disinterestedness, then, is not the beginning of an argument for the freedom of the imagination in aesthetic response from any form of external constraint, but rather the beginning of an elaborate argument for a disinterested pleasure in the order of the cosmos that is manifested in our feeling for both beauty and virtue. The key claims in this argument are, first, that what we love in all forms of beauty and virtue, free from the limits of personal interest, is order and proportion, but, second, that what we really admire in admiring order and proportion is not so much the manifestation of order and proportion in the object in which they are manifested itself, but rather the creative intelligence which is behind them, ultimately the divine intelligence which is behind all order and proportion, even when the immediate manifestation thereof might be produced by a human agent, for the latter is itself nothing but a product of the underlying divine intelligence. The first step of this argument is stated when Shaftesbury locates the object of our sense of the beauty of works of both nature and art in the order and proportion they manifest:

> Nothing surely is more strongly imprinted on our minds or more closely interwoven with our souls than the idea or sense of order and proportion. Hence all the force of numbers and those powerful arts founded on their management and use! What a difference there is between harmony and discord, cadency and convulsion! What a difference between composed and orderly motion and that which is ungoverned and accidental, between the regular and uniform pile of some noble architect and a heap of sand or stones, between an organized body and a mist or cloud driven by the wind!

He makes it explicit that we have an immediate sense for such order, and that it is the same sense that is at work in our appreciation of art and of nature:

> Now, as this difference is immediately perceived by a plain internal sensation, so there is withal in reason this account of it: that whatever things have order, the same have unity of design and concur in one, are parts constituent of one whole or are, in themselves, entire systems. Such is a tree with all its branches, an animal with all its members, an edifice with all its exterior and interior ornaments. What else is even a tune or symphony or any excellent piece of music than a certain system of proportioned sounds? (Shaftesbury 1711: 272–4)

Having in this last passage identified order with design, Shaftesbury then goes on to argue that what we really love in loving order is the designer, the mind or intelligence which we take to be the source of such order:

> [*T*]*he beautiful, the fair, the comely, were never in the matter but in the art and design, never in body itself but in the form or forming power.* Does not the beautiful form confess this and speak the beauty of the design whenever it strikes you? What is it but the design which strikes? What is it you admire but mind or the effect of mind? It is the mind alone which forms. All which is void of mind is horrid, and matter formless is deformity itself. (Shaftesbury 1711: 322)

Shaftesbury does not actually explain why if we are struck by the beauty of a design we must also or even ultimately exclusively love the designer, but perhaps this seems to him a natural and inevitable transition of the mind from effect to cause. In any case, the same assumption that our sense of beauty naturally follows the chain of effects and causes is at work in the concluding flourish of his argument, in which Theocles argues that there are actually "three degrees or orders of beauty," first, the "*dead forms* . . . which bear a fashion and are formed, whether by man or nature, but have no forming power, no action or intelligence"; second, "*the forms which form*, that is, which have intelligence, action and operation"; and finally, "*that third order of beauty, which forms not only such as we call mere forms but even the forms which form.*" Shaftesbury's justification for recognizing this third order of beauty is precisely his assumption that each of the causes of our feelings of beauty, whether proximate or ultimate, is itself an order of beauty, that is, an object of our admiration: "that which fashions even minds themselves contains in itself all the beauties fashioned in those minds and is consequently the principle, source and foundation of beauty." To all these assertions, Philocles, like one of Socrates' inter-locutors, can only respond meekly "It seems so" (Shaftesbury 1711: 323–4).

Shaftesbury's conception of the disinterestedness of our sense of beauty is thus not yet a modern conception of the freedom of imagination in aesthetic response; far from it, it is but a step toward his deeply traditional, neo-Platonic identification of beauty and goodness (with truth thrown in for good measure) (Shaftesbury 1711:, 65). In the hands of Francis Hutcheson, however, Shaftesbury's idea is transformed into a modern conception of aesthetic response as consisting in an immediate gratification in perceptual form that is free of the influence of all other forms of thought and value. Hutcheson thus introduces a clearly negative con-ception of the freedom of the imagination in aesthetic response.

Hutcheson presents himself as a follower of Shaftesbury – indeed, in the first edition of his *Inquiry* the title page stated that in it "The Principles of the late Earl of Shaftsbury [*sic*] are explain'd and defended," although by the fourth edition this statement had disappeared.[5] But his differences with Shaftesbury are as great as his similarities. Whereas Shaftesbury supposed the underlying identity of the beautiful and the good, Hutcheson treated them as fundamentally distinct, although sufficiently alike that the indisputable innateness of a natural sensibility for beauty could serve to introduce the more controversial idea of a moral sense not founded on rational calculations of self-interest:

> In the first Treatise, the Author perhaps in some Instances has gone too far, in sup-posing a greater Agreement of Mankind in their *Sense* of *Beauty*, than Experience will confirm; but all that he is sollicitous about is to show "That there is some *Sense* of *Beauty natural* to Men; that we find as great an Agreement of Men in their Relishes of *Forms* which all agree to be *natural*; and that Pleasure or Pain, Delight or Aver-sion, are *naturally* join'd to their Perceptions." If the Reader be convinc'd of this, it will be no difficult matter to apprehend another *superior Sense, natural* also to Men, determining them to be pleas'd with *Actions, Characters, Affections*. This is the *moral sense*, which makes the Subject of the second Treatise. (Hutcheson 1738: xv–xvi)

The very fact that Hutcheson divides his work into two separate treatises, the first "Concerning BEAUTY, ORDER, HARMONY, DESIGN" and the second

"Concerning MORAL GOOD and EVIL" (Hutcheson 1738: i), already argues for a difference between his view and that of Shaftesbury: the division of the unitary subject of the beautiful and the good into two separate treatises would never have occurred to the earlier writer.

Indeed, Hutcheson proceeds to demonstrate that our response to beauty should be conceived of as a sense in a way that Shaftesbury could not have, by inferring that this response can only be a sense precisely because of its distinction from any form of either cognition or volition. First, he argues that aesthetic response is not a form of cognition: "This superior Power of Perception is justly called *a Sense*, because of its Affinity to the other Senses in this, that the Pleasure is different from any *Knowledge* of Principles, Proportions, Causes, or of the Usefulness of the Object; we are struck at the first with the beauty; nor does the most accurate *Knowledge* increase this Pleasure of Beauty" (1738: 11). Then, in a passage that has already been partially quoted, Hutcheson distinguishes the response to beauty from any form of desire that necessarily determines the will to action:

> And farther, the Ideas of Beauty and Harmony, like other sensible Ideas, are *necessarily* pleasant to us, as well as immediately so; neither can any Resolution of our own, nor any *Prospect* of Advantage or Disadvantage, vary the Beauty or Deformity of an Object: For as in the external Sensations, no View of *Interest* will make an object grateful, nor View of *Detriment* distinct from immediate *Pain* in the Perception, make it disagreeable to the Sense; so propose the whole World as a *Reward*, or threaten the greatest Evil, to make us approve a deform'd Object, or disapprove a beautiful one; Dissimulation may be procur'd by Rewards or Thretnings, or we may in external Conduct abstain from any *Pursuit* of the Beautiful, and pursue the Deform'd; but our *Sentiments* of the Forms, and our *Perceptions*, would continue invariably the same. (1738, 11–12)

Now Hutcheson does not mean by this that aesthetic responses are necessarily without any effect on the will. In fact, he argues much later that since it takes so little to satisfy our basic "external" or material needs, such as our needs for food and shelter, it is actually desires for the sorts of pleasure that can be afforded by such things as "*Architecture, Musick, Gardening, Painting, Dress, Equipage, Furniture*, of which we cannot have the full Enjoyment without *Property*," that "are the *ultimate Motives* of our pursuing the greater Degrees of *Wealth*" (1738: 94–5). Rather, his starting point is simply the idea that our pleasure in beautiful things does not have a necessary and immediate effect on the will, since any effect it might have can be stayed by other considerations of the advantages or detriments of action; and thus the response to beauty cannot be identified with volition any more than it can be identified with cognition, whether of the choice-worthiness of its object or of any other property of it. Hutcheson then infers that our response to beauty should be conceived of as a sense of beauty by means of elimination: once cognition and volition have been excluded, sense is the only locus left for this response. Of course, the sense of beauty is not restricted to any one of the five senses ordinarily recognized, nor does it have any obvious organ, so for these reasons Hutcheson classifies it as an internal rather than external sense. It is not, to be sure, the only member of that class: the moral sense will also be characterized as an internal rather than external sense.

Hutcheson's basic characterization of aesthetic response is thus a negative one: it is classified as a sense on the basis of what it is not. Hutcheson then argues that there are three main kinds of objects for this sense: uniformity amidst variety in perceptual forms, which is the source of "Original or Absolute Beauty" (1738: 16); uniformity amidst variety in conceptual contents, which is the source of the "Beauty of Theorems" (1738: 30); and "Relative or Comparative Beauty," which is "that which is apprehended in any *Object*, commonly considered as an *Imitation* of some Original," and our pleasure in this beauty too "is founded on a *Conformity* or a kind of *Unity* between the Original and the Copy" (1738: 39). However, Hutcheson does not conceive of these three classes of the objects of beauty as providing a more positive characterization of the sense or feeling of beauty itself; rather, he conceives of them as three different causes of the idea of beauty, identified by empirical and inductive arguments – throughout this part of his work, he explicitly appeals to example to establish his theses (1738:, 17, 19, 73). Hutcheson's view is thus that we can say something specific about the objects of the sense of beauty, but the sense or feeling itself remains characterized essentially by what it is not – it is not a form of cognition or volition.

Thus, Hutcheson emphasizes the non-cognitive character of the sense of beauty even as he makes room for the beauty of theorems, stressing that our pleasure in this form of beauty has nothing to do with the true contents of the propositions which make up theorems, but simply "with the most exact Agreement [of] an infinite Multitude of particular Truths" in a theorem (1738: 30). He also makes clear his departure from the neo-Platonism of Shaftesbury in his concluding section "Of the *Importance* of the *internal Senses* in Life, and the *final Causes* of them" (1738: 93). Hutcheson was a pious Christian, most probably more pious than Shaftesbury, but his piety did not take the form of the latter's argument that our feeling of beauty is a direct perception of the overarching order of the universe established by its intelligent author. Instead, Hutcheson argues that it is precisely the distinction between the sense of beauty on the one hand and cognition and volition on the other that grounds a proof of God's benevolence: God did not have to constitute us so as to take an immediate pleasure in uniformity amidst variety, which also turns out to be so important for our effective thought and action, so the very fact that he did so is another proof of the goodness of God:

> And hence we see "how suitable it is to the *sagacious Bounty* which we suppose in the DEITY, to constitute our *internal Senses* in the manner in which they are; by which Pleasure is join'd to the Contemplation of *those Objects* which a finite *Mind* can best imprint and retain the Ideas of with the least Distraction to *those Actions* which are most efficacious, and fruitful in useful Effects; and to *those Theorems* which most inlarge our *Minds*." (1738: 101)

Hutcheson is by no means the secular thinker that Hume would be even a few years later. Nevertheless, the core of his aesthetic theory is secular and modern: the object of aesthetic response is not characterized in theological terms, although the existence of our capacity for aesthetic response can be given a theological explanation.

I have emphasized that Hutcheson characterizes aesthetic response in negative terms, by its contrast with cognition and volition. Does this mean that he has a negative conception of the freedom of the imagination in aesthetic response? This might seem a stretch, for Hutcheson does not make much of the concept of imagination at all. But he does in fact consider two forms of mental activity that Kant would later group together under the rubric of imagination, namely the sensory perception of present objects and the representation of absent objects through imitations of them. And in each case, his characterization of the basis of our pleasure in such objects is, to say the least, minimalist, and might well be taken to imply that a good part of our enjoyment lies in the freedom of our mental activity from external constraints. In the case of original beauty, we enjoy uniformity amidst variety in perceptual form unhampered by any other cognitive or practical concern. In the case of comparative beauty, the beauty of imitations, we enjoy the relation of conformity or correspondence between imitation and original, but do so quite independently of any other content or significance to what is imitated. Indeed, Hutcheson stresses this point in explaining how we can enjoy a beautiful representation of an original that is itself ugly: "it is by Resemblance that the *Similitudes, Metaphors* and *Allegorys* are made *beautiful* whether either the Subject or the Thing compar'd to it have *Beauty* or not" (1738: 41). In enjoying resemblance, the imagination enjoys something of significance to itself alone, independent of any other concern with the content or value of what is represented. In this sense, I think, it is fair to see Hutcheson as introducing a negative conception of the freedom of the imagination.

## 1.2 Du Bos

Jean-Baptiste Du Bos (1670–1742), diplomat and historian as well as critic and aesthetician, produced one of the most widely circulated aesthetic treatises of the eighteenth century: his *Critical Reflections on Poetry, Painting and Music* went through five French editions and was widely circulated in Britain long before Thomas Nugent's 1748 translation. It may seem as if Du Bos employs a merely negative conception of aesthetic experience as any form of escape from *ennui*, whether by watching gladiatorial combat in the coliseum or tragedy in the theater. But in fact he introduces a positive conception of the imagination as a powerful capacity to stir genuine emotions by means of representations, or as he calls them imitations, rather than by beliefs held to be true. Du Bos' conception of aesthetic response is thus diametrically opposed to Hutcheson's: instead of conceiving of our pleasure in beauty as an autonomous or even anomalous response to perceptual form, unrelated to the rest of our cognitive and practical concerns, Du Bos sees the imagination and its paradigmatic objects, artistic imitations, as distinctive means for engaging the same emotions that are relevant throughout the rest of our activities and conduct, although only too rarely aroused in quotidian life, and aroused at too great a cost. Even in cases that would seem good candidates for Hutcheson's formalist treatment, such as beautiful representations of indifferent or ugly objects, Du Bos' strategy is to find a genuine emotion that can be aroused by the engagement of the imagination. His positive conception of the power of the imagination is an important precursor of later romanticism in spite of the antiquarian style and references of his writing.

Du Bos begins his work with the claims that boredom or mental inactivity is one of the most unpleasant of human conditions, and that the arousal of the passions is one of the most effective means to dispel boredom. First, he posits that

> The soul hath its wants no less than the body; and one of the greatest wants of man is to have his mind incessantly occupied. The heaviness which quickly attends the inactivity of the mind, is a situation so very disagreeable to man, that he frequently chuses to expose himself to the most painful exercises, rather than be troubled with it. (1748: I, 5)

Then he states that

> In fact, the hurry and agitation, in which our passions keep us, even in solitude, is of so brisk a nature, that any other situation is languid and heavy, when compared to this motion. Thus we are led by instinct, in pursuit of objects capable of exciting our passions, notwithstanding those objects make impressions on us, which are frequently attended by nights and days of pain and calamity; but man in general would be exposed to greater misery, were he exempt from passions, than the very passions themselves can make him suffer. (1748: I, 9)

Thus all sorts of "frightful spectacles," from public executions and gladiatorial combats to bull-fights, as well as less bloody diversions such as gambling, will draw great crowds eager to escape boredom and lassitude (1748: I, 10, 18–19). But such stimulations come at a high cost in suffering, if not directly to ourselves then to others to whom we can be linked by the natural mechanism of sympathy,[6] and in any case such violent stimulation of our passions is rarely available in ordinary life. So humans have hit upon the use of imitations in art to engage the passions and escape *ennui* without the costs that would otherwise be paid:

> Since the most pleasing sensations that our real passions can afford us, are balanced by so many unhappy hours that succeed our enjoyments, would it not be a noble attempt of art to endeavour to separate the dismal consequences of our passions from the bewitching pleasure we receive in indulging them? Is it not in the power of art to create, as it were, beings of a new nature? Might not art contrive to produce

objects that would excite artificial passions, sufficient to occupy us while we are actually affected by them, and incapable of giving us afterwards any real pain or affliction? (1748: I, 21)

But one must be clear that by calling the passions aroused by works of artistic imitation "artificial" rather than "real," Du Bos does not mean to dissociate these emotions from those induced by executions, bull-fights, gambling, or any of the more customary events of daily life, our successes and failures in love, work, and everything else, or to imply that works of art arouse a distinct kind of feeling – such as a sentiment of beauty – that is unrelated to our other passions. Rather, his meaning is perhaps more clearly expressed in the description of the contents of the chapter that opens with the paragraph just cited: "The principal merit of poems and pictures consists in the imitation of such objects as would have excited real passions. The passions which those imitations give rise to, are only superficial." That is, the impression made by an artistic imitation is of an "inferior force" to that which would be made by the real existence of the object or events depicted,[7] it does not have the same duration as the latter, and it is "quickly therefore effaced, without leaving any permanent vestiges, such as would have been left by the impression of the object itself, which the painter or poet hath imitated" (1748: I, 23) – whether those permanent vestiges be simply unpleasant memories of excessive emotion, or other kinds of damage that might be suffered in the pursuit of passion, such as physical injury or damage to one's fortune at the gaming-table. "The pleasure we feel in contemplating the imitations made by painters and poets, of objects which would have raised in us passions attended with real pain, is a pleasure free from all impurity of mixture. It is never attended with those disagreeable consequences, which arise from the serious emotions caused by the object itself" (1748: I, 24). Yet in spite of these qualifications, which make the emotions aroused by art both more accessible and more tolerable than those aroused by exceptional occurrences in real life, it is crucial to Du Bos' whole argument that these emotions be instances of the real thing, genuine passions of love and hate, fear and joy, which may be experienced without their usual costs. Otherwise, he has no account of how art relieves the tedium of everyday life.

This is evident much later in Du Bos' argument, when he rejects the theory that the effect of the theater depends upon illusion, that is, being induced by the presentation of the play to believe to be true what is actually false. He claims that everything that goes on in the theater "shews itself there in the nature of a copy . . . we have a thousand things continually before our eyes, which remind us constantly of our real circumstances with respect to place and condition," so that not even the most inexperienced theatergoer is deluded into believing that something is really happening which is not (1748: I, 350). Nevertheless, the theatergoer is "touched in almost as lively a manner as he would have been, had he really seen Roderigue at the feet of his mistress after he had killed her father" (1748: I, 351). The pleasure of going to the theater depends precisely upon the fact that there we can experience the very same sorts of emotions we would experience if our own lives were not so humdrum, although without the great costs that we would then have to pay. And this can only happen if the imagination is a powerful alternative to cognition, but one which engages the very same emotions that would be engaged by true belief and lead to real action, not some unrelated sentiment such as a sense of the beauty of uniformity amidst variety.[8] It is in this sense that I claim that Du Bos introduces a positive conception of the imagination and its freedom: on his view, our capacity to respond to imitations – what I am perhaps slightly anachronistically referring to as the imagination – is free from the constraints of ordinary cognition and action but has a power of its own to engage our most fundamental emotions.

Du Bos draws a variety of critical conclusions from his basic conception of the function of art. Precisely because works of art engage our emotions through the imagination, but do so less forcefully than real events would, the artist must seek to make his work as engaging as possible within its natural limits. This is ordinarily done by the choice of maximally engaging subject matter or material for imitation. Thus, masters like Poussin and Rubens "are not satisfied with giving a place in their landskips to the picture of a man going along the high road, or of a woman carrying fruit to market; they commonly present us with figures that think, in order to make us think; they paint men hurried with passions, to the end that ours may be also raised" (1748: I, 45). The strength of the effect of a work of art does not depend upon formal properties, such as the degree of conformity between imitation and what is imitated; it depends upon the emotional force of what is imitated, upon the strength of its effect on the imagination. And even in a case where it might seem as if a formal relation of some sort must be the object of a special sense of beauty, such as in a painting of some emotionally indifferent subject, Du Bos rejects that approach: unlike Hutcheson, he does not explain our admiration of still life by appeal to the conformity of representation and object, but rather by appeal to the skill of the artist that is manifested in such an exercise: "when we contemplate curiously any pictures of this kind, our principal attention is not fixt on the object imitated, but upon the art of the imitator" (1748: I, p 57). This is because the exercise of human skill or artistry is something that can engage our emotions in the way that neither dead hares and copper pots nor a formal relation of resemblance between such things and images of them can.

Since the function of art is to engage our emotions by the presentation of imitations, the different possibilities for imitation that different media and genres within them afford dictate what sorts of subjects and means of representing them will best attain that end. This is the subject to which Du Bos devotes the greatest part of his book, and here too his work looks toward the future. Much of the book is devoted to a contrast between the representational potentials of painting and poetry and the emotional effects of these differences, the underlying principle of which is that "The subject of imitation ought not only be interesting of its own nature, but moreover should be adapted to painting, if intended for the pencil; and proper for poetry, if designed for verse" (1748: I, 69). Du Bos observes that "A poet can tell us several things, which a painter would find impossible to exhibit," because the latter can only present those emotions which are "particularly marked in our attitude, or precisely characterised in our countenance"; painting must therefore aim to engage just those sorts of emotions in the observer, while poetry can aim to arouse others. Further, anticipating at least part of the famous argument of Lessing's *Laocoön* by nearly half a century, Du Bos observes that because the poet can depict the evolution of an action over a period of time or a succession of actions, "he may use several strokes to express the passion and sentiment of one of his personages," and thereby to engage ours (1748: I, 75), whereas the medium of the painter confines him to the representation of a single moment of action, and therefore he "can only make use of a single touch in the expressing of a passion on each feature of the countenance, where he intends to make this passion appear," and likewise must engage the passion of the observer by means of this single touch (1748: I, 76).

Du Bos even goes so far as to extend his theory of the engagement of the passions by means of imitation to music (1748: I, ch. XLV, 360–75). He does not reject purely instrumental music in favor of vocal music on the ground that only the latter but not the former can represent human passions; instead, he argues that non-verbal music or the non-verbal aspects of music imitate the inarticulate expressions of human emotion rather than the verbal expressions of human emotion; but in both cases, whether it imitates natural signs or artificial signs, music works by engaging the imagination and arousing the represented passions in its audience.

The limits of this theory may become obvious in its application to music, which cries out for a synthesis of Hutcheson's theory of a special sense of pleasure triggered by formal relationships with Du Bos' theory of the pleasure in the arousal of our passions. A sophisticated version of such a synthesis of that sort would have to wait for Kant's work at the end of the century. But at least an adumbration of such a more complicated theory had already been suggested several years before the publication of Du Bos' treatise by Joseph Addison's popular essays on the multiple "Pleasures of the Imagination," at the very start of modern aesthetics.

## 1.3 Addison

Addison explicitly employs the concept of imagination and argues that the exercise of the imagination affords us multiple possibilities for pleasure. The different kinds of pleasure afforded to us by the imagination include both those that are unique and independent from the rest of our cognitive and affective economy and those that are intimately connected with our deepest interests in knowledge and action. Further, the pleasures of the imagination include both those that depend chiefly upon freedom from constraint from anything outside the imagination and those that are produced by images of our freedom in areas outside of the imagination itself, presumably our freedom of action in moral and political arenas. We may consider these as freedoms of the imagination in negative and positive senses. In his complex conception of the pleasures of the imagination, Addison thus puts together negative and positive conceptions of the freedom of the imagination in a way that will not be done within more professional philosophy until Kant's synthesis at the end of the century.

Early in the series of eleven papers "On the Pleasures of the Imagination" that Addison published in the *Spectator* from Saturday, June 21, to Thursday, July 3, 1712, he observes, in words very similar to those published by Shaftesbury a year earlier, that the imagination can afford us pleasure independent of the possession and therefore the use of an object:

> A man of a polite imagination is led into a great many pleasures that the vulgar are not capable of receiving. He can converse with a picture, and find an agreeable companion in a statue. He meets with a secret refreshment in a description, and often feels a greater satisfaction in the prospect of fields and meadows, than another does in the possession. It gives him, indeed, a kind of property in every thing he sees, and makes the most rude uncultivated parts of nature administer to his pleasures. (*Spectator*, 411; in Chalmers 1869: VI, 123–4)

Addison's claim that a view of a landscape can give a properly sensitive person a pleasure independent of and greater than any to be derived from the possession of it can be counted as another early appeal to the idea of disinterestedness, but, as is also the case with Shaftesbury, the kind of disinterestedness he has in mind is not supposed to entail the independence of the pleasures of the imagination from all other sources of pleasure in our lives. If anything, what Addison has in mind is that the imagination is a power that can amplify other sources of pleasure in our lives, affording us pleasure without the costs of possession and other costs of ordinary experience. To this extent, his view is also similar to that of Du Bos.

Addison clearly takes himself to be breaking new ground in his account of the imagination, and thus pauses "to fix and determine the notion" of the fancy and imagination before setting out his theory. By pleasures of the imagination, he states, he means "only such pleasures as arise originally from sight," and these are of two kinds: "primary pleasures of the imagination, which entirely proceed from such objects as are before our eyes"; and "secondary pleasures of the imagination, which flow from the ideas of visible objects, when the objects are not actually before the eyes, but are called up into our memories, or formed into agreeable visions of things that are either absent or fictitious" (*Spectator*, 411(6): 122–3). The pleasures of the imagination are thus those that we take in the visual appearance of things and in ideas of visual appearances conveyed by non-visual media. In the account of the pleasures afforded to us by various arts that Addison goes on to provide, he includes primarily visual media such as painting, sculpture, architecture, and landscape gardening, and all forms of literature, which he conceives of as employing verbal means to call up visual imagery. He does not include music in his account of the arts, although presumably he could have given an associationist account of music, as Du Bos was to do a few years later.

Before discussing the pleasures afforded by the different arts, Addison divides the primary pleasures of the imagination into three fundamental kinds – a division that would remain influential for decades to come. The three main primary pleasures of the imagination are those in grandeur, novelty, and beauty. I will discuss these in the opposite order from that in which they are discussed by Addison. Pleasure in beauty can come first, because in at least one of its forms, it seems to be the most autonomous of the pleasures of the imagination, that is, that form which is least connected to any of our other cognitive or conative interests. This is the beauty "which immediately diffuses a secret satisfaction and complacency through the imagination, and gives a finishing to any thing that is great or uncommon . . . modifications of matter, which the mind, without any previous consideration, pronounces, at first sight, beautiful" (*Spectator*, 412(6): 129). Addison illustrates this sort of beauty with the example of a male bird who may be "determined in his courtship by the single grain or tincture of a feather," which might seem to suggest that the origin of pleasure in this sort of beauty lies in the gratification of sexual desire – a common enough theory of beauty, to be sure (cf. Burke 1759: part III, secs xiii–xv). But he does not mean to derive the sense of beauty from the sexual drive. Rather, his view is that in its most fundamental form, our pleasure in beauty is simply an autonomous response to properties discerned by vision, no doubt in principle explicable by something in our individual or generic physiology, which is independent of any other drive or interest that we might have, although it can affect the direction of our choice and action due to other drives and interests. On this account, the male bird's interest in finding a female partner would not be due to the phenomenon of beauty, although his choice of a particular partner might be affected by his individual or avian conception of beauty.

Addison recognizes a "second kind of beauty that we find in the several products of art and nature," which "consists either in the gayety or variety of colors, in the symmetry and proportion of parts, in the arrangement and disposition of bodies, or in a just mixture and concurrence of all together." Without any argument, Addison claims that this sort of beauty "does not work in the imagination with that warmth and violence as the beauty that appears in our proper species," but he goes on to suggest that the paradigmatic cases of beauty in both nature and art are of this form, and also, in passing, to illustrate his associationist conception of the beauty of verbal rather than visual media:

> We nowhere meet with a more glorious or pleasing show in nature, than what appears in the heavens at the rising or the setting of the sun, which is wholly made up of those different stains of light that show themselves in clouds of a different situation. For this reason we find the poets, who are always addressing themselves to the imagination, borrowing more of their epithets from colors than from any other topic. (*Spectator*, 412(6): 130)

On Addison's theory of the primarily visual nature of beauty, all of the poets' "epithets" must ultimately be "borrowed." The main point to note here, however, is that on Addison's account this kind of beauty, which may be secondary in some order of explanation but seems primary at least in its importance in the arts, is, like Hutcheson's account of beauty due to uniformity amidst variety, similar to but not dependent on a principle of cognition. The perception of beauty is not a form of cognition, although what it responds to, symmetry and proportion, arrangement and disposition, may also be important in cognition. Whether in its simpler or more complex form, the perception of beauty is an autonomous power of the imagination.

The next pleasure of the imagination that Addison recognizes is the pleasure in novelty. Here he says that "Every thing that is new or uncommon raises a pleasure in the imagination, because it fills the soul with an agreeable surprise, gratifies its curiosity, and gives it an idea of which before it was not possessed" (*Spectator*, 412(6): 127). These could seem like positive characterizations, but much of what Addison goes on to say suggests a negative account of our pleasure in novelty, an account which, like that of Du Bos, stresses our need for relief from boredom:

> We are, indeed, so often conversant with one set of objects, and tired out with so many repeated shows of the same things, that whatever is new or uncommon contributes a little to vary human life, and to divert our minds, for a while, with the strangeness of its appearances. It serves us for a kind of refreshment, and takes off from that satiety we are apt to complain of, in our usual and ordinary entertainments. (*Spectator*, 412(6): 127–8)

The sources of our boredom or exhaustion may come from elsewhere in our lives – "our usual and ordinary entertainments" may include a great deal – but works of the imagination have a distinctive power to relieve us from those ills that arise elsewhere, a power that is not dependent upon other interests but is unique to the imagination. But it does not seem to matter much for this purpose what the form and content of the works of the imagination are, as long as they are new. This power of the imagination works by contrast, and seems neither to require nor to generate any unique or characteristic sort of form or content – this is what I mean by calling this a negative conception of the imagination or its freedom. It is a conception of the imagination simply as free from the constraints of our usual and ordinary entertainments, or of the imagination as our ability to free ourselves from those entertainments.

But Addison also recognizes a third primary pleasure of the imagination, its pleasure in greatness or grandeur. This is, of course, what would become one of the twin pillars of almost all later eighteenth-century theories under the name of the sublime. Addison really has two accounts of our pleasure in the great or sublime. In his first treatment of it, he names the usual suspects – "prospects of an open champaign country, a vast uncultivated desert, of huge heaps of mountains, high rocks and precipices, or a wide expanse of waters" – and explains our pleasure in such vistas by saying that "We are flung into a pleasing astonishment at such unbounded views" because "The mind of man naturally hates everything that looks like a restraint upon it, and is apt to fancy itself under a sort of confinement, when the sight is pent up in a narrow compass" (*Spectator*, 412(6): 126–7). This could look, again, like a negative account of the freedom of the imagination: we hate constraint as much as we hate boredom (perhaps boredom is just constraint by the familiar), so we love anything that liberates us from constraint. But as Addison continues, his account takes a subtle turn: he says that a spacious horizon is an image of liberty, where the eye has room to range abroad, to expatiate at large on the immensity of its views, and to lose itself amidst the variety of objects that offer themselves to its observation. Such wide and undetermined prospects are as pleasing to the fancy, as the speculations of eternity or infinitude are to the understanding (*Spectator*, 412(6): 127).

Addison compares the imagination in the experience of the sublime to a kind of understanding or cognition, without reducing the former to the latter. So what he seems to have in mind is that we enjoy a certain sensuous – or we might say symbolic – representation of an idea that is important to us, the idea of freedom itself. Here the imagination is not just a negative capacity to free ourselves from constraint, but a positive capacity to represent the fact or possibility of our freedom itself. In the experience of grandeur or the sublime, the imagination and its works finally acquire a special content of their own.

Addison at least tacitly recognizes a second form of pleasure in greatness ten essays later, when he writes that

> Nothing is more pleasant to the fancy than to enlarge itself by degrees, in its contemplation of the various proportions which its several objects bear to each other, when it compares the body of man to the bulk of the whole earth, the earth to the circle it describes around the sun, that circle to the sphere of the fixed stars,

and so on (*Spectator*, 420(6): 171). Now as he continues in this vein, Addison begins to speak of "the proper limits, as well as the defectiveness of the imagination," and he notes that "The understanding, indeed, opens an infinite space on every side of us," although "the imagination, after a few faint efforts, is immediately at a stand"; "our reason can pursue a particle of matter through an infinite variety of divisions; but the fancy soon looses sight of it" (*Spectator*, 420(6): 172). Yet he does not say that the imagination is frustrated by its limits in comparison to the understanding or reason, or that we are pained rather than pleased by this discovery of its limits. Instead, he continues to treat the fancy of immensity as the source of a pleasure of the imagination. Perhaps his idea here is that this exercise of the imagination is pleasing to us precisely because it launches us upon a path that needs to be completed by understanding or reason, but that we might not start upon at all were it not for the power of the imagination. In this case, then, the imagination does not please us entirely independently of our other cognitive faculties, but it plays a unique role in engaging those other capacities.

In both of these forms of the pleasure of the imagination in greatness, that where it enjoys an image of freedom and that where it starts us on the path to speculation about infinitude – which it is hard to read except as an anticipation of Kant's later distinction between the dynamical and mathematical sublime – Addison pictures the imagination as working in conjunction with rather than complete independence from our other faculties, but as playing a distinctive role in such co-operations, and as it were doubling our pleasure by means of them. This is also true in his account of the secondary pleasures of the imagination. "This secondary pleasure of the imagination proceeds from that action of the mind which compares the ideas arising from the original objects with the ideas we receive from the statue, picture, description, or sound, that represents them." Again, Addison does not reduce this pleasure in representation or imitation to a straightforward satisfaction in cognition, but regards it as an independent effect of the autonomous imagination: "It is impossible for us to give the necessary reason why this operation of the mind is attended with so much pleasure . . . but we find a great variety of entertainments derived from this single principle" (*Spectator*, 416(6): 151). At the same time, Addison clearly envisages this principle of pleasure as working in tandem with the primary pleasures of the imagination to produce complex responses to objects and intensified pleasure in them, responses in which figure both our primary pleasures in what is depicted or imagined and our secondary pleasure in its depiction or image. Thus, in comparing Homer, Virgil, and Ovid, Addison states that "The first strikes the imagination wonderfully with what is great, the second with what is beautiful, and the last with what is strange" (*Spectator*, 417(6): 156–7): each combines the secondary pleasure of the imagination generated by his skill at depiction with a different primary pleasure in what is depicted.

The same combinatory principle is also at work in Addison's treatment of the relations between nature and art. He describes at least one dimension in which each of these affords greater pleasure than the other. Thus,

> If we consider works of nature and art as they are qualified to entertain the imagination, we shall find the last very defective, in comparison with the former; for though they may sometimes appear as beautiful or strange, they can have nothing in them of that vastness or immensity which afford so great an entertainment to the mind of the beholder. The one may be as polite and delicate as the other, but can never show herself so august and magnificent in the design. There is something more bold and masterly in the rough, careless strokes of nature, than in the nice touches and embellishments of art.

This might seem to say just that nature is more sublime than art, but as Addison continues it appears that his point is rather that the immensity and variety of nature mean that it exceeds art as a source for all the primary pleasures of the imagination:

> The beauties of the most stately garden or palace lie in a narrow compass, the imagination immediately runs them over, and requires something else to gratify her; but in the wide fields of nature, the sight wanders up and down without confinement,

and is fed with an infinite variety of images, without any certain stint or number. (*Spectator*, 414(6): 138–9)

However, because of the imagination's ability to combine images in ways never found in nature, at least certain kinds of art, the fantastic or what Addison cites John Dryden as calling the "fairy way of writing" (*Spectator*, 419(6): 165), afford possibilities of pleasure not found in nature.

> Thus we see how many ways poetry addresses itself to the imagination, for it has not only the whole circle of nature for its province, but makes new worlds of its own, shows us persons who are not to be found in being, and represents even the faculties of the soul, with her several virtues and vices, in a sensible shape and character. (*Spectator*, 419(6): 168)

Thus art outstrips nature at least in its potential for the pleasure of the imagination in novelty. Finally, however, Addison observes that there is the greatest potential for pleasure when the special strengths of both nature and art are fully exploited:

> But though there are several of those wild scenes that are more delightful than any artificial shows, yet we find the works of nature still more pleasant, the more they resemble those of art; for, in this case, our pleasure rises from a double principle; from the agreeableness of the objects to the eye, and from their similitude to other objects. We are pleased as well with comparing their beauties, as with surveying them, and can represent them to our minds, either as copies or originals. (*Spectator*, 414(6): 139–40)

In observing nature as well as in creating and responding to art, the primary and secondary pleasures of the imagination can be combined.

What more professional philosophers of the same and succeeding decades held apart, Addison the popular essayist put together. He offered a complex picture of the imagination, as a capacity of mind to take pleasure in both the matter and form of objects directly present to the senses and in both the form and content of images of objects not immediately present. The imagination is also characterized as enjoying freedom from constraint whether by nature outside us or other interests within us, but at the same time as a positive power to create and enjoy images of our own liberty. It would take most of the rest of the eighteenth century before a professional philosopher, namely Kant, could achieve a synthesis as complex as that which Addison here achieved so gracefully.

## 1.4 Baumgarten

What Kant would need in order to reconstruct in his more technical terms the synthesis that Addison had achieved in his popular essays eighty years earlier would be an account of the imagination that allows it to take on symbolic and ideational content while preserving the freedom of its play with the understanding, its defining avoidance of constraint by determinate concepts. This idea was supplied by Alexander Gottlieb Baumgarten (1714–62), who in his *Philosophical Meditations* of 1735, *Metaphysics* of 1739, and *Aesthetics* of 1750 did not merely coin the term "aesthetics," but also provided a conception of the imagination as a cognitive capacity, whose products, moreover, are marked by the richness and density of their contents rather than by logical criteria such as economy and simplicity. It is tempting to use Kant's later language to characterize Baumgarten's distinction between logical and aesthetic representation, contrasting them as determinate and indeterminate, but one has to be careful here: Baumgarten's idea is actually that in order to achieve the determinacy in conception that is the ultimate desideratum of logical thought, concepts have to be kept spare and general, which means that they will apply to indeterminately many individuals; while to achieve the representation of a determinate individual that is the aim of aesthetic thought, the replete determinacy of the object can only be captured by an image that is rich, dense, and, in a sense, indeterminate. This is the origin of Kant's notion of an aesthetic idea, that is, a product of the imagination which has genuine cognitive content, paradigmatically representing an idea of reason otherwise incapable of direct sensory presentation, but which is at the same time so rich and indeterminate that it preserves our sense of the freedom of the imagination from constraint by the understanding.

Baumgarten initially introduces his idea in characterizing a poem as a "sensorily perfect form of discourse."[9] Sensory perfection consists in representing the maximal number of attributes of an object that is compatible with clearly representing that object as distinct from others at all. Thus, "The more the things are determined, the more do the representations of them comprehend; the more that is heaped up in a confused representation, the more is it extensively clear, and the more poetic is it. Thus it is *poetic to determine as much as possible about the things that are to be represented in a poem*" (1735: §xviii). But achieving a maximally determinate or concrete representation of things is not, contrary to what it might seem, a purely cognitive aim. Rather, Baumgarten's view is that it is the ultimate aim of poetry to arouse affects – here he stands in the tradition of Du Bos – while affects are more richly aroused by richer representations of affecting things. Thus he writes that "Since affects are notable degrees of displeasure and pleasure, their sensations are those that confusedly represent something as good and bad; thus they determine poetic representations; hence it is *poetic to arouse affects*" (1735: §xxv). And then he draws the conclusion that "*Stronger sensations* are clearer, hence *more poetic* than those that are less clear and *powerless*... Hence it is *more poetic to arouse stronger affects rather than less forceful ones*" (1735: §xxvii). Baumgarten's idea is thus that poetry aims to stir the emotions, a conative rather than cognitive objective, but does so through a distinctive form of cognition, the rich, dense, and "confused" imagery of the imagination rather than the spare, general, and "distinct" concepts of science.

Four years after his dissertation on poetry, the 25-year-old Baumgarten published the first edition of his *Metaphysics*, which Kant would still use as his classroom textbook half a century later. Most of this work, of course, does not concern the new discipline of aesthetics, but Baumgarten does touch upon his aesthetic theory in the chapter on psychology.[10] Here he generalizes what he had earlier said about poetry into a general theory of the perfection of sensory representation. He argues that there are two main kinds of representation, intellectual and sensory, and that the perfection or ultimate aim of representation, namely clarity, takes on a different form in each. He holds that the primary virtue of clear intellectual representations is the clarity of their component "marks" – characters or predicates – and that such clarity contributes to the "intensive" clarity of the representation, while the primary virtue of sensory representations is clarity through the number of marks, or "extensive" clarity. He then argues that extensive clarity produces liveliness: "The extensively more clear representation is lively." This is the special feature of aesthetic representations or works of the imagination: "The liveliness of representations and of speech is brilliance (splendor), its opposite is dryness (thinking and speaking in a hair-splitting manner). Both kinds of clarity signify comprehensibility. Hence comprehensibility is either lively or suitable for the understanding or both together" (1739: §531). This passage is interesting because it shows that Baumgarten, first, distinguished imagination and ordinary cognition within a generally cognitive framework; second, marked the exercise of imagination by its effect on the affects, thus breaking down any simplistic barrier between cognitive and conative analyses of aesthetic response; and, third, held that even within the response to a single work multiple kinds of cognition, a fortiori both cognitive and conative effects, could be involved. Like the more popular writer Addison,[11] Baumgarten avoided a reductionist account of the pleasures of the imagination, and undoubtedly provided a model for Kant in this regard.

Finally, Baumgarten returned to aesthetics in the first volume of his *magnum opus* under that title, published in 1750.[12] I cannot describe here the ambitious plan for this work or the wide range of topics covered even in the fragment that was completed, but will confine my commentary to the key point that would later enable Kant to complete his aesthetic synthesis. Baumgarten sums up the conception of the density of the aesthetic object developed in his earlier works by stating that

> The perfection of every kind of cognition grows from the richness, the magnitude, the truth, the clarity and certainty, and the liveliness of cognition, insofar as these harmonize within a single representation and with each other, e.g., richness and magnitude with clarity, truth and clarity with certainty, all of the rest with liveliness . . . ; when all of these perfections of cognition appear together in sensory appearance, they yield universal beauty. (1750: §22)

Here Baumgarten does not use his earlier term "confused," with its potentially negative connotations; he simply stresses that when a representation accessible to the senses is sufficiently rich and complex while still being clearly apprehensible, we have the foundations for beauty.

In the *Aesthetics*, Baumgarten also stresses that there are three dimensions of complexity in a beautiful sensory representation – the three dimensions that were to found the division of the whole work into a "heuristic," a "methodology," and a "semiotic" (1750: §13). According to Baumgarten, the "general beauty of sensory cognitions" consists, first, in "the harmony of the thoughts, insofar as we abstract from their order and their means of expression, that is, the consensus of the thoughts among themselves into a unity that presents itself in appearance, the beauty of the things and thoughts" (1750: §18); second, "since no perfection is conceivable without order, in the harmony of the order and the sequence in which we consider the beautifully conceived of things, in the internal consensus of the order with itself and in its consensus with the things" (1750: §19); and finally, "since the signified cannot be grasped without signs, in the consensus of the means of expression among themselves as well as with the order and with the things, insofar as they appear" (1750: §20). In other words, the beauty of an aesthetic representation or work of the imagination lies in the richness of the objects represented, in both the syntax and the semantics of the representation (that is, the coherence of the complex representation both with itself and with the things represented), and with the richness of the other dimensions of the representation, such as its diction and style (*dictio et elocutio*) (1750: §20). At this point, it cannot fail to escape notice that Baumgarten's aesthetics is based on and most clearly applicable to literary works, and that it is by no means obvious how well either purely visual media or other non-verbal arts such as music would fit his account. This might well be thought to be true of Kant's fully developed conception of fine art in the later sections of the *Critique of the Aesthetic Power of Judgment* as well.

Finally, Baumgarten makes explicit the fundamental implication of his account: "The beauty of sensitive cognition and the elegance of its objects are composite perfections" (*perfectiones compositae*) (1750: §24). Far from attempting to reduce beauty to a single dimension, whether perceptual form or significant content, he insists that successful works of art – the elegant objects of perfected sensory cognition – are always complex, pleasing us by means of their form, content, and material or means of expression. By this last category, he clearly has in mind verbal means of expression, where style and diction can add to the interest and coherence of the thoughts expressed; but the category could also be taken to apply to many other media where the materials of the object can add to its other beauties, as does the choice of materials in architecture, the handling of paint in painting, or instrumentation in music.

## 1.5   A Glimpse Ahead: Kant

This is hardly the place for a detailed discussion of Kant's conceptions of aesthetic judgment and fine art, although this history of the first decades of modern aesthetics has obviously been written with an eye to Kant. But a closing comment on Kant is necessary, for I have stressed that writers like Hutcheson and Du Bos separately anticipated several of the ideas that Kant was to put together, and that writers like Addison and Baumgarten anticipated the complexity of Kant's synthesis of these ideas, all of which may seem surprising given the common caricature of Kant's purported reduction of aesthetic response, whether in the case of works of nature or works of art, to perceptual form apart from all content and significance. Of course, as caricatures usually do, this one has a basis in reality: there can be no denying that in his initial analysis of aesthetic response and judgment, that is, in the "Analytic of the Beautiful," Kant characterizes paradigmatic cases of pure aesthetic response and judgment as responses to and judgments of perceptual form alone. A "pure judgment of taste" is one "on which charm and emotion have no influence . . . which thus has for its determining ground merely the purposiveness of the form" (1790: §13, 5:223). Thus, "Flowers, free designs, lines aimlessly intertwined in each other under the name of foliage, signify nothing, do not depend on any determinate concept, and yet please" (1790: §4, 5:207); "designs *à la grecque*, foliage for borders or on wallpaper, etc., signify nothing by themselves; they do not represent anything, no object under a determinate concept" (1790: §16, 5:229); and, for example, "In painting and sculpture, indeed in all the pictorial arts, in architecture and horticulture insofar as they are fine arts, the *drawing* is what is essential, in which what constitutes the ground of all arrangements for taste is not what gratifies in sensation but merely what pleases through its form" (1790: §14, 5:225). Yet as those who continue past the "Analytic of the Beautiful" cannot fail to discover, such comments may represent Kant's analysis of *pure* judgments of taste or their objects, "free beauties" (1790: §16, 5:229), but they hardly represent his analysis of paradigmatic works of art and our response to them. On the contrary, in Kant's view works of art are multidimensional and our response to them is complex, much as Addison and Baumgarten had earlier argued.

As Kant states in concluding the "Analytic of the Beautiful," all aesthetic response is an expression of the freedom of the imagination: "It turns out that everything flows from the concept of taste as a faculty for judging an object in relation to the *free lawfulness* of the imagination" (1790: General Remark following §2, 5:240), that is, a sense that a manifold of representations presented by the imagination satisfies the understanding's general interest in coherence or lawfulness but without any constraint by a determinate concept of the understanding. But when Kant turns to his explicit discussion of the fine arts – buried in the sections following the "Analytic of the Sublime" and the "Deduction of Pure Aesthetic Judgments" without the benefit of a heading of its own – it becomes clear that the free play or "free lawfulness" of the imagination is not induced by perceptual form alone. It is also induced by the content or significance of works of art, by the materials of the means of expression, and above all by the harmonious relationship among all of these elements – just as Baumgarten had asserted forty years before the third *Critique*. This is the import of Kant's conception of fine art, the product of genius, as the expression of "aesthetic ideas." Kant characterizes an aesthetic idea, as the content of a work of artistic genius, as "that representation of the imagination that occasions much thinking without it being possible for any determinate thought, i.e., *concept*, to be adequate to it, which, consequently, no language fully attains or can make intelligible" (1790: §49, 5:314). In a work of artistic genius,

> we add to a concept a representation of the imagination that belongs to its presentation, but which by itself stimulates so much thinking that it can never be grasped in a determinate concept, hence which aesthetically enlarges the concept itself in an unbounded way . . . in this case the imagination is creative, and sets the faculty of intellectual ideas (reason) into motion. (1790: §49, 5:315)

In other words, in the case of aesthetic ideas there is a free play of the imagination with content rather than form, with ideas rather than with shapes or patterns. Content is not, after all, excluded from the aesthetically relevant aspects of works of art; all that is ruled out is the constraint of content as well as of form by determinate concepts functioning as rules for the creation of and response to works of art.

Finally, Kant stresses that artistic genius is expressed in the creation of content as well as form and matter in works of art and in the creation of harmony among all these dimensions of the work of art:

> If, after these analyses, we look back to the explanation given above of what is called *genius*, then we find, *first*, that it is a talent for art . . . ; *second*, that, as a talent for art, it presupposes a determinate concept of the product, as an end, hence understanding, but also a representation (even if indeterminate) of the material, i.e., of the intuition, for the presentation of this concept, hence a relation of the imagination to the understanding; *third*, that it displays itself not so much in the execution of the proposed end in the presentation of a determinate *concept* as in the exposition or the expression of *aesthetic ideas*, which contain rich material for that aim, hence the imagination, in its freedom from all guidance by rules, is nevertheless represented as purposive for the presentation of the given concept. (1790: §49, 5:317)

Genius lies in the invention of aesthetic ideas, which is a free expression of the imagination, and in the creation of vehicles for the expression of these ideas in intuition, which in turn will involve form and matter, drawing and color, composition and instrumentation, order but also diction and style. This is Kant's development of Baumgarten's remark "The beauty of sensory cognition and the elegance of its objects display composite perfections . . . no simple perfection is given to us by the phenomenon" (Baumgarten 1750: §24).

We can now, in conclusion, explicate Kant's conception of fine art as a complex conception of the freedom of the imagination.[13] In his initial analysis of aesthetic response and judgment, Kant, like Hutcheson before him, characterizes aesthetic response in negative terms: what is essential to it is the freedom of the imagination in its play with form from constraint by determinate concepts of the understanding. The pleasure of aesthetic response

> can express nothing but its [object's] suitability to the cognitive faculties that are in play in the reflecting power of judgment, insofar as they are in play, and thus merely a subjective formal purposiveness in the object . . . Such a judgment is an aesthetic judgment on the purposiveness of the object, which is not grounded on any available concept of the object and does not furnish one. (1790: introduction, sec. vii, 5:189–90)

Or, a beautiful object provides the imagination "with a form that contains precisely such a composition of the manifold as the imagination would design in harmony with the *lawfulness of the understanding* in general if it were left free by itself" (1790: General Remark following §22, 5:240–1). But as Kant fills in the bare bones of his initial analysis, he provides a positive as well as a negative characterization of the freedom of imagination. Indeed, he provides several positive conceptions of the freedom of the imagination. First, as we have just seen, in his doctrine of aesthetic ideas Kant makes it clear that artistic imagination and aesthetic response can play freely with content as well as form. In particular, Kant maintains that the paradigmatic contents of aesthetic ideas are *ideas of reason* (1790: §49, 5:314), and ideas of reason are in turn moral ideas. But for Kant, moral ideas are ultimately ideas of human freedom, of its conditions and consequences; thus, the contents of aesthetic ideas are ultimately ideas of human freedom. So without sacrificing its negative freedom, its freedom from constraint by determinate concepts of the understanding in its free play, works of imagination have as their paradigmatic content ideas of human freedom, of its scope and limits. Second, Kant concludes the *Critique of the Aesthetic Power of Judgment* with the argument that because aesthetic response itself is an experience of the freedom of the imagination from constraint by anything external to it, aesthetic experience itself, and derivatively the objects that induce it, can be taken as a symbol of the morally good, because the essence of the latter also consists in freedom, although freedom regulated by a self-given law rather than by a merely indeterminate harmony with the understanding. The key to Kant's claim that the beautiful is the symbol of the morally good is the analogy between the "*freedom* of the imagination . . . in the judging of the beautiful" and the "freedom of the will . . . conceived as the agreement of the latter with itself in accordance with universal laws of reason" (1790: §59, 5:354). This too can be seen as a positive rather than negative characterization of the freedom of the imagination.

Thus, Kant's complex and delicate interpretation of the freedom of the imagination in the experience of beauty can be seen as the summation and synthesis of ideas set forth at the outset of the flowering of modern aesthetics in the first decades of the eighteenth century. Kant transformed the idea of the autonomy of aesthetic response that Hutcheson derived from Shaftesbury's much more limited conception of the disinterestedness of judgments of taste into his basic conception of the free play of the imagination. At the same time, he developed Baumgarten's conception of the complexity of aesthetic representation into an elaborate conception of the content of art, and the symbolic significance of aesthetic response itself into a structure that could make room both for Du Bos' conception of the engagement of the emotions through the imagination and for Addison's idea of our love for images of liberty, without sacrificing his guiding idea of the free play of the imagination. In much of the history of aesthetics after Kant, the several threads in Kant's complex fabric would often become unraveled again – but that is a long story, for another occasion.

## Notes

1 See Monk (1935), and for a recent sampler of eighteenth-century writing on the sublime, Ashfield and de Bolla (1996).

2 See Ferry (1993). An older work which emphasized *Individualität* as the key idea in eighteenth-century aesthetics is Bäumler (1923), although Bäumler, who later became a notorious Nazi spokesman, linked individuality to irrationalism, and thus saw the development of aesthetics as a locus of opposition to rationalist universalism rather than associating it with the origins of modern liberalism as does Ferry.

3 See Guyer (2000), especially chapter 9, "Moral Worth, Virtue, and Merit."

4 I have argued for this interpretation of Kant's aesthetics in Guyer (1993), especially chapter 3.

5 Contrast Hutcheson (1725: 3) and Hutcheson (1738: title-page).

6 See Du Bos (1748: I, 32). Some time ago, Peter Jones argued for the influence of Du Bos on Hume's conception of criticism and the standard of taste; I think he could also have argued for the influence of Du Bos on the more general concept of sympathy in Hume's moral psychology. See Jones (1982: 93–106).

7 Du Bos (1748: I, 22). Here too there seems to be another anticipation of one of Hume's most central ideas.

8 Du Bos' theory must thus be distinguished from what might seem to be its current counterpart, Kendall Walton's theory of mimesis as make-believe. Walton's theory is that we respond to works of art by engaging in games of make-believe, using the artworks as props, and thereby experience *analogs* of ordinary emotions, or "fictionally" rather than really experience emotions; see Walton (1990: 271), for example. Du Bos' theory is that we really experience the same emotions in observing a work of art as we would in observing or undergoing the events depicted, though in a more tolerable and less costly form, and that only the fact that we do experience such real emotions in art explains our interest in it.

9 Baumgarten (1735: §vii). Baumgarten's term *sensitiva*, translated into German as *sinnlich*, could easily be translated as "sensitive" or "sensitively." But since in contemporary English that term might connote a special degree of refinement in

discernment, I have instead adopted the translation "sensory" or "sensorily," which does not have that connotation.

10  This chapter would later be the basis for Kant's lectures on anthropology, so in fact the only place in his lectures where Kant dealt with aesthetic theory was in his lectures on anthropology.

11  Although an incurable academic, Baumgarten himself briefly tried his hand at what was intended to be a popular moral magazine along the lines of the *Spectator*, the *Philosophical Letters of Aletheophilus*. The only surprise is that with a title like that it lasted as long as twenty-six numbers in 1741!

12  There were two volumes published, in 1750 and 1758. These were an incomplete presentation of the "Heuristic," which was itself to be only one of three parts of the intended work. The massive text that we have is thus only a fragment of what Baumgarten planned to write. Unfortunately, Baumgarten never had robust health, and died in 1762, at the age of 48, leaving only the present fragment.

13  For a fuller treatment of Kant's conception of fine art, see Guyer (1997: ch. 12).

# References

Abrams, M. H. (1953). *The Mirror and the Lamp: Romantic Theory and the Critical Tradition*. Oxford: Oxford University Press.

Ashfield, Andrew and de Bolla, Peter (eds) (1996). *The Sublime: A Reader in Eighteenth-Century Aesthetic Theory*. Cambridge: Cambridge University Press.

Baumgarten, Alexander Gottlieb (1735). *Meditationes philosophicae de nonnullis ad poema pertinentibus / Philosophische Betrachtungen über einige Bedingungen des Gedichtes.* Parallel Latin and German texts ed. Heinz Paetzold. Hamburg: Felix Meiner, 1983.

——(1739). *Metaphysica*. Parallel Latin and German passages in *Texte zur Grundlegung der Ästhetik* ed. Hans Rudolf Schweizer. Hamburg: Felix Meiner, 1983.

——(1750). *Aesthetica*. Frankfurt an der Oder, 1750–8. Reprint, Hildesheim: Georg Olms, 1961. Modern edn, ed. B. Croce, Bari: Laterza, 1936. Selections, with intro. and parallel German translations, in Hans Rudolf Schweizer, *Ästhetik als Philosophie der sinnlichen Erkenntnis*. Basel and Stuttgart: Schwabe, 1973.

Bäumler, Alfred (1923). *Das Irrationalitätsproblem in der Ästhetik und Logik des 18. Jahrhunderts bis zur Kritik der Urteilskraft*. 2nd edn. Tübingen: Max Miemeyer, 1967.

Burke, Edmund (1759). *A Philosophical Enquiry into the Origin of Our Ideas of the Sublime and Beautiful*. 2nd edn, with Introduction on Taste. London: Robert and James Dodsley. Modern edns by J. T. Boulton (London: Routledge and Kegan Paul, 1958) and Adam Phillips (Oxford: Oxford University Press, 1990).

Chalmers, A. (ed.) (1869) *The Spectator, with a Historical and Biographical Preface*. 8 vols. Boston: Little, Brown.

Du Bos, [Jean-Baptiste], abbé (1748). *Critical Reflections on Poetry, Painting and Music*. Trans. Thomas Nugent, from the 5th edn. London: John Nourse.

Eagleton, Terry (1990). *The Ideology of the Aesthetic*. Oxford: Blackwell.

Ferry, Luc (1993). *Homo Aestheticus: The Invention of Taste in the Democratic Age*. Trans. Robert de Loaiza. Chicago: University of Chicago Press.

Guyer, Paul (1993). *Kant and the Experience of Freedom*. Cambridge: Cambridge University Press.

——(1997). *Kant and the Claims of Taste*. 2nd edn. Cambridge: Cambridge University Press.

——(2000). *Kant on Freedom, Law, and Happiness*. Cambridge: Cambridge University Press.

Hutcheson, Francis (1725). *An Inquiry into the Original of our Ideas of Beauty and Virtue*. London: J. Darby et al. Ed. with intro. and notes Peter Kivy. The Hague: Martinus Nijhoff, 1973.

——(1738). *An Inquiry into the Original of our Ideas of Beauty and Virtue*. 4th edn London: D. Midwinter et al.

Jones, Peter (1982). *Hume's Sentiments: Their Ciceronian and French Context*. Edinburgh: Edinburgh University Press.

Kant, Immanuel (1785). *The Groundwork for the Metaphysics of Morals*. In Immanuel Kant, *Practical Philosophy*, ed. and trans. Mary J. Gregor. Cambridge: Cambridge University Press, 1996.

——(1790). *Critique of the Power of Judgment*. Ed. Paul Guyer, trans. Paul Guyer and Eric Matthews. Cambridge: Cambridge University Press, 2000.

Kneller, Jane (1998). "Disinterestedness." In Michael Kelly (ed.), *Encyclopedia of Aesthetics*. New York: Oxford University Press: II, 59–64.

Kristeller, Paul O. (1951–2) "The Modern System of the Arts." *Journal of the History of Ideas*, 12: 496–527 and 13: 17-46. Reprinted in Kristeller (1965), *Renaissance Thought II: Papers on Humanism and the Arts*. New York: Harper Torchbooks: 163–227.

Monk, Samuel H. (1935). *The Sublime: A Study of Critical Theories in XVIII-Century England*. 2nd edn, with a new preface. Ann Arbor: University of Michigan Press, 1960.

Shaftesbury, Anthony Ashley Cooper, third earl of (1711). *Characteristics of Men, Manners, Opinions, Times*. Ed. Lawrence F. Klein. Cambridge: Cambridge University Press, 1999.

Stolnitz, Jerome (1961). "On the Origins of 'Aesthetic Disinterest'." *Journal of Aesthetics and Art Criticism*, 20: 131–43.

Walton, Kendall (1990). *Mimesis as Make-Believe: On the Foundations of the Representational Arts*. Cambridge, MA: Harvard University Press.

# Chapter 2

# Defining Art: Intension and Extension

## *George Dickie*

## 2.1

Philosophical theorizing arose, at least in the West, in ancient Greek times. There and then, the two main competitors for explaining the order that we experience were the atomists and the Platonists. The atomists explained this order as being the *result* of the micro-structure of individual things – gold has a different micro-structure from iron, tigers from lions, and so on. The atomists were theorizing about the essence of things, and they did so by talking about spatio-temporal, physical micro-structures. The Platonists also explained the order that we experience in the world, but they said that individual things fall into the types that they do because they *participate* in various Forms, these being non-spatial, non-temporal abstractions. The essence of things resides, for the Platonists, in the Forms. The atomists and the Platonists differed about the nature of the essences of things. They also differed about how the essences are responsible for the order we experience: for the atomists, *causality*[1] was responsible, whereas for the Platonists, it was *participation*.[2] Thus, at the very beginning of theorizing there was a radical disagreement over what the theorizing was about – about what is *real*.

Once the atomists had enunciated their thesis that the micro-structures of things differ from one another, they then had little else to say about those structures. They spoke of invisible micro-structures but had no means of knowing anything about these essences, although they did speculate about the movement and weight of atoms. They were so far ahead of their times that they were speechless; they were barred from inquiry into what they regarded as real by a lack of technology and developed theory. The Platonists, however, were able to speak volumes, for in addition to theorizing about the order and essence of things, they also focused on words and their meanings, which were available in great supply. They had a philosophy of language, which the atomists lacked. The atomists were as speechless about words as they were about invisible micro-structures. The

Platonists spoke of non-visible things too, but they claimed we could know them because we understand the words whose meanings were constituted by the non-visible Forms. The Forms were thus alleged to be not only responsible for the order of things but also the meanings of words. The knowing of a Form is allegedly demonstrated when a word is understood. Complete knowing of a Form is supposedly demonstrated when an adequate definition of a word – "figure," "justice," or the like – is successfully achieved.

The voluble Platonists, with a philosophy of language integrated with and underwritten by their metaphysics, won an easy victory over the speechless atomists for control of subsequent philosophizing. Theorizing about the essences of things and the definitions of words – including art and "art" – thus had its development within the Platonic vision of language and reality, with reality being understood to be a hierarchically ordered, rational structure of non-spatial, non-temporal Forms that give order to the world of experience and constitute the intensions of words in a language. The metaphysical structure is rational in the sense that it has the form that would be given by a rational arranger, although no arranger is envisaged within the system. The structure of the Forms is taken to be such that there is a genus–species relation inherent in every intension. Within this vision, the essences of all sorts of different things – gold, water, tigers, justice, art, whatever – are taken to be of the same sort and the essences themselves are subject to dialectical analysis that can yield the intensions – necessary and sufficient conditions – of the words that apply to the things with the essences. For the Platonists, inquiry about what is real was conceived of as a search into the intelligible realm of the Forms for essences and meanings or intensions; empirical inquiry was regarded as a pursuit into the illusion of sense. The intellectual agenda was thus set by the Platonists, and philosophical inquiry became an attempt to produce the essences of things and the intensions of words. Philosophical inquiry continues to have something of a Platonic flavor today.

An apparent advantage the Platonists' approach has over the atomists' is that while in principle the atomists have a way of explaining physical phenomena, there is no obvious way for them to explain how non-physical characteristics (linguistic, moral, cultural, and the like) arise from atomic configurations. On the other hand, the Platonists' metaphysics and philosophy of language supposedly deal with all kinds of phenomena from physical to moral.

As is well known, in recent times the search for the essences of art and other notions has been challenged by the claim that there are no such essences, and that "art" and other words apply to the things they do in virtue of intensions that take note of the overlapping similarities among those things. This is a challenge to whatever is left of the Platonic tradition in philosophy. There are three main difficulties with this untraditional development. First, it is unclear how the similarities are to be specified – how similar do two characteristics have to be to count as linking two works of art under the word "art" (or any two objects under the same word), and how many such similarities are required to make two objects fall under the word "art" (or any word)? Second, the reliance on similarities threatens to draw into and collect into the class of art, or any other notion specified in terms of similarities, every object in the universe because, in some way, everything resembles everything else. Third, focusing now only on art, if one tries to contain the collecting tendencies of similarities by specifying that the similarities must be to prior-established works of art, then an infinite regress of prior-established works of art is generated so that there could never have been a first work of art and hence no present works of art. Since there are works of art, the similarity conception as the whole story is wrong, and there would have to be some non-similarity ur-work or ur-works of art that have priority over "similarity" art. Thus, some kind of non-similarity foundation would be required by the similarity view.

The atomists, the Platonists, and the similarity theorists all begin by focusing on the order that they note in things: the Platonists infer Forms to explain identities in experience and to be the intensions of all kinds of words, which they take to be manifested in genus–species relationships; the atomists infer conclusions about micro-structures to explain identities of physical phenomena in experience but have nothing to say about intensions; and the similarity theorists forego inference and focus solely on experienced similarities, out of which they try to construct intensions. I shall not discuss the similarity theories further.

## 2.2

Recently, some philosophers of language have tried to work out a way to adapt the insight of the tongue-tied Greek atomists about the essences of things to the problem of the application of words to things. One of the things that has enabled these philosophers to try to do what the atomists could not try to do is that there are now well-worked-out and accepted theories of the micro-structure of things that were not available to the atomists. In general, this new technique, according to those who advance it, is said to approach the question of the application of words to things through their *extensions* rather than through intensions.[3] This new approach supposedly contrasts sharply with the traditional, Platonic-tinged approach to meaning. One begins, using the new approach, with descriptions of features that function more or less like intensions which serve to focus on some group of things (an extension), and then in the cases of natural kinds one discovers or proceeds with the assurances that an essential, underlying property of the members of the group of things (the extension) can be discovered that uniquely picks out the group of things, or some significant subset of the group of things. This underlying property, if discovered or discoverable, is what identifies this kind of thing in all possible worlds in which that kind of thing exists. Some philosophers of art have subsequently tried to apply this new technique to the philosophy of art.

The approach of Platonists is a *top-down* approach; for them, the Forms, which function as intensions, are given and complete, so that, for them, intensions come first as ready made and determine extensions, the members of which are mere appearances. The new philosophers of language, on the other hand, use a *bottom-up* approach; for them, the discovered or discoverable essential property of the members of an extension constitutes its nature.

These philosophers of language begin, not with a discussion of natural kinds, but with a discussion of proper names as *rigid designators*. According to this view, a proper name such as "Aristotle" is a rigid designator, a rigid designator being something that picks out the same object in all possible worlds where it exists. Also, according to this view, proper names are introduced by a baptism or dubbing, and we track their referents through the world by means of causal historical chains. Proper names, on this view, function by means of reference or extension rather than by intension. We in later generations have come to believe various propositions about Aristotle, and earlier philosophers of language tried to use these beliefs in one way or another as intensions to pick out Aristotle in all possible worlds. Almost all of our beliefs about Aristotle, however, could be false, and the rigid-designator approach avoids using them in any way.

These philosophers of language then go on to apply the rigid-designator approach to words for *natural kinds*. In the case of an element such as gold, various properties such as being yellow, very malleable, and so on served to focus on a group of objects (an extension); it was later discovered that all or many (a significant subset) of the objects have a particular atomic number which then henceforth serves as the essential, underlying property that picks out the group of gold things. Gold's essential property is being the element with the atomic number 79, and this means that gold is identical with the element with the atomic number 79 and that gold is necessarily the element with the atomic number 79. In the case of a compound such as water, the essential, underlying property turns out to be a particular molecular combination of elements, namely, $H_2O$; thus, water is necessarily $H_2O$. In the case of a species of plants or animals, the essential, underlying property would perhaps turn out to be something like a particular DNA profile or whatever the correct underlying property is for species. These underlying properties serve to identify, for example, gold and water in all possible worlds in which there are such substances. In the cases of elements, compounds and species, the essential properties are underlying because they are micro-structures. The discovery of the essences of natural kinds – "gold," "water," and so on – is approached through extensions. These philosophers of language have advanced the insight of the Greek atomists to a remarkable degree.

## 2.3

James Carney (1975, 1982) attempted to take the insight of the philosophers of language even further by applying the rigid-designator approach to the problem of what has been characterized in the past as the defining of "art." For this application to be possible, according to Carney, it must be the case that a paradigm set of objects had been dubbed "art" and that the dubbers believed that the objects share a universal property that is a *nature,* just as all pieces of gold share the nature of having the atomic number 79. And, for Carney, just as gold is necessarily the element with the atomic number 79, art would necessarily be whatever had the universal property. Carney suggests that it is counterintuitive not to have the belief that works of art have such an extension-determining nature. Carney then says:

> It is not unreasonable to suppose that what Danto, Dickie, and others have called the "artworld" is the subclass in a society that determines the universal property and that they rely on theories of art to do this. The artworld would be analogous to the metallurgists for "gold," and art theories would play a role similar to scientific theories and "gold" in that they would be taken as hypothesizing the extension-determining property of art. (1975: 200)

A few lines later Carney writes, "Theories such as the imitation theory or expression theory would be adequate, since they hypothesize a universal property for paradigms" (1975: 201).

What Carney is saying is that any art theory that claims that artworks share an essential property, which of course is every traditional art theory except the similarity view, is a candidate for being fitted to the rigid-designator approach. With all the historical theories of art that have been put forth, Carney's final say on the matter has to be hypothetical: "If the paradigms [of art] have a universal property, then there is a way to determine with certainty whether x is art: x is art if x has the universal property" (1975: 200).

This hypothetical resolution leaves open the possibility that different universal properties might be determined by different members of the artworld, assuming for the moment an understanding of the artworld as Carney is envisaging it. On Carney's view, this apparent difficulty is resolved because of the nature of the only two possibilities. If a disagreement arises among the members of the artworld over the common nature of artworks, then the members may decide that all the old paradigms of art do not share a single underlying nature and it will turn out that the old paradigms separate into two or more extensions, each with its underlying nature, and there will be two or more kinds of art. Or, on the other hand, if a disagreement arises within the artworld over the common nature of artworks, say, over whether a new kind of thing is art, with one side citing one nature and another side citing another nature as art-determining, the two sides either accept the two-or-more-kinds-of-art solution just discussed or can agree on one nature and there will be only one kind of art. So, the members of the artworld will either disagree and there will be more than one kind of art, or they will agree and there will be one kind of art.

Carney's view raises three questions. First, can art theories play the kind of role that scientific theories play in connection with the rigid-designator approach to natural kinds? Carney's answer is "Yes, if they assert a claim of a universal property for the paradigms." This answer raises a second question: "Which art theory is analogous to the atomic theory that yields the atomic number 79 for gold, the molecular theory that describes the molecular structure of water, or the biological theory that specifies DNA profiles?" His answer is that it is the art theory (or theories) with the universal property (or properties) determined by the members of the artworld. This answer raises a third question: "Does the artworld function as Carney envisions?" He does not answer the third question other than to say, "it is not unreasonable to suppose" that it does (1975: 200).

Peter Kivy was the first to attack Carney's suggested approach to theorizing about art (1979). Kivy does not comment on Carney's claim about actions of the members of the artworld, focusing solely on his claim of close analogy between art theories and scientific theories. Where Carney sees analogy, Kivy sees disanalogy. We are not prepared, Kivy says, to accept an art theory in the way that we "are prepared to accept a scientific account of the internal structure of a natural kind" (1979: 430). He agrees that in the scientific domain there is a history of discovering that earlier theories are false and of their being replaced by new theories, and that this bears some resemblance to art theories being replaced by later art theories. But, he says, the succession of scientific theories is different in that it reveals an increasing scope and ability to deal with the data. Such success in the scientific domain inspires a confidence that is not found in theorizing about art by philosophers.

Thomas Leddy was the next to attack Carney's view (1987). He appears to accept Kivy's point about the disanalogy between art theories and scientific theories, but he focuses on a logically prior analogy alleged in Carney's view – his contention that the artworld determines the universal property of art analogously to the way metallurgists determine the nature of gold. Carney begins by talking about artworld members "hypothesizing" about the universal property of art. Leddy notes, however, that it appears to turn out that on Carney's view the members of the artworld supposedly *determine* the nature of art by *deciding on* a universal property. This contrasts sharply with how metallurgists *determine* the nature of gold; they *discover* the universal property of gold (1987: 264). Thus, Leddy uncovers another difference where Carney's view requires similarity.

What of Carney's claim, which neither Kivy nor Leddy addresses, that the members of the artworld function to determine (even if it is only by deciding) the nature of art? Carney says that the members of what Danto, I, and others have called the artworld determine the universal property of art. This makes the artworld into something like a legislative body that deliberates and issues directives that are binding on the other members of society. First, it is not indicated who the "others" are, but the accounts that Danto and I have given of the artworld are very different, although this was perhaps not so clear in the mid-1970s, when Carney published his view, as it is now. Carney writes that Danto's statement that "It is the theory that takes it [*Brillo Box*] up into the artworld" means that we can take his statement to imply "that the extension of the term 'art' is determined by the theories of art held by the artworld" (1975: 201). Perhaps Danto's account in "The Artworld" can be construed to fit the rigid-designator approach as Carney says, but I do not think this is Danto's view, and I, for one, do not think that the artworld functions as a legislative body.

Richard Wollheim has attributed to me the view of the artworld as legislative body and then has gone on to ridicule the view (1987: 14–15). This understanding of the institutional theory of art deserves to be ridiculed because there is no reason at all to think that the artworld or any aspect of it acts like a legislative body – with meetings and decisions, and with declarations and proclamations. Fortunately, the view of the artworld that Wollheim attributes to me is not one that I have ever held (Dickie 1993: 69–71), although he and a number of other people seem to have thought I did. I have always understood the artworld to be a background for the practice of creating and experiencing art – a background that is an essential part of the practice.

So, there seem to be two strikes against Carney's view – Kivy's and Leddy's – and perhaps a third against his understanding of the nature of the artworld.

I do think the rigid-designator approach can be fitted to the imitation theory of art and to some versions of the expression theory of art, but not because these theories might be held by members of the artworld. The two theories can be fitted to the approach because they are what I have elsewhere called "natural-kind theories" (1997a: 25–8). The philosophers who were the proponents of these two theories were attempting to *identify* art with *one, single*, particular kind of human activity – imitating or the expression of emotion – that can quite reasonably be regarded as *natural* or what today would be thought of as hard-wired. Note the parallel here with gold, water, and species. In the case of gold and the other elements, it turned out that there is a fairly small number (something over a hundred) elements, and physicists discovered that each one has *one* distinct atomic number that uniquely picks it out. (Apparently, isotopes can be ignored.) In the case of water and the other compounds, it turned out that there is a very large number of compounds, but even so physicists and chemists discovered that each one has *one* distinct molecular configuration that uniquely picks it out. The case is perhaps similar for species. It is quite reasonable to suppose that some day the now-hidden, underlying nature of the behavior of imitating or expressing of emotion will be discovered by a scientist – some breed of psychologist/biologist. These two ways of acting would be natural-kind behaviors of natural-kind beings. I am speaking here of imitating and expressing as such; how such imitating and expressing are structured and directed and toward what may vary from culture to culture. By the way, these behaviors are not limited to human beings.

Unfortunately for the imitation and expression theories, there is no good reason to think that either of these behaviors is *identical* with art – some works of art are not imitations or expressions of emotion and some imitations and expressions of emotion are not art – which is why the theories have been almost universally rejected. So, although the imitation theory and the expression theory are the sort of theories that could be fitted to the rigid-designator approach, because there is reason to think that imitation and the expression of emotion have underlying essences, it would be a mistake to try to do so because those behaviors just do not match up with all our artworks. They are the wrong theories to use.

## 2.4

There is perhaps a way to fit *certain aspects* of the rigid-designator approach to art, namely, to approach through an extension, looking for an underlying property, although not one that functions in all the ways that a property such as being $H_2O$ does. Consider Carney's procedure. His account of the application of the rigid-designator approach to natural kinds can be summarized by picturing the following pairs: *gold/physicists, water/physicists and chemists*, and *species/molecular biologists*. Carney then tries to use the rigid-designator approach with the specification of the essence of art, pairing *art* and *members of the artworld*. In effect, Kivy and Leddy in different ways point out that Carney's pairing is not analogous to the earlier pairs which all involve *scientists*. In order to extend those aspects of the rigid-designator approach that I wish to use, the second place in the *art/____* pair should be filled with the name of some kind of scientist. In the above discussion of the fitting of the imitation and expression theories to the rigid-designator approach, the second place in the pair was filled by psychologists/biologists, who presumably would focus on the behavior specified by the two old theories of art. But what I am envisaging here is scientists who would focus directly on the art of our culture or other cultures.

Before trying to apply the aspects of the rigid-designator approach I wish to use to the complicated notion of *art*, consider how it might go with a simpler cultural concept. Assume an anthropologist goes to work, say, in the 1920s on a particular south Pacific island culture. In landing on the island, the anthropologist's native translator is drowned, so she must carry out her studies without the benefit of access to the islanders' language. One of her observations is that many people are referred to as *pukas* but not all. She then observes that only males are pukas, although some of them are fat and some skinny, some are short and some tall, and so on. So what is a puka? In her further observing of the social structure of the islanders, our anthropologist discovers that the teenage boys and girls regularly engage in promiscuous sexual behavior without anyone disapproving, but that about age 16 on the day of the summer solstice they are compelled to stop this behavior by everyone in the society. The 16-year-olds then have the option of participating in an elaborate ceremony in which a male and a female are paired and thereafter must maintain a monogamous relation. Those who choose not to participate in the ceremony are thereafter not permitted to engage in sexual activity with a partner without social disapproval. It is the males who do not participate in the ceremony that are thereafter pukas. So, although it was not at first evident to our anthropologist, the "underlying" feature in the case of pukas is the practice of the members of the culture, treating a male 16 years old or older who has refused to participate in the ceremony that regularizes sexual activity among persons over 16 in a certain fashion. The practice that our anthropologist takes note of is not underlying or hidden in the way that the universal properties of gold, water, and species are, but it is not as obvious as the colors of the islanders' clothes either. It takes some observing, inferring, and theorizing to arrive at an understanding of the cultural practice, but the practice in a way is transparent. The cultural practice is underlying but there to be taken note of.

When writing down her notes on the island culture, our anthropologist translates "puka" as "bachelor." When at the end of her first year on the island another native translator arrives, he says that the translation is close but incorrect and that there is no exact equivalent for "puka" in English. Our anthropologist would have discovered the underlying nature of pukas, but she would then have gone on to translate the word "puka" wrongly. American and European societies do not have pukas because we do not compel the ceremony and behavior described above. Any society that did compel the ceremony and behavior described would have pukas, even if only this island in fact had this practice. Pukas are individuals compelled and regulated as described, and they would be such in all possible worlds in which they exist. Our anthropologist would have constructed an essentially correct theory of one aspect of the island culture without the help of the intensional content of the island language, although her use of "bachelor" in her account is not quite right. Pukas and bachelors are similar in a certain central respect, but they also differ in some important central aspects, so we cannot say that they have the same underlying nature.

The underlying nature that bachelors have and the underlying nature that pukas could have, unlike the *physical* reality that gold, water, and species have, are *cultural* realities (cf. Searle 1997). Such cultural natures are or would be a small part of a larger reality that is constituted by webs of relations that are or could be instituted by a society of persons.

## 2.5

Theorizing about art began in and has been carried out throughout almost all of its history in the Platonic mode, which focuses on discovering the intensions of our words. Even when philosophers have given up on Forms, they have continued the *top-down* approach of seeking intensions – in the analysis of concepts, in ordinary language, or in just seeking definitions without saying how they are doing so. The "intensional" approach, which focuses on language, will not work for such terms as "gold," "water," and their like, but it appears to work for terms like "bachelor." Carney himself mentions that, unlike "gold," "bachelor" has a specifiable intension. He writes, "A term like 'bachelor' in its accurate adult use is introduced as a synonym for 'adult male not previously married'" (1975: 199). Carney's saying that "bachelor" is "introduced as a synonym" makes it sound as if the term was put into the language in the way a technical term is introduced by a philosopher or a logician, but of course he does not mean that it was. "Bachelor" came into the language as a co-relative term to "marriage," and both terms (and many others) ride on practices that we have instituted as a cultural group. So, "bachelor," unlike "gold," has an intension, but on the other hand, "bachelor," like "gold," can be approached through its extension; although in the case of an English word like "bachelor," we never bother to do this because, as native speakers of English, we have intensional access to its meaning. In the imagined case of pukas, the language-deprived anthropologist is forced to approach through an extension because she lacks intensional access to the islander's language.

The concepts *bachelor* and *puka*, unlike the concepts *gold, water* and *tiger*, are transparent, that is, a person who knows the culture in which the concept functions, knows the concept. The natures of bachelors and pukas are underlying in the sense that one cannot just look at an individual and see that he is a bachelor or a puka; one must know whether an individual is enmeshed in the relevant cultural relations.

The nature of bachelors and the nature of gold are similar in that they are discoverable by empirical inquiry. The natures differ in that the nature of bachelors depends on cultural developments – decisions and the like – whereas that of gold does not. So, one is tempted to say that the nature of gold cannot change, which is true, but that the nature of bachelors can, which is misleading. The use of the word "bachelor" can change in several different ways. Assume that at a given time the word has one meaning. The word could change its meaning entirely while still having only one meaning. It could change entirely and have two completely new meanings. The word could acquire a second meaning with the original meaning remaining unchanged, and so on. But even if the word "bachelor" changed in one of these ways or even if the word ceased to exist as a word in the language, the condition of being an unmarried adult male and the cultural practice of categorizing such an individual need not change. The condition and practice remain a logical possibility even if "bachelor" ceases to exist in the language and every person is in fact married or previously married.

I believe the concept *art* is like the concept *bachelor* (and the concept *puka*), and the word "art" is like the word "bachelor" (and the word "puka"). Of course, no one has ever felt the need to put forth a theory of bachelorness. Plato seems never to have felt the need to write a dialogue about it as he did about piety, friendship, and justice, or even to attack it in passing as metaphysically inferior and psychologically dangerous as he did art. Why has no one ever felt the need for a theory of bachelorness? Perhaps because "bachelor" does not serve as an evaluative weapon-word in the way that "art" does, and, no doubt, for a variety of other reasons; but probably no one has ever felt the need for a theory of bachelorness because intensional access to its meaning is so easy and uncontroversial. In any event, Plato did theorize about art and did attack art on metaphysical and psychological grounds, and philosophers have been trying to theorize about art ever since. Intensional access to "art" is obviously much more difficult than to "bachelor," and it is clearly much more controversial. We do not seem to need to apply what may be called "the extensional approach" to "bachelor," but perhaps the difficulty and controversy involved with "art" can be avoided by using the extensional approach with it.

Earlier I noted that in order to use the extensional approach to "art" the second place in the *art/___* pair should be filled with the name of some kind of scientist. Following the pattern established with the case of bachelors and pukas, I think the pair should be *art/cultural anthropologists*. Art is, I have long believed, a cultural notion, and cultural anthropologists are the scientists that deal with cultural phenomena. My own belief in art as a cultural phenomenon is demonstrated by the fact that the institutional theory of art, which I have been defending in one form or another for a long time, is clearly a cultural theory. Perhaps it is worth noting that Leddy twice alludes to art as a cultural concept by contrasting it with what he calls natural science concepts in his 1987 article that I discussed above, but that is all he says on the topic.

When I say that art is a cultural notion, I mean that it is a phenomenon that has been invented by a cultural group and that it is not a genetically determined behavior like mating, eating, and the like.[4] In saying this, I do not mean to suggest that only we or some small group of societies have art or our concept of *art*. I think that Dennis Dutton is probably right that all human societies have art (2000). Of course, there could be and might be a human society that does not yet in fact have art. I only wish to say of each society that has art that it was invented at some point in the past. It is, of course, possible that in the case of a given society art was imported from another culture before it could be invented indigenously, so in this case the point in the past referred to would be in the past of another society.

What would be the general features of the application of the extensional approach to the notion of art using the *art/cultural anthropologist* pairing? We would be looking for a cultural phenomenon that is shared by all cultures or at least many cultures, since, as noted, a given culture might not yet have art. The phenomenon would have to be of a cultural nature that is the same in all cultures that have it. That nature would have to be of a rather abstract kind, given the widely differing kinds of art that there are. And it might be that there are things that very closely resemble a kind of art that are not art; that is, there could be an arbitrariness about one thing's being art and a very closely resembling thing not being art. Such arbitrariness is perhaps inevitable where cultural matters are concerned, because cultural matters are how they are as the result of how a culture has "set things up" at some time or during some period in the past.

It would perhaps be best to begin our looking within our own culture. We would approach our own culture as the imagined anthropologist did the island culture, except that we have the advantage that we are native speakers of our own language. Of course, various aspects of language could be handicaps that lead native speakers astray. Words in their dictionary senses typically have a number of different meanings, which could be confusing. Further, we (and any native speaker of any natural language) can make a word mean almost anything by the use of inflection, irony, gestures, juxtaposition, and the like, and this too may confuse us in the cases of the meanings of some words. All of this linguistic flexibility may obscure our view of the *practices* that underlie the specific meanings of some words. We might be better able to isolate these specific meanings of these practice-dependent words if we were language-deprived observers, like the imagined anthropologist. Of course, language-deprived observers can make the kind of mistranslation imagined.

The first lesson to be derived from the imagined case of the language-deprived anthropologist's mistranslation is that in the case of the meaning of culturally determined words, access to the intensional content of the language of the members of the culture involved can be useful. The second lesson to be derived from the case of the language-deprived anthropologist (one ignored by the purely intensional approaches of historical philosophers of art) is that in the cases of certain concepts and the words that go with them, knowledge of the practices that underlie the concepts and their words is crucial to their meaning. Applying these two lessons, it may be possible to make some progress in theorizing about art.

To apply the extensional approach to the notion of art using the *art/cultural anthropologist* pairing, one needs to look for linguistic usage that is integrated with cultural practice analogous to the islanders' use of "puka" and their practice involved in organizing the cultural activities of pukas, and our use of "bachelor" and the practice involved in our organizing the cultural practice of bachelors.

If we start, as cultural anthropologists, with our own linguistic usage, the usages of "art" would have to relate to a provisional description in the way that the usages of "gold" relate to the properties of being yellow and malleable as a pro-visional description. In the way that physicists then focus on yellow and malleable objects on their way to discovering the atomic number of gold, cultural anthro-pologists will have to start by focusing on objects that satisfy the provisional description. The usages we will find with "art," however, because of our wide linguistic flexibility, will be all over the place. But note that the usages of "gold" will be too; consider, "You struck gold!" said to someone who bought Xerox stock early on or to the discoverer of an important scientific truth. Despite all of its many and varied usages, with "gold" we somehow winnowed our way down to a preliminary extension of yellow and malleable objects and then proceeded to atomic theorizing. With "art," we will have to winnow our way down to a reasonable preliminary extension and then look for a cultural practice that underlies this preliminary extension or some significant subset of it.

We can think of the history of the philosophy of art – from Plato to Danto – as a kind of winnowing of the preliminary description of "work of art," although, as we shall see, the process does not always eliminate items from the extension of works of art – sometimes it adds them.

Not even the earliest imitation theorist would have been moved to think of driftwood as art if some other ancient Greek, foreshadowing Morris Weitz and some other twentieth-century philosophers, had uttered the Greek equivalent of

"That driftwood is a lovely piece of sculpture." He would not have considered the driftwood to be within the extension of art, not only because it is not an imitation but also because it is not an artifact, that is, a human artifact. Someone has to be in the grip of a philosophical movement to think that a piece of driftwood all by itself is an artwork because it has been referred to as a lovely piece of sculpture. Thus, non-artifactuality was winnowed out of (or perhaps it should be said never got into) the preliminary description of "work of art" by virtue of something like common sense.

Imitation theorists were, however, moved – eventually anyway – by another kind of case: things that were obviously not imitations but which seemed like artworks nevertheless. Being bothered by this kind of case forced an expansion in their conception of the intension of artworks and caused them to cease being imitation theorists. The expansion of the intension of artworks by counterexamples advanced by others or just noticed has been a standard feature of theorizing about art. Notice that to work as a counterexample to someone's theory, the alleged counterexample must plausibly fit into an extension *despite* the fact that it lacks all or some part of the theorist's understanding of the intension of a term under consideration. This kind of philosophical move has been responsible, not for a winnowing out of characteristics from the preliminary description of "work of art," but for an adding of characteristics. This kind of move eliminates theories – the imitation theory of art, for example, and, I think, the expression theory as well.

I think that virtually all philosophers of art – present and past – are and always have been agreed that it is poems, painting, plays, sonatas, sonnets, sculptures, and such familiar items that are works of art and that this is the extension that they are and always have been theorizing about – trying to state the intension that fits it. There has of course been some disagreement as to whether to count Dada objects and similar things as works of art, but this is a skirmish of little significance. I have maintained that Dada objects are theoretically useful because they have helped us gain insight into the art-making context in which works of art are embedded, either because Dada objects are works of art or because they are not works of art but have been mistaken for works of art by some people. In any event, let us set aside this dispute and focus attention on the huge group of works of art about which there is complete agreement.

The philosophical problem with the large group of items that constitutes the extension of works of art has always been the great diversity of its members. This heterogeneousness has been the great barrier to the traditional attempts to extract the intension from the exhibited features of these works.[5] By "exhibited features" I mean characteristics that can be noticed by directly experiencing works of art – for example, that they are representations, are expressive, are delicate, and the like. What exhibited features could be found to be exemplified in all these many and diverse works of art? And what a ready source of counterexamples that same diversity has been against all those imitationists, expressionists, and the like who have tried to specify partial or complete conditions from among exhibited features.

Focus now on present-day theories of art. I think Danto's attempt to characterize art in terms of *aboutness* is an example of the traditional search for the intensional meaning of "work of art" among exhibited characteristics, and I believe that his theory is vulnerable to the traditional kind of counterexample attack (cf. Dickie 1993: 76–7; Carroll 1993). Beardsley's attempt to characterize art in terms of aesthetic character is also an example of the same traditional search among exhibited characteristics and is subject to the same kind of attack (1979: 729, 1983: 299). On the other hand, I think Jerrold Levinson's historical theory and my institutional theory are different from the traditional theories and can be understood as attempts to discover the underlying nature of the extension of works of art – the underlying nature being the *non-exhibited* feature of works of art that ties them together. I will not discuss Levinson's theory here because I have discussed its difficulties elsewhere (1997a: 22–4).

What would a search by a cultural anthropologist uncover in a study of "how we deal with" works of art? I believe such a search would reveal an underlying cultural structure like that envisaged by the institutional theory of art. The institutional theory is an account of the cultural structure within which works of art are produced and function, and the structure itself is specified in terms of a variety of cultural roles.

In any event, even if cultural anthropologists could not find a cultural structure identical with that described by the institutional theory, I believe they would find a structure very much like it. That is, they would find a structure of the general sort that the five declarations I gave as definitions in *The Art Circle* can serve as a summary account of. These five are as follows:

1 An artist is a person who participates with understanding in the making of a work of art.
2 A work of art is an artifact of a kind created to be presented to an artworld public.
3 A public is a set of persons the members of which are prepared in some degree to understand an object which is presented to them.
4 The artworld is the totality of all artworld systems.
5 An artworld system is a framework for the presentation of a work of art by an artist to an artworld public. (1997b: 80–2)

The structure presented by these five would be the sort of thing that constitutes the cultural essence of the institution within which art has its being. And the second declaration (definition) is the sort of thing that can be taken as a statement of the cultural essence of a work of art, namely, a statement that identifies art with the complicated property of being an artifact of a kind created to be presented to an artworld public.

## 2.6

Assume for argument's sake that "A work of art is an artifact of a kind created to be presented to an artworld public" captures the cultural essence of art because the statement has been arrived at by means of a search by anthropologists into cultural structure. Would that mean that it states the intension of "work of art"? When Carney applies the rigid-designator approach to "work of art," he concludes that "work of art" has no intension. Remember, however, what Carney says about "bachelor," namely, that it has an intension. So, Carney treats words like "bachelor" differently from the way in which he treats words like "gold." He does not explain why "bachelor" is different from "gold," and there is nothing in his article that requires him to do so. I, however, have claimed that what I am calling "the extensional approach" can be applied to "work of art" and have also tried to apply it to "bachelor." So, I need at least to show how "bachelor" has an intension if the extensional approach can be applied to it.

In effect, I have agreed with Carney that "bachelor" *means* "an adult male not previously married" and added that *being* an adult male not previously married is the underlying *cultural* nature of bachelors. How does the case of the nature of bachelors, which is derived by means of the extensional approach, differ from that of the nature of gold, which is derived by means of the rigid-designator approach? And how does the case of "bachelor" differ from "gold" so that "bachelor" can have an intension and "gold" does not?

Consider the question of how the nature of bachelors differs from the nature of gold. First, the nature of bachelors is a cultural nature; it is a cultural status. Being a bachelor is of course not a legal status, but it is related to and derived from marriage, which is a matter of law – law being an officially enacted cultural phenomenon. Marriage is a cultural (legal) way of organizing various central aspects of the lives of human beings. Being a bachelor is a cultural (non-legal) way of organizing aspects of the lives of some human males – how and under what circumstances, for example, certain human males are invited to dinner. The nature of gold, on the other hand, is not cultural, but physical. There would be gold if there were no cultures anywhere. There could not be bachelors without a culture and in fact not without a culture that has marriage. We have no control over the nature of gold, but we do have control over the nature of cultural things, although it is a complicated matter.

There is another important difference between the nature of gold and the nature of bachelors. An individual sample of gold in the actual world (the element with the atomic number 79) would be gold in all possible worlds, that is, the individual sample of gold is necessarily the element with the atomic number 79. In contrast, an individual bachelor Adam in the actual world might be a married man in some possible worlds and thus not a bachelor in all possible worlds, that is, the individual bachelor Adam is not necessarily a bachelor. Being gold is a nature that might be called an intrinsic nature, while being a bachelor is a nature that an individual acquires by fitting into a cultural context. It is worth noting in passing that particular works of art are like bachelors in this respect. For example, a particular physical object that is a work of representational art in the actual world might not be a work of art in some possible world, because that possible world lacks the cultural institution of art and that particular physical object would then merely be a representation; thus, a particular work of art in the actual world is not necessarily a work of art.

Second, in the case of discovering (or just knowing) the nature of bachelors, there is no intellectual division of labor that requires experts to discover that nature as is required in the case of gold. Gold has a hidden nature that requires highly specialized individuals – physicists, chemists, and the like – to discover its nature. The nature of bachelors, although it is underlying in being a culturally founded phenomenon, is known to virtually everyone; its nature is transparent rather than hidden.

Consider now how "bachelor" differs from "gold." First, "bachelor" is a cultural term in that it derives in part from the cultural term "married," although of course it also involves the biological terms "adult" (which may be given some cultural content by way of a roughly specified age designation) and "male." "Gold" is not a cultural term but a physical term, that is, it refers to objects with a physical nature.

Second, "bachelor" has some similarity to technical words that are stipulated to have a certain meaning. In the case of technical terms, it is typically individual persons who do the stipulating, but in the case of words like "bachelor," it is the culture that does the "stipulating" or something like stipulating that may be called cultural determination. The exact nature of this determination is vague, and furthermore the courses of the various determinations probably differ in the cases of different cultural terms. The cultural determination of the meaning of cultural words is of course closely related to the fact that we have some control over the natures of cultural matters.

There is an intimate connection between "bachelor" and the nature of bachelors – a sort of congruency in which the intension of "bachelor" and the nature of the members of the extension of "bachelor" are determined by our culture in a logically concomitant way. The word "bachelor" (and its definition) and the nature of bachelors are both the same kind of thing, namely, they are both cultural products. Both are co-ordinated and mirroring products of how we organize the intertwined pathways of our linguistic and behavioral lives. "Gold" and the nature of gold lack this intimate, mirroring relationship. We are participants in the initiating and maintaining of the cultural natures of the kinds of things of which being a bachelor is a prime example; these are cultural kinds. In contrast, we have no such "insider" relation to the natures of natural kinds.

The inarticulate Greek atomists were on the right track about gold. In a way, the Platonists would have been on the right track if they had turned their attention to transparent terms like "bachelor"; they would have had, however, to focus attention, not on rational intuition of Forms in which supposedly every sort of thing participates, but on the understanding of our participation in cultural practices that are involved with transparent terms.

The cultural term "work of art" is, I believe, like the cultural term "bachelor" and not like the physical term "gold." There is an intimate cultural connection between "work of art" and the nature of a work of art that our cultural anthropologists can discover such that that nature can be converted into a definition of "work of art." I hope it will be discovered that the definition is my institutional one.

## Notes

I wish to thank Suzanne Cunningham and Ruth Marcus for reading and commenting on earlier versions of this chapter.
1   In ancient Greek times perhaps this would have been called efficient causality.
2   In ancient Greek times this might have been called formal causality.
3   This approach is derived from the well-known work of Saul Kripke and Hilary Putnam.
4   For a discussion of cultural-kind and natural-kind theories of art, see Dickie (1997a: 25–8).
5   The distinction between the exhibited and non-exhibited features of works of art was first made and used by Maurice Mandelbaum (1965).

## References

Beardsley, M. (1979). "In Defense of Aesthetic Value." In *Proceedings and Addresses of the American Philosophical Association.* Newark, DE: American Philosophical Association.
——(1983). "Redefining Art." In M. J. Wreen and D. M. Callen (eds), *The Aesthetic Point of View: Selected Essays.* Cornell University Press.
Carney, J. (1975). "Defining Art." *British Journal of Aesthetics,* 15: 191–206.
——(1982). "A Kripkean Approach to Aesthetic Theories." *British Journal of Aesthetics* 22: 150–7.
Carroll, N. (1993). "Essence, Expression, and History." In Rollins (1993): 79–106.
——(ed.) (2000). *Theories of Art Today.* Madison: University of Wisconsin Press.
Dickie, G. (1993). "An Artistic Misunderstanding." *Journal of Aesthetics and Art Criticism,* 51: 69–71.
——(1993). "Tale of Two Artworlds." In Rollins (1993): 76–7.
——(1997a). "Art: Function or Procedure – Nature or Culture?" *Journal of Aesthetics and Art Criticism,* 55: 25–8.
——(1997b). *The Art Circle.* Evanston: Chicago Spectrum Press. Originally pub. 1984.
Dutton, D. (2000). "But They Don't Have Our Concept of Art." In Carroll (2000): 217–38.
Kivy, P. (1979). "Aesthetic Concepts: Some Fresh Considerations." *Journal of Aesthetics and Art Criticism,* 37: 423–32.
Leddy, T. (1987). "Rigid Designation in Defining Art." *Journal of Aesthetics and Art Criticism,* 45: 263–72.

Mandelbaum, M. (1965). "Family Resemblances and Generalization Concerning the Arts." *American Philosophical Quarterly*, 2: 219–28.

Rollins, M. (ed.) (1993). *Danto and his Critics*. Oxford: Blackwell.

Searle, J. (1997). *The Construction of Social Reality*. New York: Simon & Schuster.

Wollheim, R. (1987). *Painting as an Art*. Princeton, NJ: Princeton University Press.

# Chapter 3

# Art and the Aesthetic
## *Marcia Muelder Eaton*

The terms "artistic" and "aesthetic" have long histories and people disagree about exactly what they mean. I shall say much more about this later, but I begin by asking the reader to rely on his or her intuitive understanding of the words and consider the class of aesthetic objects and the class of artistic objects. What is their relationship? There are several possibilities. They might be equivalent: everything that is an aesthetic object will be an artistic object and vice versa. Or they might be totally separate. Or one class might be included in, that is, be a subset of, the other. The most common view – and one that I share – is that the last possibility holds: the class of artistic objects is included in the class of aesthetic objects, but the latter class includes more than just artistic objects. Paintings, songs, poems, dances, etc. are all aesthetic objects, but there are some things – for example, sunsets, forests, seashells, a child's laughter, or a bird in flight – that are aesthetic objects but not works of art. Another way of putting this is to say that anything can be viewed aesthetically, but only some of these things can be regarded artistically. While I believe this is correct, it is important to consider the other possibilities, for each has been thought correct by some aesthetic theorists.

1   *The class of artistic objects and the class of aesthetic objects are identical.* Not only are paintings and poems and other things typically described as works of art to be considered aesthetic, but anything regarded aesthetically will automatically be a work of art. Thus sunsets or a child's laugh are art according to this view. This is, indeed, the way some people talk. Standing on a mountaintop and gazing on the view, some individuals do describe the landscapes they see as "art." I will argue that this is an imprecise use of language. People who talk this way are speaking figuratively. And, as we shall see, some philosophers think that this way of talking can even be dangerous if taken literally.

2   *The class of artistic objects and the class of aesthetic objects are not identical; nonetheless they intersect.* People who hold this view agree that some aesthetic objects (sunsets, seashells, etc.) are not artworks. They also believe that some

artworks are not aesthetic objects – are not (cannot be or even should not be) regarded aesthetically. (I shall discuss some examples below.) Still, many works of art are aesthetic objects, and vice versa.

3 *The class of artistic objects is strictly included in the class of aesthetic objects, but is not identical to the class of aesthetic objects.* All works of art are aesthetic objects, but not all aesthetic objects are works of art. As I said above, this is the view I believe is correct.

4 It is logically possible, of course, that *the class of aesthetic objects and the class of artistic objects are totally discrete.* No works of art are or should be viewed aesthetically, and no aesthetic objects are or should be regarded as works of art, according to this possibility. I know of no one who believes this. Even theorists who insist on a strict distinction between the artistic and the aesthetic grant that aesthetic considerations to some extent, at least, are connected to at least some works of art.


The terms "art" and "artistic" have a much longer history than "aesthetic" or "aesthetic object." Even in ancient cultures where we find no word that can directly be translated into the English word "art" there were practices and concepts that at least indirectly translate as "art." (Sometimes other terms may be a more precise translation – "craft," for instance.) Still, similarities in attitudes and ideas about some skillfully created objects make it natural to talk about, say, prehistoric or Greek art. We cannot pinpoint the introduction of "art" and its equivalents in other languages, but we know it has been around for a very long time. The English word seems initially to have been used to refer to skill and then broadened to include activities that required such skill and gradually to include the products of such craft.[1]

The introduction of the term "aesthetic" can be pinpointed. It was introduced by the philosopher Alexander Baumgarten in the mid-eighteenth century, to refer to what he hoped would become a "science" of sense perception that would resemble a science of conception or logic (Baumgarten 1961). Since perception is required for the experience of beauty, he reasoned, aesthetics would provide a foundation for explaining and justifying human judgments about what is and what is not beautiful. Other philosophers responded immediately and began to say more about what is special about "the aesthetic." One of these, Immanuel Kant, devoted one of his famous Critiques, *The Critique of Judgment*, to a discussion of the nature of the aesthetic, and in this book he distinguishes the aesthetic from the scientific and the moral, and also from the artistic. His work has been extremely influential.

Human beings, Kant recognized, have a variety of different kinds of experiences and concerns. We try to make sense of the world scientifically. We care about how we treat one another. We value the way the world looks and sounds.[2] Each of these realms has its own principles and structures. Kant believed that "aesthetic" refers to the pleasure (or pain) subjects sometimes feel as we move through the world. These responses – the ways one feels – are not in the world, they are in the individual. They are not "objective" (in the objects experienced) but "subjective" (in the subject experiencing).³ When the person feels the kind of pleasure that he or she associates with beauty, the pleasure is "free." It is not tied to or dependent upon any beliefs or moral concerns that one has. One doesn't even care whether the thing one takes to be beautiful is real. If, for example, I enjoy the patterns in a stretch of wallpaper, my pleasure is not diminished by the thought that there is nothing in the world that looks that way. Indeed, if I hallucinate a pleasing design my pleasure is real and it does not matter to me *aesthetically* whether the design is or is not real. The pleasure is good in and of itself.

Paradigmatic examples of beautiful or "aesthetic" things are natural objects, Kant claimed. When I feel pleasure looking west from my window in the early evening, that pleasure is due to the "form" of my experience – the colors⁴ and shapes I perceive. The pleasure does not depend upon any knowledge that I may or may not have about why sunsets look the way they do; and my aesthetic pleasure is not diminished when I am reminded that the best sunsets occur on days when the air pollution is the worst. Science and morality are irrelevant.⁵

But, one naturally objects, surely when I have an aesthetic experience of a sonnet or sonata I must have some knowledge. I must know what a sonnet is or that a sonata is a special arrangement of sounds, not random noise. Kant would agree. And it is precisely for this reason that he distinguishes the aesthetic from the artistic. Artistic appreciation does involve knowledge, most importantly the knowledge that the object or event we are appreciating was created intentionally and skillfully by a human being. Kant provides a famous example:

> For though we like to call the product that bees make (the regularly constructed honeycombs) a work of art, we do so only by virtue of an analogy with art; for as soon as we recall that their labor is not based on any rational deliberation on their part, we say at once that the product is a product of their nature (namely, of instinct), and it is only to their creator that we ascribe it as art. (Kant 1987: 170)

Someone who doesn't know how honeycombs were made, indeed someone who doesn't know or morally care anything at all about them, could still take pleasure in the shapes and designs. This would be pure aesthetic pleasure. Now suppose a person formed some material into an object identical in appearance to a honeycomb. Again, if one did not know how it came to be, one's pleasure would be purely aesthetic. But this object will be appreciated artistically – as a *work* of art, as it were – only when one ascribes intentional human activity to its production. The pleasure we feel when we experience works of art involve something like aesthetic pleasure; but the pleasure now is not pure, not free. It is a dependent pleasure; it depends upon what we believe about the creative act that caused it to come into existence.

Strictly speaking, it may be that Kant did hold a theory that falls under the fourth possibility I mentioned above – the one I said no one has held. That is, he sometimes writes as if the class of aesthetic objects and the class of artistic objects are totally discrete. However, since he does acknowledge that something very like the pleasure we feel when we experience free or natural beauty is felt when we take pleasure in the form of art objects, he probably is best interpreted as adhering to the second or third alternative. What is of primary importance here is the fact that Kant set the stage, as it were, for distinguishing the aesthetic from the artistic.

More recently the distinction has been applied in the attempt to identify what is special about a growing concern, both in philosophy and public policy, namely, environmental aesthetics. Kant provides another example, this time one that expresses a widely shared intuition about the difference between the appreciation of art and the appreciation of nature. If both sorts of appreciation are sometimes aesthetic, but the two sorts of appreciation nonetheless differ, then there is greater support for the view that the artistic and the aesthetic are not identical.

> What do poets praise more highly than the nightingale's enchantingly beautiful song in a secluded thicket on a quiet summer evening by the soft light of the moon? And yet we have cases where some jovial innkeeper, unable to find such a songster, played a trick – received with greatest satisfaction [initially] – on the guests staying at his inn to enjoy the country air, by hiding in a bush some roguish youngster who (with a reed or rush in his mouth) knew how to copy that song in a way very similar to nature's. But as soon as one realizes that it was all a deception, no one will long endure listening to this song that before he had considered so charming. (Kant 1987: 169)

Here the knowledge that something was intentionally albeit skillfully produced – the belief that something is *art* – actually gets in the way, Kant asserts, of our having an aesthetic experience. When we learn that what we thought was the song of a bird was an imitation or recording we will feel less pleasure – or a different kind of pleasure.

The contemporary philosopher Allen Carlson agrees with Kant that there is an essential difference between appreciating art and appreciating nature. But unlike Kant, Carlson does not agree that the difference resides in there being no knowledge involved in the latter. Quite the contrary: Carlson urges that cognitive models of both types of appreciation are correct; what differs is that different cognitions or sets of cognitions are relevant in the two cases. When we appreciate art, he says, we have to know a great deal – not only that intentions and skill were involved, but that an object belongs to one genre rather than another, that it was created at one time and space rather than another, that it is made of one kind of material rather than another. In short, one must know the *category* to which it belongs (Carlson 1979: 269; Walton 1970).[6] This is true of aesthetic appreciation of nature as well. Just as one recognizes the relevance of the fact that one is watching a flute performance and not a tango, one must know that one is in a desert and not a forest if one is adequately and fully to appreciate what one sees, smells, hears, etc. "If to aesthetically appreciate art we have knowledge of artistic traditions and styles within those traditions, to aesthetically appreciate nature we must have knowledge of the different environments of nature and of the systems and elements within those environments" (Carlson 1979: 273).

Appreciating works of art and appreciating natural landscapes both require knowledge and both are genuinely aesthetic. Nonetheless, because different kinds of knowledge are required, it cannot be that the aesthetic appreciation of art can be reduced to or defined in terms of the aesthetic appreciation of nature, and vice versa. What constitutes the aesthetic, then, is not wholly confined to or to be understood in terms of the artistic. Indeed, Carlson insists that it is a serious, even dangerous, mistake to treat nature as art. If one insists on treating a landscape as if it were a landscape painting, not only is much missed or ignored, but what is "natural" about nature may be minimized, and the authenticity of a biotic system may be dismissed. The result is too often management of nature that damages or destroys important elements.

The difference between the aesthetic appreciation of nature and the aesthetic appreciation of art on such a view as Carlson's is consistent with both the second and third possibilities given above. Although Carlson is not explicit on this point (and indeed he may reject it), it is possible that not everything relevant to an evaluation of art per se is aesthetic. A work of art may be important to someone not because of its colors or shapes, but because, for example, it is worth a lot of money. Carlson is explicit about the fact that people aesthetically appreciate nature for other than artistic characteristics. Still, aesthetic consideration of nature and art do share many features – some works of art, like some landscapes, give pleasure because of their design, the patterns of colors, the proportions of volumes, the rhythms of contours, and so on. So the artistic and aesthetic certainly intersect. The artistic may even, on such a view as Carlson's, be wholly included in the aesthetic. Someone might assert that at least with respect to aesthetic value (putting aside such things as economic value, for instance), the experience one has when one regards art aesthetically is of the same sort that one has when one regards nature aesthetically. It is just that one has such experiences with respect to things other than those identified as works of art. The class of aesthetic objects is greater than the class of artistic objects, but artistic objects fall fully within this larger class.

To review what we have seen thus far, Kant said that the aesthetic and the artistic are different because the former is free of any belief or moral concern. Carlson distinguishes aesthetic appreciation of art from aesthetic appreciation of nature on the basis of the different sorts of knowledge required for each. Notice that Carlson's position suggests that insofar as *aesthetic* experience is concerned the aesthetic appreciation of art and the aesthetic appreciation of non-art (of trees or a child's laugh or a hydroelectric dam, for instance) are the same. I shall return to this suggestion later. But first we need to look further at what have been called "non-aesthetic theories of art." For, as I said above, theorists who adhere to one of these necessarily distinguish the aesthetic and the artistic.

At first blush the very phrase "non-aesthetic theory of art" may seem confusing or even contradictory. How could art be non- or un-aesthetic? Surely if anything is to be considered paradigmatically open to aesthetic consideration and evaluation, art is. And everyone (or almost everyone) would agree, I think. It simply is a fact that people associate having an aesthetic experience with art. But what does this mean? One answer comes again from Kant's analysis of *the aesthetic*, one to which I referred only obliquely above. The pleasure we feel in those experiences we identify as aesthetic is due to something's form – to what have come to be called, following Kant, something's *formal properties*. An agreeable design or relation of parts causes pleasure. Kant distances such pleasure from scientific or moral concepts. "Flowers, free designs, lines aimlessly intertwined . . . ; these have no significance, depend on no determinate concept, and yet we like [*gefallen*] them" (Kant 1987: 49). Kant's own view is very subtle and adequate treatment of it is beyond the scope of this chapter. Historically, Kantians or formalists in aesthetic theory have maintained that what makes aesthetic experience non-trivially unique is a special kind of pleasure and that what makes the pleasure special is its source, namely certain intrinsic properties of an object or event that directly manifest themselves to a viewer or hearer. Some perceptual features and their arrangements simply please one, without any external knowledge and independent of everyday purposes and concerns. A modern version of formalistic aesthetic theories of art is Monroe Beardsley's. While he holds that some aesthetic objects are not artworks, he nonetheless insists that if anything is truly an artwork it fulfills an aesthetic function – the function of evoking a pleasurable experience upon contemplating what he calls "regional properties" and ways in which they are unified (Beardsley 1958).[7] In art, the function is fulfilled by something one also recognizes as an artifact and this accounts for the fact that certain properties of artworks (for example, being ironic) cannot be attributed to things that may be aesthetically pleasing but have not been created by a human being. (A tree, for example, cannot be "ironic," except metaphorically.)

If the formalists are correct and "aesthetic" refers to those experiences which involve simply and only considering formal, immediately perceivable properties, then, some theorists have argued, art must involve more than the aesthetic, and it is not enough simply to distinguish the two in terms of artifactuality. Indeed, some have claimed, if what "aesthetic" refers to is individuals' responses, then the nature and value of art may not even involve aesthetic value in a central way. Leo Tolstoy was one such theorist. Limiting the aesthetic to certain kinds of pleasurable experiences and maintaining that the function of art is to evoke aesthetic experiences leads to a serious mistake, he thought. Like confusing the value of food with the pleasure of eating (the true function of food being nourishment), confusing the value of art with the pleasures that may accompany attending to it precludes an explanation of why it has the importance that it does to individuals and communities. That is, we cannot possibly account for the important role art plays solely in terms of pleasure. That would amount to putting art on the same level as eating chocolate or having a massage. Tolstoy argued that art is important because it enables people to communicate emotionally with one another, and the consequence of this is that these people are so bonded together that they come to treat one another better – with greater kindness or respect, for instance. Thus Tolstoy substituted a *moral* theory of art for an *aesthetic* one.

Other theorists have given primacy to other aspects of human experience. Some of these theories are quite general. They focus on the expressive or imitative powers of art. Others are more specific, concentrating on art's political, social, economic, or religious roles. Or they may emphasize some even more specific functions, such as spiritual, psychological, or physical healing.[8] All accept the formalist thesis that the *aesthetic* has at its core the possibility of evoking pleasure in the presence of the presentation of certain immediately perceivable properties, singly and in combination. Insisting that there is more to art than this, they thus distinguish between the aesthetic and the artistic. Most allow that art does have aesthetic value, but they relegate the aesthetic to a secondary function of art. Thus such theories fall under the second possibility I describe at the outset – the view that the aesthetic and the artistic are not identical but nonetheless often intersect. Notice that something may be an imitative or political success without being an aesthetic success, in this sense, for it may achieve such a goal without the formal properties arousing any pleasure. Thus the class of aesthetic and the class of artistic are not identical and one is not a subclass of the other.

Arthur Danto has used a different strategy for distinguishing between the aesthetic and the artistic and has opened the door for another way of de-emphasizing the aesthetic as it was understood by Kant and, more recently, by Beardsley. It is not intentionality or artifactuality per se that serve to subdivide the aesthetic into the artistic and the non-artistic – though they are involved indirectly, according to Danto. Rather it is how certain objects are treated within societies. Danto's work has been tremendously influenced by developments in art history – by the appearance in the last century of things like urinals displayed as "art" in museums, or stretches of silence "performed" as musical "compositions" in concert halls. Two objects or events can be indistinguishable aesthetically (may have the same manifest properties and evoke equal measures of pleasure or pain in a person who attends to their identical intrinsic properties). What makes one art and prevents the other from achieving this status depends upon the location of the first in an artworld that makes it possible for the first but not its twin to be "about" something. One can imagine two trees – one in a forest, the other in a museum – that have the same appearance. The latter but not the former may be described as "ironic" because only it communicates a human idea (Danto 1986). Only the tree that finds its way into the artworld can be art. Formal properties matter far less than the properties that emerge from theories and practices within that world.

What has been called "conceptual art" further emphasizes the difference between the aesthetic and the artistic. Conceptual art is the sort of thing "produced" at "happenings" of various kinds. A hole is dug in the ground and then filled up. Someone erases words or paints a moustache on a famous portrait. A concrete block is dropped from a tall building onto a rat in the street below. Although there is something to be seen, in such cases, the "seeable" matters little or not at all. The viewer or, more appropriately, the *experiencer* is challenged to interact with things and events – to move among objects and act upon them (for example, trip an electric eye that affects objects in an installation) as well as be acted upon by them. Even more radical is so-called art that is entirely conceptual, not perceptual at all. An "artist" thinks about dropping a concrete block on a rat or just tells someone about his or her idea for destroying an artifact. Art in this sense has been completely "dematerialized" and so there is nothing to be seen. Conceptual art objects do, typically, involve art objects or events that can be perceived or witnessed. But the perceptual is far less important than the conceptual. What always matters most is the idea and discussions that it generates. Erasures, for example, are carried out in order to get people to think about what texts hide and what they reveal or about the nature of permanence versus transience. If conceptual art genuinely is art and if the aesthetic is essentially tied to the perceptual, then, again, the aesthetic and the artistic must be distinct. For this kind of art, at least, the two seem totally discrete; there will not even be an intersection between the two classes.

But is conceptual art really art? If the answer is no, then support for the total divorce of the aesthetic and the artistic disappears. I am going to take a very strong and admittedly controversial stand on this issue and argue that conceptual art is not art – that at most "conceptual artists" are artists only metaphorically. In making my argument, I shall explain what I believe the relationship between the artistic and the aesthetic is.

One must begin by asking what it is about conceptual art that makes it a candidate for being "art" at all. How is one to distinguish a work of conceptual art from a philosophical treatise or a political demonstration? How is one to tell, indeed, if someone is having an *aesthetic* experience of a work of conceptual art? Conceptual artists may respond that they are not interested in evoking aesthetic experiences. But if what one does want to evoke is a philosophical experience, that is, the experience of participating in conceptualizing or theorizing about something, then why should one insist that one is producing art at all? Why not simply say that one is presenting an idea for consideration? The only response must be that one is presenting the sort of thing we used to call "aesthetic art" but now, in order to make it clear that more than formal properties are important, we must use this new term "conceptual art." But we have seen that many theorists rejected a view of art based purely on formalistic considerations. Persons who adhere to moral or political theories of art, for example, have always pointed to the conceptual as well as the perceptual facets of artworks. Libraries (and now the internet) are full of discussions of artworks that include references to much more than perceptual properties – to moral, political, or philosophical aspects, for instance – created long before the so-called conceptual art movement. It was only the narrowest, strictest formalists who insisted that all such artistic discussion is irrelevant to genuine or pure aesthetic experiences.

My own view is this: either there is no conceptual art or all art is conceptual. "Purely conceptual art" is an oxymoron, for art must be perceptual (for however

short a time) if it is to generate artistic discussion per se. If a thing has no perceptual dimension and generates exclusively political or philosophic (or some other
non-aesthetic) discussion then there is no basis for calling it art rather than politics or philosophy. Still, anything rightly called art is open to discussion or conceptualization of all sorts. What makes art art and not something else, such as a
philosophical or political treatise, is not the fact that people think as well as look
or listen. What makes art special is the fact that the conception is directly tied to
or dependent upon the perception. Baumgarten was right to think of the aesthetic
in terms of perception. However, he and those he so strongly influenced, such as
Kant and the twentieth-century formalists, were wrong to think of aesthetic experience exclusively in terms of perception.

How would we describe human activity and productions that did some or most
of the things we typically associate with art but did not engage aesthetic attention
and evaluation? The kind of things I have in mind are these:

participation in rituals as performer or spectator;
creating objects that are kept in special places;
creating objects used to communicate messages and feelings;
engaging in activity that is applauded in a community; and
engaging in activity that is repeated in a community.

All of these might be done without any attention to what is commonly thought
of as paying aesthetic attention. Noël Carroll has aptly described "paradigmatic
aesthetic attention" as including "tracking the formal structures of artworks, what
we might call design appreciation, along with detecting the . . . expressive properties . . . and perhaps taking note of the ways in which those properties emerge
from what are called the base properties of [things]" (Carroll 2000a: 206–7). It
is theoretically possible (though in fact uncommon, I think) to observe a ritual or
applaud an activity or do any of the other things listed above without paying attention to features like design or expressiveness. But I do not see how or why we
would ever, in this case, refer to the objects or events as "art." This is why I insist
that the class of the artistic is a subclass of the class of the aesthetic, wholly included
in it but not identical to it. Why would we applaud something or protect it or
demand that it be repeated if we cared not a whit about its intrinsic properties?
Well, we might care about its consequences – how it heals or binds the community, for instance. But if this is all that we cared about, we would probably not
object if one equally effective object or event were substituted for another. This
is not the case with artworks. Not just any poem will do for a particular occasion.
Even if we can't immediately tell the difference, we care that something was really
made by, say, Rembrandt, and not just by one of his students. (I shall say more
about this phenomenon later.) Something that is a work of art can do any of
the things in the list. But art is art because it does them via perceivable properties
and because viewers do care a whit (usually much more than a whit) about the
particular intrinsic properties of particular objects.

When individuals have aesthetic experiences, a necessary element of the experience is that attention is paid to intrinsic properties of objects and events – properties that can be perceived directly. Special knowledge may be required in order for the perception to be possible or full. For example, one needs to know what a fugue is before one can hear that a musical work is a fugue and not a tarantella. The attention demanded is what characterizes the aesthetic. This kind of attention can be given to anything that can be perceived, for anything that can be perceived has design, shape, color, etc. (though it may be boring or chaotic, clever or dull, intense or washed out). When attention is given to the particular properties of an object or an event, it is an aesthetic object or event. When this attention is given to an artifact – a thing or event intentionally created by a human being – then that artifact is on its way to becoming an artwork.

In order more fully to understand how theorists have viewed the connection (or lack of it) between concepts in aesthetic and artistic appreciation, it is helpful to return again to Kant. We have seen that he puts pleasure at the center of aesthetic experience, but it is a particular kind of pleasure. The uniqueness of the pleasure, he thought, lies in *when* it arises. We feel this kind of pleasure (one different from the pleasure we feel when we eat chocolate or do a good deed or solve a math problem) when, as he put it, our imagination engages in "free play." We experience a "quickening" of our cognitive powers. Just what Kant meant by this has been the topic of much discussion and debate. I believe that the most coherent interpretation of this part of his theory is along these lines. In moral and scientific judgments, we try to fit our perceptual experiences to our conceptual theories. We try to decide, for example, whether something is a cow or a buffalo, a wave or a particle. Or we try to determine what duty demands of us in our treatment of other people. If we succeed in such endeavors, we feel pleasure, but it is pleasure that is tied to specific concepts. In aesthetic experiences, one's pleasure is not tied to specific concepts.[9] One's imagination is free to play around with concepts – to think of something as a cow or a buffalo or maybe a cow and a buffalo at the same time. We are free to think of the wallpaper design as a school of fish and then a bouquet of flowers and then just a bunch of lines and colors and then a school of fish again and then as something entirely different, and so on. And this freedom, this "play," is delightful. When specific concepts are involved, as when, with art, we are forced to think in terms of the concepts of intention and skill, the play is restricted, and hence the playful pleasure is diminished, it seems. The pleasure is different – dependent rather than independent.

On this interpretation of Kant, both the perceptual and conceptual are involved. But Kant worried that too much of the conceptual (at least to the extent that specific concepts are involved) might erase aesthetic pleasure. Other theorists have tended to agree with him, and have emphasized the role of the perceptual in explaining the nature of the aesthetic. Frank Sibley, for instance, goes so far as to define "aesthetic" in terms of the special sensitivity people have that allows them to perceive properties like gracefulness, balance, harmony, rhythm (Sibley 1959). Having "taste" – this special sensitivity – is required for aesthetic experiences.[10]

Concepts have a role to play – they can be used by critics to draw a viewer's attention to formal properties – but as with Baumgarten, the aesthetic is to be understood and analyzed primarily in terms of perceptual experiences. Sibley believes that artworks are obvious instances of the aesthetic and probably would agree that the artistic is a subset of the aesthetic; at the very least he would agree that the two sets intersect.

One of the reasons that conceptual artists and some other contemporary theorists have wanted to separate the artistic and the aesthetic is their fear that "aesthetic" refers primarily to "the beautiful." Certainly when Kant explained the aesthetic realm of human experience he chose to do it in terms of our attribution of this quality. Until very recently in the history of philosophical aesthetics, "beauty" was at the center of attention. In ordinary discourse, people often refer to someone's "aesthetic," meaning by that the person's theory or definition of what is beautiful. In the twentieth century, at least in technological societies, "beauty" began to move from the center or at least to share it with other qualities, however. "Interesting," "dramatic," "challenging," "evocative," "moving," for example, were more and more often applied to artworks. It was difficult, for instance, to discuss urinals or repetitions of words or stretches of silence in terms of their beauty. Particularly when artists themselves insisted that beauty was not a concern of theirs, the artistic and the aesthetic part ways if one interprets the latter in terms of something's beauty. Witnessing the horrors of the wars and holocausts of their time, some theorists have thought that the pleasures of beauty were too "easy." Artists should give us more than "pretty pictures," if they are to have any real relevance to the human experience, it was often argued. Aesthetics' long association with beauty again accounts for some theorists' desire to move the artistic away from the aesthetic.

Instead of jettisoning the aesthetic, however, I think a better strategy is broadening the notion to include the very qualities that came to share the stage with beauty. Indeed, I think that retaining a connection between the aesthetic and the artistic is the only way to account for a difference between artworks and things like philosophical or political treatises. Beauty and the pleasure we take in it are paradigmatically aesthetic, but they do not exhaust the aesthetic. I suggest the following definition of "aesthetic property," and definitions or characterizations of "aesthetic experience" and "aesthetic relevance" follow immediately from it:

A is an aesthetic property of x, if and only if A is an intrinsic property of x considered worthy of attention (perception and/or reflection) in culture C.

A remark or gesture is aesthetically relevant if and only if it draws attention to an aesthetic property of an object or event.

A person has an aesthetic experience of x if and only if that person responds to an aesthetic property of an object and knows that a culture C considers it to be an aesthetic property.

Notice that this way of thinking about the aesthetic retains as a core component the perceptual element that Kant and the formalists so influenced by him emphasized. But it makes room as well for cognitive or conceptual elements that I believe also play key roles in at least most of our aesthetic experiences. Indeed, I find it hard to imagine having an aesthetic experience that is purely perceptual – where, for instance, we delight in a design in the absence of any concepts – such as the realization that we are looking at a design. A necessary component of aesthetic experience is the fact that one must look or listen or touch or feel or taste in order to know that something does in fact have a particular intrinsic property. Reports of others may give us some reason to believe that an object is well proportioned; but in order to verify the claim we must look for ourselves.

This necessary component of the aesthetic must also be a necessary component of the artistic if artworks are to be distinguished from other things that are skillfully and intentionally produced. Thus I define "art" as follows.

> X is a work of art if and only if x is an artifact and x is treated in such a way that someone who is fluent in a culture is led to direct attention (perception and/or reflection) to aesthetic properties of x.

There is nothing about these definitions of the artistic and the aesthetic that precludes the sort of discussion that conceptual artists wanted to generate. One of the best ways of drawing attention to intrinsic properties of objects and events considered aesthetically valuable within a community is precisely by talking about them. If the discussion that is generated is not tied to or grounded in the particular intrinsic properties of an object or event, then any thing that stimulates that discussion could serve as a worthy substitute. But conceptual artists would be the last to agree that anything they do or make or say is as good as anything else as long as it gets people talking about the right issues.

We do, of course, talk about works of art in ways that we do not talk about aesthetic objects that are not artworks – things and events that occur unintentionally or accidentally which nonetheless have intrinsic properties considered worthy of perception and reflection. My definition of art includes a key reference to *artifactuality*. The centrality of this notion reflects, I think, the fact that we refer to *works* of art – and this emphasizes a concern for and interest in the work, both perceptual and conceptual, that goes into the creation of art objects. Kant used his nightingale example to describe the way one's pleasure in natural objects differs from one's pleasure in art objects. It is certainly true that our evening might be spoiled if we thought we were listening to a real nightingale and then were told that what in fact we were hearing was a clever flutist or a mechanical reproduction. But might not just the opposite occur? Might we not actually get more pleasure – the pleasure that comes from realizing that one is in the presence of such a talented musician or fine recording equipment? There are many causes of aesthetic pleasure, and different people respond at different levels to different sorts of things.

The fact, however, that we do care about what is responsible for how a certain set of sounds or images or movements is produced is tied to a final issue: fakes and forgeries. Some people might think that art, but not nature, can be "faked," and that this must signal an important distinction between the aesthetic and the artistic. But does it?

First we need to look at the relevance of the possibility of forging works of art to the aesthetic or artistic experience of these things. Let's turn Kant's nightingale example around a bit. Suppose you are attending a dinner party and the host announces that the famous flutist Christina van Goedvingers will perform as coffee is served. You sit back and thrill to the sounds and the amazing skill of the performer as her fingers fly back and forth along the length of the instrument. But in the middle of a particularly wonderful passage, your neighbor whispers to you that he has learned that a trick is afoot. The sounds are really being produced by a nightingale under Christina's chair. People, as I suggested earlier, react differently, depending on what the object of their attention is. The "whole" event – the host's cleverness, the nightingale's tones, Christina's fine imitation of flute playing – is certainly a possible source of aesthetic satisfaction. But some people, at least, may be disappointed and their enjoyment may be diminished if not wiped out entirely. "She's a fake!" someone may object.

This is a very contrived example. But there are real-life counterparts. Someone thinks he or she has purchased a Rembrandt and subsequently learns that it is a fake. Or someone appreciates a film less upon learning that a stunt man filled in for the star in some scenes. Or someone thought a work was created in the sixteenth century and then finds out that it was made last week and feels cheated. There are theorists who insist that if someone cannot tell the difference between a work and a copy of it, the *aesthetic* component of the experience is stable – that whatever difference it makes to the viewer cannot be an aesthetic difference. Other theorists insist that knowledge that something is a fake or forgery does make a difference, and an aesthetic one. The aesthetic appreciation of an artwork has as an essential element the belief that something has been achieved in the work, that it is a human accomplishment. This, they argue, is why intention and skill matter. Art is a human activity and appreciation of art is appreciation of products understood as and experienced as the result of human endeavor.[11]

Suppose that we grant that artistic appreciation involves to some degree awareness of and admiration for human achievement, and that this is why one cares whether something is real or a fake. Does this constitute an important difference between art and nature (non-art), and a corresponding difference between the artistic and the aesthetic? Answering this requires asking oneself whether it would ever make sense to say that a natural object or event had been "faked." Mechanical reproductions of nature (recordings of nightingales or whale songs, for instance) might be passed off as "the real thing." But can a natural object per se ever be a fake or forgery?

I think we can imagine such cases. Suppose my husband knows that I have been looking for years for a rare orchid in a Minnesota forest. Thinking that it will please me, he buys one of the species at a florist shop and "plants" it along a trail he knows I shall be taking. Something very much like forgery or fakery takes place in such a case. Certainly deception (no matter how well intended) is involved. If I learn that the flower has come from a florist's shop, won't I be very disappointed – in much the way I am if I learn that my "Rembrandt" is not the real thing? Knowledge about the source can matter as much in nature as it can in art. Some timber companies leave enough trees along a highway to hide the denuding of land that has resulted from clear-cutting only a few yards from the road. This, too, is a kind of fakery, knowledge of which may certainly diminish the aesthetic pleasure one initially felt. It is true that appreciation of human achievement is not involved in aesthetic appreciation of nature, but knowledge is nonetheless relevant. We return to Carlson's position that knowledge is at the heart of aesthetic appreciation of both nature and of art, and again find reason to distinguish but not to separate completely the aesthetic and the artistic.

## Notes

1 For the history of uses of "art" see *The Oxford English Dictionary*.
2 It is possible to have aesthetic experiences that involve any of the senses, of course. Since the arts have historically given priority to pleasures of sights and sounds, I shall limit my discussion here to these. The reader may include the other senses where appropriate.
3 Kant argued that although aesthetic experiences are subjective, they are nonetheless universally valid. When I say something is beautiful, not only am I saying something about the pleasure I myself feel, but I also claim that everyone else should feel the same way about that thing. See *Critique of Judgment*, 1790, division I, book I. There are several editions and translations of Kant's third critique. My citations come from Kant (1987: 53–64).
4 Aestheticians disagree about whether or not colors are aesthetic properties. Some of the reasons for saying they are not will become clearer later. I believe they are. In any case, it is generally agreed that patterns and relationships of colors are aesthetic, so I shall refer to colors as well as shapes in my discussion.
5 This is a very simplified statement of Kant's view. For excellent discussions of Kant's aesthetics, see Cohen and Guyer (1982); Crawford (1974); Guyer (1997); and Kemal (1993).
6 Carlson acknowledges Kendall Walton's influential article in the development of his view.
7 See especially his chapter 1.
8 For an excellent discussion of various definitions of art, see Davies (1999). See pp. 67–71 in particular for discussion of why some theorists have said that possession of aesthetic properties is not a sufficient condition of something's being a work of art. See also Anderson (2000: 65–92).
9 Sometimes Kant writes as if aesthetic pleasure involves no concepts at all, sometimes as if it involves no specific concepts. I have settled on the latter, but Kant himself is simply not clear on this.

10  Sibley is often accused, with some justification I believe, of being elitist – of thinking that only some people are blessed with the special sensitivity that makes aesthetic experiences possible. I agree with Sibley that perception is required for aesthetic experiences, but I think all normal people are capable of having the relevant sensations. Some of these may require special learning or development of individual senses. There may be some experiences that some individuals are incapable of having – a blind person will not experience color arrangements, for example. However, a blind person may experience a work of sculpture via touch and have a richer aesthetic experience than a sighted person. It is the requirement of a general "special" sensitivity that makes Sibley's view subject to accusations of elitism.

11  For discussions of fakes and forgeries see Goodman (1976); Dutton (1979); and Lessing (1965). Part of the debate surrounding fakes and forgeries in art involves discussion of whether it is only some art forms that can be fakes – paintings but not plays, for example. This is tied to the fact that there is only one *Mona Lisa*, the one in the Louvre in Paris, but several copies of, say, *Hamlet*. Whether or not literary or musical works can be faked, and if so how, remains open to debate.

# References

Anderson, J. (2000). "Aesthetic Concepts of Art." In Carroll (2000b): 65–92.

Baumgarten, A. G. (1961). *Aesthetica*. Hildesheim: George Holms Verlagsbuchhandlung. Originally pub. 1750–8.

Beardsley, M. (1958). *Aesthetics*. New York: Harcourt Brace.

Carlson, A. (1979). "Appreciation and the Natural Environment." *Journal of Aesthetics and Art Criticism*, Spring: 269.

Carroll, N. (2000a). "Art and the Domain of the Aesthetic." *British Journal of Aesthetics*, 40(2): 206–7.

——(2000b). *Theories of Art Today*. Madison: University of Wisconsin Press.

Cohen, T. and Guyer, P. (eds) (1982). *Essays in Kant's Aesthetics*. Chicago: University of Chicago Press.

Crawford, D. (1974). *Kant's Aesthetic Theory*. Madison: University of Wisconsin Press.

Danto, A. (1986). *The Transfiguration of the Commonplace*. New York: Columbia University Press.

Davies, S. (1999). *Definitions of Art*. Ithaca, NY: Cornell University Press.

Dutton, D. (1979). "Artistic Crimes: The Problem of Forgery in the Arts." *British Journal of Aesthetics*.

Goodman, N. (1976). *Languages of Art*. Indianapolis: Hackett.

Guyer, P. (1997). *Kant and the Claims of Taste*. 2nd edn. Cambridge: Cambridge University Press.

Kant, I. (1987). *The Critique of Judgment*. Trans. Werner S. Pluhar. Indianapolis: Hackett: 53–64.

Kemal, S. (1993). *Kant's Aesthetic Theory*. New York: St Martin's Press.

Lessing, A. (1965). "What is Wrong with a Forgery?" *Journal of Aesthetics and Art Criticism*, 23.

Sibley, F. (1959). "Aesthetic Concepts." *Philosophical Review*, 68: 421–50.

Walton, K. (1970). "Categories of Art." *Philosophical Review*, 334–67.

# Chapter 4

# The Ontology of Art

## *Amie L. Thomasson*

The central question for the ontology of art is this: what sort of entities are works of art? Are they physical objects, ideal kinds, imaginary entities, or something else? How are works of art of various kinds related to the mental states of artists or viewers, to physical objects, or to abstract visual, auditory, or linguistic structures? Under what conditions do works come into existence, survive, or cease to exist?

It is important to notice that this question is quite distinct from the question of whether or how "art" may be defined. The ontological question does not ask what conditions anything must satisfy if it is to be a work of art, but rather, of various entities accepted as paradigm works of art of different genres (such as *Guernica, Clair de Lune,* or *Emma*), it asks: what sort of entity is this? And what sorts of entity in general are paintings, musical works, novels, and so on? Even the best answer to this question is unlikely to provide anything like a "definition" that will distinguish art from non-art, since the relevant ontological status(es) may be shared with a great many other things, and since works of art of different kinds may have different ontological statuses.

Although it seems that few people have a ready answer to the question of the ontological status of the work of art, some relevant considerations are built into our common-sense understanding of works of art and practices in dealing with them. We normally think of works of art as things created at a certain time, in particular cultural and historical circumstances, through the imaginative and creative acts of an artist, composer, or author. Once created, works of art are normally thought of as relatively stable and enduring public entities that may be seen, heard, or read by a number of different people who may enter legitimate arguments about at least some of the work's features. While these features characterize our understanding of all sorts of works of art, our understanding and treatment of works of different sorts diverge regarding other features.

Works of painting and (non-cast) sculpture we ordinarily treat as individual entities, such that even if exact copies are made from them, the work itself is identical with the original. We treat such works as individual entities as capable of being bought and sold directly and moved about to reside with their new owners. We also normally consider such works capable of being maintained and surviving certain changes in their physical constitution (restoring a painting, replacing a small part of a sculpture), but capable of being destroyed if the relevant canvas or piece of clay is destroyed or changed in certain ways (if solvent is applied to the pigmented surface of the canvas, or the clay is dissolved and reshaped).

Works of (traditionally scored classical) music and literature, on the other hand, may have many performances and many copies; although we may privilege the author's signed manuscript, it is only of historical interest, and may be destroyed without the work itself going out of existence. Works of music and literature themselves (as opposed to copies of the work or score or recordings of a performance) are not bought and sold as literally as diamonds, pearls, and works of painting and sculpture are; instead, performance rights, reproduction rights, or copyrights to the works may be sold, but no physical object need be shuffled from city to city for such transactions to occur. Nor does any single physical object need to be protected and maintained to prevent the work from destruction, for the work of music or literature may survive as long as some copy of it remains, though it may be destroyed if all copies and memories of it are gone.

These divergences suggest that works of art may not all be of the same ontological type – in particular, concrete works of art such as painting and non-cast sculpture may differ in status from works of music and literature. The relevant ontological divisions need not go strictly with the categories of visual art, music, drama, etc., for works of printmaking, cast sculpture, installations, and conceptual art may differ in ontological status from traditional painting and (non-cast) sculpture (and from each other); works of improvisational, folk, or popular music may differ in status from traditionally scored works of classical music; and works of performance art may differ from traditional drama. While all of these cases should ultimately be considered separately, for simplicity I will focus here on the cases of painting and (non-cast) sculpture on the one hand, and on the other hand on works of literature and music roughly of the "classical" western tradition. Remarks below should be understood as implicitly limited to those canonical forms. Any progress we can make toward answering the question in those cases may provide some guidance when investigating the ontology of other forms of art.

Although the common-sense understanding of works of art may be fairly obvious, determining the ontological status of works of art is extremely difficult, as is immediately evident from the extraordinary variety of answers among the major contenders. Indeed works of art (of some or all kinds) have been placed in just about every major ontological category – including those of mental entities, imaginary objects or activities, physical objects, and abstract kinds of various sorts. I will begin in section 4.1 by briefly surveying a range of major views. While this survey is certainly not exhaustive (and some other options will be discussed in section 4.3), it should make evident the variety of major views that have been held. But despite the great range of views available, none seems fully satisfactory, for each of them conflicts in serious ways with the common-sense understanding of art discussed above. This raises the questions addressed in section 4.2, namely whether such conflicts with common sense pose genuine problems for theories of the ontology of art, and in general how we should adjudicate among competing ontologies of art. Answering these questions will help reveal why the problem of the ontology of the work of art has proven so intractable. Perhaps more importantly, as I discuss in section 4.3, it will also suggest where we should go to look for a more adequate theory, and demonstrate why the issue of the ontology of art has widespread implications for metaphysics and for philosophy generally.

## 4.1   A Range of Views

A first, obvious view of the ontology of art is that works of art are just physical objects – lumps of marble, pigment-covered canvasses, sequences of sound waves or marks on pages – so that their ontological status is no more (or less) puzzling than that of our familiar sticks, stones, or pieces of marble. The simple physical-object hypothesis (as Wollheim [1980] calls it), however, has come under attack from a variety of directions, and its failings have inspired the development of a number of alternatives.

R. G. Collingwood famously denies that any work of art is a physical object, for two reasons. First, not only is imaginative creation necessary for creating a work of art (unlike a mere physical object), but Collingwood argues that it may also be sufficient; a composer may create a work of music merely "in his head," by imagining the relevant tune, without ever having to write a score or play a note. Thus, Collingwood concludes, the work of music (and analogously for the other arts) must be something "in the composer's head," not a series of heard notes or a physical sequence of sound waves (1958: 139). (This, however, seems at best a borderline case of artistic creation, and surely in the case of other arts such as painting, sculpture, or architecture, we in no way allow that an artist has created a work of art of the relevant sort if she has created something merely "in her head.") Second, Collingwood argues that a work of art of whatever form is not perceived by merely, say, hearing the noises of a musical performance or seeing the colors of a painting. Instead, seeing the work of art *as such* requires imagination; for example, to supplement or correct the heard sounds, subtract noises from the audience outside, and so on. Indeed, he urges, really experiencing a work of art requires a "total imaginative experience," involving, for instance, tactile as much as visual imagination in experiencing a work of painting (1958: 144–7). Thus, he concludes, works of art themselves are never painted canvasses, series of noises, or any other external objects. These are merely means that an artist may provide to help observers reconstruct for themselves something like the total imaginary experience the artist had in creating the work. This "imaginary experience of total activity" of the artist's, recreated by competent viewers, is the true work of art (1958: 149–51).[1]

Jean-Paul Sartre similarly argues that works of art are never "real" objects that can be simply perceived as painted canvases are, but rather are imaginary entities, since seeing the aesthetic object requires *imaginative* acts of consciousness (1966: 246–7). Unlike Collingwood, however, Sartre does not think of works of art as imagined *activities*, but rather as imaginary or "unreal" *objects*, created and sustained by acts of imaginative consciousness, and existing only as long as they remain the objects of such acts.

The apparently great contrast between perception of "real" objects and observation of works of art, however, seems to rely on an inadequate phenomenology of ordinary experience. It may require "imagination" – that is (as Collingwood treats it) supplementing some aspects of experience and ignoring others, grasping more than what is carried by "raw" sense perception (if there is such a thing), for a doctor to apprehend her patient's disease (just viewing red spots is not enough), or for a scientist to consider the nature of a far-away star or subatomic particle, or indeed for ordinary people to experience the houses and traffic lights, drivers' licenses and lecture halls around them rather than mere isolated visual and auditory phenomena. But while this may have various interesting implications, surely that fact alone does not demonstrate that the objects conceived in each case are merely imaginary objects "in the heads" of individual observers and existing only as long as the objects are thought of.

In any case, viewing works of art as imaginary activities or objects rather than as physical objects seems to invite more problems than it solves. Collingwood's view (1958: 142), as he admits, entails that works of music cannot be heard, nor paintings seen, since imaginative activities cannot be perceived; and both views make it extremely difficult to see how *one and the same* work of art could be experienced and discussed by many different people, since each would seem to be engaged in her own imaginative activities and experiencing her own imaginary objects. On such imaginative views no work of art can be destroyed through destroying such entities as painted canvases, since the works themselves exist only in the minds of artist and audience. Similarly, contrary to the regular practices and assumptions of the artworld, true works of art cannot be bought or sold, performed or read aloud, restored or mechanically reproduced. Finally, viewing works of art as imaginary objects or activities has the consequence that works of art exist intermittently, depending on the presence or absence of the relevant sorts of supporting mental state (Wolterstorff 1980: 43); for (assuming they are like other imaginary objects) works of art would depend for their existence and total essence on our acts of imagination (Sartre 1966: 160). Given these extreme violations of our ordinary understanding of and ways of dealing with art, the imaginary-entity hypothesis hardly seems likely to provide a superior alternative to the physical-object hypothesis.

There are, however, other, better arguments against identifying works of art of any kind with physical objects. We must first ask how to construe the thesis that works of art are physical objects: is it the strong view that they are identifiable with the *mere* lumps of matter that make them up, describable *purely* in terms of physics? So stated, the view is hardly plausible – certainly it is essential to works of art as we normally understand them that they have certain intentional, meaning-oriented, and/or aesthetic properties. Yet the prospects for describing any of these properties purely in the terminology of physics seem dim at best. Moreover, many arguments have been raised, both within aesthetics and in the literature on material constitution (Johnston 1997: 44–62; Baker 2000: 27–58), against identifying statues, paintings, and other artifacts with their constituting matter, since the two may have different identity or persistence conditions (the statue can survive the replacement of one of its fingers with a different piece of clay, while the lump of clay cannot survive such changes; and the clay can survive the reorganization of its parts into a ball, while the statue cannot) or different essential properties (the statue is essentially an artifact, created or at least selected by an artist; the lump of clay is not).

So it seems that if the physical-object hypothesis is to be made plausible, it must be construed as the weaker view that, though they might not be strictly identifiable with mere constituting matter or entities fully describable in the terms of physics, works of art are individual concreta (bearing physical properties perhaps among others) constituted by physical objects, but not identifiable with their constituting matter. While this view is clearly more plausible, the problem of determining the precise ontological status of works of art remains unresolved. For what sort of thing, exactly, is the work of art if (despite being a concrete individual, and thus not an abstract or imaginary entity) it is also not a *mere* physical entity? I will return to this issue in section 4.3.

Whatever the fate of the view that works of painting and non-cast sculpture are physical objects, there are extremely good reasons to deny that *all* works of art are physical objects in either the strong or weak sense. Thus, for example, while Wollheim and Wolterstorff both allow that *some* sorts of art (paintings, non-cast sculptures) are physical objects, both deny that this holds for *all* sorts of art. For in works of music, literature, or drama there is no particular physical object, process, or event that can plausibly be identified either with the work of art itself or with its constituting basis. In music, for example, as is often observed (Ingarden 1989: 7–16, 23–6; Wollheim 1980: 5–8), the work itself cannot be identified with any copy of the score or with any performance, since (among many other reasons) copies of the score cannot be heard, and it can survive the destruction of any copy of the score and outlast the duration of any performance. Nor can the work of music (or literature, drama, or dance) be identified with the totality of all such performances (or copies), since that would entail, for example, that the work is not complete until long after the composer's death, when the last performance is finished, and that the work itself would have been different had last night's performance been cancelled.

Given the failure of attempts to identify works of art with imaginary entities, and to identify at least many sorts of work with physical objects, the remaining option that naturally arises is to consider some or all works of art as abstract entities. Thus, for instance, Richard Wollheim holds that works of literature and music are not physical objects or classes of these; they are types (distinct from classes or universals), of which copies/performances are tokens. Nicholas Wolterstorff takes works of music, literature, drama, and even certain of the visual arts (printmaking, cast sculptures, repeatable works of architecture) to be "norm-kinds," that is, kinds determined by the properties normative within them, where the properties normative within them are precisely those selected, for example by the composer as required for the correctness of a performance.

Gregory Currie defends the more surprising view that *all* works of art are abstract types, "capable, in principle, of having multiple instances" (1989: 8). Thus, on his view, contrary to popular belief, paintings are just like novels and works of music in having multiple instances of equal ontological and aesthetic standing. So although one instance of *Guernica* happens to be Picasso's original (and people may, irrationally, care about it more or mistakenly think of *it* as the work), there is no more reason to consider it identical with *the work of painting* than there is to consider Jane Austen's original manuscript identical with the literary work *Emma*. Moreover, Currie differs from Wollheim and Wolterstorff also in viewing works of music and literature as types of *action*, namely that of discovering a certain structure (of sounds, colors, etc.) via a particular heuristic path (the way the artist used to discover the structure) (1989: 7). The action-type hypothesis (as Currie calls it), like Collingwood's proposal, has the counterintuitive consequence that works of art can never be perceived at all by observers, but can at best be reconstructed (Levinson 1992: 216–17).

Any view that identifies works of art (of any kind) with pure abstract structures immediately encounters other conflicts with the common-sense conception of art. For types and kinds, traditionally understood, exist eternally, independently from all human activities; thus, contra traditional beliefs and practices regarding the arts, works of art on such models cannot genuinely be created by artists at all, but only selected from the range of available types or kinds.[2] Moreover, despite our ordinary beliefs that many ancient works of music and literature have been destroyed, on such views the works of art can in fact never be destroyed (though tokens or instances of them may be). Moreover, pure abstract types or kinds are generally held to be individuated exclusively by their distinguishing properties – but if that is so, then, contrary to our standard means of identification, such features as authorship or historical context are entirely irrelevant to the identity of a work, while even slight alterations in the properties of the type or normative within the kind result in a different work of art.[3]

It seems, then, that despite the diversity of views available, none is completely satisfying. No work of painting, sculpture, music, or literature can be identified with an imaginary entity, a mere physical object, or an abstract type or kind without requiring us to abandon or seriously revise the ordinary understanding of art embodied in basic beliefs and behaviors in our practices in dealing with the arts. That is why the ontology of art turns out to present such a difficult philosophical problem.

## 4.2 Criteria of Assessment

It might be thought, however, that we were premature in concluding that none of the above ontologies of art is adequate. Even if each of them conflicts with aspects of our common-sense beliefs and practices regarding the arts, one might say, surely that does not show that they are wrong; perhaps it is common sense that is wrong and in need of revision on these issues, and one of the theories surveyed above may after all provide the correct account of the ontology of the work of art. Currie, for example, claims that even if the way we treat paintings "reveals a community-wide acceptance of the view that painting is singular," "It by no means follows from this that painting is singular; it is possible that we are mistaken about this" (1989: 87). To assess whether or not this is a suitable reply, we must address the larger methodological issue: what are the success criteria for developing and comparatively evaluating proposed ontologies of art? More particularly, are violations of common-sense beliefs about art a problem for these views, or only for common sense itself?

Some might say that the problems are only problems for common sense, for after all, common-sense beliefs have often in the past conflicted with scientific theories, and when they do, we readily accept that common sense must give way. So similarly, it might be suggested, our best aesthetic theories may simply require us to give up certain common-sense beliefs about works of art. As has been pointed out elsewhere (McMahan 2000: 97–8), however, the reason scientific theories sometimes warrant dismissing common-sense views is that scientific theories may be empirically extremely well confirmed, giving us strong reason to believe their direct consequences, even if they conflict with prior widely held or "common-sense" beliefs. But the same epistemic status may not be shared by philosophical theories. Not only is there no such empirical evidence available to confirm theories that hold works of art to be physical objects, action-types, or imaginary objects, but it is far from clear what sorts of empirical findings could possibly count for or against any of the major views about the ontological status of works of art. Thus even if well-confirmed scientific theories occasionally conflict with common sense, giving us reason to abandon the latter, the analogy with the scientific case gives us no reason to think that common-sense views should be tossed aside when they conflict with theories of philosophical aesthetics.

Causal theories of reference (Kripke 1972; Putnam 1975) provide the basis for another standard argument that common-sense views are fallible. For these influential theories have insisted that the reference of names and natural kind terms is determined not by concepts or descriptions that speakers of the language associate with the term, but rather by causal contact between those establishing ("grounding") the reference of a name, and the individual or kind referred to. Thus, on such theories, the reference of a name such as "Shakespeare" is not established by a relation between some description that speakers associate with the name (such as "the author of *Hamlet*") and an individual who meets the description.

Instead, it is established by a causal relation between the man referred to and the use of the name by those "grounding" it by applying it to him directly. Others may acquire the name by "borrowing" the reference from the original grounders, and thus reference back to that man may be secured and maintained, even if most commonly held beliefs about Shakespeare turn out to be false (for instance, if it turns out he did not write *Hamlet*). Similarly, according to such theories, a natural kind term such as "whale" acquires its reference not in virtue of certain animals meeting the descriptions that speakers associate with the term "whale," but by being applied directly to a certain sample of entities, after which point it refers to the kind to which all or most of those entities belong. Reference to the kind may be passed on to other speakers of the language (even if they have never seen a whale), and everyone can thereby refer to whales even if common-sense beliefs about the nature of whales are radically wrong (for example, even if everyone believes they are fish).

Thus, impressed by such theories of reference and the possibilities they leave open for radical mistakes in common-sense beliefs about both individuals and kinds, some might suggest that none of our common-sense beliefs about paintings, symphonies, novels (or things of other kinds) is inviolable, since these, like common-sense beliefs about whales, may turn out to be completely false. On such a view, the metaphysical nature of a symphony or novel is a matter for substantial discovery, about which all the beliefs and practices associated with common-sense views of art could turn out to be wrong, and so the violations of common practices or beliefs that plagued the theories above should not be counted against them.

That argument, however, relies on the idea that what might be called "art-kind" terms, such as "symphony," "novel," or "painting," like natural kind terms, refer causally. Causal theories of reference, however, were devised with natural kind terms in mind, and there has been substantial debate over whether the same theory of reference applies to artifactual kind terms or other general terms.[4] Indeed terms such as "symphony" and "novel" do not seem to be introduced by mere causal contact with independent denizens of reality, but rather to arise by stipulating their application to works of extant traditions meeting certain (perhaps vaguely specified) criteria. If one holds a descriptive theory of reference of art-kind terms, however, then the reference of terms like "symphony" is determined by the beliefs of speakers about the conditions relevant to something's being a symphony, and as a result radical revisions of such common-sense beliefs cannot be correct, for any great shift from these will prevent whatever conclusions one reaches from being *about* symphonies.

Fortunately we need not settle that debate here. For regardless of whether or not art-kind terms can be shown to function differently than natural kind terms, there is independent reason to think that complete revisions of common-sense beliefs about the *ontological status* of works of art do not make sense and cannot be justified by a causal theory of reference. As has often been noted, pure causal theories of reference (for both singular and general terms) suffer from a "qua" problem.[5] That is, in the case of naming, there are many things with which one is in causal contact: a person, her physical body, her nose, her hair color, a part of her life span, etc. A pure causal theory of the reference of names must leave it radically indeterminate which of these a particular name refers to, since the would-be grounders of a name's reference have causal contact (in part or whole) with all of these sorts of things. Similarly, in the case of general terms, the qua problem arises since any sample one attempts to ostend will have members that belong to a great variety of kinds: a single sample may contain members of the natural kinds *Homo sapiens*, mammal, and animal, as well as of the social kinds American, Republican, and self-employed individual, and many more besides. To overcome the qua problem, Devitt and Sterelny (1999: 80) (among others) have argued that pure causal theories of reference must be modified to allow that, in establishing the reference of a name, "the grounder must, at some level, 'think of' the cause of his experience under some general categorial term like 'animal' or 'material object'." Those grounding the reference of general terms, too, must have some concept of what *sort of kind* one is attempting to name – whether it is a basic natural kind (and if so, whether a species, genus, etc.), an artifactual kind, a functional kind, a property or pattern kind instantiated therein, etc. – in order to relieve the radical indeterminacy (Devitt and Sterelny 1999: 91).

Such general categorial concepts, however, are precisely those that specify the relevant *ontological category* of the entity to be referred to, that is, whether it is a person, a mere material object, a part of the whole, a property, etc. Similarly, the relevant beliefs about the sort of kind to be picked out by a general term must include beliefs about the level and sort of kind involved – whether a basic natural kind, an abstract property kind identified therein, an artifactual or social kind, etc. As a result, the *ontological category* to which the referent belongs cannot be determined after the fact, by empirical investigations that may reveal the grounders' original ontological assumptions to have been false. Instead, it is determined by the ontological category associated with the name by those who establish the reference of the term; if the term refers at all, it must refer to something of that ontological kind.

The qua problem arises with a vengeance in attempting to refer to works of art, for in addition to the usual ambiguities among part, property, and whole, in the case of works of art there are also ambiguities of level. Causal contact, at the most basic level, is with a piece of canvas or lump of marble (or perhaps with the relevant masses of subatomic particles) in the case of paintings and sculptures. To establish the work of art as the referent of a name such as "Guernica" or "David," it seems, would-be grounders of the name of this or any work of art must have an idea of what sort of thing they are trying to name (a work of painting or sculpture), and what sort of thing that is: how it relates to those physical objects, in what way its identity, individuation, and survival conditions differ from those of the physical bases, and so on (for example, that *Guernica* would be destroyed by dissolving the pigmented surface of the canvas, though the canvas would not be). Similarly, those attempting to ground the reference of a name of a work of music or literature are most directly causally connected with sound waves or pieces of paper, and can only succeed in naming the work of music or literature instead if they have at least a tacit concept of the ontological status of works of art of the relevant sort, and how they are related to physical performances and copies.[6] Similarly, would-be grounders of the reference of general terms such as "painting," "musical work," or "novel" must associate the term with certain criteria enabling them to pick out the relevant kind of work of art rather than a kind of fabric, sound wave, paper, etc. This, again, requires at least a nascent concept of the ontology of works of art of that kind, and of what distinguishes them from the physical entities in the immediate vicinity. Since those ontological conceptions determine what (ontological) sort of entity is picked out by the term (if anything is), they are not themselves open to revision through further "discoveries."

Thus one cannot appeal to causal theories of reference to motivate the view that the common-sense conceptions of artists, composers, critics, and audience regarding the ontological kinds of symphonies, paintings, or novels may all be radically mistaken, and that a theory in radical violation of those assumptions may be true. Regardless of whether a descriptive or moderated causal theory of reference is preferable for names of works of art and art-kind terms, beliefs – at least of those in the artworld establishing the reference of such singular and general terms – *determine* the ontological status of the referents of the terms.

Of course this does not mean that artists, critics, or others responsible for establishing the reference of names of works of art and of general terms such as "painting," "symphony," or "novel" must have a fully developed theory of the ontological status of works of art in formal philosophical terms. Instead, it is enough that they have basic views about the relation between works of art and the relevant physical objects, copies, and performances such as those described in the common-sense view at the outset of this chapter. It does seem reasonable to suppose that, in order to successfully name a symphony or ground the reference of the general term "symphony," for example, someone must have a concept of what sort of thing a symphony is – for instance, that it is distinct from its score or any copy of it, that it is the sort of thing that may be performed many times, more or less perfectly, and so on. It seems entirely plausible, even requisite, that artists and others in the artworld have (at some level) these kinds of beliefs; such beliefs also form the backbone of practices of selling, displaying, performing, and restoring works of art of various kinds.

Coherence with just these background practices and (tacit or explicit) beliefs is typically used in assessing various positions about the ontology of works of art, as it was in the various critical remarks of section 4.1. If the above discussion is correct, this is entirely appropriate, for – provided one accepts that at least some names of works of art and terms for kinds of works of art refer – it is such beliefs and practices that determine the ontological status of the works and kinds of works referred to.[7] In fact, it seems, if one accepts that there are works of art at all, the *only* appropriate method for determining their ontological status is to attempt to unearth and make explicit the assumptions about ontological status built into the relevant practices and beliefs of those dealing with works of art, to systematize these, and to put them into philosophical terms so that we may assess their place in an overall ontological scheme. As a result, consistency with such beliefs and practices is the main criterion of success for a theory of the ontology of works of art. While it must be allowed that these practices may be vague or leave certain issues indeterminate, so that any *precise* philosophical theory must supplement them in certain ways as well as interpreting their dictates, clearly any view that violates them too drastically is not talking about our familiar works of art and kinds of works of art at all. Thus radically revisionary views like Currie's can at best be seen as suggestions about how our practices ought to be revised (in a way that he would perhaps find more coherent and justified), not as descriptions of what sorts of things our familiar works of art "really are."[8]

## 4.3   The Road to a Solution

We are now in a position to explain why an adequate ontology of art has proven so elusive: there has been a conflict between the demands of the problem and the materials available for a solution. For the central criterion of success for theories about the ontology of art is their coherence with the ordinary beliefs and practices that determine the kinds of entities works of art are. But although different philosophers have tried placing works of art in just about all of the categories laid out by standard metaphysical systems – categories like those of imaginary objects, purely physical objects, or abstract kinds of various sorts – none of those fits completely with common-sense beliefs and practices regarding works of art. This explains both the diversity of solutions (as theorists turned from one category to another in search of an adequate solution) and the failure to find a completely satisfactory solution despite these diverse efforts.

In the conflict between the need to provide an ontology of works of art that is adequate to ordinary beliefs and practices regarding the arts, and the need to choose from the ready-made categories of familiar ontologies, the former demand must win out if we are to offer a theory of our familiar forms of art at all. So to resolve the problems of the ontology of art, we cannot simply select and appropriate available ontological categories to serve the relevant needs in aesthetics; instead we must return to fundamental metaphysics, to rethink some of the most standard bifurcations in metaphysics and develop broader and finer-grained systems of ontological categories. While the details of positive views for all of the different art forms cannot be worked out and argued for here, in closing I will suggest the direction that it seems any acceptable view should take, and why it will require broadening traditional systems of ontological categories.

It has long been common practice to divide purported entities into mind-independent physical objects on the one hand, and merely imaginary objects, projected properties, or entities that exist "only in the mind" on the other hand. But even if one accepts that there are things of both kinds, such standard divisions leave no room for entities such as paintings and sculptures. For, as we have seen, these can neither be simply identified with mind-independent physical stuff, on pain of getting the wrong existence, identity, and survival conditions, nor be treated as merely imaginary objects or activities, without denying their status as perceptible public objects. Instead, if we take seriously our ordinary beliefs and practices regarding paintings (as I have argued we must), it seems we should allow that they fall between these standard categories, as entities materially constituted by physical objects but also dependent on forms of human intentionality.[9] Thus unlike imaginary objects or activities, such works of art are mind-external, public entities, continuously existing once created, even if they are not constantly being observed or thought of. Unlike imaginary objects or abstracta, they are perceptible, are materially constituted by certain physical objects, and may be destroyed if their constituting base is. But unlike purely mind-independent physical objects, it is metaphysically necessary that they can come into existence only through intentional human activities; while it is logically possible that a pigmented canvas exist without those, it is not possible that such a thing be a *work of art*. Furthermore, unlike mere physical objects, they typically have essential visual, meaningful, and aesthetic properties, involving for example color and visual form, representation, symbols, and allusion, that depend on human perceptual capabilities, culture, and practices.[10] In short, to accommodate paintings, sculptures, and the like, we must give up the simple bifurcation between mind-independent and mind-internal entities, and acknowledge the existence of entities that depend in different ways on both the physical world and human intentionality.

Another standard division of ontological categories that has held sway at least since Plato is the divide between spatio-temporally located, changing, perishable concrete objects and non-spatio-temporally located, independent, changeless, eternal abstracta. But neither of these categories comes close to capturing central features of our beliefs and practices about works of literature and music. Such entities seem to be abstract in the sense of lacking a particular spatio-temporal location and being capable of continued existence independent of that of any *particular* copy or performance of them (or any other particular physical object). Yet at the same time, they seem not to be eternal kinds or Platonistic structures of any sort, for it is again central to our beliefs and practices about these things that they are cultural artifacts of a certain sort, which came into existence at a certain time in a particular cultural and historical context, at the hands of a particular author or composer, and which might be destroyed again if all copies, performances, and memories regarding them cease to be. Thus, although such things are not spatio-temporally located, they do have certain temporal properties, such as a temporal origin. This is a point emphasized by Ingarden (1989: 10–11), who urges that musical works thus cannot be categorized with either real (spatio-temporal) or ideal objects. Similarly Levinson (1990) takes it as a fundamental requirement of any ontology of music that it preserve the idea that musical works are brought into existence by their creator's activities. As a result, he argues, musical works cannot be pure sound structures, but must be structures of sound and performing means, *as indicated by a particular composer at a certain time –* where indicated structures, unlike pure structures, are created. Moreover, unlike the Platonist's abstracta, works of music and literature do not exist *independently*, they *can only* come into existence through forms of human intentionality, and even once created, they are not independent and eternal, but depend for their ongoing existence on that of some copy or performance, or the means for creating one (whether via a score, recording, memory, or some combination of these).

Thus taking seriously the view that there are works of music and literature, and that their ontological status is determined by central beliefs and practices regarding them, requires us to admit that there may be categories of entities between those of concrete individuals and Platonistic abstracta: a category for what I have elsewhere (1999) called "abstract artifacts." Moreover, like works of painting and sculpture, works of music and literature seem to depend for their existence on certain human intentional states without being identifiable either with the imaginary creations of individual minds or with physical objects. Thus on both counts, works of literature and music seem to fall between the cracks of traditional category systems; accommodating them will require acknowledging intervening categories for temporally determined, dependent abstracta: abstract artifacts created by human intentional activities.[11]

A careful consideration of the ontology of art has impact and applications far beyond aesthetics, for it demonstrates that standard category bifurcations are non-exhaustive, and that we need to accept a finer-grained range of ontological categories if we are to include such entities as works of art in our ontology. Developing a more adequate ontology of works of art may also lay the groundwork for a more adequate ontological treatment of social and cultural objects generally, which are so often neglected in naturalistic metaphysics. For, like paintings and sculptures, other artifacts and concrete social objects such as tables, drivers' licenses, and pieces of real estate are not merely identical with the matter that constitutes them, since they (unlike the matter) have essential relations to human intentional states. Like works of music and literature, theories, corporations, and laws of state seem to be abstract cultural entities that are created at a certain time through human activities. Broadening out familiar systems of categories in the ways required to do justice to works of art may thus also pave the way for resolving ontological problems for a variety of social and cultural objects. In short, if, rather than trying to make works of art fit into the off-the-rack categories of familiar metaphysical systems, one attempts to determine the categories that would really be suitable for works of art as we know them through our ordinary beliefs and practices, the payoff may lie not just in a better ontology of art, but in a better metaphysics.

## Notes

1  Aaron Ridley (1997) has recently argued against the traditional interpretation of Collingwood as holding works of art to be imaginary things, suggesting that when

Collingwood speaks of works of art as "in someone's head" he is only calling attention to the fact that to *understand* a work of art we must do more than experience auditory or visual phenomena. While the latter claim seems apt, it doesn't decide the ontological issue. Collingwood certainly seems to suffer from the common ontological problem of noticing that something (here, a work of art) cannot be identified with a *mere* external physical object (nor the proper experience of it with the mere experience of physical events or properties), and finding nowhere else to put it, concluding that it must be in the mind.

2 Wolterstorff and Currie accept that this consequence follows from their theories. Wollheim seems to have a less traditional concept of "type" in mind, for he treats types as existing only where particulars can be correlated "with a piece of human invention" (1980: 78). I return to this sort of option in section 4.3 below.

3 For further discussion of this point, see my (1999: 56–69).

4 See Putnam (1975), Schwartz (1978, 1980), Kornblith (1980), and my (forthcoming).

5 For a clear discussion, see Devitt and Sterelny (1999: 79–81, 90–3).

6 In fact, it might seem that since such groundings must be affixed to some or other spatio-temporal entity with which one can be in causal contact – not with any sort of abstract entity – this would rule out any views that would count any sort of work of art as being an abstract entity of any kind. I have argued elsewhere, however (1999: 43–54), that reference to *dependent* abstracta of various sorts can be made via their spatio-temporal foundations. To accept this suggestion and enable direct reference to dependent entities of various kinds, however, causal theories must be modified with an ontologically descriptive element, as described above.

7 Since the concepts of would-be grounders only establish the ontological kind of the entity referred to, *if anything is in fact referred to* (that is, if the grounding succeeds), this alone does not rule out taking the eliminativist view that there are no works of art corresponding to our common-sense concepts. I discuss why this sort of move is nonetheless misguided in my (2001).

8 This echoes Jerrold Levinson's point against Eddy Zemach's view (Zemach 1986: 245) that paintings are not individual objects, but rather can consist of different canvasses at the same time. As Levinson writes, "a revolutionary proposal as to how we might *reconceive* paintings . . . is being advanced under cover of a clarificatory thesis as to what paintings *are*" (1987: 280–1).

9 Joseph Margolis' view that works of art are physically embodied, culturally emergent entities provides one example of a view that does treat them as in between such category bifurcations (1999: 67–100).

10 Roman Ingarden provides similar arguments against identifying the architectural work of art with the real building in (1989, 262–3).

11 For further discussion of this point, see Ingarden (1989: 4–5, 1973: 9–19), and my (1999: 131–2, 141–3).

# References

Baker, Lynne Rudder (2000). *Persons and Bodies.* Cambridge: Cambridge University Press.

Collingwood, R. G. (1958). *The Principles of Art.* New York: Oxford University Press.

Currie, Gregory (1989). *An Ontology of Art*. New York: St Martin's Press.

Devitt, Michael and Sterelny, Kim (1999). *Language and Reality: An Introduction to the Philosophy of Language*. Cambridge, MA: MIT Press.

Ingarden, Roman (1973). *The Literary Work of Art*, trans. George G. Grabowicz. Evanston, IL: Northwestern University Press.

——(1989). *The Ontology of the Work of Art*, trans. Raymond Meyer with Jon T. Goldthwait. Athens, OH: Ohio University Press.

Johnston, Mark (1997). "Constitution is not Identity," in Michael C. Rea (ed.), *Material Constitution: A Reader*. Lanham, MD: Rowman and Littlefield: 44–62.

Kornblith, Hilary (1980). "Referring to Artifacts." *Philosophical Review*, LXXXIX(1): 109–14.

Kripke, Saul (1972). *Naming and Necessity*. Cambridge, MA: Harvard University Press.

Levinson, Jerrold (1987). "Zemach on Paintings." *British Journal of Aesthetics*, 27: 278–83.

——(1990). *Music, Art, and Metaphysics*. Ithaca, NY: Cornell University Press.

——(1992). Critical Notice of Gregory Currie's *An Ontology of Art. Philosophy and Phenomenological Research*, 52(1): 215–22.

Margolis, Joseph (1999). *What, After All, Is a Work of Art?* University Park, PA: Pennsylvania State University Press.

McMahan, Jeff (2000). "Moral Intuition." In Hugh LaFollette (ed.), *Blackwell Guide to Ethical Theory*. Oxford: Blackwell: 95–110.

Putnam, Hilary (1975). "The Meaning of 'Meaning'" and "Is Semantics Possible?" In *Mind, Language and Reality*. Cambridge: Cambridge University Press: 215–71, 139–52.

Ridley, Aaron (1997). "Not Ideal: Collingwood's Expression Theory." *Journal of Aesthetics and Art Criticism*, 55(3): 263–72.

Sartre, Jean-Paul (1966). *The Psychology of Imagination*, trans. Bernard Frechtman. New York: Washington Square Press.

Schwartz, Stephen P. (1978). "Putnam on Artifacts." *Philosophical Review*, LXXXVII(4): 566–74.

——(1980). "Natural Kinds and Nominal Kinds." *Mind*, 89: 182–95.

Thomasson, Amie L.(1999). *Fiction and Metaphysics*. Cambridge: Cambridge University Press.

——(2001). "Ontological Minimalism." *American Philosophical Quarterly*, 38(4): 319–32.

——(forthcoming). "Realism and Human Kinds." *Philosophy and Phenomenological Research*.

Wollheim, Richard (1980). *Art and its Objects*. 2nd edn. Cambridge: Cambridge University Press.

Wolterstorff, Nicholas (1980). *Works and Worlds of Art*. Oxford: Clarendon Press.

Zemach, Eddy (1986). "No Identification Without Evaluation." *British Journal of Aesthetics*, 26: 239–51.

# Chapter 5

# Evaluating Art
## *Alan Goldman*

### 5.1  Introduction

Evaluations of artworks pervade descriptions and discussions of them. As will be illustrated below, they are typically described in terms that are at least partially evaluative. An initial question is why this is so. There are several related parts to the answer. First, according to one common conception of art, to call something an artwork is already to grant it a positive evaluative status. What counts as a genuine work of art must meet some minimal threshold of artistic value, so that minor or mediocre works of art are still better than objects that purport to be works of art but do not merit that status. This concept relies on certain paradigms within each genre of great artworks, works that help to define an ideal of what fine art should be. Second, artworks are made to be appreciated, and we view, read, or listen to them in order to appreciate them. Appreciation is both understanding the works and recognizing and enjoying their artistic values, their values as artworks.

To understand a work is to be able to give an acceptable interpretation of it. But third, while interpretation is in some sense logically prior to (pure) evaluation, it already involves appreciating the values of various elements of a work. To interpret is to explain why those elements are there in a work, how they contribute to its overall point and value. Critics therefore naturally interpret and evaluate at the same time: they show us how to attend to the objective properties of artworks in ways that disclose their values within the works. Fourth, one common bond among people is the sharing of taste or appreciation of the same sorts of things, among them artworks. We discuss our evaluations of artworks in order to establish such bonds of shared taste, and we may view works partly because of such social aims.

One who seeks to provide a philosophical account of such discourse can make more or less ambitious claims in its defense. Most ambitious are claims that there are standards that determine the proper evaluation of artworks as artworks, that the properties indicated by such standards, in terms of which we evaluate artworks, distinguish artworks from other objects (in keeping with the evaluative concept of art), and that these properties are shared to a greater or lesser degree by all genuine artworks. Such claims have been presupposed by some of the major aesthetic theories of previous centuries (for example those of Kant or Tolstoy), but they are likely to elicit skeptical responses from contemporary aestheticians. Skeptics will argue either that there are no evaluative standards that apply across the arts, or more strongly, across artworks, or that all such standards are merely subjective or the result of social class programming.

Proponents of the first skeptical view will point out that the value of a novel may be quite different from that of a symphony or painting. The novel, unlike the symphony or painting, may provide psychological insight into the motivations behind certain patterns of behavior, while the sensuous beauty of the painting's colors or the immediate emotional impact of the symphony may be absent from the works of the other genres. The same differences might distinguish works within a genre: the value of a poem might be quite different from that of a novel or short story, the beautiful colors of a Titian or Renoir completely absent from a Braque, and the impact of a Mahler symphony completely unlike that of a Haydn string quartet. Ultimately it can and certainly has been claimed that every work of art is unique in its value. (This can be claimed even for parts of works – Desdemona's willow song aria in Verdi's *Otello* is very different from Iago's credo.)

But granting these points does not concede the skeptic's claim that there is no standard that applies across works and genres or that this standard is not different from criterial properties or standards that apply to other sorts of objects. Each artwork is indeed unique in the totality of its objective properties, and some may indeed have valuable properties that others lack. But uniqueness does not preclude shared properties that provide value. Artworks might all share the property of being valued for their uniqueness, for example. More seriously, works very different in themselves may affect us in similar ways. The skeptic will reply to this point that artworks affect us in very different ways: comedies amuse while tragedies depress us. But once more such differences do not preclude some common way of affecting us that encompasses or derives from both types of plays. Both comedies and tragedies might, for example, give us pleasure in their viewing (although I will deny below that this is true in any ordinary sense of pleasure). And those properties from which only some works within certain genres derive some of their value might not be necessary for those works to qualify as great art (or to be distinguished as art), while other shared properties might distinguish them as such. Some poems, for example, might provide psychological insight, but this is not necessarily a property of great poems, and similarly for the intense emotional impact of some pieces of music or the formal beauty of some paintings.

It remains to be seen whether different works from different genres affect us in some similar way by these very different means, and whether this similarity, if it exists, constitutes a criterion of evaluation for particular works. This will be our central question. While, as noted, it generally draws a skeptical response these days, there is some initial evidence for a positive answer. Not only is there the evaluative concept of art itself, as noted above, but there is a common distinction we draw between the aesthetic or artistic value of an artwork as an artwork, and other values it might have, for example economic. There is an artist in Miami who shall remain nameless here whose works sell for very high prices despite being in my view artistically worth very little. This distinction is all too common these days and seems to indicate some common way of distinguishing artistic or aesthetic value (even if only by a disjunctive criterion).

In aiming to answer this question, we will also be addressing some other traditional issues regarding the evaluation of artworks. Are aesthetic evaluations propositions that are true or false? Do such evaluations refer to objective properties of artworks, or are they merely expressions of subjective taste? Are they intended to be universally shared or agreed upon? What sort of reasons, if any, can be offered in support of aesthetic evaluations? Are these reasons backed by principles? Is the value of art intrinsic or instrumental? The answers to these traditional questions about the evaluation of artworks will fall out as implications from the answer to our main question regarding a type of aesthetic value that distinguishes artworks at the same time as it provides a criterion for their evaluation.

As a final preliminary, we should mention again the second version of skepticism that we noted, the position that all aesthetic value criteria are products of an upper social class strategy of cultural dominance. Sociologists have noted a strong correlation between "elitist" tastes for the finer arts and economic/social class membership, suggesting the Marxist thesis that such taste is a mere epiphenomenon without objective aesthetic basis, or, more sinister, a strategy for maintaining the sharp distinction between the upper class and others (Bourdieu 1984). Social facts themselves, however, call this skeptical thesis into question, for example the millions who attend opera performances in Central Park in New York, or, at the other end, the puzzlement that many upper-class denizens with otherwise elitist tastes feel toward some works of the avant garde.

"Taste," of course, refers both to preferences among artworks or other objects and to the ability to discern subtle differences and complex relations within such objects. That these two aspects themselves go together is to some small degree further evidence against the skeptical thesis. That taste for the finer arts tends to correlate with social privilege can be explained without reducing the former to the latter: those with economic means tend to have the leisure, education, travel, and experience that foster understanding and appreciation of painting, literature, and music. In the final analysis, however, refutation of this skeptical hypothesis, as well as of the older claim that aesthetic evaluation is the expression of purely subjective taste, depends upon the discovery of a more substantive and less pejorative basis for aesthetic evaluation.

## 5.2 Aesthetic Properties and Principles

As mentioned at the beginning, descriptions of artworks are usually cast in terms that are partly evaluative. We do not often begin with purely evaluative terms such as "good," or even "beautiful," because these are quite uninformative. But neither are we likely to first describe a painting, for example, by referring directly and only to its objective lines and colors. Instead, we use such terms as "graceful," "balanced," "unified," "vivid," "rich," "flowing," "poignant," "pulsating," "powerful," "penetrating," "subtle," "sublime," "serene," "uplifting," "delicate," "sprightly," or "dull," "grating," "plodding," "pretentious," "sentimental," "stiff," "melodramatic," "derivative," "garish," "insipid," "flaccid." These terms have more or less descriptive content – "graceful," for example, indicates, albeit imprecisely, certain formal properties – but they indicate also responses on the part of critics who apply them. More precisely, if these critics do not intend to refer only to their own responses, they refer to tendencies of their objects to produce certain reactions, positive or negative, in certain conditions in virtue of their objective properties. They refer to relational properties often called aesthetic properties.

We cannot pick out aesthetic properties by the objective, descriptive content of these terms alone, since, for one thing, what is graceful to one critic is insipid or flaccid to another. That these properties include subjective responses explains the degree of disagreement about their presence; that they have also descriptive content limits the degree of competent disagreement (what is graceful to one may be insipid to another, but should not be raucous or grating). That critics argue over the proper applications of these terms indicates that there is a normative component to their use as well: we invite or expect our listeners to agree with our uses of them, to respond in the same ways.

Reference to these properties both supports overall evaluations of works containing them and is in turn supported by more, and ultimately completely, objective properties of the works. Even the former, the link between these middle-level evaluative properties and overall evaluations, is not as simple as it might appear to be. Matters would be simple here if these properties always had the same positive or negative values, and if we could simply sum the positive ones and subtract the negative in order to derive the overall value of a work. But matters are not that way. The aesthetic properties and the objective properties on which they are based interact in ways that make context the all-determining factor. Of course, to say that a work is graceful without saying anything more suggests a positive evaluation of it, but that is because the context is normally understood, not because there is any implication here. If, for some unlikely reason, a critic called *Guernica* or the *Rite of Spring* graceful, or a literary indictment of squalid child labor elegant, it is unlikely that these would be terms of praise.

Some philosophers have tried to maintain a sense of order here by holding that these properties are inherently positive or negative even though subject to reversal by defeaters (Bender 1995). The only sense I can make of this claim is the idea that they have a certain fixed value when taken in isolation (Dickie 1988: 89). The problem with this interpretation is that they never are found in isolation, but always in the contexts of works with other aesthetic properties. Humor in a tragedy can be negative if it weakens the tragic intensity of the play, but positive if that intensity is otherwise unbearable or grating. Nor is having more of a positive aesthetic property always better. A piece by Mozart may be better than one by Salieri because it is more flowing and graceful, but this does not mean that pieces more flowing than Mozart's are better for that: they may simply be more predictable. Being unified is often a good thing in artworks, but it can also make them boring.

Hence there are no principles that link these middle-level or partly evaluative aesthetic properties to overall evaluations of works. It is more obvious that there are no principles on the more basic level linking objective properties – lines, colors, light and shade, tones, melodic and harmonic progressions, or literary devices and phrases – to these aesthetic properties. Take a musical transition in a Mozart quartet that renders the movement graceful, place it in a Bartok quartet and you have only auditory disaster. Then, too, as mentioned, what is graceful to one critic may be insipid to another: they may respond to the same objective properties differently.

Some philosophers have thought that if there are semantic criteria governing the proper uses of aesthetic terms, if we can learn to use such terms properly, then there must be principles linking such proper use to objective conditions. But there is no reason why that must be so: semantic criteria can include reference to subjective responses as well. To claim even that there are necessary conditions for aesthetic properties in objective properties is to lack imagination or experience of certain works. One who claims, for example, that pastel colors cannot be gaudy has never seen the art deco district of Miami Beach (contrast Sibley 1959).

The puzzle is that, despite the lack of principles on both levels, critics and audiences justify evaluations of artworks by appeal to their aesthetic properties, and ascription of aesthetic properties by pointing to objective properties of works (the latter may involve several steps of justifying ascription of properties with less descriptive content by appeal to those with more). A painting may be beautiful because of its grace, graceful because of delicate lines, and delicate in line because of its thin, smooth and gentle curves. But how can this justification work in the absence of principles, if ascription of the aesthetic properties represents subjective responses?

Reasons must be general in some sense, and I have denied that evaluative responses to artworks are universally shared even by competent critics. I have also asserted that there is a normative dimension to the ascription of such properties; in calling a work powerful, I do not intend to refer only to my response; I expect or invite my listener to agree, at least after experiencing the work. And I seem to invoke an evaluative standard, being powerful, that applies not only across persons, but across artworks and even genres. Yet must I not also recognize fundamental differences among genres and among tastes of different critics? There are tensions here that have haunted aesthetics from Hume and Kant on.

Clues to their resolution lie once more in the nature and use of aesthetic property terms themselves. First, the fact that all the terms mentioned at the beginning of this section apply to painting, music, and literary works alike does indeed suggest standards across the arts, although, as noted, these standards do not involve merely summing the properties to which these terms refer. Evaluative terms that naturally apply to works from different genres suggest common standards at some level of generality. Second, in applying to works across the arts, these terms also apply across the different sense modalities and mental faculties involved in apprehending these works and the properties within them to which the terms refer. In the context of artworks we refer to tones as bright and colors as muted. While such terms refer to sensuous elements of any sense modality, most aesthetic properties involve higher-order affective or cognitive responses to sensory elements and formal-perceptual structures themselves grasped cognitively or affectively. Calling a musical passage graceful, for example, reflects a higher-order, positive, affective reaction to sensuous tones and formal structures that are themselves typically grasped affectively as well as cognitively, often as a series of mild tensions and resolutions. Apprehending or appreciating such properties reflects the engagement of mental capacities from the purely sensuous through the cognitive-perceptual (grasping complex forms perceptually) to the affective and purely cognitive. That the terms referring to them apply indifferently to very different artworks in very different genres suggests that such engagement is typical in appreciating any work of fine art.

Third, we noted that use of these terms has normative force; in using them we expect or at least invite agreement. But we also recognize ultimate differences in taste, so that the reasons supporting application of these terms, ultimately objective properties of works causing certain reactions in audiences, must be general without being universal. Clearly, if there is to be normative force, not just any reactions will do. They must be reactions of the right observers in the right conditions to have any normative weight. Irreducible differences in taste at every level of competence do not imply that all evaluative judgments are on a par or that they need not be supported by reasons. The first and foremost philosopher to recognize reasons for aesthetic evaluations as general but not universal (in recognizing ultimate differences in taste) was Hume. He sought to capture the normative force of aesthetic evaluations by appeal to the notion of ideal critics (Hume 1963). That notion is still highly useful for capturing that force and the degree of generality we seek in its explication.

## 5.3 Ideal Critics

Despite the fact that the same evaluative terms apply across artworks and arts, we do not generalize our evaluations from one artwork to another that resembles it. We cannot infer that works which share some properties will share others, since all depends on the full contexts in which these properties are found. When I generalize, it must therefore be from one critic to another, or from my judgment to the expected judgment of the person to whom I express it. If we all responded to the same objective properties in the same ways, if certain properties always affected us positively, then we could limit our justifications of evaluations and their explications to reference to those objective properties. But since variable responses are involved, these responses themselves must be justified, as least when the ascription of aesthetic properties is challenged.

Only the responses of certain critics in certain conditions are guaranteed to be appropriate, therefore acquiring normative force in themselves. This suggests that the normative force of evaluative judgments that ascribe aesthetic properties can itself be captured by appeal to ideal critics suitably defined. The idea is that my evaluations are justified to the degree that they approximate to those of an ideal critic. I judge the reliability of my aesthetic judgments, those ascribing aesthetic properties, by how closely I, in making these judgments in present conditions, resemble the relevant characteristics and conditions of ideal critics. And I infer not directly from my evaluations to yours, but from mine, insofar as I take them to be sound, to those of an ideal critic, and then to yours, insofar as I expect or invite you to be competent in your judgment.

Real critics, those to whom we turn for interpretations and evaluations of artworks, are closer to ideal than average audiences. They are more knowledgeable of the traditions from which the works emerge, they are more able to discern complex relations among the elements of the works, and their interpretations show them to be more sensitive to the values or aesthetic experiences that these elements and relations can provide. From these differences we can infer the characteristics of ideal critics. Such traits as being knowledgeable of the relevant history of art and being unbiased are unproblematic in the definition of ideal critics and relatively easy to establish for actual critics. Also uncontroversial are favorable conditions for viewing or listening to works, not only physical conditions, but such factors as not being tired, irritated, or distracted, and being capable of sustained intellectual effort (Pawlowski 1989: 14). The difficulty concerns affective competence or sensitivity to aesthetic values.

A critic might theoretically be far less than ideal because, although knowledgeable and articulate, she is completely unmoved by many works to which others with experience respond most positively. But since critics at all levels of competence can disagree about particular works (Tolstoy thought Shakespeare mediocre, and Collingwood called Beethoven's music "ranting"), how can we establish this credential of adequate sensitivity, and do so without circularity? The answer is that we can have evidence of emotional normality outside of art, and we can supplement this evidence by reactions to numerous paradigms (these can be of use despite our inability to generalize directly from one artwork to another). Then, too, since, as noted, interpretations presuppose sensitive evaluations, we can and do judge critics by their ability to provide interpretations of works that help us to appreciate them. In practice, it is of course very unlikely that we will find someone with extensive knowledge of an art form who lacks sensitivity to its valuable features: one would not pursue or acquire such knowledge if insensitive to the intrinsic rewards of its pursuit and acquisition. And in practice we judge critics by their knowledge, by the freshness of their interpretations, and by whether they can point to features of works to which they react in ways we can come to share.

Instead of appealing to ideal critics, we might capture the normative force of evaluative aesthetic judgments by simply saying that the objective properties of the works merit the responses in question. But this leaves open the questions of how and why they merit such responses, and the appeal to ideal critics, once their defining properties are clear, is less mysterious. In fact, it can be thought of as providing an account of what meriting responses amounts to. A response is merited if it is one that would occur in an ideal critic. For each sort of relevant objective property, we can spell out how it might affect a fully qualified critic. We can also think about how closely we approximate to being ideal in deciding on the basis of our actual reactions whether works merit them.

We still might wonder how appeal to ideal critics captures the normative force of ascribing evaluative aesthetic properties if we compare such ascription to ascribing secondary qualities such as colors to objects. One plausible account of secondary qualities holds that to call something red, for example, is to say that it would appear red to ideal perceivers in ideal conditions. But there is no normative force behind such judgments. So why should we think that appeal to ideal critics captures the normative force of aesthetic evaluations? Two alternative answers can be given.

First, we could say that ascription of secondary qualities *is* normative in the minimal sense that agreement with such ascription is expected from those who are not color-blind or fooled by unusual lighting conditions. Because the standards are so commonly and easily met, they are tacit and typically unnoticed. Or second, we can point out that secondary quality ascriptions are not normative in the usual sense because ideal observers and conditions to which their analysis appeals reduce to normal conditions and observers, making no demands on them. By contrast, the characteristics of ideal art critics are not typical or normal. This in itself does not explain their positive normative force, but that can be explained by an additional consideration. The features that define ideal critics are those which allow for the deepest appreciation of the artworks they interpret and judge. When we are more knowledgeable of styles and more sensitive to elements and relations within works that provide aesthetic values, we are better able to grasp and enjoy those values. Thus, if we want to appreciate art maximally, we should aspire to approximate ideal critics, and their judgments will have normative force for us.

A final problem for this analysis may seem to derive from the previously noted fact that disagreement in ascribing aesthetic properties and evaluating works occurs at all levels of critical competence, implying that ideal critics will disagree as well. If ideal critics can disagree about works, then any evaluations of those works will accord with the judgments of some such critic. How, then, can these judgments provide any standards? When Tolstoy disapproves of Shakespeare and Collingwood of Beethoven, does this indeed suggest that ideal critics can disagree about any work, introducing irreducible elements of taste at all levels, or does it instead simply indicate that these critics, despite being generally competent, are less than ideal in being insensitive to the obvious values of these works?

Given the degree of disagreement among actual critics, there is no reason to believe that ideal critics won't disagree, but this does not render all judgments equal. Those that result from ignorance or insensitivity give us no reason to agree, while we do have reason to agree with competent judgments of those who share our taste. Ideal critics for a particular art form or style not only lack omniscience of all art, but also can disagree about particular works within their preferred form. This is because taste for certain works will inevitably lead one to disapprove of and remain insensitive to other works. Ideal critics of a given form will experience works within that form as deeply as their tastes allow. The most we can hope for is to approximate to ideal critics who generally share our tastes. Our judgments are to be measured against theirs. When I disagree with an ideal critic who shares my taste, I most likely lack relevant knowledge, or I am insensitive because of distraction, lack of attention, etc.

More to the point in practice, when I disagree with a peer in a real case, I must check the degree to which either of us falls short of ideal in any of these respects before I can conclude that we have an ultimate difference in taste. I support my judgment by inferring that the best explanation for my approval or disapproval is that an ideal critic would agree, that it does not result from a shortcoming on my part. I can also recognize works that are good despite my not appreciating them if I recognize that I do not approximate to an ideal critic of such works, or if I recognize that ideal critics with different taste would react favorably.

## 5.4   Engagement

While the appeal to ideal critics captures the normative force of our aesthetic evaluations, it does not yet answer our central question. That answer awaits an account of what prompts the approvals of ideal critics. Our earlier dismissal of aesthetic principles precludes reference to objective qualities of artworks as primary in that account. But it once more leaves open the possibility that the approvals of ideal critics are based on more basic ways of responding to works that they share with each other and across works and art forms. The earlier discussion of aesthetic properties alluded to what that common way of responding is. Great works of art, paradigms for appreciation, engage us on every mental level simultaneously. In them we perceptually appreciate pure sound or color, perceptually-cognitively and perhaps affectively grasp formal structure, cognitively apprehend thematic or symbolic content and historical import, emotionally react to expression, imaginatively expand upon the material present before us, and perhaps even volitionally share in pursuing the aesthetic goals of the works.

This is why medium, form, and content all always have aesthetic significance. We never simply look through the medium to the message, or through the form to the content that emerges from it. Works with the same content are not thereby equivalent, and a work with elegant form can be lessened for lacking insight. It will be objected that pure music lacks cognitive content and that literature need not engage us perceptually. But cognition is obviously challenged by and involved in appreciating the complex forms of musical compositions. Just as literary themes provide formal unity to otherwise amorphous works, so musical themes, while typically not representational, challenge and reward cognition in their development, variation, and relation to other musical elements. Cognitive virtues of art include not just insight or truth, but complexity and coherence (although these are not universally virtues). The intense thought involved in appreciating even works with significant representational content does not typically have as its goal the acquisition of knowledge separable from the works themselves, but instead is focused most often on relations internal to the works, much as it is in the appreciation of musical works. Knowledge external to works, for example knowledge of the history of the relevant art form, instead typically informs our experience of the works, heightening our appreciation of them. As for the perceptual aspect of works in which content is paramount, the appeal of the language or the pictures is precisely what raises many novels and movies to the level of fine art.

This full engrossment of our mental faculties is of intrinsic value simply because we enjoy meeting challenges to our capacities, expanding and exercising them to their fullest extent (surely there is a biological explanation for such enjoyment or satisfaction). And it is of instrumental value in the benefits that such expansion brings and in removing us, however briefly, from the real world of our practical affairs. Complete absorption in a work of art seems to take us to another world, even if one so different as a world of pure sound, and escape to such alternative worlds refreshes us and, in the case of representational arts, can suggest new possibilities for life in the real world.

This account of the primary value of art, in terms of which individual artworks can be evaluated as well, is somewhat similar to but also different from the account that sees the primary value of art as lying in its providing intrinsically valuable experience (Budd 1995: 5). The latter thesis requires distinguishing which properties belong intrinsically to experience, which in turn requires deep excursions into the philosophy of mind. Are there properties of experience that are not properties of physical objects? Is moral insight an intrinsic property of the experience of a novel? And so on. Speaking of engaging our mental capacities, holding our attention and exercising efforts on perceptual, imaginative, cognitive, and emotional levels, avoids these difficulties. Furthermore, any pleasurable experience not undergone solely for the sake of some future benefit, for example being entertained, getting a massage, or looking at a rainbow, is intrinsically valuable (the latter is also an aesthetic experience). But not all pleasurable or aesthetic experiences afford what great art does, including cognitive challenge and engagement. "Satisfaction" is a better term than "pleasure" for describing the positive feeling we derive in general from exercising our faculties and meeting challenges to them in this way. "Pleasure" is particularly inapt for describing our appreciation of tragedy or of music expressive of profound sadness, but it is clear why such art readily engages us emotionally, contributing to an overall satisfying experience.

The engagement criterion for evaluation, while it may seem disappointing in comparison to some proposal that would focus on objective properties of artworks, does explain certain more specific features of our evaluative practices. First, if a primary purpose of art is to engage all our mental capacities fully, this would explain why we define art relative to paradigms of great art that succeed in this task. The case is otherwise, for example, in the domain of morality, where we conceive moral demands not in terms of what moral saints might do, but in terms of what ordinary people can reasonably be expected to obey in the way of constraints. Second, if the criterion seems relatively unspecific when applied to individual works of art, this is not a shortcoming in relation to actual practice, but explains why our comparisons of works that engage us in different ways are themselves so rough and imprecise. Critics generally eschew such comparisons, focusing instead on properties of individual works to which we are to respond, and using such response terms as "moving," "powerful," or "affecting" as more or less synonymous with "good."

Third, as suggested above, appeal to this criterion explains why we tend to value so highly works strongly expressive of negative emotions, why we consider them generally to be more profound than other works. Again biology and the necessities of survival within groups explain why we respond more readily and forcefully to the most difficult plights of others than to their successes. In light of this fact, it is understandable that we would tend to respond more deeply and fully to tragic works of art; and the fact that we tend to evaluate them more highly as well supports the account of evaluation in terms of the engagement criterion. Fourth, the appeal to the criterion explains the emphasis on originality in art, since we are more readily challenged and engaged by works that are strikingly different from what came before, at least if they have other features worth attending to.

Fifth, and more interesting, is the account suggested of the value of truth, including moral truth or insight in art. How should our apprehension of truth or falsity, or morally praiseworthy versus blameworthy attitudes, in artworks affect our evaluations of them as artworks? Falsity or distance from reality in representational art is an artistic vice only when it turns us off, not for example in a Bosch painting or Lewis Carroll fantasy. Our interest lies in the fictional worlds created by such works, and if they allegorically suggest assertions about the real world by comparison, the truth of these is secondary. By contrast, works that favorably thematize objectionable attitudes can repel us, thereby failing to engage us on other levels even if we continue to pay some attention to them. Their false or objectionable implied claims then become artistic failings. This is not to say that we typically view or read representational art or literature in order to learn the truth or gain moral insight, both more readily available from non-fiction. But the moral viewpoint of a work can be a factor that attracts or repels us. If the former is the case, if our powers of moral judgment are challenged and engaged, then we will in the process of appreciating the work likely be expanding our moral capacities, our ability to empathize or to discriminate morally relevant differences.

Thus, in possibly engaging us on another level, both cognitive and affective, the moral dimension of a work can be an artistically relevant factor. This allows that there can be good but immoral art and, more common, bad art (or literature that fails to rise to the level of art) with a moral message. The eloquent advocacy of evil can be absorbing, but it must overcome the tendency to turn us off. We certainly with good reason tolerate far more in the worlds of artworks than in real life, but only if we are not unwilling to enter those worlds. It is easy to explain in these terms why some of the greatest literary characters, Ahab and Hamlet, to name the most prominent of all, are the most morally ambiguous. They intrigue us, inviting endless interpretation, in part because of their moral ambiguity. Morally less pat works challenge us to re-explore the moral dimensions of our experience, and so they often more readily engage us. But the moral dimension is not necessary to great art, being obviously absent from most non-representational art, and being one way among others of attracting and focusing our cognitive and affective attention.

I have noted that we can point neither to objective properties of artworks that inevitably give them positive value, nor even to aesthetic properties that do so. We can nevertheless generalize somewhat about typical ways in which works of art seek to engage us completely. First, the very constitution of the various art forms and the ways we are expected to approach works within them indicate their function of engaging us on multiple levels. As noted, we apprehend the nested melodic, harmonic, rhythmic, textural, and dynamic forms within musical works perceptually, cognitively, and affectively at the same time. Opera involves additional relations of text and overall dramatic structure to music that must be grasped simultaneously. In the visual arts, we must be aware of physical surfaces as well as representational content and expressiveness, aware of how content and expression emerge from medium and form. These relations are crucial to our evaluations of visual works. In the literary arts, as noted, the use of language, both sensuously and formally, as well as structural relations between characters, settings, and thematic elements, distinguish great art perhaps more readily than does content. Once more these relations of medium and form to content are crucial.

Second, we can be somewhat more specific about successful means across the arts for fulfilling this function. A typical means of achieving artistic excellence is to produce a sensuously pleasing, complex but intelligible formal structure that is expressive at the same time. Perhaps the best-known example of this type of structure is the sonata-allegro form typical of major musical movements in the classical style. This three-part nested form combines clarity and complexity, variation and repetition, with dramatic tension, movement, and resolution. In these respects it is not unlike the dramatic plots of many literary works, the incidents of which according to Aristotle ought to surprise when they occur, yet feel logically necessitated after the fact in relation to characters and previous episodes. In paintings too, elements such as lines, colors, light and shade, shapes, and objects can be thematized in being repeated, varied, and contrasted, creating higher-order relations such as balance or tension, and adding to the expressiveness of represented content.

That these complex forms succeed in fully engaging us is perhaps partly explained by the natural drive of the human mind to find or impose order in difficult environments, to grasp closed forms and intelligible patterns within seemingly chaotic data. This may be why we naturally seek overall thematic unity, as well as aptness of form to content, setting to character, etc., in interpreting artworks of different genres, and why we focus on personal as well as historical style to find order among works in the history of art. It is why Hutcheson's equation of beauty with unity in variety or complexity has appealed to later philosophers (Hutcheson 1971).

But that none of the above mentioned means or forms is a formula for guaranteed success in art is clear from the fact that countless first-year music theory students have learned to compose in sonata-allegro form, that high-school students learn to write Shakespearean sonnets, all with marked lack of great artistic achievement. We are often challenged by complexity, but it can also turn us off, and formally simple structures, such as those in Rothko's paintings, can be perceptually challenging as well. Originality can add to interest, but most would prefer the forty-first symphony of Mozart to a first in a completely new style by other composers. We may be intrigued by moral ambiguity, but there is little ambiguity in the wonderfully crafted characters of Charles Dickens or Jane Austen. And a painting can be unified in being intensely ugly in a complex variety of ways, leading some critics to approve and others to disapprove (contrast Beardsley 1981: 529). In short, while some generalization about successful means by appeal to objective properties of artworks is possible, there are no universally successful means to the end of fully engaging our diverse mental capacities, which alone guarantees positive evaluation of an artwork.

## 5.5   Objections and Questions

The first objection that might be raised to the above account concerns its appeal to ideal critics. A valuable work was characterized as one that would appeal to ideal critics or to those who approximate to them. An objector might claim that this description has it backwards, that a work engages because of its valuable properties, and that ideal critics are simply those who can appreciate these properties (Sharpe 2000: 325). But the problem with this position lies again in its inability to define what a valuable property is. Since we are not all engaged by or approving of the same properties, since even ideal critics differ in taste, the only way to identify valuable properties is to see or infer whether they would be responded to positively by any ideal critic, or by ones who share our tastes. Ideal critics themselves, by contrast, could be defined independently of their responses to particular objective properties of works, in terms of their knowledge and general sensitivity as reflected outside art and in their interpretations of various works. But doesn't the attractiveness of ideal critics as models still lie in their ability to appreciate the values of works they interpret? It does lie in their ability to derive deeper satisfactions from meeting challenges to their mental capacities, but once more what provides these challenges must be defined relative to the responses of these model critics. This logical priority is compatible with the fact that in judging the values of works, we normally attend to them and not to our responses to them. But in doing so, we assume that our responses are appropriate, an assumption that becomes explicit when challenged.

The usefulness of the model of ideal critics will be evident again in the answer to our second objection. This one regards the criterion of full engagement. It is that sometimes we are readily engaged by works to which we ought not to respond in these positive ways. We lap up melodrama and sentimentality in art, fall for the pretentious, the garish, or the merely skillful. The quick answer to this objection is that ideal critics would not respond in these ways, and value in art is to be measured by their responses. But how do we know that they would not respond to these works as we do, and, if engagement is what we are after, why should it matter how this is accomplished?

The answer to the first question is that melodramatic and sentimental art engages us on an emotional level too easily, while the garish, merely skillful, and pretentious engage us perceptually or cognitively that way. What is meant by "too easily" is not simply that such art does not sufficiently challenge us, but that our absorption by it is one-dimensional, blocking attention to other features of the works by other faculties. Melodramatic and garish works are often trivial in their cognitive content, while persons who react positively to sentimental art often remain focused more on their own responses and responsiveness than on various features of the works. A work that causes us to respond inappropriately causes our evaluative faculties to come apart rather than uniting them in the appreciation of the work, if it does not simply switch them off. Because one-dimensional, such art typically fades quickly in attraction and hence does not attract knowledgeable and properly sensitive critics.

The third objection is that the criterion of evaluation proposed here is ahistorical and therefore inappropriate in regard to much avant-garde and contemporary art. Much of avant-garde art, while intended to shake us up and challenge us cognitively, is perceptually insignificant or repelling. Much of it attacks earlier ahistorical standards of aesthetic value as well as the social institutions that were seen to support and be supported by those standards. Much of it can therefore be understood only in relation to the social realities from which it emerged – for example modern expressionism as a protest by the individual against technological, mass-oriented society, constructivism and pop art as different celebrations of that society.

In brief response, while the emphasis in much of this art may lie in prompting interpretations or cognitive responses, it does so by assaulting our senses and feelings as well as our intellects. This is presumably why Duchamp, for example, famously displayed a urinal instead of some other commercial object – not for its traditional type of aesthetic value or formal qualities, but for the affective shock of *seeing* it on display. Whatever philosophical question was raised or high-brow joke was made, it was done by these artistic means. It is certainly true that such art does not aim at aesthetic value by traditional means, by creating works with formal beauty or elegance to produce a self-contained aesthetic experience. But avant-garde art remains distinct from art-historical interpretive essays, however many of those it prompts through attention to its perceptible features. If artists address problems of earlier art in their works, or reject those problems, they do so by means of objects to be seen or heard, in which the medium remains crucial to the work. This is why the best artistic attacks on traditional art institutions ended up in their museums.

As for the criterion of full engagement being ahistorical, it is not so in its application. Presently composed works in Beethoven's style would (presumably) not engage ideal music critics. But Beethoven's place in musical history, both his dramatic departures from the classical style of Haydn and Mozart and his influence on later Romantic composers, certainly informs the way we hear his works, being a major part of our cognitive engagement with them and altering the ways we hear their formal and expressive qualities.

In closing, we can make good on our claim that the answer to our question regarding an evaluative criterion across the arts that distinguishes artworks from other artifacts implies answers to other traditional questions about aesthetic judgments. Are evaluations of art objective? This admits of only a complex answer. We have seen that evaluations are usually couched in terms that refer to relational properties, relating objective properties of works to responses of ideal critics. Objectivists must explain disagreement in terms of mistake by one of the parties, but if ideal critics disagree as well, this explanation will not always work. Our evaluations must be relativized to those who share our tastes. At the same time, there are standards for judgments deriving from standards for judges that our evaluations must satisfy in order to have the normative force we intend. If art has a function, then it might seem that there must be an objective fact of the matter whether a given work fulfills it. But if the function of art is to fully engage our mental faculties, and a work does so for some critics but not others, then the correctness of an evaluation of it is not so straightforward.

Does each artwork have unique value? Each may be unique in the ways its objective properties prompt our responses, but not unique in the type of value afforded by this process. Is this value intrinsic or instrumental? Our answer has been "Both." We take satisfaction in the challenge to and full absorption of our perception, thought, imagination, and feeling in appreciation of great artworks, and we benefit from the escape this provides, from the comparison of artistic worlds to the real world, and from the expansion of our capacities in their full exercise. The best works are those that meet this standard.

# References

Aristotle (1941). *Poetics*. In R. McKeon (ed.), *The Basic Works of Aristotle*. New York: Random House: 1455–87.

Beardsley, M. (1981). *Aesthetics*. Indianapolis: Hackett.

Bender, J. (1995). "General but Defeasible Reasons in Aesthetic Evaluation." *Journal of Aesthetics and Art Criticism*, 53: 379–92.

Bourdieu, P. (1984). *Distinction: A Social Critique of the Judgment of Taste*, trans. R. Nice. Cambridge, MA: Harvard University Press. (Original work pub. 1979.)

Budd, M. (1995). *Values of Art*. London: Penguin.

Dickie, G. (1988). *Evaluating Art*. Philadelphia: Temple University Press.

Hume, D. (1963). "Of the Standard of Taste," in *Essays Moral, Political, and Literary*. Oxford: Oxford University Press: 231–55. (Original work pub. 1757.)

Hutcheson, F. (1971). *An Inquiry into the Original of our Ideas of Beauty and Virtue*. New York: Garland. (Original work pub. 1726.)

Pawlowski, T. (1989). *Aesthetic Values*. Dordrecht: Kluwer.

Sharpe, R. A. (2000). "The Empiricist Theory of Artistic Value." *Journal of Aesthetics and Art Criticism*, 58: 321–32.

Sibley, F. (1959). "A Contemporary Theory of Aesthetic Qualities: Aesthetic Concepts." *Philosophical Review*, 68: 421–50.

# Further reading

Burger, P. (1990). "The Problem of Aesthetic Value." In P. Collier and H. Geyer-Ryan (eds), *Literary Theory Today*. Ithaca, NY: Cornell University Press: 23–34.

Carroll, N. (2000). "Art and Ethical Criticism." *Ethics*, 110: 350–87.

Davies, S. (1994). "The Evaluation of Music." In P. Alperson (ed.), *What Is Music?* University Park, PA: Penn State University Press: 307–25.

Goldman, A. (1995). *Aesthetic Value*. Boulder, CO: Westview Press.

Graham, G. (1995). "The Value of Music." *Journal of Aesthetics and Art Criticism*, 53: 139–53.

Levinson, J. (1998). "Evaluating Music." In P. Alperson (ed.), *Musical Worlds*. University Park, PA: Penn State University Press: 93–107.

Meynell, H. (1986). *The Nature of Aesthetic Value*. Albany, NY: SUNY Press.

Scruton, R. (1997). *The Aesthetics of Music*. Oxford: Clarendon Press.

Shusterman, R. (1980). "The Logic of Evaluation." *Philosophical Quarterly*, 30: 327–41.

# Chapter 6

# Interpretation in Aesthetics
### *Laurent Stern*

For earlier writers in aesthetics, judgment or evaluation was the topic of choice in the discussion of criticism. Its gradual replacement by understanding or interpretation, since the early nineteenth century, brought about a re-evaluation of major problems in aesthetics. No doubt problems of interpretation were discussed long before Schleiermacher, and problems of evaluation remained in the background of the discussion in the last two centuries. Yet contemporary aesthetics would be incomprehensible if we did not focus on the most exhaustively discussed touchstone of understanding or interpreting: intentionality. The role of intentionality in criticism is central for both professionals and lay persons. At issue in the debate about intentionalism is a philosophical problem. By insisting on the philosophical character of this problem, I expect to convey the conviction that there is no decisive argument on one or the other side of the debate. If there were such a decisive argument, we would be dealing with issues concerning facts, and we would have to admit that the role of intentionality in criticism was never a philosophical problem. One epistemologist believes that he sees sense data, another that she sees physical objects – but, when they cross a busy intersection, they both dodge cars. Similarly, critics of either intentionalist or anti-intentionalist conviction must be prepared to deal with problems in practical criticism, presented to them by their opponents. If they are equally good critics, it can be expected that they will agree in their critical judgments, even if they differ about the reasons they provide for their judgments. So, why should we be concerned about this problem? The answer is that fundamental questions in aesthetics require different answers, depending on the stand we take concerning intentionalism.

## 6.1  Understanding on the Ground Level

Wimsatt and Beardsley argued in their justly famous paper "The Intentional Fallacy" (1946) that the intention of the author was neither available nor desirable as a standard for the interpretation and evaluation of the literary text. The authors of that paper and their readers both broadened and refined the scope of this thesis. In the more than half a century since its publication, we have come to think of the intentional fallacy not only in the context of literary artworks, but also in the context of visual or musical works of art. Also, anti-intentionalism has become fully compatible with an inquiry into the history of artworks. Originally there may have been a rigid demarcation line between what is within the limits of an artwork and what is beyond those limits. Once we admit an artwork's history and elements of its surrounding world within these limits, the demarcation line between what is admitted and what is ruled out becomes quite elastic. Nonetheless, what is at issue between intentionalists and their opponents is not trivial. Charles Rosen – pianist, musicologist, historian of music, art, and literature, and a more gifted philosopher than most professionals in our field – wrote: "It is the moral duty of a performer to choose what he thinks is the musically superior version, whatever the composer's clearly marked intention – it is also the moral responsibility of a pianist to try to convince himself that the composer knew what he was doing" (Rosen 1994: 22). As long as they are sensible and moderate, both intentionalists and anti-intentionalists can use Rosen's words in support of their own convictions. If this is the case, what is the import of the debate about intentionalism?

Creating an artwork is not the same as interpreting that artwork. The poet, painter, or composer may be the first interpreter of his own work, but he is not necessarily its most qualified interpreter. The artist must satisfy his own standard of correctness for the artwork he is creating. If dissatisfied, he may change his own work. The interpreter may not change the artist's work, unless she can demonstrate that the change serves a textually superior version of the work. Even the medieval scribes who were only concerned about sequences of letters followed by spaces in copying the text of the Hebrew Bible changed Genesis 18.22 to *but Abraham stood yet before the Lord*, although they found in their master copy the positions of Abraham and the Lord reversed. The interpreter's standard of correctness is the same as the standard we have in ordinary contexts: if the interpreter claims that she understood what she was told, and we do not have evidence to the contrary, then we must agree with her claim. In the context of artworks, if the interpreter is "at home" with the artwork she is concerned about, if she is comfortable with that artwork, then we must agree: as long as her belief is not challenged, she understood it. In both contexts the burden of proof is on those who disagree with an interpreter's belief that she understood or was comfortable with what was presented to her.

In both contexts, understanding rests on the interpreter's persuasion that further clarification is not needed. Proof is required to show that her persuasion is mistaken. To be sure, it may be proven that the interpreter's initial understanding was mistaken or too shallow or too deep – but if she is comfortable with her understanding of what was said or done in ordinary contexts, or if she is "at home" with her understanding of a given artwork, she is under no obligation to collect evidence against her interpretation until she is challenged. Interpretations are self-confirming until they are challenged. Amateur or professional critics who wish to convince others of the correctness of their interpretations will seek such challenges. After all, the best defense of a given interpretation is that it is better than other available interpretations for a given purpose.

The artist's dissatisfaction with his creation is a criterion for his failure to satisfy his own standard of correctness. In the large majority of cases, and as long as his creation is not in the public domain, he can change it to suit his own purposes. Except in extreme cases, an interpreter is not free to change another person's creation. No doubt artists painted over another artist's artwork long before the twentieth century. These cases do not undermine the fundamental difference between the role of the artist and that of the interpreter. Legislators create laws, judges interpret them; artists create works of art, professional or amateur critics interpret them. It can be argued that such neat divisions betray a shallow understanding of these different roles. But even arguments against these divisions presuppose that they must be taken seriously.

Our standards for understanding or interpretation are quite low. If at a more advanced stage of our thinking about what another person has said or done we raise factual or philosophical questions about our own or another person's understanding, we can do so only because we start from some ground level of understanding. Similarly, our being "at home" or being comfortable with a given artwork provides a ground level for raising issues of criticism about our own or another person's understanding of that artwork. Most of the time we are satisfied with that ground-level understanding, and we raise questions only in exceptional cases. Readers of literary artworks, visitors at art galleries, listeners at concerts have at least the level of understanding of what is presented that is available to each of us when we are comfortable with a given artwork. Even if they cover their eyes or ears or skip pages of a book, when confronted with an artwork they consider sensationalist, jarring, pornographic, or obscene, they react to an initial ground-level understanding that is the precondition of further engagement in the activity of interpreting. After conceding the claim of their having understood an artwork at this ground level, we may turn around and show that their understanding was wide of the mark or off the wall. In arguing against the acceptance of their understanding or interpretation of that artwork, we claim that they partially projected or totally superimposed on the artwork what is their contribution to the artwork, but cannot be found in it.

In everyday contexts we refrain from saying about others that they do not understand what they are told or what they see or hear until we have evidence for such claims. Prompted by elitism or snobbism, amateur and professional critics often suggest that most visitors to museums and art galleries, the majority of listeners at musical performances, and many readers of literary artworks do not understand the artworks they confront. Until we have evidence for such wild claims, there are no good reasons to believe that they are true. If we wish to become clear about the role of amateur and professional interpreters, we must take it for granted that comfort, pleasure, delight with a given artwork is sufficient evidence for a ground-level understanding of that artwork. At the same time, critics must account for the discontent with or complaint about a given artwork. Is this the viewer's, listener's, or reader's fault? Or is that artwork a failure?

## 6.2   The Critic's Role

When engaged in the activity of interpreting artworks we are performing the tasks of a critic, either on the amateur's or on the professional's level. Disagreements between two critics who are of the same level or of different levels arise for one of two reasons: one of the critics expresses her complaint about a given artwork, while the other registers her delight with that artwork, or both express their complaint or give voice to their delight, but for different reasons. Both critics must focus on what they have seen, heard or read when confronting a given artwork. This means that both critics must focus on the realized intentions of the artwork's creator. Occasionally, they will also find unintended consequences of the artist's mistaken performances: a slip of the pen or an unintended brushstroke that escaped the artist's last correction of his creation. If both the intentionalist and the anti-intentionalist critic confront one and the same artwork, then the disagreement about the artist's realized intentions must be negotiated by reference to that artwork. Any disagreement about the artist's unrealized intentions is a disagreement about the artist, and not about his creation. The question arises: is there a disagreement that requires reference to the artist's intentions?

When confused about what has been said or done in ordinary contexts, we ask the speaker or agent for clarification. If artworks were communications between an artist and his public, we would consider it natural to ask the artist for clarifications about his work. The artist is an expert on the standard of correctness that he wanted to satisfy in his work. If he is sufficiently articulate about these standards, he may provide us with information about the genesis of the work we are confronting, he may tell us about rejected variants that did not satisfy his own standard of correctness. Yet as a critic he must tell us about the standards of correctness that are satisfied in his work – and about these he is not in a better position than any other critic. Romantics may believe that only the artist understands his own creation – and they may be right as long as we focus on the process leading up to the creation of an artwork. If we focus on the finished artwork and the artist's realized intentions, then the artist's interpretation of his own work must compete against all other available interpretations.

## 6.3  Conflicting Interpretations

Initially, amateur or professional critics must make sense of the artwork they confront. The anonymous medieval scribes who changed the positions of Abraham and the Lord in copying the received text were amateurs. Charles Rosen – second to none among professional interpreters – admitted that the A-sharp in the first movement of Beethoven's *Hammerklavier* Sonata, Op. 106, was probably a misprint. Yet, regardless of what could be found in the printed score or gleaned from the manuscript copy – should it reappear – Rosen has been playing the musically more interesting A-sharp, although he considered the A-natural probably correct. In the interpreter's view, the changes were warranted, for they make better sense of the text or the score. Perhaps other interpreters can avoid such changes. In a debate of this kind, we accept the reasons presented by one side or the other, and agree or disagree with the changes suggested. At different times we may agree with either side, and show tolerance about the matter, at least as long as we do not care about the topic of the debate. Yet interpreters recommending such changes care about them passionately. If they did not believe their interpretations, if they did not hold them to be true, they would not suggest the changes. Detached observers of the available alternatives may counsel tolerance of opposing views, and argue that interpretations are neither true nor false, but more or less plausible, apt, to the point, or relevant. However, if we argue for or actively support one interpretation, can we be tolerant of its contrary?

The urgency of this question cannot be overestimated, whenever a disagreement about interpretations is debated. One critic is comfortable with an artwork, while the other is not "at home" with it. Both may be professionals, or amateurs, or one may be a professional and the other an amateur. The critic who is comfortable with, derives pleasure or delight from, that artwork will find his opponent wanting. Since he is comfortable with that artwork, he must ascribe some fault to the other interpreter, if she fails to appreciate and understand it. Her eyes or ears and her understanding must be at fault if she does not agree with him. At the same time, she will blame him for appreciating and misunderstanding something as an artwork that in her judgment is empty. According to her, he will have superimposed on a thing what is in his imagination, and not in that thing. Overtly, the debate between the two critics is about one and the same thing, but as soon as intolerance concerning a contrary judgment raises its head, the focus of the debate changes from a thing to the critic who happens to disagree with another critic. Moreover, intolerance can enter the discussion even if two critics agree about a thing that purports to be an artwork. Both could be comfortable with that artwork or both could reject it as an artwork, while they do so for different reasons. Again, each of the two critics could argue that the other must be blamed for superimposing on an artwork or on what purports to be an artwork what the other imagines is seen or heard rather than what is seen or heard. Debates between two critics who disagree in their judgments, or two critics who agree on a given judgment and disagree on their reasons for that judgment, are debates between interpreters and not between philosophers. Philosophers will find it easy to assign relative merit to each interpretation; interpreters must choose between competing interpretations. From the interpreters' perspective, the philosophers who assign relative merit to competing interpretations don't care about the issues of the debate, they don't care about the facts of the matter, and they don't care about the truth.

But it is precisely because philosophers care so much about the facts of the matter and about truth that they are unwilling to assign a truth value to either one of the two competing interpretations. This does not mean that there is one truth for interpreters and another for philosophers, or that what is a fact for one need not be a fact for the other. It means that we do not know what is the case in these circumstances. Interpreters arguing for or defending a given interpretation hold that it is true, but just because we agree that they would not argue for that interpretation if they did not hold it to be true, it does not follow that it is true. In arguing for that interpretation they may believe that they have established a fact, and for all that we know, they may have come close to having established a fact. But not even the best available or most successful interpretation can become transubstantiated into a fact. After all, if we knew what the facts were, we would not need interpretations.

Some critics may be tempted to support one of the competing interpretations by trying to discover the intentions of the artwork's creator. Only intentions that are unrealized in the artwork are at issue in this search, for the realized intentions are available for both competing interpretations. But the interpretation of an artwork cannot be transubstantiated into a fact, just because it is supported by its creator's unrealized intentions. Artworks are finished only if they satisfy their creators' standards of correctness. By imposing on a finished artwork its creator's unrealized intentions, the critic changes that artwork. If artworks were communications between an artist and his or her audience, then such changes would be appropriate. A letter-writer's slip of the pen can be easily corrected by reference to the writer's intentions. After correcting it, we may wonder what, if anything, the mistaken performance says about the writer. But we would not ask whether the mistaken performance makes the letter more or less valuable. By contrast, a slip of the pen in a poem can make that poem more or less valuable. If the slip makes it a more valuable poem, then we would not remove it, even if this has been recommended by the poet. If the slip makes it a less valuable poem, then we would remove it, even if the poet recommended the contrary. Interpreters correct a text or a score, if this is warranted in the process of making sense and bringing out the value of that text or score.

Communications may contain secrets; our awareness of a letter-writer's unrealized intentions may uncover those secrets. Artworks are not communications, and they contain no secrets. Interpretations can only show what is publicly available in a given artwork that – as far as we know – satisfied its creator's standard of correctness. An artwork's interpretation is weakened rather than strengthened by a reference to its creator's unrealized intentions. By taking account of these intentions, critics admit their failure in understanding and appreciating that artwork. Even if the artwork's creator tells us about his unrealized intentions, he can do so only if he takes on the role of a critic who happens to interpret his own creation. Compared to other critics of his creation, he is in a privileged position only about his unrealized intentions. Concerning his realized intentions, he may be even less privileged than any other critic, especially if he sees or reads into his artwork what others cannot find there. Yet, we must not conclude that the available evidence overwhelmingly supports anti-intentionalism.

## 6.4   The Artwork's World

Intentionalist critics correctly insist that an artwork's interpretation requires the inclusion of parts of its surrounding world. For example, the understanding of a literary artwork requires not only the reader's acquaintance with its language, but also some knowledge of the practices, conventions, and culture that is part of the world surrounding that artwork. Even the understanding of a simple story requires that we use our imagination in filling the gaps between events that are told in that story. What we learn from one artwork, we bring to our understanding of other artworks. We have learnt most of our empirical generalizations about human nature from reading stories or seeing movies at an early age. Armed with that store of knowledge, we came to understand the more complex artworks we have encountered at later stages in our lives. We do not read, see, or hear an artwork as if it was the first of its kind we ever confronted. Since we always add elements that cannot be found within a given artwork, the question arises: why do anti-intentionalist critics object specifically to the inclusion of the unrealized intentions of an artwork's creator within that artwork? Why don't we treat his unrealized intentions – as far as they are known to us – as extensions of his realized intentions? Moral principles are at issue for both intentionalist and anti-intentionalist critics.

According to intentionalist critics, it is our duty to understand an artwork as its creator wanted it to be understood. Kantian morality requires that we act in such a way that we always treat humanity in ourselves and in others never simply as a means but always at the same time as an end. Extending this demand to literary artworks, E. D. Hirsch, Jr, writes: "To treat an author's words merely as grist for one's own mill is ethically analogous to using another man for one's own purposes" (Hirsch 1976: 90). The insight hidden in this claim is worth preserving independently of its appeal to Kantian morality. Other moral principles are invoked in support of anti-intentionalism. The anti-intentionalist critic asks: what authority permits an intentionalist critic to rely on the unrealized intentions of an artwork's creator in interpreting that artwork? The author, artist, or composer did not include them in his artwork; in judging that he finished his artwork, he proclaimed that it satisfied his own standards of correctness. It is now an autonomous work, and we may not add to it what its creator left out. According to Beardsley, "it is just as important not to read something into a poem as it is [not] to overlook something" (Beardsley 1958: 26). The anti-intentionalist critic's insights also deserve to be preserved. Both arguments will be called arguments of connoisseurs – or, to be brief: "c-arguments." Moralizing claims leading to arguments are also entered by the dilettante – we will call them "d-arguments."

Visitors to an art museum who are uncomfortable with the artworks that are exhibited are sometimes overheard saying after looking at a painting by Mondrian or Pollock: "My 12-year-old daughter or 9-year-old son could do that." A seasoned curator can only answer: "Let them try it, and see whether they succeed." It is unlikely that youngsters imitating what they see in a Mondrian or Pollock would like what they are doing, and even if they learn to like it, they will need some time for developing their own standard of correctness that they would need to satisfy. Obviously, at one time our great painters were amateurish youngsters; the dilettante is merely mistaken in believing that they remained such youngsters. Yet his indignation has a point. If the creator of an artwork does not like his own artwork, if he is not "at home" with that artwork, if he does not derive pleasure or aesthetic delight from that artwork, while at the same time he pretends the contrary, both connoisseur and dilettante will call him a fraud. The connoisseur will also call him a fraud if he has not satisfied his own standard of correctness or if he does not have a standard of correctness, and nonetheless actively pursues the entry of his work into the public domain. The dilettante has a further cause for complaint. If an artwork's creator and his connoisseur public are "at home" with that artwork, if they derive pleasure or aesthetic delight from it, then either they are frauds or something is wrong with him. Neither of these options provides much comfort. Finally, the connoisseur has cause for complaint if she is uncomfortable with an artwork although its creator and at least some connoisseurs are "at home" with it. Is she witnessing a small conspiracy to commit fraud, or are her eyes, ears, and understanding at fault? Both c- and d-arguments point to a surprising connection between the interpretation of artworks and moral considerations. Second, both covertly imply an equally surprising connection between the evaluation and the interpretation of artworks. Finally, both seem to assume that there ought to be a convergence of tastes, despite the long history of the suggestion that there is no disputing about them.

## 6.5   Misinterpretations and Off-the-Wall Interpretations

The interpretation of artworks is inseparable from their evaluation. It always makes sense to ask whether the interpreter was "at home" or uncomfortable with a given artwork, whether she was entertained or bored by it, whether she derived pleasure or aesthetic delight from it, or whether she found it offensive. Unless we become aware of both her attitudes and her beliefs concerning a given artwork, we cannot appreciate her contribution to criticism. Discussions about interpretations of artworks that are fully separated from value considerations miss the point of criticism in the arts. Such discussions are closer to the debates among medieval intellectuals about texts sacred and profane than to literary or art criticism. Our literary critics tell us about issues of race, class, and gender, while purporting to write about literary artworks (Ellis 1997). I am in sympathy with their stand on these issues, but even the political sermon would be more effective if we were told about its connection to the artwork, and if we knew whether the critic derived some pleasure from the artwork, or whether she found it offensive.

Intentionalist critics believe that they can stem the tide of unwarranted social or political commentary within literary and art criticism by insisting that the authors or artists being discussed could not have meant what is attributed to them by the politically committed critics. The intentionalists have stronger weapons at their disposal when they wish to defend criticism against ideologies, discredited or newfangled. They can use these weapons even if they happen to agree with the social agenda of their politically committed colleagues. The central issue in criticism is not what the creator of an artwork may have meant or what a critic makes him say, but what can be discovered in his artwork. Ideologies are damaging to criticism only if they prompt the interpreter to cover rather than reveal what can be found in an artwork. No doubt we do not have innocent eyes or ears when we approach an artwork, and we must bring to it what we have learnt about art and life in order to bring out what becomes available for discovery. The question arises: how can the interpreter avoid superimposing on an artwork what is in her and thereby obscuring rather than illuminating the object of her interpretation?

Interpretations have a natural limit: they are rejected if they contradict facts known to the interpreter. In ordinary contexts, outside of the arts, the interpreting activity is often triggered by a contradiction between the words of a speaker or writer and what is accepted as a fact by the interpreter. Within the arts, the interpreting activity is at times triggered by the tension between our expectations – based on facts that we accept – and what is found in an artwork. More frequently, interpreting is prompted by our being uncomfortable with an artwork or by the need to provide an interpretation for those who are not "at home" with that artwork. If readers, viewers or listeners are uncomfortable with an artwork, then either they did not understand what they found in the artwork they confronted, or there was nothing to understand in that object that purports to be an artwork, or they were situated somewhere between the two previously mentioned extremes. The visitor to the art museum must acquire some knowledge of art and art history before he can discover what there is to see in a painting by Mondrian or Pollock. What the visitor must bring to these paintings will enable him to see in them more than just arbitrary markings on a contrasting surface. Given sufficient additional education, he may even come to see what professionals in the field of art see in these paintings. Yet what he brings to the painting may be sufficient for him for seeing an artwork in what he noticed, even if his contribution partially obscures rather than illuminates what can be found in it. What he brings to it may be fertile ground for its misinterpretation. However, misinterpretations are still interpretations, even if they are off the mark or wide of the mark. It is also possible that his contribution completely obscures what is in that artwork, in which case we can no longer speak about a misinterpretation: what the visitor attributes to that artwork is an off-the-wall interpretation, not at all an interpretation of the artwork.

The distinction between misinterpretations and off-the-wall interpretations is fundamental for understanding interpretation in the arts. Interpretations are expected to bring out what can be found in artworks. If a professional critic brings to an artwork anything that partially obscures what can be found in it, her criticism will be understood as merely a subjective response to that artwork. To be sure, subjective responses must be rejected only if they obscure what can be found in the artwork that is interpreted. Even if we are more inclined to be guided by subjective responses of professional than amateur critics, we expect from a professional – and exemplary – critic that she brings to notice what can be found in an artwork without partially obscuring it. If we see it as a better artwork due to her interpretation, we will prefer her interpretation to other available alternatives. Included among these will be interpretations based on merely subjective responses by other critics, professional or amateur. In everyday contexts, outside of the arts, we accept only the best available interpretation for our purposes. Matters are not different in the context of the arts. To be sure, yesterday's best interpretation may become today's second-best interpretation, but as soon as it is judged second best, it is discredited; it becomes a misinterpretation.

If we accept only the best available interpretation for our purposes, then merely subjective responses that partially obscure what is found in an artwork must yield to the interpretations of an exemplary critic. The exemplary critic provides us with interpretations that are so unobtrusive that we come to believe that we are presented with a description of what can be found in an artwork rather than an interpretation. "The elucidations of a poem," wrote Heidegger, "must strive to make themselves superfluous. The last, but also most difficult step of every interpretation is this: to disappear with its elucidations before the pure presence of the poem" (Heidegger 1951: 8). It is an ideal of criticism that we rely on nothing but the internal evidence available in interpreting an artwork, and when we are provided with such an interpretation, we read, see, hear, or understand that artwork as if no interpretation had taken place. Guided by the exemplary critic, not only do we come to understand a given artwork in light of an interpretation, but also we come to believe that we are guided by facts about that artwork rather than an interpretation.

Unfortunately, neither connoisseurs nor dilettantes have criteria at their disposal that would permit them to distinguish among interpretations provided by exemplary, professional, or amateur critics. There are no internal bells that start to ring when interpreters offer their audiences a misinterpretation or an off-the-wall interpretation. It may happen to connoisseurs as well as to dilettantes that they stand before a painting and spread over it what they wish to see. It happened even to

Heidegger that he superimposed his phantasies and free associations on a van Gogh painting of shoes: what he saw as peasant shoes or a peasant woman's shoes were actually van Gogh's own shoes (Schapiro 1994). If this happens to a dilettante, we dismiss the interpretation; if it happens to a connoisseur, we may want to save the speculation leading to the interpretation (Derrida 1978; Stern 1999). In either case, off-the-wall interpretations are not taken seriously. Since misinterpretations compete against each other for the position of the best interpretation available for a given purpose, they must be taken seriously, even if they are dated or discredited.

If an interpreter merely argues against an off-the-wall interpretation, it is sufficient to call attention to the facts that contradict that interpretation. If she argues against a misinterpretation, she must provide us with reasons for preferring her interpretation. As a critic, she will be found wanting if she merely tells us about her subjective responses to an artwork. For example, it won't do to say that she likes that artwork, while expecting the agreement of her audience because she happens to have good taste. She must draw attention to the object of her interpretation and convince her audience that if they come to understand it as she does, they will also appreciate it. If she satisfies in this task, then an additional overt or covert social or political agenda does not change her qualifications as a critic. No doubt some will be alienated by her agenda, while others will become converts to her views. But there are no valid objections to the inclusion of her agenda within her critical essays. For a critic finds her audience and a reliable following primarily among those who share her social or political agenda. In her role as a critic, her primary responsibility is speaking or writing about the artwork she is interpreting for her audience in the expectation of their agreement concerning its appreciation. There are no safeguards against a misinterpretation or an off-the-wall interpretation; the best that she can do is to show and describe what is in an artwork and to defend her interpretation against available alternatives.

Intentionalist critics may wish to argue for an interpretation, and the exclusion of misinterpretations or off-the-wall interpretations, by reference to the intentions of the artwork's creator. Suppose we discovered a letter by Piero della Francesca informing us that he used wooden horses as models for the horses he painted. Or suppose a letter of Vincent van Gogh's informed us that he used his own shoes as models for painting a peasant's shoes or a peasant woman's shoes. No doubt the letters would be valued as sources for biographical information about their authors. But Piero's letter would contain no news about his frescoes: good observers see that theater props were the models for the horses in them. On the other hand, the best observers could not discover in the paintings of shoes that they were peasant shoes, even if they were prompted by van Gogh himself. Anti-intentionalist critics will dismiss such testimony, intentionalists will consider it seriously – their attitudes toward the testimony may be different, while at the same time they will agree in their beliefs about these artworks.

## 6.6  Universalizability

We are now in a better position to understand conflicting interpretations in the arts. Interpretive conflicts about an artwork may arise between two connoisseurs, grounding their conclusions on how to read, see, or hear a given artwork on what I have called competing c-arguments; it may arise between a connoisseur and a dilettante, based on competing c- and d-arguments; finally, it may be grounded on two different d-arguments. Conflicts between d-arguments can be disregarded: they are either uninformed, or mirror the conflict between c- and d-arguments. Debates between two connoisseurs or between a connoisseur and a dilettante deserve detailed discussion. In both kinds of debates, the connoisseurs insist that they show and describe what is in a given artwork, and exhibit its value; moreover, what they say about it is available for discovery by all reasonably well-informed readers, viewers, or listeners.

Two connoisseurs may have the same attitude to an artwork – for example, they both highly appreciate it – but offer different reasons in support of their interpretations. Or, although they provide similar reasons in supporting them, they may have different attitudes toward one and the same artwork: while one appreciates it, the other finds it rather shallow. Such issues arise also in the context of debates between connoisseurs and dilettantes. In all these debates we pay lip service to the platitude that there is no disputing about tastes, while our debates are in fact animated by such disputes. Connoisseurs argue against each other and against dilettantes while believing that, if their opponents had good taste and sufficient knowledge about art, they would come to agree on the understanding and appreciation of the artwork discussed. Even if some of their opponents co-operate and come to agree with them, as long as they cannot convince all of their opponents, they must face a problem presented by the very existence of such opponents. If they had good taste and were sufficiently informed, why wouldn't they agree with the interpretation and appreciation that are being offered to them? The suspicion arises that either their taste or their education is at fault: something is wrong with them, if they dig in their heels and refuse to accept the dictates of good taste, superior knowledge, and education. On what grounds do they dare to resist the authority of the best critical judgment?

They have good grounds, and they have been lent a voice by Hans Christian Andersen's little child in "The Emperor's New Clothes": "But the Emperor has nothing at all on!" Moreover, the dilettantes may at times be joined by some connoisseurs who agree that there is nothing at all to a given object that is exhibited in an art gallery. If there are connoisseurs who claim that the pile of bricks exhibited at the Tate Gallery is an artwork, they must superimpose on that object what is in them rather than in the object exhibited. Are there any standards of correctness that are satisfied by that object? Does it have some kind of shock value? Does it provide amusement, entertainment, pleasure, or aesthetic delight to the connoisseur who supports the claim that it is an artwork? If none of these questions can be satisfactorily answered, then the dilettante is right: the object exhibited is not an artwork. Unless the conflicts can be terminated by convincing the opponents, suspicions follow in the wake of interpretive conflicts in the arts. The dilettantes suspect the connoisseurs of being part of a conspiracy to commit fraud on an unsuspecting public for supporting the claim that the pile of bricks is an artwork. The connoisseurs suspect the dilettantes for being insufficiently knowledgeable or lacking in taste.

The mutual suspicions are seldom justified, but they are unavoidable. C-arguments must be presented with a universal voice. Implied in such arguments is the claim that given sufficient knowledge and adequate taste, all readers, viewers, or listeners of a given artwork will find what the professional or exemplary critic found in that artwork. Yet anyone speaking with a universal voice must face the probability that she will not find universal agreement. Confronted by disagreement, the critic must choose among three alternatives. She can withdraw her judgment about the artwork; she can maintain her judgment, but surrender the claim that she is speaking with a universal voice; finally, she can maintain her judgment and speak with a universal voice, while standing up against the disagreement of some of her listeners and readers. The first choice is of no interest. The second permits her to withdraw to a safer ground, but at a high price. She can tell her audience about her subjective response to a given artwork. But she can no longer argue that the basis for her subjective response must be understood as if it were a quality of that artwork, that this basis can be found by all who confront it, and finally, that given this basis they must all share her subjective response to that artwork. The third choice is to continue speaking with a universal voice, while standing up against the disagreement of what is often a majority. Some will admire such bravery, others will be offended by the universal voice.

D-arguments against the universal voice question the very idea that there are professional or exemplary critics who know the arts in the sense in which professional mathematicians or physicists know their subject matter: practical criticism in the arts is close to practical criticism in politics, but far from the practice of professionals in mathematics or physics. According to this view, the professional critic's universal voice must be drowned out by the little child's voice – "But the Emperor has nothing at all on!" C-arguments enter a more sophisticated objection against the professional or exemplary critics' universal voice. Some agree with the dilettantes that there are no professional critics, while others are worried about the claims of knowledge and insight of the professional critics. They claim to know what others don't know – but isn't that claim just an expression of authoritarianism? Within the tradition of philosophical critics who speak with a universal voice there is indeed a streak of authoritarianism, elitism, and even a barely disguised contempt for those who are not sufficiently knowledgeable to formulate c-arguments with a universal voice.

The philosophical tradition of a universal voice in aesthetics can be traced to Kant's *Critique of the Power of Judgment* (2000: 96–7 [1790 § 6]):

For one cannot judge that about which he is aware that the satisfaction in it is without any interest in his own case in any way except that it must contain a ground of satisfaction for everyone. For since it is not grounded in any inclination of the subject (nor in any other underlying interest), but rather the person making the judgment feels himself completely free with regard to the satisfaction that he devotes to the object, he cannot discover as grounds of the satisfaction any private conditions, pertaining to his subject alone, and must therefore regard it as grounded in those that he can also presuppose in everyone else; consequently he must believe himself to have grounds for expecting a similar pleasure of everyone.

The professional critic who speaks with a universal voice does not ask whether others agree with him, but demands that they agree (Kant 2000: 97 [1790 § 7]). Confronted with such a demand, some readers will agree that it is occasionally justified, and at times they too will issue such demands; others will argue that it is not justified, and they will never issue such demands. Both c- and d-arguments against the professional critics' universal voice must be understood as part of the revolt against the dominant tradition in aesthetics. Proponents of d-arguments claim not only that the artworld's emperors are naked, but also that they abuse their positions of authority within our society by imposing their taste on the artworld's public. C-arguments against the dominant tradition insist on the separation of classificatory and evaluative issues concerning objects that are considered to be artworks. The role of institutions and persons who confer the status of art is clearer in these arguments than the reasons for conferring that status on one object rather than another. Supporters of the dominant tradition in aesthetics are suspicious of the proponents of these c-arguments: are they trying to replace the universal voice of the professional or exemplary critic with sociological considerations? Regardless of how we answer this question, it must be admitted that the professional critic's universal voice deserves to be questioned. No doubt we tolerate and often follow their judgments, at least as long as they do not have the power to enforce their views. Yet wouldn't we consider them to be petty tyrants, if they did have such power?

## 6.7 Two Mistakes

We do not always interpret artworks. Interpreting is an activity, and it is a mistake to attribute an activity to others or to ourselves without adequate evidence. It will not do to say that lack of evidence merely shows that most of the time this activity is unconscious. If this were the case, our engagement with artworks would be more on an unconscious than on a conscious level. We interpret only when a text, a score, or a visual artwork is in need of interpretation for others or for ourselves. In other cases we simply understand and like, appreciate, dislike, or dismiss what is presented to us. The second mistake is to distinguish between surface- and deep-level interpretation in the context of artworks. The first mistake serves the goals of anti-intentionalist critics: it permits the attribution of a characteristic that is consistent with a given artwork but cannot be discovered in it. The second mistake serves the purposes of intentionalist critics: it permits the attribution of an unconscious intention to the creator of an artwork when a characteristic of that artwork cannot be attributed to his conscious intentions. Both mistakes indicate an over-intellectualization of the interpreting activity: many c-arguments – especially by critics who accept a confused version of the continental European philosophical tradition – are theory-driven rather than triggered by problems that arise from the understanding of an individual artwork. Critics can compensate for both mistakes if they can show that interpreting where no interpretation is needed, or deep-level interpreting where this is not needed, brings out the value of that artwork for some segment of its audience.

In ordinary contexts – outside of the arts – we interpret only when there is a need to interpret and we invoke methods of deep-level interpretation only when natural or surface-level interpretation does not explain sufficiently what others have said or done. Methods of deep-level interpretation often permit us to understand what others try to keep for themselves or of what they are not completely conscious. These methods rely primarily on paying attention not only to what others say, but also on how they say it – their tone of voice, the words and gestures they are using, and their behavior. Surface-level interpretation is sufficient for what others confess; deep-level interpretation is required for what they betray. In the context of interpreting artworks, we may ask: do we need to interpret when we understand directly what is presented to us in an artwork? Is there ever a need to distinguish between surface- and deep-level interpretation in the context of interpreting in the arts? The answer to both questions is that the decision about these matters is subject to a normative constraint. In judging interpretations, we accept only the best one available for our purposes. In the context of art interpretation, this implies that if an interpretation brings out the value of an artwork better than other available interpretations, it will be accepted by at least a part of the artworld's public. In some cases it may even happen that one and the same interpretation – Heidegger's discussion of van Gogh's painting of shoes is a case in point – is accepted by some as the best available interpretation, while it is dismissed by others as either an off-the-wall interpretation or a misinterpretation.

## 6.8 Envoy

In a discussion of interpreting in the arts we must aim at providing neutral descriptions of the interpreting activity that may be useful for professional or amateur critics even if they don't share the author's bias for or against intentionalism. While I happen to favor the anti-intentionalist side of the debate, and I find the over-intellectualization of interpreting in the arts unfortunate, the prospect of a continuing debate on these matters is more important than converting opponents to the side where I have been led by what lawyers call the preponderance of the evidence.

## References

Beardsley, Monroe C. (1958). *Aesthetics: Problems in the Philosophy of Criticism*. New York: Harcourt Brace & World.

Derrida, Jacques (1978). *La vérité en peinture*. Paris: Flammarion.

Ellis, John M. (1997). *Literature Lost: Social Agendas and the Corruption of the Humanities*. New Haven, CT: Yale University Press.

Heidegger, Martin (1951). *Erläuterungen zu Hölderlins Dichtung*. Frankfurt: Vittorio Klostermann.

Hirsch, E. D. Jr (1976). *The Aims of Interpretation*. Chicago: University of Chicago Press.

Kant, I. (2000). *Critique of the Power of Judgment*, ed. and trans. Paul Guyer. Cambridge: Cambridge University Press.

Rosen, Charles (1994). *The Frontiers of Meaning*. New York: Hill and Wang.

Schapiro, Meyer (1994). "The Still Life as a Personal Object – A Note on Heidegger and van Gogh." In *Theory and Philosophy of Art: Style Artist and Society*. New York: George Braziller: 135–42. (Original work pub. 1968.)

Stern, Laurent (1999). "Some Aspects of Interpreting." In M. Krausz and R. Shusterman (eds), *Interpretation, Relativism, and the Metaphysics of Culture: Themes in the Philosophy of Joseph Margolis*. Amherst, NY: Humanity Books: 15–40.

## Further reading

Armstrong, Paul B. (1990). *Conflicting Readings: Variety and Validity in Interpretation*. Chapel Hill: University of North Carolina Press.

Cavell, Stanley (1987). *Disowning Knowledge: In Six Plays of Shakespeare*. Cambridge: Cambridge University Press.

Danto, Arthur C. (1981). *The Transfiguration of the Commonplace: A Philosophy of Art*. Cambridge, MA: Harvard University Press.

——(1997). *After the End of Art: Contemporary Art and the Pale of History*. Princeton, NJ: Princeton University Press.

Gadamer, Hans Georg (1989). *Truth and Method*. 2nd edn, trans. revised. New York: Crossroads. (Original work pub. 1960.)

Goodman, Nelson (1976). *Languages of Art*. 2nd edn. Indianapolis: Hackett.

Irwin, William (1999). *Intentionalist Interpretation: A Philosophical Interpretation and Defense*. Westport, CT: Greenwood Press.

Iseminger, Gary (1992). *Intention and Interpretation*. Philadelphia: Temple University Press.

Iser, Wolfgang (2000). *The Range of Interpretation*. New York: Columbia University Press.

Kivy, Peter (1990) *Music Alone: Philosophical Reflections on the Purely Musical Experience*. Ithaca, NY: Cornell University Press.

Lamarque, Peter and Olsen, Stein Haugom (1994). *Truth, Fiction, and Literature: A Philosophical Perspective*. Oxford: Clarendon University Press.

Rosen, Charles (1998). *Romantic Poets, Critics and Other Madmen*. Cambridge, MA: Harvard University Press.

Schapiro, Meyer (1973). *Words and Pictures: On the Literal and the Symbolic in the Illustration of a Text*. The Hague: Mouton.

Smith, Barbara Herrnstein (1988). *Contingencies of Value: Alternative Perspectives for Critical Theory*. Cambridge, MA: Harvard University Press.

Sternberg, Meir (1987). "Gaps, Ambiguity and the Reading Process." In *The Poetics of Biblical Narrative*. Bloomington: Indiana University Press: 186–229.

Walton, Kendall L. (1990). *Mimesis as Make-Believe: On the Foundations of the Representational Arts*. Cambridge, MA: Harvard University Press.

Wollheim, Richard (1974). *On Art and the Mind*. Cambridge, MA: Harvard University Press.

——(1987). *Painting as an Art*. Princeton, NJ: Princeton University Press.

Wolterstorff, Nicholas (1980). *Works and Worlds of Art*. Oxford: Clarendon Press.

# Chapter 7

# Art and the Moral Realm
## *Noël Carroll*

## 7.1 Introduction

The relation of art and morality is enduring and complex. Indeed, it is so complex that it is better to speak of the relation*s* of art and morality, rather than to talk as though there were only one relation here. In all probability, art and morality arrived on the cultural scene at roughly the same moment, inasmuch as the earliest tribal moralities and values of the race were articulated and disseminated through the songs, poems, dances, narratives, and visual arts of our early forebears. In the *Iliad*, for example, Homer taught the Greeks the virtues and vices of vengeance (French 2001: ch. 1). Much early art, as well, was a vehicle of religious expression and belief which involved tutoring audiences in the obligations and ideals of their cultures, while also, at times, criticizing them, as Christ does in many of his parables in the New Testament (Parker 1994: 48).

In the West, medieval art and much of that to follow was devoted to expressing the tenets of Christianity in almost every imaginable medium, including words, song, sculpture, architecture, stained glass, painting, and so on. So many cathedrals are, in effect, encyclopedias of Catholic culture, repositories of Christian values expressed in visual narratives that serve to recall exemplary moments. And the same doctrinal function occurs in the artifacts of non-western cultures. In short, there can be little doubt that one of the primary functions of art through the ages has been the presentation and exploration of morality.

Art is a primary means for enculturating peoples in the ethos of their society – where that ethos has, as one of its central components, morality narrowly construed. Art introduces us to that ethos and its morality, reinforces and clarifies our commitments to it, often through exemplary stories and characters; art inspires us morally by equipping us with ideals, and it can even suggest ways of criticizing prevailing forms of moral blindness.

Of all the services that art performs, none seems more longstanding than its involvement in the ongoing enculturation of its audiences, which process encom-

passes their moral education in diverse ways. This is not to say that moral education is the only significant thing that art does. But imprinting and interrogating
the ethos of a people, including its morality, for its audiences is one of the tasks
art excels in discharging; perhaps it does this as well as anything else it does. Moreover, this is not only a function of the art of yesteryear; it continues in the literature, drama, film, dance, fine art, and song of artists everywhere today.

For these reasons, it is not surprising that much art is discussed and evaluated
in terms of morality. It is not odd, for example, to read a critic chiding Philip
Roth's recent novel, *The Dying Animal,* for its apparent inability to think of
women as other than sexual beings (Scott 2001). This sort of criticism seems to
be an appropriate response to the kind of novel *The Dying Animal* is.

Admittedly, not all art is equally suitable for moral evaluation. Some absolute
music and some abstract painting may be bereft of moral content altogether,
thereby rendering moral criticism inapposite in such cases. However, so much art
traffics in moral matters and presents moral viewpoints that when moral considerations are raised with respect to the relevant artworks, nothing seems amiss – at
least to the plain reader, viewer, or listener.

But common sense and philosophy often diverge. And when it comes to assessing the pertinence of art to morality and of morality to art, that divergence can
be quite pronounced. On the one hand, since Plato, some philosophers have disparaged art's epistemic credentials as a source of moral education, suggesting that
art has little to offer by way of instruction concerning the moral life. That is, art
is not relevant to morality.

On the other hand, many philosophers, especially since the eighteenth century,
have argued that the realm of art is essentially independent from the realm of
morality. Thus, moral criticism is not germane in evaluating artworks as artworks.
Or, in other words, morality is not truly relevant to art. Indeed, some even might
say that it makes no sense, ontologically speaking, to criticize artworks morally,
since only agents can be criticized in this way and artworks are not, strictly speaking, agents.

We can organize these arguments against the common-sense view – that art or,
at least, some art can be evaluated morally – under three headings: cognitive or
epistemic arguments; ontological arguments; and aesthetic arguments. In order to
appreciate what is at stake in the debate between philosophy and common sense
on the issue of the ethical criticism of art, something needs to be said about each
of these challenges.

The cognitive or epistemic arguments against the moral evaluation of artworks
challenge the notion that artworks can serve as vehicles for moral education. Such
arguments raise concerns about whether artworks are such that they possess the
capacity to provide genuine ethical instruction. For if artworks lack the resources
to provide genuine ethical instruction, it makes no sense to commend them for
doing so. Moreover, if artworks are really outside the instruction game altogether,
then there is little point in criticizing them for failing to do what they cannot do
anyway.[1]

The sorts of considerations that lead some philosophers to challenge the capacity of artworks to contribute to ethical learning include the following: that the ethical knowledge supposedly dispensed by artworks is too trivial to count as real knowledge acquisition (so it is scarcely reasonable to say audiences learn from artworks); that the putative knowledge claims in artworks are empirically unsubstantiated (fictions, for example, are made up; they are hardly evidential); and third, that the moral implications attributed to artworks are not supported by the kind of argumentation and analysis that one typically expects to accompany and to authenticate ethical claims in the realm of moral debate and contestation.

That is, according to what we can call the banality argument, the moral insights attributed to, for instance, literary fictions are too threadbare to count as something a novel teaches its readers. In most cases, the readers must already grasp the relevant truisms – such as that gratuitous cruelty toward innocent victims is evil – in order to understand the novel. Thus, it strains credibility to suggest that the novel teaches this to readers. You cannot teach someone what they already know. Moreover, since the so-called knowledge that most artworks allegedly impart is of this truistic variety, the claim that art contributes to moral education is vastly, if not entirely, exaggerated.

Furthermore, if moral education requires something to teach, namely knowledge, then some philosophers worry that art is not up to the job at hand. For knowledge, properly so called, is not simply a matter of belief, but involves belief warranted by evidence, argument, and analysis. And though artworks may imply or presuppose many beliefs, they do not substantiate them by evidence, argument, or analysis. Most artworks (excepting certain avant-garde attempts) do not include experimental or observational data in support of their claims (Beardsley 1981: 379–80); nor do they contain the sort of explicit argumentation and analysis in support of their moral views that one finds in newspaper editorials, policy statements, sermons, and philosophical treatises, and on the other platforms from which moral claims are advanced.[2]

Thus, though one finds common sense incessantly recommending artistic achievements for their contributions to moral enlightenment, the philosophical skeptic insinuates that this is so much blather, uplifting perhaps, but ultimately empty-headed. For epistemic reasons, art cannot be praised for its cognitive additions to moral knowledge, because what it brokers is neither knowledge (*justified*, true beliefs) nor even new beliefs (rather than merely truisms). Nor, the philosopher may add, should artworks be criticized for failing to provide moral education, if that is not something they were ever equipped to do.

But epistemic objections are not the only ones philosophers raise with regard to the relation of art to morality. The epistemic line of attack supposes that it makes no sense to evaluate artworks morally, where such evaluation rests on the presumption that artworks have the capacity to afford moral education. But suppose, contra the epistemic arguments just rehearsed, that artworks could be shown to facilitate moral education, and that, in consequence, it does make sense to evaluate them morally. In that event, many skeptical aestheticians will say: "OK, evaluate the relevant artworks morally, *but* the moral evaluation of said artworks is strictly independent of and irrelevant to their aesthetic evaluation." That is, an artwork may be evil, but that evil need not figure at all in the question of whether it is aesthetically good or bad.

Suppose that Nero incinerated Rome because he thought it would be an enthralling spectacle for the eye (and for the ear too, since he was fiddling all the while). Though the resulting spectacle was unquestionably evil, it does not follow, so the philosophical skeptic suggests, that it was not also beautiful, for aesthetics and ethics are twain. Thus, even if the epistemic arguments against the ethical criticism of art fail, there are aesthetic arguments that may also be introduced to challenge the common-sense assumption that some, indeed many, artworks can be intelligibly evaluated ethically.[3]

Of course, the epistemic arguments and the aesthetic arguments against the ethical criticism of art make different points. The former claim that artworks cannot be evaluated morally, whereas the latter claim that, even if artworks can be evaluated morally, their moral evaluation is never relevant to their aesthetic evaluation. Thus, one might reject the epistemic arguments, while accepting the aesthetic argument. But there is also another option: one might accept the epistemic arguments as a way of reaching the aesthetic conclusion by contending that, since artworks do not really involve moral knowledge, assessing them, qua artworks, in that light is never appropriate. Rather, they should only ever be assessed aesthetically, despite the commonsensical inclination to suppose that the moral viewpoint of an artwork, at least sometimes, might have something to do with its artistic merit or demerit.

Lastly, the philosopher might charge common sense with speaking nonsense when we talk of artworks as being moral or immoral. People, it might be said, are moral or immoral, not things. This is the aesthetician's variant of the notion that "guns don't kill, people do." Likewise, "artworks are not immoral, people are." It is a category error to think otherwise. Thus, on ontological grounds, the skeptical philosopher bridles at the basic assumption of ethical criticism, however entrenched the idea appears in our artistic practices.

Whether our commonsensical assumptions about the ethical criticism of art can be defended against these philosophical arguments is the question that this chapter addresses. In what follows, I will examine, in turn, the epistemic, ontological, and aesthetic arguments against the ethical criticism of art. By way of preview it is only fair, in the interests of full disclosure, that I confess before the ball starts rolling that I belong to the party of common sense.

## 7.2   The Epistemic Arguments

Because of the multifarious roles that art appears to play in the enculturation of value, a natural first thought about the relation of art to morality is that art participates in the process of moral education. This, then, suggests a basis for the ethical criticism of the arts. Put schematically, art that enhances moral cognition, to the extent that it does so, is morally good; whereas art that distorts moral cognition, to the extent that it does so, is morally defective. This is the commonsensical presumption that the epistemic arguments seek to undercut.

First, it is argued that it is mistaken to suggest that art educates audiences morally, since the beliefs it conveys to audiences – even if true – are so banal that it makes no sense to say that it *teaches* them to anyone. No one needs a novel as intricate as *Crime and Punishment* to learn that murder is wrong.[4] In fact, knowing that murder is wrong is probably a precondition for understanding the novel. Thus, it is implausible to allege that readers learn this by reading Dostoevsky.

Second, if artworks are genuinely educative, it is alleged, they must not only be transmitting new, hitherto unrecognized, interesting, non-trivial beliefs; those beliefs must also amount to knowledge – they must be true and justified. But artworks characteristically neither supply the kind of evidence that would be required to warrant the empirical claims they often presuppose, nor support their moral claims with arguments and explicit analysis. Thus, the beliefs proffered by artworks do not constitute genuine knowledge, since they are not justified.

Underlying these epistemic arguments is, of course, a view of what genuine moral education would require. It takes as its paradigm the transmission of a kind of propositional knowledge. If art is educational, it is presumed, it would convey to audiences propositions that are of the order of discoveries – that relay new, interesting (non-trivial), general information – which, in turn, the art in question supports with evidence, argument, and analysis. If art does not communicate propositional knowledge of this sort, either overtly or by implication, then it is not genuinely educative. Moreover, it is argued that art does not characteristically afford propositional knowledge of this sort. So, it is not genuinely educational.

Perhaps the first thing to note about this set of epistemic arguments is that its conception of moral education appears unduly constricted. Let us temporarily grant, for the purposes of argument, the skeptic's assertion that art does not characteristically afford knowledge of the sort that he has in mind. Does this preclude the possibility that art is morally educative? Surely it does not, if there are dimensions of moral education that this model excludes which, as well, can be exemplified by artworks. Furthermore, it is not the case that there is just one type of moral education of this variety that the skeptic's model neglects. There are many.

For example, artworks may expand our powers of moral judgment. Many moral rules are of a highly abstract nature and may be very difficult to apply in practice. Artworks, especially narrative ones, can enable us to begin to apply them. Jane Austen gives flesh to the principle that we should refrain from treating others merely as means to our own ends through the concrete case of Emma's meddling in Harriet's love life. In Austen's encouraging us to see what is wrong in Emma's behavior – in being encouraged to judge it wrongful – we are brought to see the relevance of such abstract principles in everyday affairs in such a way that we can become more adept at issuing comparable judgments in real life. In this regard it is the process that engagement with the novel encourages that is educative rather than the product construed as a newly acquired moral maxim.

Narrative artworks require audiences to become involved in a continuous process of making moral judgments about characters, situations, and even the points of view of artworks as a whole. In this, they provide occasions for practice in the application to particulars of abstract moral principles and concepts, such as those of virtue and vice. Without such practice in matching concrete cases to our moral abstractions, moral judgment would remain impoverished, if not inert (Carroll 1998a).

Though art is not the only opportunity we have for acquiring such practice, it remains a culturally important, as well as a sanctioned, one. Indeed, narrative artworks may enlarge our awareness of the range of variables pertinent in making moral judgments – in applying moral principles and concepts to concrete particular cases. In this way, artworks, or at least some of them, may hone our overall skills in making moral judgments.

The enhancement of skills – of our knowing how to do something, such as issuing moral judgments – should count as education on anyone's view of learning. It may not be reducible to the skeptic's paradigm of the acquisition of a certain sort of propositional knowledge, but that is no reason to discount this kind of moral learning as a contribution that art can make to moral cognition. One of the morals of *Emma* – treat others as ends, not means – may in some sense be a truism. But coming to see that that principle can apply to the circumstances Austen portrays – and to similar situations in everyday life – may enrich one's capacities of moral perception and even enable one to increase one's command of the principle in such a way that one sees its applicability to cases unimagined by Austen.

Integral to the ability to make sound moral judgments is the capacity to scope out situations sensitively – to be alert precisely to variables, often not immediately obvious ones, that carry moral significance. Art, especially narrative art, is a leading cultural vehicle for developing this talent. Thus, in *David Copperfield*, the reader (with Charles Dickens's help) detects, when first encountering Steerforth, a note of callous manipulation beneath his superficial charm and congeniality. It may be close to a truism that charm can cloak opportunism, but it need not be the acquisition of that proposition upon which the case for the educative value of *David Copperfield*, in part, rests. Rather, what Dickens helps the reader acquire is finesse in sussing out characters like Steerforth – in perceiving the tell-tale signs of moral flaws in a concrete context, one that is complex in the sense that it admits of mixed messages.[5]

Indeed, arguably, art, especially narrative art, can improve our overall attentiveness to the kinds of nuanced behavioral details that are relevant for delivering accurate moral judgments. Just as exercising our capacity to hit a ball against a variety of pitchers develops our batting skills, notably in terms of flexibility and adaptability to new circumstances, so reading novels may expand the acuity of our moral perceptions.

Augmenting our skills in moral judgment and perception, then, is a contribution to moral education that artworks can make that is not defeated by the skeptic's banality argument. Thus, where artworks enlarge our powers of moral judgment, common sense will adjudge them, all things being equal, to be morally good (or morally bad, should the artworks in question befuddle or confuse or otherwise impede our powers of moral judgment). Moreover, there are other sorts of skills besides those just mentioned that art may nurture which are also morally educative, despite the skeptic's objections.

Art, for example, engages our emotions, including our moral emotions, such as righteous indignation.[6] Furthermore, our emotions are educable. A large part of enculturation involves, following Aristotle, learning to mobilize the right emotion in response to appropriate objects with the suitable level of intensity. By exercising our emotions, including our moral emotions, artworks may tutor them – through directed practice – to love and hate the right things for the right reasons and with the right quotient of energy.[7]

Among the emotions that artworks, especially narrative ones, shape are our sympathies. In this regard, artworks have the power to enlarge our sympathies – to elicit our concern for people whom we might otherwise ignore, such as peoples of other races, genders, ethnicities, nationalities, sexual preferences, the physically and mentally disabled, the elderly, and so on. Much contemporary literary fiction, theater, film, and TV is dedicated to this project, for instance Athol Fugard's "*Master Harold*" . . . *and the Boys*. It is hard to see why the cultivation of moral feelings through commerce with artworks should not count as moral education.

The skeptic cannot accept it as such, because the narrow view of education he presupposes entertains as education only the acquisition of novel, general, epistemically warranted propositions. But this seems too limited. Moreover, if the skeptic defends this viewpoint by arguing that education is tied to cognition, and that the emotions are not cognitive, then this can be countered from two directions.

First, it may be pointed out that making a sharp distinction between emotion and cognition is too draconian. Emotions, inasmuch as they are generally guided by reasons, possess a cognitive dimension; indeed, audiences may be made aware by their emotional reactions of some of their hitherto unacknowledged beliefs through exposure to certain artworks. And second, even if the emotions are not cognitive in the narrow sense of being tied to the relevant sort of propositions, education – such as learning to swim or to ride a bicycle – need not be narrowly cognitive in the skeptic's sense.

Thus, contra the skeptic, it makes sense to evaluate artworks that enlarge our emotions or that reinforce our authentic moral sentiments as *pro tanto* morally good, and those that corrupt said emotions as *pro tanto* morally defective. That is, the skeptic's epistemic arguments do not cut against this sort of moral evaluation of – at least some – artworks.

Related to the enhancement of our emotional repertory, especially our talent for sympathy, is another skill that some artworks can promote. Many narrative art-

works excel in giving us access to alien points of view. They enable us to understand others from the inside, so to speak. They give us moral insight into behaviors that we might not otherwise comprehend and, for lack of comprehension,
morally condemn out of hand. Toni Morrison's *Beloved*, for instance, puts readers
in a position to see how the slave-mother's destruction of her own child is not an
act of moral depravity, but is motivated by genuinely compelling reasons.

And, apart from the specific moral insights that such novels afford, engaging
with works of this kind also, arguably, may in general enhance our moral sensitivity to unfamiliar points of view. That is, immersion in this sort of art can make
us more practiced at appreciating the viewpoints of others – can make us more
empathetic – thereby dislodging us from our natural inclination toward egocen-
tric and/or ethnocentric partiality. Artworks, then, can augment our powers of
moral reflection, not only by undermining specific prejudices through the exploration of alien viewpoints, but by cultivating a general attitude of impartiality in
the sense of an openness to the moral claims of others.

So far the kinds of moral skills that we have claimed that some artworks can
cultivate are moral in the very narrow sense. That is, they pertain primarily to judgments that employ concepts of right and wrong, obligation and duty, virtue and
vice, especially with regard to others or with regard to ourselves in relation to our
conduct toward others. However, there is a broader conception of morality, sometimes denominated by the term *ethics*, which concerns questions of the nature of
the good life or the meaningful life.[8] Such ethical concerns – while canvassing
narrow moral preoccupations with obligations to others, with justice and fairness,
with right and wrong – ask, more broadly, what makes a life worth living.

Clearly an answer to this sort of question is not reducible to a history of our
rightful actions in our conduct toward others. Our lives encompass so much more
than following the Ten Commandments or some other, suitably expanded moral
code. But how are we to begin to approach the existentially pressing, ethical (in
the broad sense) issue of assessing the worthiness or significance of our lives as a
whole?

That is, for many the question of the meaningfulness of their lives arises
unavoidably. In our culture, there is scant guidance as to how to negotiate this
challenge, outside religious guidance. In fact, it may be that in our culture
artworks – certain kinds of artworks, notably certain kinds of literature – have
the best claim to mentorship in this regard. For to answer the question of
whether our life is worthy, we need a holistic sense of it, and that holistic sense is
best captured by narrative – an incomparable device for organizing or colligating
or collecting the diversity of our experiences into a unity. To see our lives as significant requires at least an ability to configure them as meaningful stories. But
whence do we learn the skill of rendering or configuring our lives as meaningful
stories?

Of course, we hear others recount their lives; and the various roles we inhabit
have subtending, if sketchy, scenarios. And for believers, religious traditions offer
narrative paradigms. But for secularists, the most sophisticated narrative exemplars

for exploring the unity of lives we have are, in the main, to be found in literary fictions, movies, dramas, and the like. Such narratives can give a holistic sense of a life, exploring it from the inside and the outside, and from beginning to end (or, at least, from nodal turning points to life-determining choices and events).[9]

Genres like the bildungsroman are predicated upon telling life stories. In novels such as *The Magic Mountain*, *A Portrait of the Artist as a Young Man*, and *Nausea*, we encounter stories of characters deciding the course of their lives as those decisions emerge from a barrage of jostling alternatives. What we learn from these stories, I submit, is not so much a template of a life story to be slavishly emulated as a sense of how to narrate or to structure or to configure the evolution of a life into a unity. That is, mindful exposure to sophisticated life narratives communicates to us the knack of how to begin to tell our own life stories, if only to ourselves, and, in that way, they augment our capacity to find holistic significance and unity in what otherwise may feel like the rush of one god-damned, desultory thing after another.[10] And acquiring and/or refining this skill for divining the significance or meaning of a life through our intercourse with the relevant sorts of fiction, then, puts us in position – supplies a necessary condition – for ascertaining whether that life-structure is a worthwhile one.[11]

Some artworks, especially narrative ones, contribute to moral education by developing important moral skills with respect to moral judgment, perception, emotional responsiveness, sympathy, empathy, and the capacity to narrate our lives (and those of others) as significant unities. These claims on behalf of the educative potential of art are not defeated by the skeptic's banality argument. Rather, they outflank that argument by finding sources of moral education available in some artworks – notably, in terms of the development of skills (know-how) – that the skeptic, at his own peril, ignores, because of his requirement that moral education afford the acquisition of a certain sort of propositional knowledge (knowledge *that*). However, it is not simply on the basis of skills that one may defend the commensensical notion that (some) art may be defended as a source of moral education.

The skeptic denies a cognitive role to art on the grounds that the propositions obtainable through art are truisms, generally known by audiences in advance of the artwork. Suppose we grant that this is the case (though later we will find reason to contest it). Nevertheless, this dismisses, in effect, the possibility that artworks may function to recall to mind truths the audience already knows, in some sense, but has forgotten or neglected, or truths whose full seriousness and relevance they have not retained or do not access or have suppressed, or that they simply never realized completely to begin with. That is, artworks may serve to remind audiences of what they already know by posing it vividly and concretely.

The poor and the oppressed, for example, may always be with us, and though we know it, it is quite easy to lose sight of this and of its moral implications. Artworks like the activist performances of Dario Fo, the San Francisco Mime Troupe, and Bread and Puppet Theater may not only recall our attention to such mundane facts of life, but also remind us of their moral weight vis-à-vis our responsibilities.

Abetting recollection is a leading function of (much) art, while recovering what is already known and bringing back to mind its significance is undoubtedly a contribution to cognition. Thus, even if artworks only traded in moral truisms, that would not show that artworks could not be enlightening, if it could also be demonstrated that frequently artworks function to activate memory and to recall to mind what is already known, but negligently or remissly so, in a way that underscores its importance.

This, it would appear, has been a major function of art through the ages, and it does not seem appropriate to disparage art as a form of education on the grounds of the alleged triviality of what is presented. For we are often unmindful or forgetful of simple moral truths learned long ago, and, however banal those truths may be said to be, to be reminded of their relevance is hardly trivial. Call this art in the service of memory, which, by anyone's account, should be regarded as an element of cognition.

Artworks may serve cognition not only by promoting recollection of moral knowledge already known, if only dormantly or passively, but also by deepening our understanding of that which we already know. That is, we may possess many beliefs in isolation, or serially, so to speak, but fail to see the interconnections between them. We may know, for instance, that all persons should be treated equitably and that women are treated differently than men, but fail to realize that this differential amounts to a violation of the principle of equal treatment.[12]

In this regard, a feminist novel, such as Marilyn French's *The Woman's Room* – by vividly portraying how this differential treatment adversely affects a person, a woman, shown to have justifiable aspirations and needs just like ours (if we are males or male-identified females) and about whom we are encouraged to be concerned – can remove the scales from our eyes, thereby prompting us to reorganize our cognitive stock, to see or to comprehend, where we were previously blinkered, the plight of women as falling under the principle of the equality of persons.

In this way, an artwork can render our belief set more coherent by making the implications and connections between what we know more explicit, perspicuous, and consistent. This sort of gestalt shift in our grasp of what we already know may be best described not as the acquisition of the sort of proposition the skeptic privileges – since the generalization about equal treatment is putatively already in our cognitive stock – but as a deepening of our understanding of a principle we already possess, as an insight into the implications of and interconnections between that which we already know, in short, a re-membering of our moral mapping.[13]

That the relevant principle may be of the order of a truism would appear to provide no reason for dismissing the insight in question as unenlightening. For the novel at issue serves to reorganize our conceptual map, drawing links where before there were none in a way that enables the reader to find new connections in his knowledge stock, thereby engendering new understanding. "Education," we should remind ourselves, comes from the Latin root "educere," which means to draw forth or bring out or lead out, often in terms of what is latent or potential. Hence, artworks that educe deeper understanding of what is in some sense already known should have a fair claim to being educative.

If the preceding considerations permit us to challenge the allegation that art cannot be educative because it merely rehashes general propositions that, since they are already known, are trivial and, therefore, not appropriately regarded as something that requires learning, we still have not yet addressed the epistemic arguments that maintain that art has no claim to be morally educative, since the beliefs it allegedly advertises do not amount to knowledge, lacking, as they typically do, warrant in terms of evidence, argument, and/or analysis. Zola, for instance, believed that his novels supported the theory of inherited traits. But how could they? His cases were made up – indeed, they were made up expressly to serve his purposes. Would that biologists had it so easy. Likewise, *The Cabinet of Dr Caligari* is said to show that authority breeds madness. But where is the argument?

This set of objections against the educative potential of art is rooted in a very demanding requirement as to what shall count as communicating knowledge, viz., that the relevant knowledge claim carry with it its own warrant, on its sleeve, so to speak. As we shall see, this may be an unrealistic demand. But that nothwithstanding, it can be shown that at least some artworks can meet even this very exacting criterion for knowledge communication. In order to see this, it pays to remember that much of the art that we have in mind when we are talking about moral education is fiction. This has led some philosophers to deny that it lacks the wherewithal to warrant the claims it advances. However, it is strange that philosophers should field this objection, since they use fictions all of the time in order to secure their claims.

That is, standard fixtures in the philosopher's repertoire are thought experiments, examples, and counterexamples that are fictional in nature. Thus, if philosophical thought experiments produce knowledge – warranted belief – why cannot it be the case that artistic fictions, conceived of as thought experiments, function analogously?[14]

Philosophical thought experiments can be fictional because the knowledge they aim to produce is conceptual, not empirical. Confronting the doctrine that justice requires never lying, Socrates imagines the case where the question arises of whether it is just to tell an enraged friend, bent on revenge, where he can find his sword. It makes no difference that the case is made up, since on hearing the case, one realizes that it is a possible one, and that its possibility refutes the universal prohibition against lying – it shows that such a universal constraint is not consistent with our concept of what justice demands. The knowledge unearthed by this thought experiment is perhaps something we already knew, but the thought experiment recalls it to mind and makes its pertinence shine forth. Moreover, since the knowledge in question is conceptual – concerning our concept of justice and its conditions of application – it need not rest on empirical evidence.

Clearly, many artistic counterexamples function like this one from Plato. Perhaps Bertolt Brecht's *Galileo* can be interpreted as a refutation of the axiom "never lie," while Martha Nussbaum convincingly reads Henry James's *The Ambassadors* as a challenge to the conception of rule-dominated moral reasoning (Nussbaum 1990). Such cases force us to amend initially attractive or common-place conceptions of morality by confronting us with eminently possible cases through which the content of our concept of what is moral is interrogated and clarified. Since we are dealing with conceptual knowledge here, it makes no dif-ference that the cases are fictional, thus rendering as beside the point the skepti-cal allegation that artworks always lack sufficient empirical warrant.

Moreover, since the thought experiment itself is an argumentative strategy – in literature no less than philosophy – the skeptic cannot maintain that art lacks the appropriate argumentative resources, since it shares the thought experiment with philosophy. That is, a thought experiment functions to excavate conceptual knowl-edge by pointing to neglected possibilities in such a way that listeners come to the relevant conclusions on their own, so to speak. The thought experiment moves the argument or analysis into the minds of the audience, where they make the per-tinent connections. Such knowledge may be propositional – propositional knowl-edge about the conditions of application of our concepts – thereby meeting the skeptic's most stringent demands. Furthermore, there is no reason to suppose that literary counterexamples cannot function as effectively in refuting generalizations as those found in purely philosophical texts, since, among other things, philoso-phers sometimes uncontroversially use literary examples in this way; considering the Socratic doctrine that a person who knows the good cannot choose to do evil, a philosopher can reach for Milton's Satan, Shakespeare's Iago, and Melville's Claggart as counterexamples.

Literary thought experiments do not only yield propositional knowledge about our concepts negatively, by way of imagined counterexamples to general claims. They may also function to afford positive knowledge of concepts. Philosophical thought experiments are often designed to promote conceptual discrimination by setting forth a polarized, graduated array of contrasting fictional cases that sys-tematically vary the factors that contribute to enabling us to identify conceptual distinctions, dependencies, and other relations. Kant, for example, imagines two merchants – one who counts out the correct change because it is right to do so and another who performs the same action so as to avoid incurring a bad reputa-tion – in order to limn the distinction between moral action and prudent action. The reader, contemplating Kant's contrasting examples against the background of her own conceptual stock, sees the point and performs the analysis on her own; the argument, to the extent that there is one, is supplied by the reader.

Similarly, fictions are often designed in such a way that they can provoke com-parable exercises in conceptual discrimination by means of structured arrays of contrasting cases. Dickens's *Great Expectations*, for example, explores the concept of virtuous parenting by constructing a gallery of varied parental figures who instantiate the concept of virtuous parenting to greater, or more often lesser, degrees; Pip's sister, her husband Joe Gargery, Miss Havisham, and Abel Mag-witch. Reflecting on this array, we are able to clarify our concept of virtuous parenting. Only Joe qualifies under the concept, since he alone shows selfless love in relation to his charge. Moreover, his possession of this qualification is illuminated by contrast to the other parental figures, who, in varying ways, suggest defective and even vicious modes of parenting.

Pip's sister fails to meet the criterion of virtuous parenting, since she regards Pip as a chore, simply to be disciplined "by hand," as she says. Miss Havisham and Magwitch, in turn, are defective parental figures, since they treat their wards as a means to satisfy their own fantasies – Estella and Pip are not ends in themselves, but means to achieve vicarious wish-fulfillments for Magwitch and Miss Havisham respectively.

The structure of character contrasts in *Great Expectations* enables us simultaneously to clarify our concept of virtuous parenting – it allows us to reflect upon the conditions where we would apply or withhold it – and sharpen our sense of when the concept is defectively or even viciously instantiated.[15] The text makes these conceptual discoveries available to us, if not as we read along, then in the reflective afterlife of the text or in conversation with others about our reaction to it. In this way a literary fiction may serve the purposes of conceptual discrimination by means of employing a structure analogous to the philosophical thought experiment.[16] And inasmuch as the philosophical thought experiment is warranted by the argument and analysis it elicits in the thinking of the reader, so should we regard at least some artistic thought experiments as warranted in the same way in terms of argument and analysis.[17]

Thus, even allowing the skeptic his extremely exacting requirement of what it would take for an artwork, such as a literary fiction, to communicate knowledge, it can be shown that some artworks possess the wherewithal to do so. For some artworks, construed as counterexamples and/or thought experiments, have the capacity to engender the sort of reflection that yields propositional knowledge about the conditions of application of our concepts in the same way as philosophical thought experiments do. That is, the force of the skeptic's epistemic arguments is too strong. They can only succeed by denying the enlightening potential of thought experiments, a gambit that would consign too much philosophy to the flames.

Up to this point, we have played along with the skeptic's supposition about what would be required for art to communicate knowledge. We have shown that even under this somewhat austere conception, some art, notably some fiction, can pass the test. However, it is important to note that the skeptic's demands are unrealistic, and, once we see that, of course, then even more art than has so far been reclaimed for moral education can be shown to have a legitimate title to communicating knowledge, especially moral knowledge.

*Pace* the skeptic, we do not characteristically require that knowledge claims come with all the relevant empirical evidence, argument, or analysis written on their sleeves. Claims are typically advanced in newspaper editorials, science textbooks, and even philosophical texts without marshalling all the pertinent documentation or argumentation. Authors rely on readers to bring a stock of empirical and conceptual knowledge to the text and to use that stock to assess the claims they make. Most arguments in historical works, for instance, are enthymematic, notably in terms of the presuppositions about human psychology upon which they depend. Authors, in such cases, rely on their audience to use what they already know about the subject at hand and their understanding of the world to test their conclusions.

We do not epistemically disparage a newspaper editorial about the national budget because it comes unaccompanied with yards of graphs and footnotes; nor do we discount, as potential knowledge, claims about the motivations of world leaders because said articles lack experimental data, argument, and/or conceptual analysis. In fact, it is extremely rare that knowledge claims are advanced with anything near full documentation and argumentation. But if this is how we treat knowledge communication in general, why should the standards shift when it comes to art?

The skeptic, in short, has set the epistemic bar higher for artistic knowledge communication than for ordinary, including most formal, discourse. Once we see that, we realize that the scope for deriving moral knowledge from art is even more ample than we have canvassed so far. Fictions can be a source of information about our obligations without exhaustive documentation and argumentation, just as op-ed page articles can be.

Fictions, as well, can be especially useful as sources of insight concerning moral psychology. Mary Shelley's *Frankenstein* presents us with a scenario of the way in which the denial of affection gives rise to a kind of raging envy best understood as a species of revenge. We do not need mountains of data on developmental psychology to appreciate Shelley's perceptiveness, nor an argument. We can discern the inner logic of the Frankenstein Monster's behavior by reflecting on our own feelings.

Such insight into moral psychology is one of the staples of great fiction. It provides us with knowledge relevant for moral self-understanding and for understanding and judging others morally. That it originates in art should not stop us from helping ourselves to it, since comparable knowledge claims are frequently and reliably derived from non-artistic sources without the benefit of full empirical documentation, argumentation, and analysis. That is, despite the skeptic, art is not, in principle, worse off than most of our other venues of knowledge communication.

Thus far, I have rushed through an inventory of ways in which art may function as a source of moral knowledge. It is a large and varied list, because, as I mentioned at the outset, the relations of art and morality are complex and varied.[18] I have not discussed every way in which art may be morally educative, but only those that address the skeptic's arguments against the very possibility that art can deliver moral knowledge. Many of my examples have involved the ways in which art can develop pertinent moral skills, since knowledge of how to conduct moral reflection demarcates an area of moral education that the skeptic, with his emphasis on the acquisition of a certain sort of propositional knowledge, has ignored altogether.

However, we have seen, as well, that it is also possible for art to deliver even this sort of knowledge, once we recall that artworks can function as thought experiments that either refute universal generalizations or abet conceptual discrimination. Moreover, we have pointed out additionally that the skeptic's epistemic arguments may rest on too high a standard of what is required to advance knowledge claims. And if that is true, then common sense has all the more reason to expect moral insight from artists – to commend them when they afford it and to chide them when they mislead or confuse us.

## 7.3   The Ontological Argument[19]

Though there may not be epistemic obstacles to evaluating art morally, it appears that there may be a metaphysical one. For artworks are things, albeit artifacts, and we do not ordinarily morally evaluate things as such. Moral judgment is reserved for persons or beings with the right sort of psychological capacities. Thus, it is a category mistake, so the skeptic might argue, to call artworks morally good or bad. Perhaps this is the thinking that motivates Oscar Wilde, in his preface to *The Picture of Dorian Gray*, to say famously: "There is no such thing as a moral or an immoral book. Books are well written or badly written. That is all."[20]

Stated less elliptically, the argument would seem to be this:

1   If artworks can be evaluated morally, then they must be the kinds of things that can bear moral properties, viz., persons or person-like entities to whom the relevant mental properties apply.
2   Artworks are not the kinds of things that can bear moral properties; they are not persons or person-like entities to whom the relevant mental properties apply.
3   Therefore, artworks cannot be evaluated morally.

Let us grant the first premise, for purposes of argument. The question then becomes whether artworks are the sorts of things that can bear mental properties. Certainly parts of some artworks appear to be the right sort of thing, namely characters. Nothing seems out of place in judging Dr No to be evil. Of course, here the skeptic is apt to respond that typically when we evaluate novels morally, it is not the characters whom we are judging – for evil characters can inhabit morally upright fictions – but it is the novel as a whole, so to say, that is the object of evaluation. And, furthermore, the novel, unlike a character, is not a person-like thing.

Nevertheless, the recognition that characters can be evaluated morally suggests the way in which it may be appropriate to assess novels as such morally. For novels are narrated from points of view. As discussed above, Philip Roth's *The Dying Animal*, for example, characterizes women in a certain way, as primarily, indeed almost exclusively and mythically, sexual beings, and encourages readers to view them similarly. This point of view, moreover, belongs either to a person (the actual author) or to a person-like thing (the implied author) or, most probably, to both. And, of course, either the actual author and/or the implied author is the appropriate object for the application of the mental properties relevant to moral attributions.

Consequently, there should be no problem in morally evaluating the author(s)' point of view.[21] Where that point of view affords moral insight, to that extent, a novel can be said to be morally good. Where a novel unreflexively obscures moral perception, as *The Dying Animal* arguably does, it is to that extent morally bad.[22] There does not seem to be a category error here, since points of view are necessarily attached to persons (actual authors) or person-like things (implied authors). Therefore, at least artworks that possess points of view would appear to evade the preceding ontological argument. And that amounts to quite a few works of art.

It might be said that if it is the point of view of the actual artist that is at issue, then we are not really morally evaluating the artwork, but the artist. This does not seem right, however, for two reasons. First, the point of view is something that the novelist has constructed and, therefore, is part of the artwork proper. Second, though intimately related, even in everyday life, we can distinguish between moral judgments of a person and his point of view. Thus, we can render differential judgments of the moral character of a conscientious Brahmin who is unacquainted with other views about caste-relations. Similarly, we may in principle distinguish between our judgments of a novelist's moral character and his viewpoint, even if these often do converge.

It might also be objected that the implied author is not really the kind of thing to which moral predicates can be applied. However, if characters can be judged morally, then implied authors should be as well. For the implied author, where he or she diverges from the real author, is really a persona or role or mask that the actual author invents or takes on, much as an actor plays a character. Though of a different order, an implied author is a fictional character of sorts. Hence, if fictional characters can be judged morally, so can implied authors. Moreover, just as fictional characters can be criticized morally where they provide attractive exemplars of moral viciousness, so can implied authors be criticized where they present depraved points of view as lustrous. Nor can it be denied that implied authors qua characters and their related points of view are part of the artwork proper, since they compose, in large measure, what the novelist has constructed.

Oscar Wilde alleges that books can only be written well or badly; that they are not moral or immoral. However, inasmuch as that writing is involved in the construction and expression of points of view, it may be susceptible to moral evaluation. Moreover, artworks other than literary fictions also possess points of view. Thus, in a vast number of cases, common sense has little to fear from the skeptic's ontological argument.

## 7.4   The Aesthetic Argument

If successful, our rejoinders so far to the philosophical skeptic show that it can be appropriate to evaluate some art morally. But the skeptic may be quick to note that even if an artwork is morally bad, it may still be aesthetically good, just as moral goodness does not guarantee aesthetic quality or preclude aesthetic awfulness. A movie that exalts the career of a remorseless jewel thief may still be aesthetically exciting, while one that commends the teachings of a paragon may be aesthetically boring.

This is hard to deny. However, the skeptic frequently extrapolates a rather expansive principle from these commonplaces, namely that the moral blemishes in an artwork never count against its aesthetic merit and that the moral worthiness of an artwork never counts toward aesthetic worthiness. That is, aesthetic value and moral value are strictly independent or autonomous from each other. This position can be called autonomism.[23]

Obviously, the autonomist's argument is based on the presupposition that the aesthetic realm and the moral realm are utterly discrete, with no possibility of substantive interaction between them. But whether this hypothesis can be sustained, of course, depends on how we are to understand the notion of the aesthetic presumed in the aesthetic argument.

One way to construe this vexed notion is to regard the aesthetic as pertaining to experience – the experience of the artwork – and to hold that that experience is aesthetic only if it is valued for its own sake. An element in an artwork is aesthetically valuable, then, if it promotes aesthetic experiences. This may be thought to exclude moral insight as an aesthetic element in an artwork, furthermore, on the grounds that moral insight is not valued for its own sake, but for other reasons, such as its conduciveness to good conduct.

However, this will not do. For if one believes that experiences are valuable for their own sake, surely one must concede that moral insight can be. Can a proponent of such value deny that learning that the social practices of an extinct civilization were evil can be appreciated (in his sense) for its own sake, even though it has no possible ramifications whatsoever for the appreciator's present conduct? If purely theoretical, mathematical insights can be valued for their own sake, why can't moral insights be so valued? Consequently, the conception of aesthetic value that ties it simply to experiences valued for their own sake cannot do the job of hiving off the aesthetic from the moral, in the way the aesthetic argument requires, undoubtedly because this view of the aesthetic is not sufficiently contentful.

A perhaps more promising way of crafting the concept of the aesthetic for autonomist purposes is to associate the aesthetic with the formal. On this view, an aesthetic experience has a certain content – the form of an artwork – and aesthetic value is calibrated in terms of the capacity of the formal structure of the work to engage aesthetic experience productively. As William Gass puts it: "Artistic quality depends upon a work's internal, formal, organic character, upon its inner system of relations, upon its structure and its style, and not upon the morality it is presumed to recommend or upon the benevolence of its author, or its emblematic character, when it is seen as especially representative of some situation or society" (1993: 113).

Of course, the autonomist cannot deny that many artworks contain moral content, often forcefully presented. But she contends that this content is only ever relevant to the aesthetic evaluation of an artwork insofar as it relates to the form or structure of the work – does it contribute to the unity or coherence of the work, or does it detract from it? Arnold Isenberg says: "Any issue of moral ideas may be an aesthetic object. But a didactic poem is a work of *art* – which means that ethical material is not merely utilized but is worked into a structure. Now there are structures built of other than ethical materials; and there it is common enough for critics to employ such criteria as 'unity' and 'coherence'" (1973: 280). Likwise, Isenberg implies, ethical features of artworks play into aesthetic evaluation to the extent that they contribute to the form of the artwork. That is, the evil viewpoint that a work sponsors, no matter how morally noxious, is not an aesthetic demerit, unless it renders the work formally incoherent, as it would if it inadvertently endorsed inconsistent moral views (1973: 281).

Whether or not the identification of aesthetics with form is to serve the autonomist's agenda, needless to say, rests on the notion of form – a notoriously difficult concept to define – that the autonomist adopts. Some notions of form will clearly be inadmissible – such as that the form of an artwork comprises only its non-representational elements – since they would appear false from the outset to the scope of aesthetic experience. But perhaps a clue to the relevant notion of form is our widespread tendency to associate form with the *how* of an artwork – how it is phrased, how it is painted, how it is constructed. The form of the work pertains in some way to the manner in which it has been contrived. But in what way?

Not just any answer to a how-question about an artwork will suffice to instruct us about the form of the work. Being told that the words on the page of a novel got there by printing does not identify a formal aspect of the novel. Rather, the how-questions that are pertinent to the formal structure of the work have to do with the elements and relations in the work that function to realize the point(s) and/or purpose(s) of the work.[24] As Louis Sullivan said, "Form follows function."

It is a formal feature of a narrative painting that it leads our eye to the subject of the picture, since the point of the work is to encourage our contemplation of, say, the Madonna and child. Likewise, the rapid montage of the Odessa Steps sequence of the film *Potemkin* is a formal element, because it visually enhances the chaos of the scene which the director, Sergei Eisenstein, wishes to communicate to the audience. That is, artworks possess points or purposes – themes they are designed to convey or mental states, like emotions, moods, or even visual pleasure – that they seek to engender in viewers, listeners, and readers; and the elements and relations in the work that realize those points and purposes constitute the formal structure(s) of the work. Like the human form, the form of the work is its outward manifestation (of its point[s] and purpose[s]) – the way in which it presents or embodies them.

In constructing an artwork, the artist chooses how to proceed relative to the point or purpose of the work – to make the line thick or thin, to alliterate or not, to opt for a major or minor key, to portray a character as harsh or gentle in view of the point or purpose of the work (or of a part thereof). The sum of these choices embodies the relevant *how* of the work, its form, the manner in which it pursues its end. Or, to state the matter formulaically: the form of an artwork is the ensemble of choices intended to realize the point(s) or purpose(s) of the artwork.

Supposing this to be an idea of form that the autonomist acknowledges, then we can state the conclusion of her aesthetic argument thus: a moral defect in an artwork is never a formal defect in a work and a moral virtue in an artwork never counts as a formal virtue. Admittedly, the autonomist may be correct in observing that not every moral defect is a formal one, just as not every moral virtue is a formal one. But is she correct in alleging that moral properties of artworks are *never* relevant to their formal, that is to say, their aesthetic, evaluation?

One very common purpose of artworks is to arouse our emotions. The emotions, of course, are criterially governed. In order to fear something, a percipient must regard it as harmful. Moreover, the criteria that govern many emotions are moral; to be angry, I must regard the object of my state as someone who has done wrong to me or mine. And, there are straightforwardly moral emotions, such as righteous indignation. Thus, in order to arouse certain emotions, the relevant artworks must design the characters and situations they portray in a way that is morally appropriate to the emotion they are meant to elicit. It would be an error in the design, *ceteris paribus*, in an artwork predicated on raising a sense of injustice in normal audiences, were it to represent as utterly saintly the commandant of a heinous slave camp. That is, it would be a formal error insofar as the way in which the commandant has been designed impedes the work's functioning as intended.

Similarly, had Nero ignited Rome with the intention of engaging emotions like the awe that occasions the display of fireworks, his conflagration would have been a failure from the perspective of normal viewers, who, aware of the grievous costs to life and property involved, greeted it with horror rather than wonder. The error here would have been formal, since Nero's design choices, notably roasting people, did not serve the putative purpose of the incineration. But it is also, needless to say, a moral outrage. Moreover, it is the fact that it is a moral outrage that, in large measure, accounts for its incapacity to function to realize its purpose, since it is the perception of the moral outrageousness of Nero's action that blocks the intended response in the normal audience member. That is, the moral defectiveness of Nero's fire is intimately connected to its compromised aesthetic design; the immoral or evil nature of Nero's choice is the major reason that his fire-work failed to secure its purpose.

For a case closer to home, consider again Philip Roth's *The Dying Animal*. The novel aims to paint the life of male desire in a morally heroic, albeit melancholy, light. But the manipulative central character, David Kepesh, is transparently a sexual predator, and his apparent view of women as essentially sexual beings, while intended to be complimentary (even mystically so), is morally impoverished. The moral defects in the character and the novel's point of view are apt to thwart the morally sensitive reader's enthusiastic response to this paean to libertinage, which seems locked in a sixties time warp, somewhere between *Playboy* and the Woodstock nation. If there is a way to craft the representation of Kepesh's *modus vivendi* in a way that would secure the sought-after effect of admiration, Roth has not found it.

Furthermore, the formal flaw in Roth's design is traceable, to a great degree, to the morally defective point of view he invites and encourages morally sensitive readers to embrace. That they cannot embrace it because of its immorality is the central reason for the ultimate emotional unintelligibility of the book (Kieran 2001: 34). The reason it is formally incoherent is primarily due to its moral defectiveness.[25] That is, part of the design of many artworks is their moral-emotive address. Where that capsizes, for reasons of moral defectiveness, the design of the work is likewise flawed.

Thus, in cases like this, ethical criticism and aesthetic criticism merge. Our best explanation of why *The Dying Animal* is aesthetically defective is that it is morally blemished. That is, the design of the work misfires because the moral short-sightedness it proffers is unacceptable to the morally sensitive audience. Therefore, sometimes a moral defect in an artwork is relevant to evaluating it aesthetically, inasmuch as the moral address of the work can be an integral part of its design. Moreover, in cases where the moral defect qua moral defect in the work explains the failure of the work to discharge its purposes, the moral defect is also a bad formal choice, which is to say, contra autonomism, an aesthetic defect (Carroll 1998b). That is, the reason that explains the formal failure of the work is a moral one – for example, that it is too immoral to be countenanced by a morally sensitive audience.[26] Hence, sometimes a moral defect in a work can also figure as an aesthetic defect.

This argument does not show that every moral defect is an aesthetic defect, but only that *some* are – namely, those that compromise the design of the work. Some moral defects in a work may be insignificant or adventitious to the presiding purposes of the artwork. Furthermore, artworks can be immensely subtle and complex in terms of their moral commitments and implications. Moral defects in such works may only be identified by sustained and recondite interpretations. Consequently, some moral defects may elude even morally sensitive and informed audiences, due to the work's subtlety, obscurity, and/or intricacy. Where that happens and, as a result, the moral defect in question is not likely to retard the morally sensitive reader, viewer, or listener's emotive uptake of the work, the moral defect will not count as a formal or an aesthetic defect, though, of course, it remains a moral defect.[27]

Additionally, it should be clear that even where an artwork contains a moral defect – that is also a formal or aesthetic defect – that does not entail that the work overall is necessarily bad aesthetically, since the work may contain, as well, compensating aesthetic virtues that render the work, on balance, aesthetically good. And this, along with the considerations from the previous paragraph, rather than autonomism, accounts for the commonplace observation that it is possible for a work that contains moral defects to be aesthetically successful.

If we have shown, against the aesthetic argument, that sometimes a moral blemish in an artwork amounts to a formal or aesthetic flaw, it remains to be pointed out that sometimes the positive moral features of an artwork can contribute to the aesthetic value of a work. Narrative artworks especially are constructed in such a way as to engage readers, viewers, and listeners in virtually continuous processes of moral judgment – moral assessments of characters, situations, and points of view. Obviously, then, if these elements are designed in a way that makes it possible for audiences to make insightful and enlightening connections between the moral variables in the story, the story, all things being equal, will be better for it – that is, more absorbing. And inasmuch as it is a purpose of most art to be absorbing, design choices of this sort will be aesthetically good, just because they stimulate the audience's moral imagination in productive activity that the audience finds rewarding.

We saw earlier that artworks may be adjudged morally good for exercising our moral powers. Insofar as this can also contribute to absorbing the audience in the work, it can also be an aesthetic virtue of the work for morally sensitive audiences. Moreover, for such audiences, the moral insights must be reasonably authentic, if they are to mobilize said audience's participation and not deter it. Thus, making apposite moral observations can be part of the design of an artwork. Oscar Wilde was just wrong if he thought that good writing, as it is normally assessed, is always utterly divorced from moral content.

The autonomist's aesthetic argument maintains that a moral defect in an artwork is never an aesthetic defect and that a moral virtue is never an aesthetic virtue. Perhaps this argument has been attractive for so long because it functions like a firebrake against aggressive moralists who would counterintuitively brand every moral defect an aesthetic defect and declare all right-thinking artworks aesthetic masterpieces. Nevertheless, however serviceable in the struggle against puritanism and censorship, the aesthetic argument is too ambitious. For sometimes, *pace* autonomism, aesthetic and ethical evaluation converge.


## 7.5  Conclusion


Art and morality have been linked together for so long and in so many ways that it appears commonsensical for plain readers, viewers, and listeners to assume that it is natural – at least some of the time – to treat the latter as a source of enlightenment about the former, and – again, at least some of the time – to suppose that sometimes the moral evaluation of an artwork may be relevant to its aesthetic evaluation. Maybe that is one reason that ordinary critics typically feel so free to move without comment between the moral evaluation of the point of view of an artwork and its artistic evaluation.

However, as we have seen, there are formidable philosophical objections to this practice – particularly epistemic objections, ontological objections, and aesthetic objections. These philosophical arguments raise important questions about our practices with regard to art. Nevertheless, the considerations they advance are not insurmountable, as I have attempted to demonstrate. In fact, these objections serve as a salutary pretext for attempting to clarify what we are doing and why we are doing it when it comes to speaking about art. In that sense, philosophy needs to be thought of as not inimical to common sense, but as an impetus to its greater refinement and sophistication.

## Notes

1 This is not the only conclusion the philosopher can opt for at this juncture. For instance, Plato maintained that artworks could not provide knowledge, ethical or otherwise, but this did not lead him to conclude that artworks should not be criticized morally. For Plato, artworks could not afford ethical knowledge, but they could – indeed they necessarily did – promote immorality, and, therefore, they could be disparaged morally. However, since the Platonic position about art in this regard has already been subjected to mountains of criticism, I will not dwell on it in this chapter.

2 This argument against the claims of art to supply knowledge has been identified by Kivy in his (1997–8: 22).

3 The French poet Laurent Tailhade, hearing of an anarchist bomb thrown into the Chamber of Deputies, said "Who cares for the death of vague human beings, if the gesture be beautiful?" Quoted by Guerard (1963: 71).

4 It should be clear that in using this intuition pump about *Crime and Punishment*, I am representing the position of the philosophical skeptic. It is not my position that this is the only thing that *Crime and Punishment* might have to teach. Rather, I only intend to be advancing the skeptic's point in a rhetorically effective and well-precedented way. Unfortunately, some commentators, like Connolly and Haydar, have misinterpreted my expositional deployment of such intuition pumps as my considered view of works like *Crime and Punishment*. Throughout this chapter, I attempt to portray the skeptic's arguments as forcefully as I can in order to attempt to defeat them on their own terms. This should not be taken as a sign that I agree with all the presuppositions of the skeptical arguments. See Connolly and Haydar (2001: 122).

5 The capacity of literature to refine moral perception is a major theme of Martha Nussbaum's. See especially her (1990).

6 Views of the ways in which art might engage the emotions educatively can be found in Currie (1995); Walton (1990).

7 The capacity of art to educate our emotions, of course, is not necessarily distinct from its capacity to enhance our skills with respect to moral perception, since the emotions and perception are linked in important respects. Likewise, the refinement of our moral emotions is also connected to our powers of moral judgment.

8 Goldberg labels this distinction between two senses of morality as the conduct-centered sense versus the life-centered sense. See Goldberg (1993: 113).

9 Goldberg points out that there is a dimension of moral judgment that involves taking lives as a whole. This is a matter of seeing their unity. This, moreover, is a dimension of moral judgment that literature excels in modeling. He says "Literature has always been concerned with making moral sense of lives" (1993: 113).

10 Literature educates us in the ways of structuring not only our own lives as unities, but also the lives of others. And as Goldberg notes, one dimension of moral insight involves "the capacity to make sense of people's lives in a holistic way . . . a capacity to find terms appropriate to each particular life." This species of moral insight might also be called the moral imagination, due to its capacity to construct unities. See Goldberg (1993: 109).

11 Of course, the importance of narrative art for exhibiting life stories is not only relevant for introducing audiences to ways of beginning to configure their own life stories. By displaying lives, often lives very different from our own, narratives provide access to information about possible lives – what Mill referred to as life experiments. Fictions, in this regard, might be construed as life–thought experiments, cost-free opportunities to contemplate alternative lifestyles. This is an approach emphasized especially by Putnam (1978).

12 Oliver Connolly and Bashshar Haydar contend that this sort of function of novels has greater application to political cases than to personal moral cases. But this is not correct. One could regard the case of *Emma*, discussed earlier, as also vividly underscoring and deepening the principle that persons should be treated as ends, not means, in the personal moral realm. See Connolly and Haydar (2001: 121).

13 I first advanced this response to the skeptic's banality argument in my (1998a). Since then, Oliver Connolly and Bashshar Haydar have criticized that article by presupposing that I claim that only moral understanding of this sort can be derived from narratives, and that propositional knowledge, of the kind recommended by the skeptic, cannot be so derived. This is a misinterpretation of my original article and of my view. In my (1998a: 158n.16), for example, I explicitly admit, citing *Native Son*, that some narrative artworks supply the kind of propositions the skeptic requires. And in the body of the text, when I talk about the "standard case" and "the vast majority" of narratives (1998a: 141), the implicit hedge is meant to acknowledge that there are cases of learning from fiction that meet the skeptic's requirements. Connolly and Haydar confuse my giving the skeptic his strongest case for the purpose of refuting it with my own position, despite the fact that I implicitly and explicitly part company with the skeptic's claim that narrative art cannot provide access to non-trivial, propositional, knowledge claims. See Connolly and Haydar (2001: 109–24).

14 The notion that some artworks may be conceived of as thought experiments is defended at length in my (forthcoming). Subsequent to writing that article, I have discovered that a similar view is advanced by Zemach (1997: 198–200). Likewise, Helen Reed, the novelist in David Lodge's recent novel *Thinks . . .* , suggests that "novels could be called thought experiments," after she hears various thought experiments from the character Ralph Messenger, the director of the Holt Belting Center for Cognitive Science.

15 Marshall Cohen and Eileen John have pointed out to me that my use of the notion of conceptual knowledge may be too strained here. Perhaps it might be better to call the kind of knowledge I have in mind philosophical knowledge.

16 Some literary thought experiments may serve to identify necessary conditions for the application of a concept, as *Great Expectations* zeroes in on selfless love as a condition for virtuous parenting. Other literary thought experiments may function to remind us of the importance of certain properties as variables to consider when rendering moral judgments. For an example of the latter case, see my (forthcoming) treatment of *Howards End*.

17 Another function of philosophical thought experiments is to set up a problem, as Plato does with the myth of Gyges in his *Republic*; perhaps needless to say, this can also be a function of literary fictions.

18 It is not my contention that the types of moral education rehearsed above are utterly discrete and mutually exclusive. For example, our emotional responses to fiction may be enlisted in the process of encouraging us to make finer conceptual discriminations. And there are other ways of combining the activities sketched above. My purpose here is not to erect a rigorous, iron-clad taxonomy of moral responses to art, but only to remind the reader of the various ways in which our experience of art contests the skeptic's epistemic arguments. Furthermore, it should go without saying that I do not pretend that my brief list of possibilities here is an exhaustive one.

19 This argument was identified by Devereaux (2001). The response that I develop to this argument here parallels Devereaux's, though where she speaks of posited authors, I prefer to speak of points of view, due to my reservations about the notion of posited authorship.

20 Devereaux cites Oscar Wilde as a representative of this position.

21 This argument parallels that against expressive properties being necessarily metaphorical that I make in my (1999: 95–9).

22 The hedge "unreflexively" is included here in order to accommodate the possibility that a novelist might project an evil viewpoint ironically or reflexively for the purpose of unmasking it.

23 Elsewhere I have referred to this position as moderate autonomism. Radical autonomism maintains that it is never appropriate to evaluate artworks morally. The preceding two sections of this chapter are intended to undermine radical autonomism. Moderate autonomism – which I am now simply calling "autonomism" for expositional purposes – holds that moral evaluation of artworks is possible but is never to be confused with aesthetic evaluation. See my (1996, 2000).

24 This view of artistic form is defended in my (1999: 142–8).

25 The sense of incoherence here is different from that suggested by Arnold Isenberg in the quotation above. Isenberg appears to think that moral elements in an artwork are formally incoherent when they jar with each other (1973: 281); that they are evil is not important, so long as they are consistent. That is why Isenberg appears to think that ethical and aesthetic evaluation can always be kept separate.

However, the kind of incoherence I have in mind is pragmatic – that the immoral viewpoint of the work undermines the prescribed uptake to which the work aspires. The reason it misfires can only be explained by calling attention to the fact that the moral viewpoint it advocates is too defective to enlist the co-operation of the morally sensitive audience member. Thus, the reason it fails aesthetically in terms of actualizing its purposes is that it is morally defective. Its aesthetic failure and its moral failure are explained by reference to the same feature of the work – its moral defectiveness. Thus, in these cases, unlike Isenberg's, the kind of incoherence in question does not support the idea that ethical and aesthetic evaluation can always be kept apart.

26  Here it needs to be added that we must understand the morally sensitive audience in counterfactual terms. The reason for this is that we expect artistic merit to stand the test of time. Thus, genuine aesthetic evaluations track the reactions that morally sensitive audiences would have to the work, not the reactions that the actual audience has to the work. For a contemporary audience to a work – such as Nazi audiences to Riefenstahl's *Triumph of the Will* – may, in the heat of the ideological/patriotic moment, be blinded to the moral defects of the artwork.

27  It is for this reason that in the past I have referred to this position as moderate moralism. This view contrasts with Gaut's position, which he calls ethicism, which contends that every moral defect in a work is, *pro tanto*, an aesthetic defect. My argument covers less ground than Gaut's does and, though I am not completely unsympathetic with Gaut's inclinations, my argument explicitly does not go as far as his.

However, several commentators – including Connolly, Harold, and Kieran – have argued that my position collapses into Gaut's. Their reason for this is that since the morally sensitive viewing I consider relevant for tracking moral defects is to be understood counterfactually – in terms of how a morally sensitive viewer would respond to a work – then any moral defect in a work will, allegedly, disturb its implementation of the work's point and/or purpose. I deny this for the reasons stated above: not every moral defect – for example, an off-hand agist aside – will be structurally undermining of the presiding purposes of the work, and some moral defects will not be obvious enough in a work to attract the attention of even the morally sensitive audience member.

Perhaps Connolly, Harold, and Kieran think that it is impossible for a viewer, reader, or listener, construed counterfactually, to count as morally sensitive, if some moral defect would elude them. However, this seems to me to be talking about morally hypersensitive audiences, not just morally sensitive ones. One can be morally sensitive and still not pick up on very subtle or recessive moral defects in a complex artwork. Morally sensitive audiences should not be conceived of as ethical superpersons. Thus, moderate moralism does not collapse into the stronger position, ethicism, though like ethicism it must be thought of in terms of the counterfactual responses of morally sensitive audiences, since ideally, aesthetic evaluations are expected to converge on the results of the test of time.

See Gaut (1998); Connolly (2000); Kieran (2001); Harold (2000).

# References

Beardsley, Monroe C. (1981). *Aesthetics: Problems in the Philosophy of Criticism*. Indianapolis: Hackett.

Carroll, Noël (1996). "Moderate Moralism." *British Journal of Aesthetics*, 36: 223–37.

——(1998a). "Art, Narrative, and Moral Understanding." In Jerrold Levinson (ed.), *Aesthetics and Ethics*. Cambridge: Cambridge University Press: 128–60.

——(1998b). "Moderate Moralism versus Moderate Autonomism." *British Journal of Aesthetics*, 38(2): 419–24.

——(1999). *Philosophy of Art: A Contemporary Introduction*. London: Routledge.

——(2000). "Art and Ethical Criticism." *Ethics*, 110: 350–87.

——(forthcoming). "The Wheel of Virtue: Art, Literature, and Moral Knowledge." *Journal of Aesthetics and Art Criticism.*

Connolly, Oliver (2000). "Ethicism and Moderate Moralism." *British Journal of Aesthetics*, 40(3): 302–16.

Connolly, Oliver and Haydar, Bashshar (2001). "Narrative Art and Moral Knowledge." *British Journal of Aesthetics*, 41(2).

Currie, Gregory (1995). "The Moral Psychology of Fiction." *Australasian Journal of Philosophy*, 73: 250–9.

Devereaux, Mary (2001). "Moral Judgments and Works of Art." Paper at conference on Art and Morality, University of California at Riverside, April.

French, Peter A. (2001). *The Virtues of Vengeance.* Lawrence, KA: University of Kansas Press.

Gass, William H. (1993). "Goodness Knows Nothing of Beauty: On the Distance between Morality and Art." In John Andrew Fisher (ed.), *Reflecting on Art.* Mountain View, CA: Mayfield.

Gaut, Berys (1998). "The Ethical Criticism of Art." In Jerrold Levinson (ed.), *Aesthetics and Ethics.* Cambridge: Cambridge University Press.

Goldberg, S. L. (1993). *Agents and Lives.* Cambridge: Cambridge University Press.

Guerard, Albert L. (1963). *Art for Art's Sake.* New York: Schocken Books.

Harold, James (2000). "Moralism and Autonomism." Talk at Central Division Meetings of American Philosophical Association, Chicago, April.

Isenberg, Arnold (1973). "Ethical and Aesthetic Criticism." In *Aesthetics and the Theory of Criticism: Selected Essays of Arnold Isenberg.* Chicago: University of Chicago Press.

Kieran, Matthew (2001). "In Defence of the Ethical Evaluation of Narrative Art." *British Journal of Aesthetics*, 41(1): 26–38.

Kivy, Peter (1997–8). "On the Banality of Literary Truths." *Philosophic Exchange*, 28.

Nussbaum, Martha (1990). *Love's Knowledge.* Oxford: Oxford University Press.

Parker, David (1994). *Ethics, Theory and the Novel.* Cambridge: Cambridge University Press.

Putnam, Hilary (1978). "Literature, Science, and Reflection." In *Meaning and the Moral Sciences.* London: Routledge and Kegan Paul.

Scott, A. O. (2001). "Alter Alter Ego." *New York Times Book Review*, 27 May: 8.

Walton, Kendall (1990). *Mimesis as Make-Believe: On the Foundations of the Representational Arts.* Cambridge, MA: Harvard University Press.

Zemach, Eddy M. (1997). *Real Beauty.* University Park: Pennsylvania State University Press.

# Chapter 8

# Beauty and the Critic's Judgment: Remapping Aesthetics
## *Mary Mothersill*

## 8.1

Philosophers, unlike physicists, are attracted by the thought that their work addresses, even if indirectly, concerns of non-philosophers. Here there is a grain of truth, although the day is past when one could warn undergraduates that unless they signed up for a course in ethics, they would never be able to tell the difference between right and wrong. C. I. Lewis once observed that in philosophy we study what we already know – which is certainly not true of physics. (Of course an objector might argue that "what we already know" is a phrase that leads straight into thorny epistemological thickets.) But surely the impression of a breath of fresh air that comes from reading J. L. Austin for the first time is enough to convince us that whether or not an appeal to ordinary language can settle a disputed issue, it is not a bad place to start. Occam's razor dictates that technical language be kept to a minimum and adopted only when necessary. Philosophical aesthetics has been remiss in this respect, and my aim in the following pages is, first, to argue that the terminology and idiom familiar to aestheticians are in need of revision and, second, to see what can be done in the way of aesthetic theory once the revisions are accepted.

The first step is to get rid of the term "aesthetic value." It purports to pick out the central concept of aesthetics. In the eighteenth century that concept was said to be beauty and the aim of aesthetics to study the beautiful in nature and in art. When and why the shift to "aesthetic value"? It is fairly recent – within the past half century or so. Standard dictionary entries under "aesthetics" speak of "beauty." The motives for changing the conventions are a matter for speculation but some of the obvious factors are historical. The idea of developing a science of the beautiful first emerges in the context of German rationalism in the eighteenth century. Alexander Baumgarten, credited with coining the term "aesthetics" in 1735 (Baumgarten 1954), thought of founding a subject cognate with ethics, metaphysics, and epistemology, hence in need of an overarching theory. Although

British authors of the same period – Shaftesbury, Hutcheson, Burke, Kames, and Hume – did not adopt Baumgarten's label or share his academic predilection for abstract theory, they did explore the realm of taste and offered worthwhile suggestions about the psychological aspects of beauty.

What is important is that while both the British and the Germans thought of beauty as a genus exemplified both in natural phenomena and in artistic productions, their real interest was in the arts, more narrowly in talk *about* the arts. With a passing nod to rural landscapes and sunsets, they moved on to the main topic – investigation of the claims of critical judgment, where what is in question is the merit of a work of art. This bias has very few antecedents in classical or medieval philosophy. Plato took beauty to be a form, allied to the form of the good. It bears on human experience in the role that it plays in the soul's struggle to transcend delusive appearance and gain acquaintance with reality. In Plato's view, beauty is instantiated in an object of love. The process begins with infatuation, the love of a particular person, and then moves on, if all goes well, to love of an ideal beauty, thence to an appreciation of the beauty of a just state, and thence to what is the most beautiful of all and the most lovable, the form of beauty itself. Plato does not deny that artifacts may be beautiful; he discusses the matter in the *Hippias Major* and elsewhere. But he took the arts, mainly poetry and music, to be a topic for political philosophy and educational theory and held that their production should be strictly controlled, if necessary prohibited, because of their pernicious influence on impressionable audiences. Aristotle took a less exalted view of beauty, and modern aestheticians find his thoughts about the arts comparatively congenial. In the *Poetics* and the *Rhetoric* he explores the dimensions of a well-made tragedy and argues that the emotional involvement of the spectator has a cathartic effect and is thus benign from a moral point of view. The aesthetic theories of early medieval philosophers were Platonic and metaphysical in spirit, although Aquinas, for one, proposed a definition of beauty that was supposed to hold across the board for mundane objects as well as for "transcendentals."[1]

Aesthetics as we understand it today is restricted almost entirely to the theory of criticism, as is evident in its beginnings. The British authors mentioned above were chiefly interested in literature, and poetry in particular. Addison, for example, in his *Spectator* essays, saw his task as identifying particular passages as "beauties" in contrast with "blemishes" or "deformities," and his theoretical excursions, as appears from the series of papers on the imagination, are closely linked with reflections about the appreciation and creation of poetry (Addison 1965). Among the German theorists, the preoccupation with literary criticism is less immediately obvious. Baumgarten's project sounds less like a guide for critics than a theory of perception. He argued that appreciation illustrates a distinctive form of knowledge; he called it *scientia intuitiva*. On the other hand, the examples he offers are almost all from literature. Kant knew Baumgarten's *Aesthetica* (it is interesting that it was left unfinished) and also the work of Baumgarten's student, G. F. Meir, author of *Foundations of all Beautiful Arts and Sciences* (1748, 1750). In the first part of the *Critique of Judgment*, Kant himself undertook a systematic account of beauty, a concept he regarded as philosophically important, on a level with those of pure and practical reason. Indeed he refers to the third *Critique* as the "crown and coping stone" of his whole system. He offered a definition of the concept of beauty and, under the title "The Antinomy of Taste," posed the following question:

> How is a judgment possible which, going merely upon the individual's *own* feeling of pleasure in an object, independent of the concept of it, estimates this as a plea-sure attached to the representation of the same object *in every other individual* and does so *a priori*, i.e. without being allowed to wait and see whether other people will be of the same mind? (1964: 145)

Kant attempted to answer this question, and although his answer – both com-plicated and in many ways obscure – has received mixed reviews, nobody denies that the question itself is crucial for philosophical aesthetics. Since Kant says repeat-edly that no work of art is as beautiful as some natural objects and phenomena, it may seem that he is a counterinstance to the generalization that links aesthetics to the theory of criticism. Note, on the other hand, that critical judgment – in Kant's term, the "Judgment of Taste" – although often a source of conflict among those who profess authority with respect to poetry, rarely arises when the topic is comparative judgments of natural beauty. *A* may be puzzled or disappointed by the discovery that a rural vista that he finds beautiful strikes his companion *B* as unattractive, but it would be exaggerating to say that *A requires B* to share his pleasure and does so, as Kant puts it, on a priori grounds. Experience and obser-vation suggest that, when it comes to the beauties of nature, there is nothing as it were for the Antinomy of Taste to get a grip on. People do not come to blows over differences about the beauty of natural landscapes. Indeed there is something a bit strained in characterizing appreciation (Kant's examples) of a birdsong or a rose as a "judgment" of *any* kind.

A further point: Kant himself, although not the philistine caricatured by some commentators, was a man whose tastes in literature were conventional and some-what old-fashioned. He did, however, make a big point of differentiating the beau-tiful from the sublime. Following Burke, who was his model, he chooses natural phenomena as examples of the sublime:

> Bold, overhanging . . . threatening rocks, thunder clouds piled up the vault of heaven, borne along with flashes and peals, volcanoes in all their violence of destruction, hur-ricanes leaving desolation in their track, the boundless ocean rising with rebellious force, the high waterfall of some mighty river . . . make our power of resistance of trifling moment in comparison with their might. But, provided that our own posi-tion is secure, their aspect is all the more attractive for its fearfulness. (Kant 1964: 110)

The history of the sublime, starting with Longinus, treats it as a rhetorical mode, an aspect of the art of persuasive speech-making, and it is hard not to see Kant as drawing on literary or perhaps architectural examples (he *does* cite the pyramids and St Peter's) rather than on experience of the awe-inspiring phenomena themselves (which is certainly understandable, given the low incidence in Königsberg and its environs of items immeasurably great or immeasurably powerful). But speculations about Kant's own experience with the beautiful and the sublime are beside the point. What is important to recognize is that the first part of the third *Critique*, an attempt to develop a systematic aesthetic theory, makes much more sense if we take it to be an analysis of critical judgment coupled with an analysis of beauty rather than a disquisition on the beauties of nature. The same could be said of Hume, whose much less ambitious essay, "Of the Standard of Taste" (1965) – Kant, I am told, had read it – finds that the heart of the problem lies in evaluating competing claims about the merits of particular epic poems or dramatic works.

Remember the social background. Patronage of the arts, formerly the prerogative of princes, their high born hangers-on, and ecclesiastical notables, was taken over to an increasing extent by prosperous middle-class enthusiasts – people who had the time and money to buy books, attend concerts, and collect paintings. Part of the new scene was an increasing concern with the question of who had or lacked taste, as evinced in his selection of artworks. In response, professional critics or at any rate commercially funded arbiters began to attract readers. Alexander Pope and Samuel Johnson are examples; in France, Denis Diderot and members of his circle proposed principles and examples to guide the amateur's choice. What we think of as aesthetics today has its academic underpinnings, but its real roots are in the eighteenth-century salons and coffee-houses. When Hume in his essay says that the standard of taste, the rule by which disputes are settled, is the joint verdict of the "true judges," he is acknowledging the influence of respected critics of his day.

As people paid more attention to literary, visual, and musical works, their vocabulary changed. Beauty, instead of being seen as a quality shared by every genuine artistic achievement, began to be restricted to particular genres or styles. Witness the distinction between the beautiful and the sublime. The beautiful is what is perceived as pleasing in a non-strenuous way, relatively small, dainty, graceful, and feminine. The sublime is large, immeasurably large, overwhelming, awe-inspiring, masculine – the source, in Kant's odd phrase, of "negative pleasure." Although the crude sexist ideology is apt to set our teeth on edge, the division does serve as a way of classifying what Frank Sibley (1959) called "aesthetic properties." How many times have you been reminded that "beauty" is misapplied to works that are challenging, are dissonant, depict suffering and violence, but count as great achievements?

It was Hegel who first made explicit the idea that it is works of art, their analysis and interpretation, that take center stage. Although he continued to speak of beauty, he held that there is a categorial difference between art and nature, a view that he expressed as follows:

> in common life we are in the habit of speaking of a beautiful color, a beautiful sky,
> a beautiful river...of beautiful flowers, beautiful animals and, above all, of

beautiful human beings . . . We may begin by asserting that artisitic beauty stands *higher* than nature. For the beauty of art is the beauty that is born – born again, that is, of the mind; and by as much as the mind and its products are higher than nature and its appearances, so much the beauty of art is higher than the beauty of nature. (1905: ch. 1)

It is not just that works of art – the great ones anyway – are more beautiful than any river or flower or human being; they do not belong on the same scale. Hegel continues: "The mind and its artistic beauty, in being 'higher,' have a distinction which is not simply relative. Mind and mind only is capable of truth and comprehends in itself all that is, so that whatever is beautiful can only be really and truly beautiful as partaking in this higher element and as created thereby." Croce, in a similar vein, writes: "Nature is beautiful only for him who contemplates her with *the eyes of the artist* . . . without the *aid of the imagination*, no part of nature is beautiful . . . and . . . a natural beauty that an artist would not *to some extent correct* does not exist" (1929).

One can imagine a thoughtful person in the middle of the twentieth century reasoning as follows:

Aesthetics is a going concern and Baumgarten was right: if it is going to be a genuine philosophical subject, it must organize theory around a distinctive concept, and spell out the conditions for its application, which is to say, must provide an analysis of the distinctive form of judgment. It used to be assumed that the key concept was beauty and that the judgment of taste is an assertion to the effect that a particular item is beautiful. Then Kant's Antinomy comes into play and it is up to us aestheticians to decide whether such judgments are objective or subjective and how, if at all, they can be justified or confirmed. But we are frequently advised to study the work of practicing critics, and critics appraise works of art, not natural phenomena. So whether one thinks, like Hegel, that what is born again of the mind stands higher than natural phenomena, or, like Kant, that the converse is true, we must recognize that Art is very different from Nature. The predicate "*X* is beautiful," as expressing the response of a nature-lover, means something different when it is understood as a critical verdict. So how about replacing "beauty" with "aesthetic value"? Portraits as well as sitters, birdsongs as well as musical performances, have aesthetic value, and the term has the degree of generality required for aesthetic theory.

My contention is that, however motivated, this move is a bad one. Why? It cuts us off from common parlance. "Aesthetic value" is academic jargon, a term rarely heard outside the classroom. Consider: "My daughter is brilliant and virtuous; the only thing she lacks is aesthetic value." (Parallels in other fields are equally grotesque, for example, "My daughter is beautiful and virtuous; the difficulty is that most of what she claims to know lacks cognitive value" or "My daughter is learned and beautiful, but the way she treats other people has ethical value that is decidedly negative.")

## 8.2

What is the alternative? We have a choice and there is no point in trying to sound revolutionary. Aesthetics today is understood to have as its province the fine arts and their interpretation. A student who signs up for a course expects to learn something about poetry or painting or ballet, and would have reason to complain if the only examples discussed in class were sunsets and wild flowers. So why not just acknowledge the facts: aesthetics *is* the philosophy of art and theory of criticism? When it comes to the Judgment of Taste, drop the cumbersome "aesthetic value" and say that our interest is in critical verdicts – assertions to the effect that such-and-such is a good novel or string quartet or portrait. The other possibility would be to go back to the tradition, say that aesthetics explores the concept of beauty, and just wait and see how far such exploration gets you in understanding the arts. My inclination is to adopt the second plan, and for the following reasons.

Beauty is a distinctive and a timeless concept. The term itself has cognates in every language, and in every language it plays a role in pretheoretical informal talk. Like truth, it is a basic concept, but whether, like truth (at least on Frege's [1956] view), it is indefinable is an open question. Aquinas, and after him Kant, made a start at a definition, and that is a project worth exploring. The concept of art is a different matter. Historians tell us that the very idea of there being some set of essential features that mark off works of art from other artifacts is one that emerged gradually over time (Kristeller 1951, 1952), and that it was only Hegel and his successors that made it seem like a plausible assumption. We could keep the term "art" while recognizing that what counts as art varies dramatically from one culture or historical period to another. Perhaps it would be better to talk about a *family* of concepts, although even that may be presuming too much. Hegel himself, one of the few philosophers who had first-hand knowledge of the arts and had sound critical instincts, held that the philosophy of art has substance only when it is identified with the history of art (properly interpreted, of course). In the past fifty years or so, much time and effort have been devoted to the exploration of Kant's Antinomy and to the epistemology of the Judgment of Taste, where what is estimated is a claim to artistic achievement. The results are inconclusive, partly because of widespread disagreement about what qualifies as a candidate. The artworld, like other elements in a consumer capitalist culture, has continuously shifting borders. What was dismissed twenty years ago as mere craft or mere entertainment has acquired a more august status, while the masterpieces of yesteryear end up in yard sales or the family attic. Practitioners – at least the upwardly mobile, entrepreneurial ones – are intent on having their handiwork recognized as art, that is, as having a serious claim to respect, interpretation, and public attention. How can one hope to construct a theory of *Phi* where there is an ongoing conflict about the extension of *Phi*? (Imagine you have a small child who wants a pet, and you want to know what breed of dog would be most suitable. There can be disputes; but what if there were conflicting opinions as to what counts as a dog? Is a fox a kind of dog? How about a docile wolf?)

The starting point should be an account of pretheoretical notions of beauty. (Without that, there would be nothing against which to check out theories.) A claim that some particular item is beautiful is familiar and well understood, but may seem unpromising as a topic of inquiry, since it is so frequently off the cuff – a sort of witless exclamation. But it is always in order to ask "Why do you say that?" or "What makes you think so?" If no answer is forthcoming, it does not follow that the speaker is stupid or that what he says is unintelligible. Perhaps what he responds to seems to himself evident and unanalyzable, as it were, a simple, non-natural property. Or perhaps without rejecting the question, he finds that he cannot say what features account for what he takes to be beautiful. (This often happens where what is in question is a work of art; hence the critical vocabulary includes the handy phrase, "*je ne sais quoi*.") Suppose, however, that the subject, although no theorist, is willing to reflect on his own usage and what he intends his hearers to understand. My hypothesis is that there will emerge a number of substantive points on which everyday opinions converge. There is a core of non-esoteric beliefs about beauty that is taken for granted and can be elicited by direct questions.

In what follows I will couch my findings in the first person plural, as "what we believe," meaning what I (MM) and whoever agrees with me believe. But I do not lay claim to any special authority and do not wish to implicate readers in views that they do not share. It would be illuminating to discover genuine disagreements.

To begin with, ask not what things *are* found to be beautiful but what *sorts* of things might turn *out* to be beautiful. The answer, I suggest, is that anything (or almost anything) that can be counted as an individual and is described in non-question-begging terms, such as "a dress," not "an elegant dress," is a possible candidate. We can think of unlikely items: a pile of sand, a dead rabbit, for example. But imagine possible settings and illumination of the sort exploited by photographers. Imagine the way in which the elements of one of his still lifes may have appeared to Chardin and see whether beauty can be excluded on a priori grounds. Or consider the range and variety of the items which we actually *take* to be beautiful: a tree, a sports car, a tennis stroke, a mathematical proof, a woman, a street scene, a gesture, a tulip, a sonatina, a Christmas tree, and so on indefinitely. Some works of art are beautiful (since anything may be); some are prized for their beauty and some for other reasons.

The tradition that finds exhaustive the division of art and nature is false to the facts of experience and takes no account of unclassified items. A coiffure, wind chimes, a letter of condolence, an herb garden: where do they belong? We may be struck by the beauty of everyday objects that would not, even by the most liberal criteria, be counted as works of art. And what about human beings? Plato thought that using make-up was a form of deception and therefore deplored the cosmetician's art – a view that does seem rather far-fetched. (To be an entrant in a beauty contest, you have to begin with a scrub-up.) Moreover, artifactuality itself, a minimal requirement, is a matter of history and not discoverable simply by inspection. Hegel and his successors, who held that works of art have a different and a stronger claim to beauty than products of nature, understood Art as comprising canonical works and understood Nature as what is radically uncultivated and unimproved – the Northern Lights, virgin forests, remote rivers and mountains. It is true that we think differently about the clear cases, admire the technical skills displayed in works of art but not – unless impressed by the Argument from Design – in nature. But note that even in the clear cases, the distinctions observed are determined not by the historical facts but by our *beliefs* about where agency and intention has played a role. Nature unimproved, including what is revealed by microscopes and telescopes, abounds in items that look as if they had been planned. That is what keeps creationism afloat, and the converse is also true: genuine artistic achievements, as Kant observed, often strike us as emerging all on their own from nature without authorial help.

### 8.3

What do we *mean* – what do we convey – when we say of a particular item $X$ that it is beautiful? Assuming that we speak from the heart and are not merely babbling, I think there is an answer that is subject to confirmation, and in what follows I list some beliefs and argue that they are sufficiently well grounded to count as knowledge. (Of course, if successfully challenged, they will *not* count as knowledge, but what I include are things that I [MM] at any rate claim to know.)

(1)   *When we say that an individual X is beautiful, we give our hearers to understand that X is something we like, that our encounter with X pleases us.* This connection is one that always holds; it is a Gricean *implicatur* (Grice 1989). What if someone says "$X$ is beautiful and I find it revolting?" That is not unintelligible, but we wait for an explanation. A common one puts the predicate in scare quotes: "So-called 'experts' (pretentious snobs!) call $X$ beautiful but the truth is that $X$ is revolting."

(2)   *There are widespread differences of taste. What one person loves and appreciates, another finds boring or ugly.* It is not necessary to be a world traveller or a highly sophisticated person to be aware of this fact. Hume (1965) puts it nicely: "Men of the most confined knowledge are able to remark a difference of taste in the narrow circle of their acquaintance, even where the persons have been educated under the same government, and have early imbibed the same prejudices."

(3)   *Within limits, differences of taste should be tolerated. Where conflicts arise, there is no way of proving that one opinion is true or correct. Nonetheless there are cases in which one opinion is true or correct and the other is not.* Our overall answer to the question of objectivity lacks coherence. We may be led to consult philosophers

who offer to resolve what looks like a paradox. Any resolution must take account of both of our pretheoretical assumptions.

Two illustrations follow, one from Kant and one from Hume, of how to set up the issue. Kant's version, the "Antinomy of Taste", is formally stated as a contradiction:

> *Thesis.* The judgment of taste is not based upon concepts; for if it were, it would be open to dispute (decision by means of proofs).

> *Antithesis.* The judgment of taste is based upon concepts; for otherwise, despite diversity of judgment, there would be no room even for contention in the matter (a claim to the necessary agreement of others with this judgment). (Kant 1964: 206)

It is hard for someone who has not studied the first two *Critiques* to follow Kant's presentation. What does he mean by "concept"? What is it to be "based on concepts"? What is the difference between "dispute" and "contention"? What does it mean to say that the judgment of taste claims "necessary agreement of others"?

Hume's version is less daunting. He speaks of two species of common sense. The first holds that someone who finds a poem beautiful is not making a judgment but expressing his sentiments, and so what he says is neither true nor false:

> a thousand different sentiments, excited by the same object, are all right because no sentiment represents what is really in the object . . . Beauty is no quality of things themselves; it exists merely in the mind which contemplates them; and each mind perceives a different beauty. One person may even perceive deformity where another is sensible of beauty and every individual ought to acquiesce in his own sentiment without pretending to regulate those of others. (Hume 1965)

The second species of common sense, according to Hume, opposes the first, holding that comparative judgments at least *are* either true or false:

> Whoever would assert an equality of genius between Ogilby and Milton, or Bunyan and Addison, would be thought to defend no less an extravagance than if he had maintained a mole-hill to be as high as Teneriffe or a pond as extensive as the ocean. Though there may be found persons who give preference to the former authors, no one pays attention to such a taste and we pronounce, without scruple, the sentiment of these pretended critics to be absurd and ridiculous. (Hume 1965)

Kant believed that the only way to resolve the antinomy is by way of a "transcendental deduction." Only someone who knows what Kant means by that phrase will be competent to decide how successful his resolution is. Hume (1965) thought that the "joint verdict" of competent critics (the "true judges") is the "true standard of taste and beauty." Well, maybe.

Because my aim is to make explicit what we know or believe with good reason without benefit of theory, where our opinion is confused, uncertain, possibly inconsistent, I register it as such without trying to provide a resolution. Assuming (1) and (2) above, I propose to go no further than the "subjectivist" view and say that we know what we mean when we call something beautiful even if we are not bothered by the question: "Right! So it seems to you, but is it *really* beautiful? Could you be mistaken? Is your critical judgment objective?"

(4)  *When we say of some X that it is beautiful, we give our hearers to understand that we are (or have been) acquainted with X. If it is a person or a portrait, we have seen it; if it is a quintet, we have heard it; if it is a novel, we have read it, and so forth.* (4), like (1), is seen to be true if we consider the oddity of apparent counterexamples: "Pianist A played beautifully last night. Sorry I missed the recital." "Donne's *Holy Sonnets* are very beautiful. I must get around to reading them sometime." To make such remarks plausible, we have to understand them as referring to the findings of an actual witness – someone we trust – one of Hume's "true judges."

(5)  *The only generalizations we can rely on are those that hold for denumerable classes of encountered particular items.* (5) follows from (4) and is worth noting only because we are careless about invalid inferences. Having ascertained that each of my grandchildren is beautiful, I can be confident in my generalization. But if my encounters with kittens, daffodils, and sonatinas have been consistently rewarding, I may conclude that there is some inherent beauty in kittens, daffodils, and sonatinas and so extend my claims to hitherto unexamined cases. A risky business! The next certifiable kitten I see may be diseased and mangy or have been recently squashed by a car. Predictions about daffodils and sonatinas are open to analogous risks.

(6)  *There are no principles of taste and there are no laws of taste that are both interesting and true.* Since both laws and principles purport to cover future cases as well as present and past cases, (6) follows from (5). A principle would spell out sufficient conditions for an item's qualifying as beautiful. A principle plus a suitable minor premise would validate the claim that a particular *X* is beautiful by deductive inference. Such a possibility is ruled out by (4) above. A law of taste, dodging the objectivity issue, would specify conditions under which members of a specified set of subjects would be moved to ascribe beauty to items within a particular range. Generalizations are lawlike only if they are projectible. (5) above rules out this possibility. Changing and recurrent trends in the various fashion industries suggest statistical generalizations. Artworks are commodities, and fluctuations of the market can be recorded as well as promoted. A particular artist gets to be everybody's favorite for a while and then is heard of no more. Statistics influence the impressionable but cannot tell us where we will find what we take to be beautiful.

(7)  *Perceptions of an item as beautiful are possible only to subjects who are in a particular mood and frame of mind.* A headache or an anxiety attack is enough to incapacitate us. Recognition of (7) is what has seemed to justify philosophers' talk of the "aesthetic attitude." That is another term that we would do well to expunge. Not that (7) is *false*, but, as characterized by the theorists, it serves only to remind us of a commonplace that has no peculiar relevance to aesthetics. It is connected with the idea, familiar in the eighteenth century and emphasized by Kant, that the pleasure we take in beauty is a "disinterested" one. A pleasure is disinterested and an attitude aesthetic only if the subject has the object in focus. To have an object in focus is said to be an achievement and mildly abnormal. "Psychical distance" is

what you have in a fog at sea, once you stop worrying about collisions and ship-
wreck and realize the beauty of the fog itself. "Intransitive attention" and "absorption in the immediate" describe the state in which you concentrate on the item
you find beautiful and not on something else. George Dickie, who has given a
succinct account of a deflationary view, speaks of the "myth" of the aesthetic attitude (1964). But it is not a myth; it is a truism, and fairly trivial at that. Granted
that if the pleasure you take in a scenic vista is linked to the thought of what a
terrific parking lot it would make, it is not just the *beauty* of the rural landscape
that enchants you. You are distracted. But the so-called aesthetic attitude is
demanded by *any* activity that requires concentration – conjugating irregular
verbs, hitting a fly to center field, removing an appendix without perforating the
patient's colon, making eggs Benedict, completing a crossword puzzle. A frame
of mind that is calm but not somnolent is a condition of getting on with any
demanding enterprise. So (7), though true and not unimportant – in trying to get
the hang of a poem or a concerto, we may be distracted not by thoughts about
real estate but by self-indulgent fantasy – is true a fortiori.

(8)  *If explanation demands covering laws, then there is no explanation of why we
find one individual beautiful and another not. What often is possible is to tell someone
what we think it is that makes a particular item beautiful, and sometimes we can
get our companion to see what we mean and come to agree with our judgment.* Notice
that (8) does not prejudge the issue of objectivity. If by the exercise of my critical skills, I enable you to understand what I understand and to enjoy what pleases
me, it does not follow that beauty is a property discoverable in the object judged,
rather than what Santayana (1986: ch. 1) defines as "pleasure objectified." That
question remains open.

   If the purpose of aesthetics is to provide an analysis of the concept of beauty,
the eight points listed above provide a good basis for an aesthetic theory. The
burden of proof must be accepted by anyone who projects a theory which entails
that one or more of the eight claims is false.

## 8.4

A difficulty: "aesthetic value" was supposed to bridge the gap between the merit of
notable works of art and an indefinitely various set of non-works of art – admired
artifacts, unimproved natural objects and events. My suggestion has been that with
a view to constructing an aesthetic theory, the prospects are brighter if we concentrate on beauty and trust the intuitions of non-philosophers. At the same time, I
have maintained that the philosophy of art and theory of criticism have been the
preoccupation of modern aesthetics from its eighteenth-century beginnings. Unless
the theory of beauty sketched above has some bearing on criticism and the arts, it
simply gives up on the problems that make aesthetics interesting in the first place.

   Some comments: in considering what the non-philosopher sees herself as com-
mited to in claiming that an item is beautiful, I assumed that the subjects were

serious and reflective people. But some great works of art, especially on first acquaintance, are breathtaking and leave us speechless, deprive us of our powers of discrimination. In such a situation "It's beautiful" may be pure exclamation, a way of registering astonishment and delight rather than an attempt at characterization.

There is no reason to think that the predicate "*X* is beautiful" is equivocal as between Art and Nature, but there are important differences in our responses. For one thing, the sort of dispute that motivates the search for a decision procedure – a criterion or a canon – rarely arises when there are differences of opinion about a natural beauty. If I admire the hills of west Virginia while you compare them unfavorably with Mount McKinley, you need not *despise* me or call for an umpire. My taste in movies or poetry or music, however, like my taste in clothes, reflects my income bracket, my educational background, my social status (or the status to which I aspire). To have what I find beautiful dismissed as junk calls for retaliation – or at least for refutation.

A further point: many natural beauties are evanescent, and to pinpoint the features of, say, a particular sunset or birdsong, in line with (3) above, my audience must be someone at my side at the right place and the right time. Note also that there is no canon of natural beauties. There are famous, well-advertised sites, but the Seven Wonders of the World are all artifacts. And bear in mind that what counts is not the facts of the matter but what, with or without reason, we *believe*. We can see a man playing the French horn or a child building a sandcastle or a poet declaiming her verses, but being the product of intentional action is not a feature announced by the product itself, and occasionally doubts arise. Even when we are pretty sure that we are dealing with an artifact, we may not know what function it is designed to serve.

Imagine someone whose project is to follow (literally) in the steps of Cézanne. He will have occasion to observe that Mont Ste-Victoire is visible from many points of view and that it is scenically more interesting in some perspectives than in others. He will know or can easily find out where Cézanne set up his easel to do a particular version. He can compare the portrait, so to speak, with its subject. The question of which is the more beautiful, though unlikely, is intelligible, but no matter how closely the painting resembles its original, it is not just one among many views of Mont Ste-Victoire. Of the mountain one does not ask whether the juxtaposition of greens and blues is effective, whether the visual space is well organized, how closely in his practice the artist hewed to his theory about what three-dimensional shapes are basic. Of the painting one does not ask whether judicious terracing might not make the slopes suitable for farming. What the Cézanne offers is the work of a master craftsman and a visionary genius.

To speak from the heart about a work that one admires is not to tell us very much. From a critic we expect something more than an "It's beautiful – Oh wow!" reaction. The concept of beauty in the critical vernacular plays a limited role. We do expect a critical *verdict* to emerge, but a reference to beauty is understood to offer *support* for a positive verdict and rarely appears in the overall judgment of taste. For one thing, it has a limited range: it may apply to a particular singer's rendition of an aria, but it would be odd to describe a whole opera as a "beautiful work" and even odder to apply the predicate "*X* is beautiful" to a drama or a novel. Nor is "beautiful" always a term of commendation. Stanley Cavell (1969) has a good example:

"He plays beautifully, doesn't he?"
"Yes, *too* beautifully. Beethoven is not Chopin."

To describe a work as beautiful is to characterize it. That is why I said earlier that the distinction between the beautiful and the sublime, forgetting about its sexist overtones, marks a genuine difference and provides an example of critical characterization. Characterization involves the use of what Frank Sibley (1959), in an influential paper, called "aesthetic concepts." To describe one work as tragic, dramatic, intense and another as tranquil, light-hearted, and witty is to make a claim that is either justified in the event or not. Sibley distinguishes aesthetic concepts from non-aesthetic concepts. The difference on his view is that non-aesthetic concepts can be correctly applied by any unimpaired intelligent subject, whereas it requires sensitivity and taste to know where and how an aesthetic concept is instantiated. An important point for Sibley is that there are no sufficient conditions for the application of aesthetic concepts – no description of an unexamined item of which we can say: "If this description fits, then the item must be, say, tragic, dynamic, witty, or tranquil." As noted in sections (5) and (6) in the sketch of a theory I have presented, the predicate "*X* is beautiful" is not condition governed and cannot be the outcome of deductive inference. Here is a point at which an analysis of beauty intersects with the theory of criticism.

Beauty is one among many factors that a critic must take into account. For every artist, there is the question of how well he or she handles a particular medium – a question about technical skills. Such skills may be graded and assessed, and there are generally recognized standards of assessment with which the critic is supposed to be familiar. Not an easy assignment! You have to know a lot about baroque musical theory, and you have to have listened to a lot of Telemann and a lot of Bach, to be confident in the assertion that while Telemann's counterpoint is often imaginative and always competent, Bach was a creative genius whose achievements go beyond any comparison with his contemporaries.

Many signal achievements in the arts manifest high degrees of technical skill, and in particular cases, this fact is critically relevant. (Consider Dürer, Hopkins, and Haydn.) But as has often been observed, technical skill in itself is no guarantee of signal achievement. An author or a photographer or a painter can qualify as highly proficient although what he or she produces is paradigmatic kitsch.

The problem of objectivity, I have argued, comes to the fore only in contexts where a critical verdict is called for. It may help to notice that assessment of an artist's technical competence, always relevant though never decisive, may be based on independent grounds, and we are not tempted by the thought that such assessment is purely subjective. No one thinks that recognition that a composer has figured out how to manage a difficult modulation without breaking the conventional rules is "only in the mind of the observer." If that consideration has any weight, it may mitigate the force of what Hume and later Kant regarded as a paradox or an antinomy.

## 8.5   Conclusion

Philosophical aesthetics has as its charge to explicate the concept of beauty and to explain the practice of criticism in the arts. Since there is no non-question-begging definition of "work of art," there can be no such thing as the "philosophy of art," unless one accepts Hegel's good idea that the philosophy of art is identical with the history of art. What the so-called "institutional" theory claimed, namely that what counts as art is whatever the received authorities in the artworld acknowledge and hence varies from one place or time to another – a theory that I once dismissed as a bit of cynical nominalism – actually gets things about right. But critical theory, in this respect like the concept of beauty, can lay claim to a status that is not linked to the fashions of a particular historical period and culture.

## Note

1   "Pulchrum dicatur id cujus apprehensio ipsa placet."("The beautiful is said to be that of which the mere apprehension pleases.") Aquinas, *Summa Theologica*, a, II ae. 27. Reply to Objection 3.

## References

Addison, J. (1965). "The Pleasures of the Imagination." In D. F. Bond (ed.), *The Spectator*. 5 vols. Oxford: Clarendon Press.

Baumgarten, A. (1954). *Meditationes Philosophicae de Nonnullis ad Poema Pertinentibus*, trans. K. Aschenbrenner and W. B. Hollther as *Reflections on Poetry*. Berkeley: University of California Press.

Cavell, S. (1969). "Music Discomposed." In *Must We Mean What We Say?* Cambridge: Cambridge University Press.

Croce, B. (1929). *Aesthetic*, trans. D. Ainslie. London: Macmillan: 99ff.

Dickie, G. (1964). "The Myth of the Aesthetic Attitude." *American Philosophical Quarterly*, I(1): 56–65.

Frege, G. (1956). "The Thought: A Logical Enquiry," trans. A. Quinton and M. Quinton. *Mind*, 65: 289–311.

Grice, H. P. (1989). "Logic and Conversation." In *Studies in the Way of Words*. Cambridge, MA: Harvard University Press: 1–138.

Hegel, G. W. F. (1905). *Philosophy of Fine Art*, trans. B. Bosanquet. London: Routledge and Kegan Paul.

Hume, D. (1965). "Of the Standard of Taste." In J. W. Lenz (ed.), *"Of the Standard of Taste" and Other Essays*. New York: Bobbs-Merrill: 3–24.

Kant, I. (1964). *Critique of Judgement*, trans. J. Meredith. Oxford: Clarendon Press.

Kristeller, P. O. (1951, 1952). "The Modern System of the Arts." *Journal of the History of Ideas*, 12: 496–527 and 13:17–46.

Meir, G. F. (1748, 1750). *Foundations of all Beautiful Arts and Sciences*. Halle.

Santayana, G. (1986). *The Sense of Beauty*. New York: Scribners.

Sibley, F. (1959). "Aesthetic Concepts." *Philosophical Review*, 68: 421–50.

# Chapter 9

# The Philosophy of Taste: Thoughts on the Idea
### Ted Cohen

The idea of *taste*, both in ordinary and in philosophical uses, has more than one sense. On the one hand, taste suggests a preference for better things, as in "his taste in music is impeccable," and on the other hand, taste can suggest an ability to discriminate between various items, to distinguish them one from another, as in "his taste in wine is infallible, he always identifies the vineyard and the year." These uses of the word "taste" must somehow be related to the word's use in reference to the sense of taste, housed in the taste buds.

Whether it is taste in the restricted sense, having to do with the sensation of things in one's mouth, or in the broader sense, where one speaks of taste in works of art, for instance, the two components in the idea of taste may well be connected. It seems plausible to suppose that the connoisseur, someone of considerable taste, has a range of preferences at least partly on account of his ability to discriminate the components of whatever he is exercising his taste on. Thus the person of better taste prefers *A* to *B*, while others do not, and he does this because he is aware of elements of *A* and *B* not recognized by others.

Both conceptions are present in the work of one of the earliest and best theorists of taste, David Hume. He thinks of both senses of "taste," calling one of them the "mental" or "metaphorical" sense of "taste," and the other the "bodily" or "literal" sense. It seems clear that, in the first instance, Hume regards taste as a capacity to feel pleasure, and thus, in "Of the Delicacy of Taste" (1987a), he declares that having a more delicate taste means having a greater capacity to feel pleasure. But in the longer essay "Of the Standard of Taste" (1987b) he, in effect, defines taste as "the ability to detect all the ingredients in a composition." And in that longer essay he proposes to illustrate what it is to possess delicacy of taste by recounting an episode from *Don Quixote*. What Sancho's kinsman actually says there suggests that both conceptions of taste have somehow been run together. Before getting to that passage I will quote a few other lines from Hume, as background:

In short, delicacy of taste has the same effect as delicacy of passion: It enlarges the sphere both of our happiness and misery, and makes us sensible to pains as well as pleasures, which escape the rest of mankind. (1987a: 5)

When you present a poem or a picture to a man possessed of this talent, the delicacy of his feeling makes him be sensibly touched with every part of it; nor are the masterly strokes perceived with more exquisite relish and satisfaction, than the negligences or absurdities with disgust and uneasiness. (1987a: 4)

Where the organs are so fine, as to allow nothing to escape them; and at the same time so exact as to perceive every ingredient in the composition: This we call delicacy of taste, whether we employ these terms in the literal or metaphorical sense. (1987b: 235)

As all the perceptions of the mind may be divided into *impressions* and *ideas,* so the impressions admit of another division into *original* and *secondary* . . . The reflective impressions may be divided into two kinds, viz. the *calm* and the *violent.* Of the first kind is the sense of beauty and deformity in action, composition, and external objects. (2000, Bk. II, Pt. I, Sec. I: 275–6)

So perhaps these two conceptions have been run together in this way. When you, having more delicate taste than I, obtain pleasure from some object that leaves me unmoved, you therein exhibit your greater delicacy of taste, but your pleasure is the direct result of your identification of qualities of the object that escape me. That is, it is precisely because you can "perceive every ingredient in the composition" (second sense of "delicacy") that you are "sensible to [a pleasure that escapes me]" (first sense of "delicacy"). But Hume's exposition of this congruence is not unproblematic on this point. Here is his description of the triumph of Sancho's kinsmen, as Hume paraphrases Sancho's remarks:

Two of my kinsmen were once called to give their opinion of a hogshead, which was supposed to be excellent, being old and of a good vintage. One of them tastes it; considers it; and after mature reflection pronounces the wine to be good, were it not for a small taste of leather, which he perceived in it. The other, after using the same precautions, gives also his verdict in favour of the wine; but with the reserve of a taste of iron, which he could easily distinguish. You cannot imagine how much they were both ridiculed for their judgment. But who laughed in the end? On emptying the hogshead, there was found at the bottom, an old key with a leathern thong tied to it. (1987b: 234–5)

This is a very fanciful version of the passage actually to be found in *Don Quixote,* and I have long wondered how Hume came to tell the story as he does. Did Hume have an inaccurate translation of the novel, or no translation but only word of mouth, or did he alter it to suit his own purposes? I must leave that question to better scholars than I. It is enough for me to note that in Hume's version (although not in the original Cervantes), Sancho's kinsmen report both what they taste (iron in one case, leather in the other) *and* that the wine has a certain merit (less than it would have if it lacked the iron and leather tastes). One report is of an "ingredient" in the "composition." The other is of the quality of the wine. I believe Hume takes both reports to be an exhibition of the kinsmen's delicacy of taste.[1]

Let us look a little more deeply into what is at stake, for a moment simply accepting Hume's idea that the beauty of a thing is nothing more or less than the thing's capacity to induce certain feelings of pleasure in certain kinds of people. So: you are pleased by something, and I am not. Furthermore, you can identify aspects of the thing that escaped me. Might we say, on that basis alone, that, in a sense, you have judged the object itself more accurately than I, that is, that you have responded more to what the object truly is than have I?

It may be helpful to have a concrete example. Here is one involving the proposition that my friend Richard Strier has better taste in wine than I. It is not only that this proposition might mean any of these things (all of which are true), but that it might mean more than one in various combinations:

1   Richard can tell one wine from another with greater accuracy than I, identifying types of grapes and vintages that escape me.
2   In many cases Richard prefers one wine to another when it makes no difference to me.
3   Richard can *describe* wines more copiously than I, not merely by identifying vintages, but by using words like "earthy," "bold," "complex," and so on, while I do not even connect those words with the wines in question.

Now as a matter of fact, these subpropositions are logically independent, that is, any one of them might be true without either of the others being true – as a matter of logic alone; but typically there will be some connection, most obviously, perhaps, in the fact that Richard's preference for wine $X$ over wine $Y$, while I have no relative preference, is accompanied by Richard's being able to describe the two wines in words that escape me, and in his being able to identify the actual ingredients of the wine (the kind of grapes from which it was made, the year in which those grapes were harvested, etc.) while I cannot.

I will try to go a little more deeply into this "logic" presently, but first let me make a somewhat different beginning.

There are two outstanding questions, one obvious and direct, and the other somewhat surprising. The first question is whether there is any way to make sense of the idea that one person's taste is better than another's. This is the way the question typically appears, and it certainly appeared that way to Hume. But there is a variation on this question that may be at least as fruitful to pursue. Hume thinks that his readers will feel compelled to agree that in some sense Milton is better than Ogilby, and Addison is better than Bunyan, or, perhaps, that the pleasure to be gotten from reading Milton is greater than that to be had from reading Ogilby. It is to accommodate this commitment that Hume develops his thesis that some pleasures are more natural or appropriate than others, referring these pleasures to the experience of especially qualified tasters. But what if a reader of Hume simply does not have this conviction about Milton and Ogilby?[2] Hume's overture might be more compelling if he referred not to an interpersonal case, in which one person's taste is to be compared with another's, but to an intrapersonal case, in which a single person reflects on changes in his personal taste. One might ask oneself, with regard to the changes in one's taste, changes that seem to be part of everyone's history, whether he is content to regard these simply as *changes*, or whether he feels a need to say that his taste has *improved*. Suppose I say, truthfully, that at some earlier time in my life I enjoyed the music of Smetana more than I cared for the music of Mozart or Bach, but that it is no longer like that with me. I now derive more pleasure from Mozart than from Smetana. Do I think only that my taste has changed, or do I think it has improved? It is important to ask this question innocuously and innocently at first, and without regard to the soon-to-be-pressing philosophical questions of whether I can justify this idea of improvement, or even explain it. First let us see whether there is something to be justified and explained. I will go no further into this matter here, but only note, and then move on, that I believe that virtually everyone, responding ingenuously, will think that there have been improvements in his taste, that his taste has, so to speak, *developed*, and at least in that sense his taste is now better. (It may also be in some cases that one may think his taste has deteriorated, perhaps as a result of a decline in one's ability to discriminate musical pitches, or an inability to concentrate as hard for as long.)

I understand Hume's argument fundamentally to be this: if you wish to say that your taste is not simply different from what it once was, but that it has improved (or deteriorated), then you must suppose that there is, in Hume's sense, a "standard of taste," because except against the background of such a standard, there is no way to make sense of the idea of improved taste. Thus I understand Hume to have offered a "transcendental" argument well before the argument of Kant's *Critique of Judgment*.

The second question, I think, is unsuspected but extremely interesting. It is this: if there is a difference between better and worse taste, why should anyone wish to have better taste? It may seem obvious, virtually analytic, that better taste is something one must wish for, or at least should wish for, but in fact it is far from obvious, and whether it is even true depends absolutely upon how one understands just what it is for one taste to be better than another.

In whatever sense of "taste" is at hand, why should I want my taste to be more like Richard's? If, in some sense of "taste," Richard has better taste than I, why should I want my taste to be better?

With this example in mind, or any you care to supply, the questions seem to be these, among others: should one have better taste? Should one want to have better taste? Is it better to have better taste?

These questions may seem ridiculous, or at best invitations to academic exercises, for it might seem that it is somehow carried in the very word "better" that it is better to have better taste, and that, therefore, one should want to be in the better condition. But the questions are not at all ridiculous. If having better taste means either being able to detect more of what is there in an object, or being disposed to feel pleasure when others, of lesser taste, do not, even then it would be true that it is better to have better taste even if, as philosophers say, all things were equal. But it is never the case that all things are equal.[3] There are costs in the acquisition of better taste, in any sense of "better taste." In the first place, it will undoubtedly take time to refine one's taste, and it will require effort. On what grounds would one say that no matter how else one might have spent this time and effort, it would be better to have spent it in improving one's taste? Well, one replies, once the time and effort have been expended, one will be permanently suited to experience pleasures otherwise unobtainable. Perhaps. But what pleasures might one find if one had forsaken the development of taste and instead devoted oneself, say, to learning to play pool very well, or learning to read other languages, or learning to dance, or simply improving one's health by exercising and dieting? I see no way to treat this other than as an empirical question, and if it is a matter of what the facts happen to be, then the putative advantages in having better taste are themselves matters of fact, and they may or may not be worth it when measured against whatever has been lost.

There is yet another cost if, as I believe, Hume is right to attribute to elevated taste an increased capacity for feeling pleasure but also an increased liability to experience pain. A very common experience in the history of one's dealing with music or literature or painting is indeed a coming to delight in things that once failed to move one, but an attendant consequence is almost inevitably to lose the pleasure that once came from things that now seem inferior.

Suppose that at a certain time, as a young person, your taste in music runs toward orchestral works like Tchaikovsky's *1812 Overture*, Ravel's *Bolero*, Grofé's *Grand Canyon Suite*, and similar pieces. You find very little to respond to in Bach's fugues, Beethoven's late quartets, or Berg's *Lyric Suite*. For whatever reason, you set about improving your musical taste. (Perhaps we should not be so fast to say *improving* your taste, and settle, cautiously, for saying that you will be *changing* your taste.) At some later time you do indeed derive great enjoyment from Bach, Beethoven, Mozart, Haydn, Berg, Schönberg, and others. But now you don't care much for the cannon and church bells in the *1812*, and you are mainly bored by Ravel's experiment. Surely you have lost something, lost a source of pleasure in your life. And I think you may well have lost more. You cannot learn to listen to Bach overnight. You will have spent much time listening without much pleasure, and maybe time reading about Bach's music, and perhaps even getting instruction from others. What else might you have done in that time? Is the newly gained musical delight worth what you have lost, including those musical delights that used to be yours? Surely this is an open question.

But, one might say, it is simply true, analytically, axiomatically, a priori, that it is better to like better things.[4] It is just the same as it is obviously true that what one should do is what one ought to do. A moral saint is someone who always does the right thing. An aesthetical saint is someone who always likes the better things.

That sounds persuasive, but only for a time. In the end, I think, one will come to the brute assertion that the pleasure (or whatever it is) available from the presumably better music is just better than that available from the presumably lesser music. I see no reason to assent to this assertion.

It is a central feature of Hume's conception of taste, and, I think, of any plausible conception, that the ability to detect ingredients in things, as well as to obtain pleasure when responding to those ingredients, is relative in this sense: one may have taste in objects *of a certain kind* and have little or no taste in other kinds of things. In a well-known reminiscence, Norman Malcolm has recorded this about Wittgenstein's eating preference when they were together at Cornell: "Wittgenstein declared that it did not much matter to him what he ate, so long as it was always the same" (1958: 85).

This remark has delighted many Wittgenstein admirers, especially those who find him precious and agreeably eccentric. But just what is to be made of this declaration of Wittgenstein's? It is part of the Wittgenstein myth that he was a man of considerable and even fastidious taste, the designer of a house, a women's fashion consultant, a connoisseur of music (in which connection he despised Tovey's discussion of Beethoven), an appreciator of American detective fiction who preferred it to Dorothy Sayers. What has happened when it came to food? Is it that he did not want his taste to be exercised in this regard? Did he want not to have to judge? Did he wish to give his keen sensibility a rest? Is it, perhaps, exhausting always to be a discriminator? But then why be an aesthetical referee in some cases but not in others? Is it that taste in music, say, is more important than taste in food? Why would that be? Is it that the rewards available to a musical connoisseur are very great, while those available to a gastronome are not so great?

Finally, let me return to the question of what might connect taste in the sense of an ability to detect things with taste in the sense of the possession of a capacity to feel pleasure and therefore to have a set of preferences. Could one say that my friend Richard is somehow "right" to feel the pleasure he feels when drinking his wine, while I have erred in failing to be pleased by that wine? Perhaps it is that those ingredients Richard responds to – the ones I fail to detect – are really there, are in fact properties of the wine, and so in some sense Richard is truly responding to the object in a way in which I am not, almost as if he were seeing colors while I am color-blind. Now of course the feeling of pleasure does not follow "logically" from detecting those ingredients: as Arnold Isenberg remarks in a different context (1973: 163), a "sameness of vision" may or may not be followed by a "community of feeling," but let us overlook that gap. Suppose it is true that if I did detect what Richard detects, I would feel as Richard does, and I would have his preferences in wine. There is still the question, why should I do that? Is it that Richard's experience of the wine is more accurate than mine, more adequate to the wine itself, as if I have not really experienced *the wine* at all? There are philosophers, and many other thoughtful people as well, who would say that. But I demur, speaking only for myself. This way of thinking of things is reminiscent of Aristotle's idea that there is an essence of tragedy, and therefore a "proper" and somehow correct way of responding to tragedies. That idea has a logical feel to it, but I do not think it is compelling. And that leaves me embracing a curious proposition: I can see that Richard's taste is more apt, more properly attuned to the objects being tasted, and in that sense more accurate than mine, but I see no reason to wish to have his taste. A curious proposition, indeed, but it may be true. In moral matters, one might say that seeing that $X$ is the right thing to do brings with it a wish that one would oneself do $X$. But in matters of taste there is a gap between a recognition of "accurate" taste and the desire to have accurate taste. This somehow sounds wrong, but I think it may well be right.

## Notes

1  I have done my best to make sense of Hume's use of this passage, in Cohen (1994).
2  The Addison/Bunyan comparison is especially problematic. Among readers of Hume today, the likelihood is that they will have a reasonably good opinion of Bunyan and will know nothing of Addison, whereas Hume thought much better of Addison than of Bunyan.
3  Think of the propositions that, all things being equal, one should not lie, not commit murder, not take steroids, etc. One might very well assent to these, but all the interesting questions arise when not all things are equal, and it might well be that lying, murdering, and steroid-taking are exactly the right things to do.
4  Augustine (1998: bk XIX, ch. 24) thought that one "people" is better than another if it loves better things. One might say, similarly, that one person is "better" than another if he likes better things, but it is very difficult to say *why*.

## References

Augustine (1998). *The City of God Against the Pagans*. Cambridge: Cambridge University Press.

Cohen, T. (1994). "Partial Enchantments of the *Quixote* Story in Hume's Essay on Taste." In Robert J. Yanal (ed.), *Institutions of Art: Reconsiderations of George Dickie's Philosophy*. University Park, PA: Pennsylvania State University Press: 145–56.

Hume, D. (1987a). "Of the Delicacy of Taste and Passion." In *David Hume: Essays Moral, Political and Literary*. Indianapolis: Liberty Classics: 5.

——(1987b). "Of the Standard of Taste." In *David Hume: Essays Moral, Political and Literary*. Indianapolis: Liberty Classics: 4.

——(2000). *A Treatise of Human Nature*. Oxford: Oxford University Press.

Isenberg, A. (1973). "Critical Communication." In W. Callaghan et al. (eds), *Aesthetics and the Theory of Criticism*. Chicago: University of Chicago Press.

Malcolm, N. (1958). *Ludwig Wittgenstein: A Memoir*. London: Oxford University Press.

Yanal, Robert J., ed. (1994). *Institutions of Art: Reconsiderations of George Dickie's Philosophy*. University Park, PA: Pennsylvania State University Press.

# Chapter 10

# The Emotions in Art
## *Jenefer Robinson*

### 10.1  The Emotions in Art: A Thumbnail Sketch

Beginning with the early treatises on the arts by Plato and Aristotle, thinkers in the western tradition have often commented on the close connection between the arts and the emotions. Plato and Aristotle both thought that the arts evoke or arouse emotions, although for Plato this was a weakness in the arts, whereas for Aristotle it was a strength. Indeed, as we shall see later, Aristotle thought that the evocation of emotion by dramatic works of tragedy can help to teach us about life. In later eras the emphasis shifted from the evocation to the representation of emotion, although the two ideas were not always clearly distinguished. In the seventeenth and eighteenth centuries it was a commonplace that the arts of painting, poetry, and music were to represent or "paint the passions." Later still in the Romantic and post-Romantic periods, the emphasis shifted again: the Romantic artist typically saw himself as expressing his own emotions in his work rather than representing emotions or evoking emotions in other people. If the audience experienced emotion on reading or looking at or listening to the artist's work, then it was by means of recreating in themselves the emotional experience of the artist captured in the work. Most theories in the history of western aesthetics which link art to emotion have assumed that the emotions evoked or represented or expressed by the arts are ordinary ones from life, such as pity, fear, joy, sadness, love, etc.

One apparent exception to this generalization is the theory that works of art evoke a special emotion or kind of emotion called the "aesthetic emotion," a theory defended by the early twentieth-century art critic Clive Bell and associated with the overtly formalist views of the "Aesthetic" movement (Bell 1914). Bell thought that there is a special kind of emotion evoked by form, primarily in the visual arts and music. However, what he seems to have had in mind is simply the idea of being moved by particularly beautiful, harmonious, or powerful forms, such as can be found in the work of Cézanne and Gauguin (1914: 6–10). The "aesthetic emotion" is nothing but a special kind of wonder, awe, and/or joy which is evoked by successfully created form rather than by representational content, that is, it is actually a familiar "life" emotion, which has a special kind of object, namely artistic form.

Although theories of art have focused on the connections between the arts and the emotions, attention has rarely been paid to what the emotions really are and why and how they function in relation to the arts. Recently, however, there has been an explosion of research on the emotions in several different disciplines – philosophy, psychology, anthropology, neuroscience, linguistics, etc. – so that we are now in a better position to clarify how the emotions function in the arts. In this chapter I will first explain something about current emotion theory (section 10.2). Then I will turn my attention to the two main ways in which emotion enters discussion about the arts: the idea of emotional expression (section 10.3) and the role of emotional evocation in our understanding and appreciation of the arts (section 10.4). In general, I will try to illuminate these ancient topics in aesthetics by reference to contemporary emotion theory.

## 10.2   Emotion

Although the theory of emotion is still in its infancy and there are still large areas of disagreement among theorists, there is nevertheless a growing consensus about some of the major questions about emotion. In what follows I shall somewhat arbitrarily lay down seven dicta which I think are crucial to understanding the emotions. Although none of them is accepted by every theorist, I have sought to stress theses that have gained fairly wide acceptance.

(1)   When do emotions arise? What kind of stimuli set off an emotional response? There is widespread agreement among emotion theorists that emotional responses occur when our wants, goals, and interests, and/or those of our kin or our social group, are perceived to be at stake. I respond angrily when I think you have offended me (or mine); I respond with anxiety when I very much wish something not to happen and I am uncertain whether or not it will happen (Gordon 1987: 70); I respond with joy when I think something wonderful has happened, with sorrow when I think I have suffered a loss of some kind.

(2)   What are emotions? Different emotion theorists with different agendas have tended to identify emotions in somewhat different ways. Some people think of emotions as long-term dispositions, such as a life-long love for one's children or contempt for racists. Others who study facial expressions of emotion think of emotions as short-term episodes lasting for only a few seconds. While recognizing that the word "emotion" is used in diverse ways, I think of an emotion primarily as an episode, albeit one that involves more than a change in facial expression and which typically lasts for more than a few seconds. I find useful R. S. Lazarus's concep-

tion of emotion as a transaction or interaction between a person and the environment, such that each emotion is characterized by a distinct and specific "relational meaning." On this conception, an emotion is a *response* by a person (I ignore other species in this chapter) to some particular situation or event in the environment, which is registered as significant to that person's wants, goals, and interests. Each emotion is distinguished by a "unique and specifiable relational meaning," which "summarizes the personal harms and benefits residing in each person–environment relationship" (Lazarus 1991: 39). Thus an angry response is to "a demeaning offense against me and mine"; compassion is "being moved by another's suffering and wanting to help" (1991: 122).

(3) Emotions involve a focusing of attention on a select subset of total environmental input (De Sousa 1987). What I pay attention to in an emotional episode is a function of my wants, goals, and interests (and those of my kin or social group). We cannot identify emotions with paying attention, of course, since I pay attention to all sorts of things for all sorts of reasons, but a focus of attention on something registered as important to me seems to be a minimum requirement for emotion. When I am afraid of the approaching grizzly bear, my fear rivets my attention upon it. When I am angry with you, my attention is insistently drawn to the offense (I think) you have committed. In general, emotions require a focus of attention on some aspect of the environment that seems to be of significance to us in light of our wants, goals, values, and interests (Robinson 1995b).

(4) Emotions do not merely get us to pay attention to certain aspects of the environment rather than others. They also involve evaluating those aspects of the environment in one way rather than another. In an emotional episode we focus on those aspects of the environment which we deem relevant to our wants, goals, and interests, and we evaluate those aspects *in terms of* our wants, goals, and interests. In anger, for example, I evaluate your remarks as "an offense," as violating some norm that I hold dear, and I focus my attention on your remarks perceived in that light. In Lazarus's terms, the "relational meaning" of the anger episode is an interaction between the offensive environment and my angry response (which in turn will usually change the environment, perhaps causing you to back off and apologize, thereby removing the offense, or perhaps leading you to retaliate with anger of your own, thereby compounding the offense).

Many recent philosophers writing on emotion have argued that an evaluative judgment or belief forms the core of an emotion. Different evaluative beliefs identify the different emotions. Thus Robert C. Solomon, in a book that reignited interest in the emotions among philosophers in the Anglo-American philosophical tradition, went so far as to say that anger *is* a judgment or set of judgments to the effect that "someone has wronged or offended me," and that my embarrassment *is* my "judgment to the effect that I am in an exceedingly awkward situation" (1976: 187).

However, the evaluative component of emotion does not always amount to a belief but is more like a kind of "seeing-as," a stance or a way of focusing on the world. In anger I see the world as offensive even if on reflection I do not *believe* that the world is ganging up on me. If I am afraid of spiders, I see them as threatening, even while I am perfectly aware that they are not threatening at all. I have a fearful "vision" of spiders, as nasty, hairy, threatening creatures that descend suddenly and silently through the air (and possibly on my head). Similarly, in joy I see the world as a wonderful place, even though I know that objectively speaking there is a lot wrong with it. The evaluations that are central to emotion are best thought of not as beliefs, but as ways of seeing the world. They are not all-things-considered evaluations, but are based on a narrow set of interests and goals. That is why I can be joyful (since from my partial point of view everything is going swimmingly), while simultaneously convinced that in general the world is in a shambles (Rorty 1980; Greenspan 1980).

To corroborate the idea that the "evaluation" in emotion is not a "judgment" in the normal sense of that term, some remarkable experiments in empirical psychology suggest that in some "primitive" cases of emotion the evaluations occur too fast for any higher cognitive processes to be involved, and certainly below the level of consciousness. Robert Zajonc's "mere exposure" results and Lazarus's "subception" experiments, for example, seem to show that some emotional responses may consist in nothing but an "instinctive," unthinking response of pleasure or fear (Robinson 1995b).

(5)   Whatever the evaluative component of emotion turns out to be, it also seems to be true that an evaluation all by itself is not *sufficient* for an emotion. Whatever the evaluative belief or the "way of seeing" one comes up with as the distinctive feature of a particular emotion, it is always possible to imagine a situation in which a person has the relevant belief or sees things in the relevant way, yet does not experience the corresponding emotion. For example, I can *believe* that you have insulted and offended me or I can *see* your behavior as insulting and offensive, yet fail to be angry. Something more seems to be required. Dating from William James, the "something more" has usually been identified with physiological responses and action tendencies of some kind (James 1890).

Ever since James, psychologists have tended to emphasize the physiological aspects of emotion. An episode of emotion typically begins when one's attention is drawn to something which is evaluated as important in some way to one's wants, goals, or interests (it is an offense, a loss, a friend or enemy, etc.). If the episode is to be a truly emotional episode, however, this evaluation produces a response, which consists in physiological changes, especially autonomic nervous system changes and cardiovascular changes, as well as action tendencies. Some of these bodily changes probably serve to ready the person for subsequent action, as in fight-or-flight responses. Many of these changes probably serve to reinforce the focus of attention on whatever it is that has set off the emotional response in the first place. And many theorists – especially those in the Darwinian tradition – have pointed out the important function that changes in facial expression, tone of voice, posture, and gesture serve in communication: we "read" other people's expressions and gestures in order to figure out their state of mind and possible future actions. For social animals like us, this is a very useful capacity. (Ekman 1993).

(6)   Emotions clearly have a biological basis, yet they are also highly dependent on social and cultural norms. Apart from some "basic" emotions such as (perhaps)

the fear of falling or infantile attachment to the predominant care-giver, emotions involve evaluations that are culturally specific. Anger may involve an evaluation that one has been offended, for example, but in different cultures what constitutes an "offense" will be very different. What's more, not every culture will have the exact same concept of "an offense." Different cultures carve up the emotional landscape in different ways. In many cultures there will be no one word exactly corresponding to "anger" in English (Russell 1991). This is no doubt due to the fact that different cultures have different "world views," and hence different ideas about what matters to people: since emotional responses are always in terms of one's wants, interests, and goals, different value systems are likely to produce different emotions.

(7) Particular emotion words, such as "anger," "fear," and "compassion," are sometimes used to refer to the particular kind of evaluation characteristic of those emotions, even when the physiological aspects of the emotion are not present. We might think of "anger" in this sense as an "emotional attitude" rather than a full-fledged emotional state. Thus I may calmly say that I am very angry about government policy toward the environment, where what I mean to convey is not that I am in a physiologically aroused state or about to go on the attack, but simply that I have a certain perspective on the policy, from the point of view of my own wants, interests, and values.

Finally, I will say nothing here about feelings, perhaps the least understood aspect of emotion.

## 10.3 Emotional Expression in the Arts

"Expression theory" took its rise from the Romantic movement, with its emphasis on the artist's emotions, rather than those of the spectator or audience. According to the poet Wordsworth in his preface to the *Lyrical Ballads*, poetry is the "spontaneous overflow of powerful feelings," which are "recollected in tranquillity" (Richter 1989: 295). Beethoven is reputed to have said in conversation with Louis Schlosser that "stimulated by those moods which poets turn into words, I turn my ideas into tones which resound, roar and rage until at last they stand before me in the form of notes" (Morgenstern 1956: 87). In other words, one of the chief goals of the Romantic artist is the sincere expression of his own emotions in his art.

We find this Romantic emphasis on the artist's expression of emotion in the post-Romantic theories of such diverse thinkers as Dewey (1958) and Collingwood. In Collingwood's *The Principles of Art* (1938), "art proper" is characterized as "expression," which for him meant the exploration and elucidation of the artist's emotions in a work of art. Collingwood described expression as a process in which the artist gets clear about his emotional states by working through them imaginatively in a medium. Expression thus consists in the outward manifestation of the artist's emotion in an artwork, but unlike what he calls the "betrayal" of emotion, it is not the mere manifestation of *symptoms* of emotion like the red face, clenched fist, and trembling limbs of the angry person, but a cognitive process in which the emotions expressed are thereby clarified and articulated. Expression for Collingwood is not a generalized "description" of an emotion, as when I say "I am sad," but is particularized by specific images, metaphors, rhythms, etc. Nor is it the same as the evocation or arousal of emotion (1938: 109–24). Collingwood was heavily influenced by the Italian Hegelian philosopher Croce, who thought of art as a means to a special kind of intuitive knowledge distinct from discursive knowledge. In Collingwood's theory the artist's special "intuition" becomes his knowledge of his emotional state as expressed in the creation of a new, original, unique work of art.

Over the past fifty years or so the Croce–Collingwood theory of art has been roundly criticized by a number of analytic philosophers, including John Hospers (1955) and Alan Tormey (1971). Tormey gave what is often considered to be the definitive refutation of the theory in his book *The Concept of Expression*. There he outlines a generic "expression theory" (E-T), which he claims is common to many expression theorists including Dewey and Collingwood: "(E-T) If art object O has an expressive quality Q, then there was a prior activity C of the artist A such that in doing C, A expressed his F for X by imparting Q to O (where F is a feeling state and Q is the qualitative analog of F)" (1971: 103). Tormey then argues that a work of art can have *expressive qualities* – melancholy, cheerfulness, nostalgia, and the like – without there necessarily being a prior *act of expression* by an artist. A work can be melancholy without the artist's expressing his own melancholy in the work. Moreover, the evidence that a piece of music is melancholy, say, lies in its harmonic progressions, rhythm, timbre, dynamics, etc., not in any act performed by the composer while creating it.

The idea that emotional expression in the arts is nothing but the possession of an emotional character has been taken up enthusiastically by many analytic philosophers. A novel twist on the idea was added by Nelson Goodman in *Languages of Art*, who argued that the possession of emotional character was metaphorical, not literal, and that the emotional character was not just possessed but exemplified, referred to, or shown forth by the work (1968: ch. 2). Goodman also extended the notion of expression so that not just emotional qualities but any aesthetically significant qualities – such as fluidity, weight, or dynamism – which are metaphorically possessed and exemplified can be said to be expressed. Goodman's semantic notion of expression would seem to be very different from Collingwood's psychological notion, but it retains the idea that expression involves both possessing and communicating a certain manifest character.

Tormey's arguments are perfectly sound as arguments against the generic "expression theory" he outlines, but unfortunately the theory is virtually unrecognizable as an account of Dewey's or Collingwood's actual views. In particular, as Francis Sparshott has pointed out, E-T is not a theory of what artistic expression *is*; it is really a causal account of how artworks acquire their expressive qualities (1982: 623–4). Clearly, artworks acquire their expressive qualities by virtue of having a particular gestalt whether or not they are the end result of the causal process described by E-T. But the expression theory is not usually put forward as a causal account of how artworks acquire expressive qualities, but rather as an account of what art *is*, namely (in this view) expression, as well as what this *means*, that is, what it is for a work of art to be an expression of emotion. And it is not implausible to think of expression as the articulation of the artist's emotions in the manifest character of his work.

Tormey distinguished between being a "φ expression," from which we cannot infer that there is any φ being expressed, and being an "expression of φ," for which the inference holds. If a man has a melancholy expression on his face, this does not necessarily mean that he is expressing his own personal feeling of melancholy in his facial expression. Like the Saint Bernard dog, with which Peter Kivy illustrates this same point, the man may just have been born with a melancholy-looking face (1980: 3). By contrast, if his melancholy expression were an expression *of his melancholy*, we can legitimately infer that the man is indeed manifesting his own state of mind in his melancholy expression. Tormey argues that an aesthetic interest in artistic expression is always an interest in "φ expressions" rather than "expressions of φ." Although it may be true that a person is expressing his melancholy in the way he writes a piece of music (say), the music itself need not have a melancholy character, and it is only the *expressive character* of a piece which the rest of us can detect in it that is of any interest aesthetically. Moreover, if the music itself expresses melancholy this simply means that the music has a particular "perceptible quality, aspect, or gestalt" (Tormey 1971: 121): it has a melancholy character. We cannot infer from the melancholy character of the music to any melancholy in the artist. The music is a "melancholy expression," not an "expression of melancholy."

What Tormey overlooks, however, is the fact that the expressive character of an artwork is thus and so precisely because it *seems* to be a manifestation of thus and so emotional state in someone or other. For example, the melancholy character of the music may indeed be due to its harmonic progressions, timbre, dynamics, and rhythm, but what makes us call it an *expression of melancholy* is that its character seems to be the manifestation of someone's melancholy. Collingwood's position needs modifying rather than rejecting: the emotions expressed in a work may not belong to the artist himself but only to an *implied* artist, a narrator, or a character or persona in the work. What remains true from Collingwood's view is that "expression" means the manifestation and elucidation of someone's inner states in an artistic medium. Furthermore, it is the expressive character of a piece of music (say) which manifests the emotional states expressed, whether they belong to the actual composer, to an implied composer, or to a "persona" or "character" in the music such as Melisande or the Swan of Tuonela.

Collingwood's theory clearly has limitations as a general theory of art, since much art is not an expression of emotion in his sense. Think of Albers's *Homage* to the *Square* or Vasarely's Op-art paintings, for example, which have very little to do with emotion in any sense. However, as a theory of what artistic expression is, Collingwood's theory is by no means as silly as Tormey and others have made out. Many works of art do indeed seem to articulate and clarify some emotional state, and it is the expressive *character* of the poem or piece of music or whatever which manifests the person's or persona's emotional state.

As Jerrold Levinson has stressed, two different questions often get entangled in discussions of expression in the arts. On the one hand there is the question "What is expression?" And on the other hand there is the question "How do works of art achieve expression?" (1990: 337–8). The expression theory, suitably modified, suggests a plausible answer to the first question: that artistic expression is the manifestation and elucidation of an emotional state of an artist, implied artist, narrator, character, or persona in the expressive character of a poem, a painting, a piece of music, etc. This answer is plausible because it ties the expression of a person's or persona's emotional state to the expressive character of the artwork, just as the expressive character of a person's face or gestures or tone of voice may (although not infallibly) reveal the emotional state of that person.

The second question asks about *how* emotional states can be manifested in works of art. In an emotional encounter with the environment a person reacts to the situation (person, event), forms assessments of the situation in terms of his wants and interests, and responds with physiological changes, action tendencies, facial expressions, tones of voice, gestures, etc. At the same time, in an emotional encounter the environment takes on a particular aspect; it looks a certain way to a person under the influence of an emotion: the angry person sees offense; the person in the throes of happy love sees welcome and beauty; the anxious person sees threats; the melancholy person sees a dark, drab world. In general, artworks can manifest emotions either by analogy with a person who is expressing an emotion or by mirroring the way the world appears to a person in an emotional state.

The main way in which we distinguish one emotion from another is in terms of how something is evaluated or "seen," as when in anger I see your action as an offense, and in fear as a threat. As Collingwood noted, poetry and other literary works are particularly good at articulating and clarifying the evaluative component in an emotional state. Instead of merely saying that he longs for a world of beauty beyond the world of human suffering, Keats writes his *Ode to a Nightingale*, in which he articulates his thoughts and feelings by reference to the nightingale, a symbol for him of artistic beauty for which the poet (or his persona) yearns. Even poetry which is not primarily conceived of as "an expression of emotion" normally has an expressive aspect. Although Pope, for example, is not very interested in "expressing his individual emotions" in his work, the author's dry, ironic wit is clearly manifest in his poetry. In novels and plays, too, the implied author may be unobtrusive, but nevertheless give an overall tone to the work which is the result of his own emotional attitudes. In Molière's plays we find the expression of his love of the ridiculous as well as his underlying good humor and affectionate tolerance for the foibles of humanity. By contrast, the world of *Madame Bovary* is a stiflingly complacent and conventional one of second-rate people, which seems to reveal a contempt for humanity in the author Flaubert.

Representational paintings are particularly good at capturing a vision of the world when viewed with a particular state of mind or emotion. In Munch's *The Scream*, for example, we have a representation of a "character," the screaming person in lower right, who seems – from her (his? its?) exaggerated facial expression – to be in the throes of some powerful emotion of alienation and anxiety. At the same time we are shown the way the world appears to this character and the way that it feels emotionally: the person is scrunched up against and constrained by the picture plane; she (or he) is distanced from the indistinct, shadowy, black figures at the other end of the bridge, who seem to be threatening and rejecting; the whole picture echoes the scream, as if the whole world is infected with the screamer's anxiety: it is a justly celebrated picture because it expresses so well – articulates and clarifies – a particular state of mind. This painting is primarily intended as an "expression" – it is an "expressionist" painting – but many paintings in the western tradition from the Renaissance onward are expressive in a similar way, even if, as in Pope, the emphasis is not on the fact that they are expressions. Thus Wollheim has described Monet's painting of *The Seine in Thaw* as a work of mourning that expresses the painter's ambiguous feelings on the death of his wife (1987: 95). Similarly, Chardin's depictions of the ordinary objects of everyday life can be seen as expressions of his love and respect for ordinary things and people. In his painting of *The Copper Cauldron*, for example, Chardin's loving attention to the cauldron transforms an ordinary household object into something rich, gleaming, and noble.

The expression of emotion is not always – or even typically – the manifestation of thoughts or evaluative attitudes. Very often it take the form of bodily gestures, facial expressions, tones of voice, and actions and action tendencies. In the art form of dance these are the main ways in which emotions are expressed. Dancers "articulate" emotions by subtle nuances of movement and gesture, just as actors do. Emotions can be expressed with beauty and grace or with raw power, depending upon the style of the dance, while still articulating and clarifying fine shades of emotion in the characters. Thus the loving gestures in a passionate pas de deux may express the passionate love between Romeo and Juliet, just as the brutal, pounding movements of the sacrificial dance express a state of religious ecstasy in *The Rite of Spring*. A contemporary abstract dance may articulate emotion in a similar way. The expression of anger, fear, love, or grief in the stylized movements of the dance can be profoundly moving whether or not they are part of a narrative line or story.

Like dance, music can be expressive of the inner states of a persona or character by means of dynamic gestures that seem to be a manifestation of some inner psychological state in that persona or character. Indeed, Jerrold Levinson defines musical expression in terms of the hearability of music (by a "suitably backgrounded listener") as an expression of some psychological state in a musical persona "in a sui generis 'musical' manner" (1996: 107). Thus, the sweeping pianistic gestures in a Rachmaninoff piano concerto may seem to issue from the very heart of the Romantic hero who is the music's persona.

Of course by far the preponderance of music in the world is music with words: song and its derivatives, such as oratorio and opera. In a song the singer, whether regarded as a character, such as *Gretchen am Spinnrade*, a narrator, such as the teller of the tale in a folk ballad, or both, as in the mini-drama of Schubert's *Erlkönig* (Cone 1974), may well be expressing his or her emotions in just the same way as the lyric poet: the words articulate and clarify the speaker's/singer's state of mind. At the same time, the music itself (its harmony, rhythm, melody, timbre, and so on) may be expressive in a way similar to dance: the movements and gestures in the music may be expressive of some emotion or attitude. The music can represent in a stylized way the drooping posture of the melancholy person or the leaping for joy of the joyful person.

Unlike dance, however, music can also express emotion by a stylized version of tone of voice, another of the important ways in which emotions can be characterized. As Peter Kivy has emphasized, music often mimics the passionate speaking voice (1980: 20–1). One thinks, for example, of Monteverdi's Arianna pleading "Lasciate me morire" or Purcell's Dido crying in anguish, "Remember me." To say that such music is bitterly unhappy is implicitly to compare it to vocal gestures characteristic of bitter unhappiness. If this is right, then it is misleading to say that *all* attributions of emotional predicates to music are metaphorical, as Goodman suggests. A piece of music is melancholy in just the same literal way as a tone of voice, a facial expression, or a drooping posture is melancholy. As Leo Treitler has emphasized, the marking "*mesto*" in a piece of music is no more metaphorical than "*piano*" or "*espressivo*" (1997: 36–9). It simply prescribes the character of the music for the performer. Much musical expression consists in a stylized version of literal human modes of expression in gesture, action tendency, tone of voice, etc.

Not just any painting of ice floes will be an expression of mourning, and not just any painting of a copper cauldron will be an expression of respect. Painters draw on a web of social, religious, and cultural associations surrounding both objects and forms in order to convey their expressive vision of the world. When a painter depicts the world in a particular way, he inevitably draws on this kind of cultural knowledge. Color symbolism is particularly important. Thus Watteau's expression of nostalgia for a graceful Arcadian world depicts that world in tones of pink, yellow, and violet, the colors of ball gowns and draperies at elegant court soirées, evoking a world of galanterie. By contrast, Corot's depiction of placid rural scenes in greens and browns expresses a contented view of a solid, prosperous, pastoral world which is domesticated, serene, and abundant. Abstract works omit the representational clues that help to disambiguate expressiveness. But we can still distinguish the bright, vibrant, dynamic canvasses of Kandinsky, which seem to express passion and energy, from his cooler, calmer paintings. As Kandinsky himself wrote, colors have their own character which is to some extent independent of context. Similarly, the expressive qualities we perceive musical tones as having, although no doubt influenced by cultural associations, are perceived as inherent in them, so that, for example, we in our culture cannot help experiencing the minor key as suggestive of the darker emotions.

Human beings inevitably experience the world as steeped in emotional significance. Even when we attribute non-emotional properties such as warmth, iciness, flamboyance, dullness, buoyancy, or weight to the world, we are describing the world as experienced in terms of its human significance. That is why there is some justification for Goodman's treating such properties as *expressed* by a work of art, like more psychological properties. We see the world as expressive and that expressiveness mirrored in art, because humans see so many of their encounters with the environment in emotional terms, in terms of their own wants, wishes, values, and interests.

## 10.4   The Emotional Experience of the Arts

Our discussion of expression in the arts makes it clear that expression is not the same thing as the evocation or arousal of emotions by a work of art. It is true that according to Collingwood understanding what emotions an artist expresses in his work requires recreating in oneself the emotions expressed, but there is also a great deal of art that should not be conceived of primarily as the "expression of emotion" but which nevertheless arouses our emotions. The ancient Greek tragedians would no doubt have thought it very odd if someone had told them their dramas were an expression of their personal "inner" feelings, but to this day their works *evoke* powerful feelings in audiences. Indeed, this is one of Plato's chief complaints about them.

In the *Republic* (1974), Plato complained about the way in which the tragic drama and the Homeric epics work on our emotions, so that, for example, we may weep at seeing a dramatic enactment of a man's grief at the death of his son. Plato tut-tuts that emotions weaken the moral fiber; warriors in particular should govern their emotions by their reason and should maintain a stern resolve in the face of personal calamity. Aristotle, by contrast, thought that the very function and goal of a tragedy is to induce a *katharsis* of pity and fear. Aristotle had a very different model from Plato of what emotions are; he was a "judgment theorist" and thought that reason or judgment was an important *component* of emotion, and that Plato was wrong to think that emotion is necessarily an enemy of reason (Aristotle 1984).

The tragedy of *Oedipus the King*, which seems to be Aristotle's paradigm of a tragedy, arouses our pity for Oedipus' misfortunes at the hands of fate and our fear that fate could deal us ourselves a similar devastating blow (1987). People differ on their interpretations of what a "*katharsis*" is, but most theorists think that Aristotle means that we are *purged* of our pity and fear by working through these emotions as we respond to the play. Others emphasize that in working through these emotions our experience of the play *clarifies* for us the nature of our pity and fear. It is clear that whatever the correct reading of "*katharsis*" is, Aristotle thinks that a well-told story or drama both can and should arouse our emotions, and that contrary to Plato's view, the arousal of the emotions in this way can teach us something valuable about what it is to be human.

Many recent writers, however, have thought that there is something puzzling about our responding emotionally to stories, when the stories are "made up." How can it be, they say, that we feel some powerful emotion for a fictional character, while knowing full well that the character is fictional? This is the so-called "paradox of fiction," which is generated by the apparently incompatible assertions that a reader feels some emotion toward a fictional character while at the same time being perfectly aware that the character does not exist (Walton 1990; Neill 1993). These two assertions are typically said to be incompatible because being in an emotional state of compassion is supposed to entail having a particular *belief* about the object of one's compassion – I believe, for example, that Anna Karenina has had a raw deal – whereas if I know that Anna does not exist, I cannot believe that *she* has had a raw deal, since there is no "*she*" for me to have the belief about (and I know this).

A lot of ink has been spilled and words processed on this so-called paradox, which has always seemed to me to be a non-problem. It is a non-problem because, as I explained in section 10.2, emotions are ongoing interactions between an individual and the environment, and "the environment" includes not only the world present to our senses but the world as it appears to us in our thoughts and imaginings. This "inner environment" is peopled with events and situations and people who may or may not exist in reality, but I can have emotional reactions to the contents of my thoughts and imaginings just as I can to the objects of perception. I can "see" Anna Karenina as in a no-win situation even if she is only a figment of Tolstoy's – and now my – imagination. If Anna is an "object" of emotion, she is so in the sense that she is an object of thought and imagination, of wishes and interests. If I feel my interests and values to be at stake in my encounter with this object of imagination, then I can respond emotionally to it ("her"). Just as I can get all worked up imagining my parents dying in a car crash, so I can get all worked up imagining someone called Anna Karenina going through all the wrenching experiences Tolstoy describes her as having. This is just a fact about how human emotions function. Furthermore, as we have seen, emotions do not require *beliefs* about anything, but only a perspective on things, in terms of our own wants, interests, and values. What Tolstoy succeeds in doing so masterfully is in getting us to find our own wants, interests, and values to be at stake in Anna's story, so that we respond emotionally to her. Indeed, there are scenes in the novel which can induce almost the full panoply of emotional responses: physiological changes, facial and vocal expression, and action tendencies. We may weep for Anna, moan and groan, tremble, sweat, and tense our muscles, as a result of an "evaluation" of her situation as pathetic and an intense *wish* to help the poor woman. The main feature of emotion which is lacking in our encounters with fictional stories is appropriate action. Despite my compassion for Anna Karenina, I cannot act to promote her welfare, whereas in real life compassion usually requires some attempt to help the object of our feelings.

Not only is it possible to respond emotionally to works of art; for very many works it is mandatory to respond emotionally if we want to understand the work as fully as possible as well as its "lessons" for our own lives. This is strikingly true of Romantic works in which the artist is attempting to express his emotions. Unless we feel something of Keats's wistful yearning after the song of the nightingale, we will not understand what he is driving at in this poem. He surely wants to evoke in the reader the feelings he is trying to articulate. But it is not just Romantic poems that encourage us to respond emotionally to them. Very often, important facts about the characters and events depicted in a novel or painting are made manifest to us through our emotional responses to them. Thus my sorrow and pity for Anna Karenina may be what alert me to her vulnerability. My feelings of shock and alarm in front of Munch's *The Scream* may sensitize me to the alienation and anguish expressed in the painting. My feelings of disgust and contempt for Macbeth's wanton murders may reveal to me the horror that he is perpetrating. Similarly, it may be by responding to Molière's Alceste with both amusement and compassion that I discover that, although ridiculous, he is also pitiable. Again, as Aristotle recognized, in order to grasp Oedipus' predicament and to learn from it, we have to feel pity for Oedipus – that fate has dealt him such a blow – and fear for ourselves – because fate might at any moment lay us low in a similar way.

Some thinkers have argued that we empathize with the emotions experienced by the characters in a novel or play, or, in the fashionable language of cognitive psychology, we *simulate* the emotions they feel by imaginatively inducing them in ourselves (Feagin 1996). Tolstoy, for example, describes Anna's fate in such a way that we imaginatively share her wants and goals and the evaluations she makes of her situation in light of these wants, goals, and evaluations; and in sharing these wants, goals, and evaluations, we come to understand the motivation for her behavior. However, we do not always have to empathize with the characters in a story. Very often we take a third-person perspective: we contemplate the characters' doings and feelings and feel *for* them rather than *with* them (Feagin 1996). Rather than feel Anna's fears and her sense of hopelessness, we feel compassion. Rather than feel self-satisfaction along with Jane Austen's Emma, we feel amused and fond of her. When we respond in this way, we are responding *with* the author or implied author rather than *with* the characters. Of course, we may be able to feel *for* the characters more easily if we are first able to feel *with* them. Both Tolstoy and Jane Austen in their very different ways guide our emotional responses to the characters, enabling us to both empathize (feel with them) and sympathize (feel for them).

In *What is Art?* Leo Tolstoy defends the view that the function of art is to *communicate* emotion. His idea is that the artist should sincerely express a particular emotion that he himself has experienced by giving his work a particular emotional character, and this character will in turn evoke the artist's original emotion in the spectator or audience (Tolstoy 1930). We see the tortured Van Gogh landscape and we are "infected" with the tortured emotional state expressed in the painting by the artist. Or we read *Ode to a Nightingale* and we feel the same wistful yearning as the poet expresses in his poem. However, even those who are willing to concede that artists can express their emotions by imparting a particular emotional character to their artworks usually balk at the suggestion that the audience should feel exactly the same emotion as was originally experienced by the artist. I may feel *pity* for Van Gogh upon seeing his tortured landscapes rather than identifying with the tortured emotions of the artist himself. I may feel *shocked* and *alarmed* by the anguish and alienation expressed by Munch in *The Scream*.

However, although this is true, it does not follow that we never either can or should experience the emotions that the artist communicates in a work. Indeed, it could be argued that it is only because we feel the tortured quality in the Van Gogh or the alienation in the Munch that we respond with pity or alarm. Tolstoy no doubt overstates his case, and, like Collingwood, he ignores the possibility that it may be a persona's, a narrator's, or an implied author's emotions that are being communicated, rather than the artist's. Nevertheless, there is some plausibility to the idea that the emotions communicated by an (implied) artist in an artwork sometimes at least can – and maybe should – "infect" the audience, as Tolstoy says, if we are to understand the work properly and experience it as it was meant to be experienced.

One problem with Tolstoy's theory, however, is that it emphasizes the arousal of emotion in an audience as though that were always a valuable thing to do. But some of the emotions aroused are unpleasant, as when we weep for Anna Karenina (Feagin 1983). Moreover, it is not just the great classics of western literature that evoke these emotions: lots of trashy novels, such as Harlequin romances and dime-store horror stories, can make us weepy or terrified. The important point to notice here is that a good novel or play, besides evoking emotions, also invites and encourages us to *reflect* upon the emotions of the characters and upon our own emotional experiences of them. A novel such as *Emma* or *Anna Karenina* demands constant reflection as we read, and also after we have finished reading. We are invited to reflect on the emotional experience of the characters, to see how and why they react as they do, and also to reflect on our own emotional experience as a whole and how and why it unfolded as it did (cf. Nussbaum 1990). If this is right, then our emotional reactions – however dark – are necessary in order both to understand the novel and to learn from it, because in order to understand and learn from our emotional reactions to a novel, we must first have had an emotional experience of it. The same is true for many works of painting and music (Davies 1994).

How do works of art "teach us about life"? One way that novels and movies are often said to do this is by enlarging our emotional range. Novels, for example, present us with characters and situations that we have never met in the flesh but which are recognizably human. Stories often hinge on an emotional encounter: a love affair, a loss, a wrong. They show us the emotional experiences of the characters, the way they view the situations in which they find themselves, and their responses to those situations. Good stories demonstrate how emotions grow out of social contexts and the interactions of different people, and they detail the clash of different people's goals, wants, and interests, including moral interests (Nussbaum 1990). In this way good novels expand our emotional repertoire by giving us a better understanding of the many varieties of fear, anger, love, anxiety, and the other emotions that have names in our language, as well as illustrating emotional states for which there may be no word in our lexicon. John Benson once remarked that it would be nice to have a word for the emotional state exemplified by J. Alfred Prufrock in Eliot's poem, as in "I've been feeling rather prufish lately" (1967: 339). What Eliot's poem does is to explain and illustrate an emotional state for which there is – currently at least – no one-word description. I for one now have a clear idea of what it would be to feel prufish, a piece of knowledge I lacked prior to reading the poem. As C. G. Prado puts it, novels and other literary works give us "practice in engaging in other forms of life" (1984: 105). In general, novels and other literary works can teach us the social and cultural meanings of emotions and emotional behavior; they are thus a means of teaching us about our culture as well as being exemplary products of that culture.

The kind of education that novels offer is a *sentimental* education. It is an *experiential* education. It would be silly to say that all we acquire from *Anna Karenina* is the dispassionate belief that life's a bummer. We are able to find out what it is like to be in a particular emotional state, to understand how one can come to be in that state, what happens when you are in such a state, how it affects other people, how it affects your motives and future plans, how to escape from it, and so on and so forth. To get an emotional education from novels, you need to have your own emotions aroused (Robinson 1995a). If you think that Anna is just another tedious Russian heroine, that she should get a life and take up some sort of social work to distract her from her many miseries, then you have failed to grasp a vital aspect of the novel: you have failed to grasp Anna's character and what it is that makes her tick. In order to grasp *emotionally* what is going on in the novel, we have to have our own wants and interests engaged; we have to care about Anna, so that even if we find her exasperating at times, we nevertheless sympathize with her predicament. Again, our chief guide in this endeavor is the author, or implied author, who tries to get us to care about his characters and influence how we respond emotionally to them (Carroll 1997). And of course it is the author or implied author who tries to guide our reflections about the emotional experiences of the characters and the emotional experiences we are having as we read about them.

Our emotional responses to painting are not guided by a temporal unfolding as in literature or music, but we can gain a similar kind of understanding from paintings if we respond emotionally to them and then reflect back on our emotional responses. I may be moved to compassion not just by the story of Anna Karenina but by a late Rembrandt self-portrait: my attention is insistently drawn to certain aspects of the face (they are made salient) which are of significance to me and hold my interest. And by reflecting on this emotional experience I may come to realize that Rembrandt has shown us something about the poignancy of old age, how it melds wisdom and long experience with frailty and bodily deterioration. Or I find myself moved by Chardin's *Copper Cauldron*, by the beauty and simplicity of the objects it depicts and the harmony of their composition. By reflecting on my emotional experience, I come to realize that Chardin has shown us the nobility of everyday objects and everyday life.

What of the non-representational arts of music, architecture, and abstract painting? Music is often said to be the most expressive art form and that which evokes emotion the most readily. If we are listening to a song, then we may respond emotionally to the character or persona in the music just as we do to a character or persona in a poem or a novel, but in a song we have words to help us understand what is being communicated. Some instrumental music without words lends itself to interpretation as a psychological drama with a musical persona as protagonist, and we may respond emotionally to such music as we do to a literary drama (Karl and Robinson 1995). But music can also "infect" us in a more direct way. There is some evidence that in ordinary life the expression of emotion in facial expression and tone of voice is contagious. It seems possible that music in imitating expressive vocal and other gestures may also "infect" its hearers directly with the emotions it expresses. Perhaps we respond empathetically, as we may respond empathetically to people's emotional gestures or tones of voice. Similar empathetic responses seem likely when we experience dance.

Moreover, as Zajonc and others have shown, some emotions can be evoked directly by a stimulus, without the intervention of any cognitive evaluation (Robinson 1995a). It seems plausible to suppose that some aspects of music can evoke emotions directly in this way, by acting immediately on our bodies, inducing physiological changes (especially cardiac changes) and action tendencies. In particular, music with a strong rhythm makes us want to move to the rhythm and induces joy or ebullience, whereas music with a regular beat at about the same speed as the heart has a calming effect.

Similar emotional effects may be directly aroused by architecture. Some buildings seem capable of evoking emotions in a direct, non-cognitive way, as when large spaces make us feel small, vulnerable, and insignificant, or low ceilings and narrow corridors make us feel constricted and imprisoned, or perhaps when well-proportioned, noble, graceful rooms give us an enhanced sense of human dignity. Some paintings also seem able to evoke emotions directly in this way. Rothko's huge canvasses are not particularly interesting formally; they are not particularly beautiful; and they have no figurative content. But they are enormously powerful because they can directly induce a quasi-mystical state of serene contemplation.

None of this is meant to suggest that the abstract arts cannot also evoke emotions with cognitive content. And indeed emotions evoked "directly" no doubt serve to reinforce the more cognitively complex emotions that we may also experience. If a piece of music makes me feel nervous with its jagged rhythms and unexpected harmonic leaps, that may help me to empathize with the anxiety of the "persona" in the music (Robinson 1994). And if it evokes this anxiety in eloquent, well-constructed musical phrases, I may be emotionally moved by the clever way the composer has expressed these feelings in the music (cf. Kivy 1990). Similarly, if a building makes me feel an enhanced sense of human dignity, this may reinforce my awed admiration of its graceful, harmonious design.

## 10.5  Conclusion

Obviously, evoking emotion is hardly unique to art: it is not a feature of art that distinguishes it from play or, for that matter, from life. Just because the arts are capable of evoking and expressing emotion, it does not mean that all or even most art actually does. In fact the current trend in many of the arts is to move away from the emotions, especially the more "passionate" passions, such as love and hate, anger and fear, jealousy and compassion. The subject of a novel might still be jealousy or hatred, but the odds are that a contemporary novelist would treat these emotions from a relatively unemotional point of view. I think, for example, of all the hatred and jealousy in Ian McEwan's *Amsterdam*, the tone of which is unrelentingly cool and sardonic. Indeed in the *New York Times Book Review* for January 7, 2001, there is an article called "The Big Chill" commenting on this change in literary fashion. The author points out that the characters in the most acclaimed recent novels "often seem stunned and affectless, emotionally absent," and that it is hard for readers to feel much for characters who feel so little themselves. We might add that it is not just the characters who leave us cold; the voices that tell these stories, the narrators and implied authors, are often just as chilly.

What this means is that much of this fiction does not intend to get us emotionally engaged by appealing to our wants, interests, values, and goals. It might want to amuse us in a cerebral sort of way, or it may want us to admire its technical prowess. But most of these novels are aiming at the intellect rather than the heart. I think of Robert Coover, Don DeLillo, even Penelope Fitzgerald. So it is appropriate to end this chapter on the emotions in art by reminding you that there is much good art that is really not very interested in the emotions. Nor is this merely a recent phenomenon. The great sculptures of pre-dynastic Egypt, Byzantine icons, Persian rugs, do not have as a primary aesthetic goal the expression or evocation of emotion. The emotions have been important in art over the centuries, but they are not a sine qua non for artistic achievement.

## References

Aristotle (1984). *Rhetoric*, 2nd edn, trans. W. R. Roberts. New York: Random House.
——(1987). *Poetics*, trans. R. Janko. Indianapolis: Hackett.

Bell, C. (1914). *Art*. London: Chatto and Windus.

Benson, J. (1967). "Emotion and Expression." *Philosophical Review*, 76: 335–57.

Carroll, N. (1997). "Art, Narrative, and Emotion." In M. Hjort and S. Laver (eds), *Emotion and the Arts*. Oxford: Oxford University Press: 190–211.

Collingwood, R. G. (1938). *The Principles of Art*. Oxford: Clarendon Press.

Cone, Edward T. (1974). *The Composer's Voice*. Berkeley: University of California Press.

Davies, S. (1994) *Musical Meaning and Expression*. Ithaca, NY: Cornell University Press.

De Sousa, R. (1987). *The Rationality of Emotion*. Cambridge: MA: MIT Press.

Dewey, J. (1958). *Art as Experience*. New York: Putnam's Sons.

Ekman, P. (1993). "Facial Expression and Emotion." *American Psychologist*, 48: 384–92.

Feagin, S. (1983). "The Pleasures of Tragedy." *American Philosophical Quarterly*, 20: 95–104.

——(1996). *Reading with Feeling*. Ithaca, NY: Cornell University Press.

Goodman, N. (1968). *Languages of Art*. Indianapolis: Bobbs-Merrill.

Gordon, R. M. (1987). *The Structure of Emotions*. Cambridge: Cambridge University Press.

Greenspan, G. (1980). "A Case of Mixed Feelings." In A. Rorty (ed.), *Explaining Emotions*. University of California Press: 223–50.

Hospers, J. (1955). "The Concept of Expression." *Proceedings of the Aristotelian Society*, 55: 313–44.

James, W. (1890). *The Principles of Psychology*. New York: Holt.

Karl, G. and Robinson, J. M. (1997). "Shostakovich's Tenth Symphony and the Musical Expression of Cognitively Complex Emotions." In J. M. Robinson (ed.), *Music and Meaning*. Ithaca, NY: Cornell University Press: 154–78. (Original work pub. 1995.)

Kivy, P. (1980). *The Corded Shell*. Princeton, NJ: Princeton University Press.

——(1990). *Music Alone*. Ithaca, NY: Cornell University Press.

Lazarus, R. S. (1991). *Emotion and Adaptation*. Oxford: Oxford University Press.

Levinson, J. (1990). *Music, Art, and Metaphysics*. Ithaca, NY: Cornell University Press.

——(1996). "Musical Expressiveness." In *The Pleasures of Aesthetics*. Ithaca, NY: Cornell University Press: 90–125.

Morgenstern, S., ed. (1956). *Composers on Music*. New York: Pantheon.

Neill, A. (1993). "Fiction and the Emotions." *American Philosophical Quarterly*, 30: 1–13.

Nussbaum, M. (1990). *Love's Knowledge*. Oxford: Oxford University Press.

Plato (1974). *Republic*, trans. D. Lee. Harmondsworth: Penguin.

Prado, C. G. (1984). *Making Believe*. Westport, CT: Greenwood Press.

Richter, D., ed. (1989). *The Critical Tradition*. New York: St Martin's Press.

Robinson, J. M. (1994). "The Expression and Arousal of Emotion in Music." *Journal of Aesthetics and Art Criticism*, 52:13–22. Reprinted in P. Alperson (ed.), *Musical Worlds*. University Park: Pennsylvania State University Press: 13–22.

——(1995a). "L'education sentimentale." *Australasian Journal of Philosophy*, 73: 212–26. Reprinted in S. Davies (ed.), *Art and its Messages*. University Park: Pennsylvania State University Press: 34–48.

——(1995b). "Startle." *Journal of Philosophy*, 92: 53–74.

Rorty, A. (1980). "Explaining Emotions." In A. Rorty (ed.), *Explaining Emotions*. Berkeley: University of California Press: 103–26.

Russell. J. A. (1991). "Culture and the Categorization of Emotions." *Psychological Bulletin*, 110: 426–50.

Solomon, R. C. (1976). *The Passions*. Garden City, NY: Anchor Press and Doubleday.

Sparshott, F. (1982). *The Theory of the Arts*. Princeton, NJ: Princeton University Press.

Tolstoy, L. (1930). *What is Art?*, trans. A. Maude. Oxford: Oxford University Press. (Original work pub. 1896.)

Tormey, A. (1971). *The Concept of Expression*. Princeton, NJ: Princeton University Press.

Treitler, L. (1997). "Language and the Interpretation of Music." In J. M. Robinson (ed.), *Music and Meaning*. Ithaca, NY: Cornell University Press: 23–56.

Walton, K. (1990). *Mimesis as Make-Believe*. Cambridge, MA: Harvard University Press.

Wollheim, R. (1987). *Painting as an Art*. Princeton, NJ: Princeton University Press.

# Part II

# The Arts and
# Other Matters

# Chapter 11

# The Philosophy of Literature: Pleasure Restored

*Peter Lamarque and*
*Stein Haugom Olsen*

## 11.1 Background

### 11.1.1 A Platonic invitation

A few lines after the famous reference to the ancient quarrel between poetry and philosophy in book 10 of Plato's *Republic* (X, 607, b–c) Socrates issues the following invitation:

> Shall I propose, then, that she [poetry] be allowed to return from exile, but upon this condition only – that she make a defence of herself in some lyrical or other meter?
> Certainly.
> And we may further grant to those of her defenders who are lovers of poetry and yet not poets the permission to speak in prose on her behalf: let them show not only that she is pleasant but also useful to States and to human life, and we will listen in a kindly spirit; for we shall surely be the gainers if this can be proved, that there is a use in poetry as well as a delight? (607, d–e)

The invitation is not an invitation to philosophy, to an inquiry into "the principles and theory of literature, its nature, its creation, its function, its effects, its relations to the other activities of man, its kinds, devices, and techniques, its origins" (Wellek 1955: v), but an invitation to defend literature in terms of its usefulness. And it is not an invitation to philosophers but to poets and lovers of poetry.

It is remarkable to what extent the history of criticism can be seen as a response to this invitation by those to whom it was issued. For there is no tradition of sustained philosophical reflection on literature within philosophy. Instead there is a tradition of criticism with its own separate if not totally independent history. The contributors to this tradition are only occasionally philosophers. Mostly they are "poets" and "lovers of poetry." "The greatest bequest of Classical criticism to later centuries," says George A. Kennedy in the first volume of *The Cambridge History of Literary Criticism*, "has doubtless been its three seminal texts: *Poetics, Ars poetica, On Sublimity*" (Kennedy 1993: 346). Of these, only the *Poetics* is a philosophical work. Neither Horace nor "Longinus"[1] wrote as philosophers. *Ars poetica* is a treatise on how to write poetry presented by a master of the craft, a poet. *On Sublimity* consists of "a few notes" for the addressee of the work, Postumius Terentianus, which "may be useful to public men" (*On Sublimity*, I.1, in Russell and Winterbottom 1972: 462) and is written by an enthusiast, a lover of poetry. Horace and "Longinus" propound general principles, but they do not do so systematically, nor do they support these principles by philosophical argument.

As a rule, poets and lovers of poetry have not been concerned with disinterested philosophical inquiry. Reflections on the nature and function of literature from the Renaissance to the middle of the nineteenth century only rarely take the form of systematic philosophical treatises modeled on Aristotle's *Poetics*. More often they are prefaces, dialogues, etc. written to defend a certain practice (Dryden [1970: 19], Fielding, Wordsworth), advice to poets and critics based on the model of Horace's *Ars poetica* (Boileau, Pope), or defenses against moralists or other enemies of poetry (Sidney, Shelley).

Above all, poets and lovers of poetry are concerned to establish the cultural legitimacy of literature. Plato had challenged this legitimacy by arguing that poetry is morally, as well as epistemically, unsound, and the question of poetry's cultural standing has throughout the critical tradition been construed as a question of its epistemic and moral function, the latter taking precedence over the former. When Horace declares the aim of the poet to be "to do good or to give pleasure – or, thirdly, to say things which are both pleasing and serviceable for life" (*Ars poetica*, 333–4, in Russell and Winterbottom 1972: 288), and that "The man who combines pleasure with usefulness wins every suffrage, delighting the reader and also giving him advice" (*Ars poetica*, 343–4), the good ("prodesse") and the useful ("utile") are taken to be a kind of edification. This was the way in which Renaissance critics interpreted Horace: "To the overwhelming majority of Renaissance critics," says M. H. Abrams, "as to Sir Philip Sidney, the moral effect was the terminal aim, to which delight and emotion were auxiliary" (Abrams 1953: 16). Sidney was defending poetry against attacks from "poet-haters" (Sidney 1973: 99) who challenged poetry on moral grounds, and he defended poetry while accepting the terms of the attackers. Even in the relatively short period in England between 1660, when the Puritan grip on English intellectual life and society was loosened, and the beginning of the nineteenth century, when the Evangelical spirit became a central influence in all spheres of intellectual life, "poetry without profit was often held to be trivial" (Abrams 1953: 16). "There were a few writers," says Wellek about this period, "who thought that poetry should only delight, but the majority of critics accepted moral utility as the primary aim of literature" (Wellek 1955: 21).

## 11.1.2 Defending the cultural legitimacy of literature

English criticism in the nineteenth century sees three important developments bearing on the way in which the cultural legitimacy of literature is established. The first grew out of the Romantic view that poetry was not imitation of external reality but expression of the inner subjective self ("the spontaneous overflow of powerful feeling"). This changed the conception of how poetry contributed to the reader's moral improvement:

> if early nineteenth-century writers made the traditional claim that valid art has a use beyond beauty, it was with an important and characteristic difference. Earlier critics had defined poems primarily as a delightful way of changing the reader's mind; the Wordsworthian critic, primarily as a way of expressing his own. The product effects human betterment, but only by expressing, hence evoking, those states of feeling and imagination which are the essential conditions of human happiness, moral decision, and conduct. By placing the reader in his own affective state of mind, the poet, without inculcating doctrines, directly forms character. (Abrams 1953: 329)

Poetry was no longer conceived as moral "instruction" to the reader, but as forming character directly, "without inculcating doctrines." Thus was the moral effectiveness of poetry guaranteed and its cultural legitimacy established. This view gained wide currency in nineteenth-century England not only among poets and lovers of poetry, but among the whole reading audience. Literature in England in the nineteenth century became accepted as a main source of moral improvement. The extent to which this view gained acceptance is perhaps best illustrated not by quoting from the great Victorian authors who had an interest in presenting their work as edificatory (for example, George Eliot 1963: 270) or from the great critics who championed the view (for example, Matthew Arnold 1973: 162), but rather from a public figure like John Morley, journalist, Member of Parliament, and biographer, "that very busy man,"

> when, despite more pressing demands on his time, he agreed to address a gathering of the University Extension movement in 1887 on the topic of "The study of literature." Among the generalities we might expect from that conjunction of speaker, topic, and audience, we find Morley emphasizing the special modern need "to find some effective agency for cherishing within us the ideal." This, he could declare without fear of being inappropriately controversial, "is the business and function of literature." And in spelling out the manner in which it might discharge this function, he reached for a similarly uncontentious litany of phrases: literature acts by "the cultivation of the sympathies and imagination, the quickening of the moral sensibilities, and the enlargement of the moral vision." (Collini 1991: 79; see also Morley 1890: 201; and for further examples, Baldick 1983: ch. 3)

The second development from the nineteenth century saw the literary critical tradition transform itself into cultural criticism. This cultural criticism came into being in the early and mid-Victorian periods as a sustained attack on the kind of society that developed in Britain during that period as a result of industrialization. The criticism was voiced in the periodicals which dominated the intellectual and social debate at the time, in pamphlets, lectures, speeches, reports, and sometimes also in full-length books. Cultural criticism was social and moral criticism, but it gained its peculiar character because of the role it assigned to a humanist education in the preservation and development of national culture. Central to this humanist education was literature (Baldick 1983: 19). Through its humanizing influence literature established not only its own cultural legitimacy but also the cultural legitimacy and moral mission of criticism. Criticism became as important as literature (Arnold 1962: 161–2), and poetry, in Arnold's famous phrase, was, in so far as it was good poetry, "criticism of life" (Arnold 1973: 46, 163).

Third, nineteenth-century criticism saw the beginning of a trend that was to become fully developed in the twentieth century. Critics became self-conscious about the a-philosophical nature of criticism and sometimes even adopted an anti-philosophical attitude. It was not so much that critics came to see literature as superior to philosophy or merely that literature should not, in spite of being concerned with the moral question "how to live" (Arnold 1973: 46), be reduced to philosophy. It was partly that criticism itself with its newfound responsibilities and social mission made a claim to be as important as philosophy, and partly that an explicit claim was made that criticism had a different logic from that of philosophical discourse. Critics like Arnold reject the relevance of principles and methods of argument to the critical conclusions that they want to establish. Thus Arnold's famous touchstone method does not involve principled argument. In examples of great literature "the substance and matter on the one hand, the style and manner on the other, have a mark, an accent, of high beauty, worth, and power" (Arnold 1973: 171). However, no theoretical account can be given of this "mark" or "accent": "if we are asked to define this mark and accent in the abstract, our answer must be: No, for we should thereby be darkening the question, not clearing it" (Arnold 1973: 171).

### 11.1.3 Anti-philosophical trends in criticism

In the twentieth century this rejection of philosophy took two forms. First, it became a major element in the practical criticism that developed in England from nineteenth-century cultural criticism in the early decades of the twentieth. One main representative of this type of criticism was F. R. Leavis, who carried on the social mission of criticism at the same time as he emphasized criticism, or "English," as a discipline of thought different from and opposed to philosophy (Leavis 1975: esp. pts 1 and 2). While practical criticism was anti-theoretical as well as anti-philosophical, a second development from cultural criticism also involved a rejection of philosophy:

> Beginning in the days of Goethe and Macaulay and Carlyle and Emerson, a kind of writing has developed which is neither the evaluation of the relative merits of literary productions, nor intellectual history, nor moral philosophy, nor epistemology, nor social prophecy but all these things mingled together into a new genre. This genre is often still *called* "literary criticism," however, for an excellent reason. (Rorty 1982: 66)

This "new genre" is a special form of literary criticism that has been given its own label:

> The most convenient designation of this new genre is simply the nickname "theory," which today has come to designate works that succeed in challenging and reorienting thinking in fields other than those to which they ostensibly belong because their analyses of language, or mind, or history, or culture offer novel and persuasive accounts of signification. (Culler 1988: 15)

It might seem odd that "theory" or Critical Theory is anti-philosophical, given that in one sense it is not anti-theoretical, but it is presented by some of its proponents as a new master-discipline that relegates philosophy to the sidelines: "I think that in England and America philosophy has already been displaced by literary criticism in its principal cultural function – as a source for youth's self-description of its own difference from the past" (Rorty 1980: 168 n6). In other versions "theory" becomes at the very least a genre of writing that deals more illuminatingly with the "same" problems as philosophy (de Man 1986: 8). However, one also finds within Critical Theory a suspicion of rational argument akin to that found in Arnold. This suspicion occurs on two different levels. First of all, as a new genre of writing, Critical Theory is trans-disciplinary and cannot therefore answer to disciplinary norms of argument:

> As instances of the genre of "theory," these works exceed the disciplinary framework within which they would normally be evaluated and which would help to identify their solid contributions to knowledge. To put it another way, what distinguishes the members of this genre is their ability to function not as demonstrations within the parameters of a discipline but as redescriptions that challenge disciplinary boundaries . . . Though they may rely on familiar techniques of demonstration and argument, their force comes – and this is what places them in the genre I am identifying – not from the accepted procedures of a particular discipline but from the persuasive novelty of their redescriptions. (Culler 1983: 8)

And, second, the later phase of Critical Theory that comprises poststructuralism and deconstruction also embraces a form of anti-rationalism the consequence of which is to construe all sorts of argument merely as forms of rhetoric which do not, because they cannot, answer to any normative standards. The notion of correctness is swallowed up by the notion of persuasion. At the same time Critical Theory is driven by an ethical imperative that takes on a strong political coloring.

"Literary theory, in the forms in which we know it," says Terry Eagleton, "is a child of the social and political convulsions of the 1960s" (Eagleton 1984: 88). The aspect of "theory" which aims to undermine the notion of rational argument and truth, and which consequently also removes the foundation of all moral, social, and aesthetic values, is motivated by a liberation ideology and has a political purpose. The notions of moral, social, and aesthetic value, as well as the notions of truth and of personal identity, serve, it is argued, to repress "voices" that would present political agendas based on values different from those on which the present social or cultural order is based. The exposure of the values on which this order rests as unfounded in reason or in nature deprives that order of its legitimacy and opens the way for a challenge to the ideas which this order embodies. So with Critical Theory too the moral mission motivates the theoretical stance.

### 11.1.4   Toward a refocusing of philosophical approaches to literature

A philosophy of literature has to contend with these two dominant features of the critical tradition: an a-philosophical practice that is not concerned with disinterested philosophical inquiry and an overriding concern with establishing the cultural legitimacy of literature by proving its moral worth. This is not an easy legacy to deal with from a philosophical perspective, not least because it has determined the framework for theoretical reflection about literature for more than two thousand years. Even today this legacy tends to dictate the concerns of philosophical reflection on literature. But it is a pernicious legacy because it has channeled thought about literature away from some obvious features that have received very little attention.

One of the central features of literature (or "poetry" broadly conceived) that was noted by Plato is the aim to please. That literature pleases and gives joy has been an experience recognizable in different cultures and different periods, and was noted by every critic until the beginning of the nineteenth century. It was considered a characteristic feature. "The end of writing is to instruct," says Johnson, "the end of poetry is to instruct by pleasing" (Johnson 1969 ll. 280–2). If there had been a tradition of philosophical inquiry dealing with literature, the constitution, nature, and quality of this experience would most probably have been one of its prime objects. However, in the absence of such a tradition and given the overriding concern with the moral worth of literature, the underlying logic of the apprehension that constitutes this recognizably valuable but non-instrumental experience has been left largely unexplored. When, in the philosophy of literature, the question of how a literary work is apprehended has arisen, the terms used to ask the question as well as the conceptual framework employed to give the answer have characteristically foreclosed any reference to such a value-experience.

Two different but related frameworks have been used to formulate, and provide terms for answering, the question of how literature is apprehended. When hermeneutics ceased to be merely a practical method for interpreting biblical or classical texts and, starting with Schleiermacher in 1817 (Schleiermacher 1998: 5), was developed into a general theory of understanding, literature was subsumed under a paradigm of apprehension that made the notions of understanding and interpretation central. Moreover, it was assumed that although different types of texts may need different hermeneutic methods, there is an underlying unity between these differences. Apprehending literary works involved the same epistemic process as understanding a legal document, a religious text, a historical account, and so on. In fact, in Dilthey the notion of "understanding" becomes the key concept designating how all forms of expression (*Ausdrück*) of what he calls "Erlebnis" or "lived experience" are apprehended and thus the key concept for characterizing the way in which "human studies" (*Geisteswissenschaften*) can yield knowledge of their object (Dilthey 1992: 102).

The second kind of framework used to formulate and answer the question of how literary works are apprehended has been the linguistic/semantic framework, giving prominence to the concept of word or sentence meaning. The literary work was supposed to be first and foremost a linguistic fact possessing meaning, and apprehending the work of literary art was fundamentally a matter of reconstructing its meaning. The linguistic/semantic perspective dominated twentieth-century criticism in all its forms from New Criticism through structuralism and poststructuralism.

Neither of these frameworks can integrate into the apprehension of the literary work the recognizably valuable but non-instrumental experience that has traditionally been referred to by the term "pleasure." Both frameworks go on to defend literature in terms of morally (politically or socially) beneficial insights, but exposure to these insights is taken to be external to the apprehension of a literary work. Neither framework takes up the challenge of explaining the distinctive pleasure of literature, not as an extra psychological bonus, but as something that is inherent in the very mode of apprehension that literature demands.

In order to give some idea what these frameworks cannot accommodate it may be useful to look at a passage from a little essay by Virginia Woolf entitled "Reading," from *The Common Reader*. Here she tries to render the experience of immersing oneself in imaginative literature. She does not give an analysis in abstract terms, but instead attempts to convey the content and importance of this kind of experience. The works she refers to, Elizabethan travel literature, are not paradigmatically "literary" in the manner of poetry or the novel, but they make certain demands on the reader also made by paradigmatic literary works, demands that constitute an important aspect of the reader's experience. "There is," she says,

> balm for our restlessness in conjuring up visions of Elizabethan magnanimity; the very flow and fall of the sentences lulls us asleep, or carries us along as upon the back of a large smooth-paced cart horse, through green pastures. It is the pleasantest atmosphere on a hot summer's day. They talk of their commodities and there you see them; more clearly and separately in bulk, color, and variety than the goods

brought by steamer and piled upon docks; they talk of fruit; the red and yellow globes hang unpicked on virgin trees; so with the lands they sight; the morning mist is only just now lifting and not a flower has been plucked. The grass has long whitened tracks upon it for the first time. With the towns too discovered for the first time it is the same thing. And so, as you read on across the broad pages with as many slips and somnolences as you like, the illusion rises and holds you of banks slipping by on either side, of glades opening out, of white towers revealed, of gilt domes and ivory minarets. It is, indeed, an atmosphere, not only soft and fine, but rich, too, with more than one can grasp at any single reading.

So that, if at last I shut the book, it was only that my mind was sated, not the treasure exhausted. Moreover, what with reading and ceasing to read, taking a few steps this way and then pausing to look at the view, that same view has lost its colors, and the yellow page was almost too dim to decipher. (Woolf 1966: 21–2)

The experience is one of enjoyment, and one ceases to read only when it gets too dark. One loses oneself in what one reads. And it is a highly articulated experience. It has, borrowing a term from photography or television technology, what may be called *high definition*. Such an experience does not, however, simply occur. It demands that the reader perceive the particularities and minute nuances that the work presents through its use of language, structure, and plot (if there is one). Reading is an act and to be successful it requires the exercise of the reader's own abilities. And for the act of reading imaginative literature, the abilities a reader needs most are imagination, discrimination, and sensibility. It is the exercise of these abilities in the reading of a work that *constitutes* the enjoyment. Virginia Woolf's enjoyment of Elizabethan travel literature is defined by her perception of what it says and how it says it. It is this perception that her essay on "Reading" is about.

The kind of experience that Virginia Woolf tries to render for us is central to the role and status of imaginative literature in our culture. The love of literature that springs from enjoyment has been *the* central force in the development and conservation of a literary tradition and a literary culture. This love for literature was movingly illustrated in *Fahrenheit 451*, where those who cared for imaginative literature formed their own outcast community in a book-burning society and *became* each and every one a work of literature by memorizing it and adopting the title as their future name.

## 11.2  The Way Forward

### 11.2.1  A framework for the enjoyment of literature

An adequate conceptual framework for describing the apprehension of a literary work would have to be able to accommodate this experience of enjoyment. The concepts of "meaning," "understanding," and "interpretation" are too narrow to capture this. So what would a philosophy of literature look like that restored to a central role the love of literature and the pleasurable experience that literature affords? An adequate theory would need to operate under fairly demanding constraints so as not to fall back into either sentimentalism or vague platitudes. What is needed is a robust *aesthetics* of literature, drawing on all that the discipline of aesthetics has to offer, and capturing a conception of literature that is true to the literary tradition.

### 11.2.1.1   Constraints on the theory

Some constraints are of paramount importance:

1   The theory should not remove the concepts of *meaning or interpretation* altogether from the critical vocabulary, for any critical practice without such terms would be impoverished indeed. The point is to incorporate the quest for meaning without letting it dominate the ends of critical practice.
2   The theory should not remove, but rather find the appropriate context for and the appropriate characterization of, the *cognitive values* traditionally associated with literature.
3   The theory should not be narrowly *hedonistic*. There have been attempts to explain the pleasures of reading in purely "sensory" terms, or even as "erotic." Famous modern exponents would include Roland Barthes (1976), who distinguishes *plaisir* and *jouissance* to describe modes of reading, and Susan Sontag (1994), who argued that "In place of a hermeneutics we need an erotics of art" (Sontag 1994: 23). Both ideas are playful and provocative but neither is the basis for a *philosophical* theory.
4   Nor should the theory be *formalistic* or *reductive* in characterizing the "love of poetry." It should not seek to reduce the complex nature of a literary response to any one aspect of literary pleasure, such as poetic imagery or plot structure or character development.
5   The theory should provide a context in which *literary value* is integrated into the very conception of literature and the literary response, not merely a by-product of the reading process.
6   Finally, the theory should incorporate all literary forms – lyric poetry, epic, drama, the novel, the short story – without giving implicit priority to one form over another (as New Criticism did to poetry, for example, and structuralism to narrative).

The point of highlighting these constraints – what follows will show, in general terms, how each constraint might be met – is to emphasize that an adequate framework for placing the enjoyment of literature at the center of a literary aesthetics need not abandon more traditional critical concerns, nor need it lead to a narrowing of focus. On the contrary, putting *appreciation* in central position does not eliminate but *refocuses* the principal theoretical concepts in literary criticism: meaning, interpretation, cognition, truth, form, value.

### 11.2.1.2  The notion of "appreciation"

A few preliminaries are needed about "appreciation." The term is used in different, often ill-defined, ways applied to all the arts and to literature. In appropriat-
ing it as a central concept in literary aesthetics it is important to keep the meaning
broad even if clearly bounded. It is broad because it covers all aspects of a literary response to a work; it is bounded because it covers precisely *literary* responses,
those responses to a work *as* literature. It is integral to this usage that the experience of literature *as literature* is sui generis, not reducible to, or merely an instance
of, responses to other kinds of linguistic products, whether they be philosophical
works, conversations, or one-off utterances. The point will come up again later.
Appreciation involves the recognition of, and the pleasurable experience in, distinctively literary (or aesthetic) features of a literary work. This is an active mode
of response, constrained by conventional expectations and procedures, calling for
perceptiveness, discrimination, and judgment. It is a learned response, requiring
training, and it is normative; there are correct ways of going about it. One consequence is that not every pleasure induced by reading literature, however warranted or legitimate, should be characterized as a literary pleasure or a pleasure
directed at literary qualities. Susan Feagin has offered an account of literary appreciation based essentially on affective response and emotion (Feagin 1996). Even
though she builds into appreciation elements of interpretation, reflection, and
meta-reflection, it becomes apparent that her focus on affect is too narrow, giving
prominence only to local responses to character and incident, and not providing
a framework for explaining global judgments of value (over a whole work) or able
to account for the pleasures of unity and coherence in a work (Lamarque 2000).

### 11.2.2  The role of meaning

The first constraint in developing a philosophy of literature based on appreciation
concerned the role of meaning. In analytical aesthetics (quite apart from the
hermeneutic and structuralist traditions) no topic has occupied more attention
than that of literary meaning and interpretation. The reason is clear, given the centrality of the theory of meaning in analytical philosophy. However, arguably, the
importation of philosophy of language into the philosophy of literature has had
badly distorting effects. Before addressing these distortions, an obvious premise
must first, and unequivocally, be acknowledged, namely, that literary works, of all
kinds, are essentially linguistic (in this they contrast with pictorial, sculptural, or
musical art forms). Clearly a necessary condition for appreciating a literary work
is that the meanings of its component words and sentences be grasped. Nor should
the potential difficulties of this preliminary condition be underplayed, for "explication," the determining of "contextual meanings" (the terms come from Beardsley 1981: 130ff), faces all the normal problems of meaning assignment, as well
as additional problems relating to the "hermeneutic circle," the influence of the

whole over the part and the part over the whole. It is clear that at the level of explication, *meaning* is central, and if there is a role for philosophical theories of meaning then it is here that they have their most natural application. However, it should be equally clear that explication of textual meaning is not all there is to literary appreciation. It is not an end in itself, at best only a stage in the interpretive process.

The mistake of many analytical philosophers of literature is to generalize the methods, and indeed the problems, of *explication* to literary interpretation in the round, and by implication import meaning to the very core of literary appreciation. This mistake is evident in a number of facets of recent debate. One is the elevation of the *intention* issue to the highest priority in the philosophy of literature. The question of what importance to assign authorial intention in literary criticism, whether there is an "intentional fallacy" involved, has been around for over half a century (see the collections of essays in Newton-de-Molina 1976; Iseminger 1992). But a notable trend, among philosophers, in the past twenty years or so has been to pursue the debate in terms drawn from outside literary criticism. Thus, in not untypical examples, Noël Carroll defends a version of intentionalism by appeal to the model of *conversation* (see his essay in Iseminger 1992), and Robert Stecker utilizes the speech-act notion of "utterance meaning" (Stecker 1997: ch. 9). Both accounts, it could be argued, are reductive, failing to capture what is distinctive about literature (Lamarque 2001). If the debate on intention restricted itself to the proper domain of meaning in literary criticism, namely, explication, then there might be some justification in it. But it is apparent that little heed is given to the distinction between textual meaning at a sentential level and interpretation applied to whole works.

It is here that a second distortion enters: an uncritical use of the expression "the meaning of the work." It is far from clear what sense, if any, could be given to the phrase "the meaning of *Pride and Prejudice*," or how the sentence "*Macbeth* means . . ." might be completed, as if those expressions identified, or could identify, some determinate entity (see the essays "Text and Meaning" and "The 'Meaning' of a Literary Work" in Olsen 1987). But even more problematic is the common assumption that such meaning as a whole work might have is on a par with the meaning that individual sentences have (an assumption explicit in Stecker [1997], who uses "utterance meaning" to apply to both). To think of a work of literature as a complex sentence or "utterance" calling for construal either in semantic terms or in terms of what a speaker intended is to miss the fact that literary works conform to their own conventional purposes (Olsen 1978) and are not reducible to conversational modes of communication (Lamarque 2001). To interpret a literary work as a whole is not just to recover its semantic content or to understand its component sentences; it is to appreciate how its aesthetically relevant features "hang together," what interest or value it has from a literary point of view, why it rewards close attention. Here we see the refocusing that an emphasis on appreciation brings to interpretation. Of course there is a element of meaning involved – it is readily conceded that a grasp of word and sentence meaning is a pre-condition for appreciation – but the pleasure associated with taking a literary interest in a work calls for much more than attention to linguistic meaning.

### 11.2.3   Cognitive values and the truth debate

Terms drawn from general aesthetics, such as coherence, unity, aesthetic feature, aesthetic value, are more useful for explaining literary-specific responses than terms drawn from philosophy of language. So it is, arguably, with the complex issue of cognitive values in literature. The highlighting of appreciation does not entail rejecting cognitivist elements in literary criticism – the idea, suitably refined, of *edification* in responses to literature – but demands a proper characterization of it which both does justice to the critical tradition and preserves the autonomy of literature among cognitive discourses, including the sciences and philosophy.

Clearly the interest readers take in literature is partly an interest in what particular works are *about*, and it can be argued that a special kind of *aboutness* – not mere reference, but thematic content – captures best the cognitive aspects of appreciation (Lamarque and Olsen 1994: ch. 16). A theme gives unity to a work, and one function of literary appreciation is to elicit themes through attention to the work's subject matter. Echoing the earlier point about meaning, thematic content is not semantic content, and someone fully apprised of a work's semantic content might still fail to appreciate what it is *about* in this literary sense. It is a mark of a work's enduring interest that it sustains themes of a universal or "perennial" nature (Lamarque and Olsen 1994: ch. 16). Perhaps that is at the heart of Aristotle's defense of poetry.

Appeal to thematic content or "vision" offers a more promising focus for characterizing the cognitive element of literature than does too hasty an evocation of "poetic truth." The trouble with "truth" is that it comes heavy-laden with connotations from the scientific or philosophical enterprise – verification, proof, argument, debate, refutation, the practice of inquiry – none of which is well suited to the values properly associated with poetry. Appeals to truth in literature always start off on the wrong foot, trying to distance the desired kind of truth from the familiar kind (see Hospers 1946; Falck 1989). But a work's thematic content is integral to the work that it is, not merely under general descriptions, for many works can be about duty and desire, public and private morality, pride and prejudice, but in the specific way that the themes emerge from character and incident or image and symbol. Those over the centuries who have sought to defend the cultural legitimacy of literature in terms of its moral truth would have been better concentrating on the moral content in the sense described. Many of the perennial themes associated with literature are of a moral nature and much of the interest in literature is in the way it develops its moral content. But those who seek moral *truth* simply distort the specific contribution that literary works can make, judging literature against a philosophical or theological standard that misses all that is peculiar and distinctive about the literary. To characterize what a work is about, thematically, in moral terms and to derive (and find support for) moral principles from a work are two utterly different kinds of enterprise (Lamarque 1996: ch. 8).

A key feature of the pleasure that literature affords is the demands it makes on the imagination. It is through the imaginative reconstruction of a work's content that readers come to see what value or interest the work holds. Literature has long been associated with the imagination, not just as a product of the imagination but also as a prompt for it (on the latter, see Walton 1990). Even the most passionate defenders of the cognitive benefits of literature are likely to appeal as much to imagination as to truth. Shelley, for example, who famously described poets as the "unacknowledged legislators of the world," praised poetry not for its truth but for the way it "enlarges the circumference of the imagination by replenishing it with thoughts of ever new delight" (from *A Defence of Poetry* [1821], in Seldon 1988: 484). And Iris Murdoch, who does not shy from the truth idiom, puts most emphasis on the "liberated truth-seeking creative *imagination*" (Murdoch 1993: 321, italics in original) associated with literature. Literary appreciation is partially but crucially an exercise in the imagination. Only through the imagination can a reader grasp the connectedness of a work's elements round its core themes. In this lies the pleasure of literature and also, through reflection on universal themes, its edification. Those who defend the integration of Horace's *utile* and *dulce* would be well advised to start here.

### 11.2.4 *Appreciation and formalism*

It is often assumed that a focus on the pleasures of literature, especially poetry, is primarily a focus on formal features, such as fine writing, powerful imagery, mellifluous prose, and well-structured plots. Distinctively literary qualities have come to be thought of as formal qualities, verbal, structural, stylistic, or rhetorical. Part of the reason stems from the popular conception that what makes poetry distinctive is precisely its use of language, its "poetic devices," like rhyme, meter, image, or symbol. Behind this conception lies a general classification of literature as "belles-lettres." But there has also been theoretical encouragement in the pervasive formalism in twentieth-century criticism. Russian and Czech formalism in the early decades of the century sought to identify "literariness" through language functions such as "the palpability of signs" (Jan Mukarovsky) or "foregrounding" (Roman Jakobson). In Anglo-American New Criticism, distinctive literary qualities were found in "paradox" (Cleanth Brooks) or "ambiguity" (William Empson), again formal properties of language. And post-World War II structuralism introduced formalism into studies of narrative, for example, identifying *metaphoric* and *metonymic* modes of narrative (Lodge 1977) or distinguishing "readerly" from "writerly" texts (Barthes 1975).

Such formalism is of little use for an adequate theory of literary appreciation. Formal properties, including those listed, occur in all kinds of texts to different degrees, so they do not themselves mark off what is of value in literature. More pertinently, no formal feature of a text is *intrinsically* of literary interest or value. What matters is the aesthetic function assigned to formal features within an overall conception of a work. An aesthetic (thus literary) feature *emerges* only within the context of a literary reading. In other contexts it remains merely inert, merely a formal textual property. If seven types of ambiguity were discerned in a philosophical text this would be a flaw in the text, a nuisance, or a problem to be overcome. Ambiguity is a value in poetry only to the extent that it contributes to a valued end, for example, exploring depths of meaning or rendering a complex emotion.

Other conceptions of the pleasure of reading focus less on formal features, more on the treatment of character. Here is George Henry Lewes extolling the virtues of Charlotte Bronte's *Jane Eyre*, in an early review (1847):

> Almost all that we require of a novelist she has: perception of character, and power of delineating it; picturesqueness; passion; and knowledge of life. The story is not only of singular interest, naturally evolved, unflagging to the last, but it fastens itself upon your attention, and will not leave you. The book closed, the enchantment continues. With the disentanglement of the plot, and the final release of the heroine from her difficulties, your interest does not cease. You go back again in memory to the various scenes in which she has figured; you linger on the way, and muse upon the several incidents in the life which has just been unrolled before you, affected by them as if they were the austere instructions drawn upon a sorrowing existence, and not merely the cunning devices of an author's craft. (Lewes 1847: 690)

The experience described here will be familiar to readers of literature and valued by them, but it can only be part of a full literary appreciation. Again, character development, like formal features of a text, can hold literary or aesthetic interest only to the extent that it contributes to a more global achievement of a work. A finely drawn or memorable character in a novel or drama is of little satisfaction if in the end it distracts from, and does not cohere with, other elements. Herein lies one difference between literary narrative and biography or history. We do not demand of a minor character in a biography – one that captures our interest momentarily – that it fit into a pattern or contribute to the aesthetic effect of the whole. However, the pleasures of reading literature are (partially) aesthetic pleasures of connectedness, where appreciation is directed to an overall achievement and to an imaginative vision in which the means are consonant with the ends. This is far from an arid formalism, nor is it reductive in giving priority to any specific aspect, be it "literary language," character development, or moral truth.

### 11.2.5   *Literary value*

Value has been integral to the account sketched above. Associating literature with a distinctive kind of appreciation is already to associate it with a distinctive kind of value. What are appreciated are the values that the work manifests. Note how different this is from *understanding*, for it is possible to understand something without valuing it. The prevailing formalism in twentieth-century criticism, previously noted, has encouraged a value-free criticism (if that is not a solecism), where mere description has replaced judgment. But literature cannot be cut off from value, for to attend to literature *as* literature is already to submit to an expectation of value, to an assumption, defeasible of course, that a work will reward literary attention, that there is interest to be found and pleasure to be gained.

Any adequate account of literary value will be tied to a conception of what makes literature distinctive among discourses. Those who deny, or merely relativize, literary value are most likely to deny any distinctiveness about literature, a position common within poststructuralism (see Herrnstein Smith 1988). On the view that all texts are undifferentiated and all values instrumental, there are no values attached to literature per se. But on theories which do seek out defining attributes of literature, criteria for literary value will be linked to these attributes. For example, meaning-based accounts will promote the value of *complexity of meaning*. Works with hidden or multiple meanings or works calling for complicated processes of interpretation will be more highly valued (at least receive more attention) than works whose meaning is relatively accessible. Thus it was that New Critics preferred poetry to narrative and the poetry of Donne or T. S. Eliot to that of Shelley or Rupert Brooke. Those critics, like F. R. Leavis, who give prominence to moral truth as a literary end will postulate a "great tradition" which elevates George Eliot and Henry James over Laurence Sterne and Thomas Hardy (Leavis 1960).

Setting aside particular literary judgments, it is clear that an account of reading in terms of appreciation will foreground the values sought by this mode of apprehension. It is a truism that what is valued is what is appreciated, just as it is a truism that what makes literature valuable is what makes something literature in the first place (given the evaluative nature of the concept "literature"). But the focus on appreciation and on attending to a work *as literature* is by no means empty and yields values different from those theories that give prominence to literary language or moral truth. The values reside in the pleasurable experience that literature can provide, which in turn rests on the aesthetic qualities (not formalistically defined) that literature exhibits.

An objection to equating literary value with the pleasures of literature might be that a higher value will be placed on "pleasing" works than on those that are troubling, dissident, or tragic. Indeed, how could tragedies, often thought to be the pinnacle of literary excellence, have any value on an account that stresses "pleasurable experience"? In fact there is a long-standing debate about the precise nature of the "pleasures of tragedy" (see Hume 1993; Feagin 1983; Nuttall 1996), yet few would deny that tragic drama can afford a kind of pleasure, indeed a pleasure associated with aesthetic qualities, broadly conceived, and literary presentation. The objection wrongly associates literary pleasure with merely sensuous forms of delight. In fact the works – comedies, light dramas, humorous verse – which do most to lighten the spirit through laughter and playfulness are often deemed to be less rewarding for literary appreciation than those of a more reflective or even darker tone. There is nothing in the theory of appreciation that contradicts this.

### 11.2.6  The diversity of literature and literary practice

It is often a stumbling block for attempts to define literature that literary works take such diverse forms, from short lyric poems to triple-decker novels, from comic verses to the great tragedies. Any essentialist focus on local formal features – language, structure, or rhetoric – seems to run up against a ready supply of counterexamples. Correspondingly, it might be thought that the pleasures afforded by literature are themselves too diverse to yield substantial generalizations across all literary types and instances.

It is no part of a philosophical analysis of literary appreciation to play down the variety of literary works. But just as moral philosophers can reflect on moral choice, say, or the difference between moral and prudential reasons, without denying the limitless range of human action and character, so the philosopher exploring the distinctiveness of literature and the logic of literary appreciation need not postulate a false homogeneity among literary works. That the expectations raised, and the rewards gained, from reading a novel, watching a drama, or pondering a lyric should be radically different in important respects does not affect the premise that in virtue of inviting *literary attention* all three can yield experiences that should have some equally important aspects in common. The distinctions that matter in this context are less those between literary genres than those between different kinds of reading practices and kinds of interest. To adopt a *literary point of view* on a text, whatever literary genre that text belongs to, is to follow conventions of a broadly prescriptive nature (Lamarque and Olsen 1994; Lamarque 1996). Training in literary appreciation is not, *pace* Richard Rorty, indistinguishable from training in philosophy, the social sciences, or psychology. The practices associated with these modes of discourse are different, as standard educational divisions acknowledge.

Literary education is an education in how to read and enjoy works of literature. It should not be presumed that appreciating literature as literature is an innate or natural aptitude, for which training is superfluous, any more than appreciation of any art form is merely intuitive. Nor is the appreciation of literature – given formal expression in literary criticism – reducible to modes of understanding or interpretation found in other practices. Literary education is an initiation into its own practice, and those who have skills in the practice learn how to make the appropriate discriminations and how to enhance the experience of value conventionally sought. Acquiring a critical vocabulary is not sufficient, nor arguably necessary, for appreciation; the use of critical concepts is at best a means to, not a sign of, appreciation. Those with knowledge of literature and a feel for the literary seek a special kind of pleasure from the works they read; a pleasure that demands further readings, that discerns emergent aesthetic qualities easily missable by those whose interests are purely linguistic or those driven single-mindedly by thoughts of moral edification; a pleasure in the coherence and connectedness in a work, the way that thematic content gives shape to subject and image; and a pleasure that is not instrumental or utilitarian but a pleasure in the literary for its own sake.

## Note

1 The literary treatise *On Sublimity*, of which about two-thirds survives, is ascribed by the medieval tradition to "Dionysius Longinus" or "Dionysius or Longinus." Until the early nineteenth century, it was generally believed to be by the third-century rhetorician Cassius Longinus. Internal evidence, especially the chapter on the decline of oratory (44), points, however, to an earlier date, some time in the first century AD. However, the treatise is still referred to as Longinus' *On Sublimity*.

## References

Abrams, M. H. (1953). *The Mirror and the Lamp: Romantic Theory and the Critical Tradition*. New York: Oxford University Press.

Arnold, Matthew (1962). "The Function of Criticism at the Present Time." In R. H. Super (ed.), *The Complete Prose Works of Matthew Arnold*. Vol. III: *Lectures and Essays in Criticism*. Ann Arbor: University of Michigan Press: 258–85.

——(1973). "Wordsworth" and "The Study of Poetry." In R. H. Super (ed.), *The Complete Prose Works of Matthew Arnold*. Vol. IX: *English Literature and Irish Politics*. Ann Arbor: University of Michigan Press: 36–55, 161–88.

Baldick, Chris (1983). *The Social Mission of English Criticism 1848–1932*. Oxford: Clarendon Press.

Barthes, R. (1975). *S/Z*, trans. R. Miller. London: Cape. (Original work pub. Paris: Seuil, 1970.)

——(1976). *The Pleasure of the Text* trans. R. Miller. London: Cape. (Originally pub. as *Le Plaisir du Texte*. Paris: Seuil, 1975.)

Beardsley, Monroe C. (1981). *Aesthetics: Problems in the Philosophy of Criticism*. 2nd edn. Indianapolis: Hackett.

Collini, Stefan (1991). *Public Moralists: Political Thought and Intellectual Life in Britain 1850–1930*. Oxford: Oxford University Press.

Culler, J. (1983). *On Deconstruction: Theory and Criticism after Structuralism*. London: Routledge and Kegan Paul.

——(1988). "Literary Criticism and the American University." In *Framing the Sign: Criticism and its Institutions*. Oxford: Blackwell: 3–40.

de Man, Paul (1986). "The Resistance to Theory." In *The Resistance to Theory*. Manchester: Manchester University Press: 3–40.

Dilthey, Wilhelm (1992). "The Rise of Hermeneutics." In Gayle L. Ormiston and Alan D. Schrift (eds), *The Hermeneutic Tradition: From Ast to Ricoeur*. Albany, NY: State University of New York Press: 101–14. (Originally pub. as "Die Enstehung der Hemeneutik," *Gesammelte Schriften*, Vol. V. Stuttgart: B.G. Teubner; Göttingen: Vandenhoeck and Ruprecht, 1964: 317–31.)

Dryden, John (1970). "Of Dramatic Poesy: An Essay." In James Kinsley and George Parfit (eds), *John Dryden: Selected Criticism*. Oxford: Oxford University Press: 16–76. (Originally pub. 1668.)

Eagleton, Terry (1984). *The Function of Criticism: From The Spectator to Post-Structuralism*. London: Verso.

Eliot, George (1963). "The Natural History of German Life." In Thomas Pinney (ed.), *The Essays of George Eliot*. New York: Columbia University Press: 266–99. (Originally pub. 1856.)

Falck, C. (1989). *Myth, Truth and Literature*. Cambridge: Cambridge University Press.

Feagin, Susan L. (1983). "The Pleasures of Tragedy." *American Philosophical Quarterly*, 20: 95–104.

——(1996). *Reading with Feeling: The Aesthetics of Appreciation*. Ithaca, NY: Cornell University Press.

Herrnstein Smith, Barbara (1988). *Contingencies of Value: Alternative Perspectives for Critical Theory*. Cambridge, MA: Harvard University Press.

Hospers, John (1946). *Meaning and Truth in the Arts*. Chapel Hill, NC: University of North Carolina Press.

Hume, David (1993). "Of Tragedy." In Stephen Copley and Andrew Edgar (eds), *Selected Essays*. Oxford: Oxford University Press: 126–32.

Iseminger, G., ed. (1992). *Intention and Interpretation*. Philadelphia: Temple University Press.

Johnson, Samuel (1969). *Preface to Shakespeare's Plays*. London: Scholar Press.

Kennedy, George A. (1993). "Christianity and Criticism." In George A. Kennedy (ed.), *The Cambridge History of Literary Criticism. Vol. 1: Classical Criticism*. Cambridge: Cambridge University Press: 300–46.

Lamarque, P. V. (1996). *Fictional Points of View*. Ithaca, NY: Cornell University Press.

——(2000). Review of Susan L. Feagin, *Reading With Feeling*. *Mind*, 109: 145–9.

——(2001). "Appreciation and Literary Interpretation." In M. Krausz (ed.), *Is There a Single Right Interpretation?* University Park, PA: Penn State University Press: 285–306.

Lamarque, P. V. and Olsen, S. H. (1994). *Truth, Fiction, and Literature: A Philosophical Perspective*. Oxford: Clarendon Press.

Leavis, F. R. (1960). *The Great Tradition*. London: Chatto & Windus.

——(1975). *The Living Principle: "English" as a Discipline of Thought*. London: Chatto & Windus.

Lewes, George Henry (1847). Review of Charlotte Bronte, *Jane Eyre*. *Fraser's Magazine*, December. (Extract reprinted in Charlotte Bronte, *Jane Eyre*, ed. Richard J. Dunn. New York: Norton 1971: 447.)

Lodge, D. (1977). *The Modes of Modern Writing: Metaphor, Metonymy, and the Typology of Modern Literature*. London: Edward Arnold.

Morley, John (1890). "On the Study of Literature." In John Morley, *Studies in Literature*. London: Macmillan: 189–228.

Murdoch, Iris (1993). *Metaphysics as a Guide to Morals*. Harmondsworth: Penguin.

Newton-de-Molina, D., ed. (1976). *On Literary Intention*. Edinburgh: Edinburgh University Press.

Nuttall, A. D. (1996). *Why Does Tragedy Give Pleasure?* Oxford: Oxford University Press.

Olsen, S. H. (1978). *The Structure of Literary Understanding*. Cambridge: Cambridge University Press.

——(1987). *The End of Literary Theory*. Cambridge: Cambridge University Press.

Plato (1953). *Republic*. In *The Dialogues of Plato*, trans. Benjamin Jowett. Vol. II. 4th edn. Oxford: Oxford University Press.

Rorty, R. (1980). *Philosophy and the Mirror of Nature*. Oxford: Blackwell.

——(1982). "Professionalized Philosophy and Transcendentalist Culture." In *Consequences of Pragmatism: Essays: 1972–1980*. Brighton: Harvester: 60–71.

Russell, D. A. and Winterbottom, M., eds (1972). *Ancient Literary Criticism: The Principal Texts in New Translations*. Oxford: Oxford University Press.

Schleiermacher, Friedrich (1998). *Hermeneutics and Criticism: And Other Writings*, ed. and trans. Andrew Bowie. Cambridge: Cambridge University Press.

Seldon, R., ed. (1988). *The Theory of Criticism: From Plato to the Present*. London and New York: Longman.

Sidney, Sir Philip (1973). *A Defence of Poetry*. In Katherine Duncan-Jones and Jan van Dorsten (eds), *Miscellaneous Prose of Sir Philip Sidney*. Oxford: Clarendon Press: 73–121.

Sontag, S. (1994). "Against Interpretation." In *Against Interpretation*. London: Vintage: 3–14.

Stecker, R. (1997). *Artworks: Definition, Meaning, Value*. University Park, PA: Penn State University Press.

Walton, Kendall (1990). *Mimesis as Make-Believe: On the Foundations of the Representational Arts*. Cambridge, MA: Harvard University Press.

Wellek, René (1955). *A History of Modern Criticism 1750–1950. Vol. 1: The Later Eighteenth Century*. New Haven, CT: Yale University Press.

Woolf, Virginia (1966). "Reading." In *Collected Essays*. Vol. II. London: Hogarth Press: 12–33.

## Further reading

Booth, Wayne (1992). *The Company We Keep: An Ethics of Fiction*. Berkeley: University of California Press.

Cavell, Stanley (1979). *The Claim of Reason: Wittgenstein, Skepticism, Morality, and Tragedy*. Oxford: Oxford University Press.

Danto, Arthur (1987). "Philosophy and/as/of Literature." In Anthony J. Cascardi (ed.), *Literature and the Question of Philosophy*. Baltimore: Johns Hopkins University Press: 1–23.

Eldridge, Richard (1989). *On Moral Personhood: Philosophy, Literature, Criticism, and Self-Understanding*. Chicago: Chicago University Press.

Griffiths, A. Phillips, ed. (1984). *Philosophy and Literature*. Royal Institute of Philosophy Lecture Series 16. Cambridge: Cambridge University Press.

Ingarden, Roman (1973). *The Literary Work of Art: An Investigation on the Borderlines of Ontology, Logic, and Theory of Literature*, trans. George G. Grabowicz. Evanston, IL: Northwestern University Press.

Lamarque, Peter (2000). "Literature." In B. Gaut and D. M. Lopes (eds), *The Routledge Companion to Aesthetics*. London: Routledge.

Levinson, Jerrold, ed. (1998). *Aesthetics and Ethics*. Cambridge: Cambridge University Press.

Livingston, Paisley (1990). *Literary Knowledge: Humanistic Enquiry and the Philosophy of Science*. Ithaca, NY: Cornell University Press.

New, Christopher (1999). *Philosophy of Literature: An Introduction*. London: Routledge.

Nussbaum, Martha (1990). *Love's Knowledge: Essays on Philosophy and Literature*. Oxford: Oxford University Press.

——(1995). *Poetic Justice: The Literary Imagination and Public Life*. Boston: Beacon Press.

Palmer, Frank (1992). *Literature and Moral Understanding*. Oxford: Clarendon Press.

Skilleås, Ole Martin (2001). *Philosophy and Literature: An Introduction*. Edinburgh: Edinburgh University Press.

# Chapter 12

# The Philosophy of the Visual Arts: Perceiving Paintings
## *Joseph Margolis*

### 12.1

In speaking broadly of "the visual arts" one may intend to collect artworks of the most diverse kinds: architecture, for instance, landscaping, décor, couture, decoration, and other forms of design. But conventional usage singles out painting and sculpture without prejudice to whatever else may be included, except that painting and sculpture (already categories that threaten to be too protean for useful generalization) are assumed to collect the principal specimens of what we have in mind when we wish to theorize about "the visual arts"; where, that is, the addition of architecture or décor is likely to introduce considerations very different from what would be featured in speaking of painting and sculpture. This is not always so, of course, as when we resist treating van der Weyden's triptych *The Adoration of the Lamb* as a painting separable from its place near the altar of St Baaf's. Usually, one thinks of easel painting to provide a sense of acceptable exemplars, though not so as to disallow Michelangelo's Sistine ceiling or Frank Stella's shaped panels, or Anselm Kiefer's mixed media hangings, or Chartres' windows, or Schwitters's collages, or Mapplethorpe's photographs. But when we consider a goodly selection of "canonical" paintings – perhaps more than sculpture – we are drawn to admit that the salient philosophical questions ask: "What is a painting?," meaning by that to specify something of its peculiar ontological features and why we are interested in the distinctive way a painting "works" as a painting; and "What is it to see a painting as a painting?," meaning by that to specify something of the conditions peculiar to the epistemological achievement of viewing paintings as paintings, and what such viewing yields in the way of understanding paintings as such.

No sooner do we admit the laxity, even prejudice, of the concept than we are led to concede that, as distinct from the modern tradition of western painting (and sculpture), much that we now include as art or fine art, the "art" of the medieval church for instance, could not have been included, except by a deformation (or transformation) of what was prized in such visual work, before the visual image (in the modern sense) displaced the visual presence of the sacred (Belting 1994). So the classificatory effort carries in its wake a changeable notion of what is of focal importance in addressing visual art itself. James Elkins, for instance, has formulated a very strong brief against the privileging of what in the West we tend to think of as the visual arts, reminding us of the very different practices and traditions of non-western visual "art" and the "popular" arts and, most significantly today, the "non-art" images of science, technology, and communicating "information," which provide the preponderant bulk of visual images. That they tend to be discounted as "non-art" (that is, that they are simply excluded from the canons of the West) does not justify denying the fact (Elkins argues persuasively) that "visual expressiveness, eloquence, and complexity are not the proprietary traits of 'high' or 'low' art, and . . . that we have reason to consider the history of art as a branch of the history of images, whether those images are nominally in science, art, writing, archaeology, or other disciplines" (1999: 4).

The principal thing is that, though our two questions are hardly the same, they are inseparable; for, in general, there is no way to specify the perceivable features of the world without implicating our perceiving them; what we take the objective world to be like must be adequated to our competence to discern those features. That is in fact the supreme lesson, construed in very different ways, developed by Kant and deepened by Hegel (allowing for perception's being historicized), which sets a *conditio sine qua non* for all defensible, genuinely modern theories of knowledge and reality. Furthermore, if we agree that the paradigm of perception is what humans can actually report they perceive – or concede, by their own lights, what other creatures perceive though those creatures cannot themselves report the fact – then, if perception is theory-laden and subject to historical variation, to different saliences, and to different forms of habituation, and if (more pointedly) artworks are deliberately contrived artifacts and *their* perception conformably disciplined (also artifactual), then it is doubtful that either artworks or their perception will yield universal regularities or necessities ranging over the whole of the visual arts (no matter how carefully the visual arts are defined). In that case, we may as well feature whatever we take to be most central and important for what are indisputably included in the West's conception of the great arts of the world.

For example, Brunelleschi and Alberti are said to have been the first to have discovered the vanishing point in linear-perspective drawings; that is, a certain visual illusion constant to eyes trained to view two-dimensional representations of space as having three-dimensional import. In this sense Brunelleschi began to formulate the "universal," so-called "natural" elements of perspective; if so, then Masaccio and Masolino were the first to apply Brunelleschi's rules in the form of what has been called "horizon line isocephaly" in the frescoes of the Brancacci Chapel (Santa Maria della Carmine, Florence): that is, lining up the heads of figures in the same perceived depth in a receding distance. The important point to notice, however, in Masaccio's *Tribute Money* and *The Healing of the Lame Man*

*and the Resurrection of Tabitha* (attributed to Masolino), is that the linear align-
ment tolerates a measure of perceptible deviation controlled by an interpreted
grasp of what may be said to be the pictorial and perceptual "intent" of the entire
array; so that we see that what is perceived is itself informed by (does not risk too
great a deviation from – but could) the supposed perspectival rules of the *artifactual* (perceived) space. The point to bear in mind is that the visual structures
of the painting *cannot be perceived* at all if we disallow the corollary that the *perception* of such structures is itself an *artifact of our theory of perceiving paintings*
(White 1987: ch. 9; Edgerton 1975: ch. 2; contrast Danto 1991).

Jan van Eyck's intriguing painting, *Portrait of Giovanni Arnolfini and his Wife
Giovanna Cenami,* poses (according to Hubert Damisch) the problem of two vanishing points fixed by the ambiguous function of the mirror: the point at which
the artist witnesses the marriage (from where he actually stands viewing it) and
the point reflected in the mirror (signifying his assigned position in the painting),
both within the space of the mirror's circle (Damisch 1994: 130–1). This is said
to be not unusual in Flemish work of the period; and indeed Erwin Panofsky
counts several other vanishing points in the *Arnolfini* which are apparently visually acceptable in the composition as a whole. In fact, Panofsky counts "four central
vanishing points instead of one" in the Arnolfini study (1434) as opposed to the
"nearly contemporary and relatively comparable Italian work," Masolino's *Death
of Saint Ambrose* (*c.*1430), which is "fairly 'correctly' constructed," that is, constructed in accord with Brunelleschi's rules. Van Eyck, it seems, was not familiar
with Brunelleschi's findings (Panofsky 1971: 3, 7). But both Panofsky and
Damisch think of perspective in paintings as *perspectiva artificialis* (rather than
merely *naturalis* – the perspective of natural optics). Hence, Damisch views perspective as "a model for thought" (1994: xiii, 446–7); and Panofsky thinks of perspective as a "symbolic form" – more or less a matter of cultural convention
(1991). Damisch views perspective, then, in his structuralist way and Panofsky
does so as a supporter of Ernst Cassirer's vision.

Seen thus, the "rules" of pictorial perspective can hardly fail to be at least partly
"heuristic" or intentionally adjusted to the purpose of the artist's rendering of pictorial space. Damisch's "shaggy dog" story of the "Urbino perspectives" – in the
rendering of the "*città ideale*" (the Urbino panel, pre-eminently) – certainly confirms how the development of "scientific" perspective (Brunelleschi's objective)
inevitably yields, and must yield, in the construction of "artificial" perspectives
ranging from architecture to theater to decoration (as Damisch summarizes the
matter), as in the choice of a perspectival mode *or* the mingling of various such
modes, possibly even answering to the artist's "need" to invent ever more complicated modes of composition. (That is, Damisch notes the perceptual tolerance
of "incompatible," even "incommensurable," perspective schemes within the same
painting, distinguishing between *perspectiva artificialis* and *naturalis*.) Certainly,
something of such complication informs Michel Foucault's (1970) perceptive
analysis of the baffling perspective of Velasquez's *Las Meninas* (that is, *if* perspective must be unified in terms of Brunelleschi's peep-hole). There seems always to

have been a certain yielding to Alberti's advice to favor a "sensate wisdom" over the "strict" geometry of natural perspective: the variations, here, clearly defy any single perspectival reading (Damisch 1994: 425–32; Steinberg 1981, cited by Damisch).

But if that is so, then Rudolf Arnheim's (1974) gestalt conception of the "universality of perceptual patterns" is subtly, even if heroically, off the mark. Arnheim has always favored Köhler's notion of a "causal foundation" of perceived visual patterns in the physical structures of the nervous system (even if those structures are not themselves perceived). But his attractive heuristic schema – I can only call it that – of "centricity and eccentricity" (that is, the centrifugal centering of vectorial forces emanating from an individual center, say a person, and the admission of other similar centers among which the first counts only as one) is not really a distinction that *could* be construed in purely gestalt terms grounded in the physical, or somehow segregated (within visual perception) from any influences of an intentional or narrative or historical or interpretive nature.

Arnheim nowhere quite concedes the import of his own admission that his visual schema is itself infected by the understanding that the two "principles" he espouses apply "universally" to human life itself:

> I began to see that the interaction of centricity and eccentricity directly reflected the twofold task of human beings, namely, the spread of action from the generating core of the self and the interaction with other such centers in the social field. The task in life of trying to find the proper ratio between the demands of the self and the power and needs of other entities was also the task of composition. This psychological relevance justified the concern with the formalities of composition. (1988: ix; see also ch. 11)

But surely Arnheim has a metaphorical ratio in mind, one that affects his account of visual perception as well. He himself supplies a telltale (unintended) counterinstance in his much-admired *Art and Perception*: there, he mentions a fifteenth-century painting in which St Michael weighs "one frail little nude [man]" who "outweighs four big devils plus two millstones" in a pair of scales (1974). The colors and the forms and even certain tricks of visual emphasis are (really) insufficient (in any plausible gestalt sense) to tip the balance in the virtuous soul's favor. The only satisfactory explanation for the "visual" balance requires the executive role of the narrative interpretation of the scene! Nothing that Arnheim offers offsets the fatal implication. Even more compelling cases may be mentioned: for instance, James Ensor's canvasses of grotesque figures deliberately crowded into a smallish corner of the picture space that reminds us (by its absence) of the "normal" spacing and balance of such spaces. But Ensor's paintings, complete with garish colors, are hardly out of balance: their representational import justifies the visual order and makes it acceptable.

The most developed version of the position most opposed to Arnheim's is advanced by Marx Wartofsky. Wartofsky treats the perception of artworks (and more) as "a cultural and historical product of the creative activity of making pictures." He draws two radical conclusions: first, "that all theoretical attempts to construct a theory of vision, which presuppose that seeing is an essential, unchanging structure of [sic: 'or'?] process; or that the human eye is describable in some generic physiological way, are, if not fundamentally mistaken, then essentially incomplete"; and, second, "that there is no intrinsically veridical, or 'correct', mode of representation, that is, there is no criterion of veridicality that is not itself a product of the social and historical choices of norms and visual representation" (Wartofsky 1979: 272; see also Wartofsky 1972). Ultimately, there is no way to assign disjunctive contributions between biological nature and cultural history that contribute to perceptual functioning: we must think of vision as an indissolubly 'hybrid' competence, paradigmatically identified in cultural space (by dint of human reporting); this is the point of Hegel's contribution to the theory of knowledge and perception – in effect, against the perception of any *ding-an-sich*. Whatever is assigned as the stable underlying ingredient of the neurophysiology of perception is entirely inferential at the explanatory level; it cannot be perceptually compared.

The weighting of these two seeming sources of perception is confused (on both sides) in the well-known debate between E. H. Gombrich and Nelson Goodman (Gombrich 1972). "Visual" balance, perspectival "correctness," and the like – in two-dimensional representations – cannot in principle be freed from the narrative or interpreted coherence of their intentional order, but they cannot of course violate the bare physical conditions of sensory perception either. There simply is no direct inference from the perception of the physical world to the rule-like conditions for two-dimensional representation of any "intended" visual "world." What, for instance, are the perspectival constraints on the peculiar space (which possesses *some* three-dimensional import) in Picasso's *Three Musicians*? (or, indeed, in Picasso's variations on *Las Meninas*?)

Gombrich rather graciously concedes that "Nelson Goodman has persuasively argued against J. J. Gibson and me that 'the behavior of light sanctions neither our usual nor any other way of rendering space; and perspective provides no absolute or independent standard of fidelity'." But of course Gombrich is a great admirer of Constable's "scientific" solution of representing landscapes; and so he rightly asks: "Fidelity to what?" (Gombrich 1972: 129). Goodman is certainly right in what he is reported to have said here (Goodman 1968: 10–19). (Gombrich concedes he himself muddled his own thesis.) But Goodman appears to draw too extreme a conclusion from this dispute (and Gombrich's concession) – Gombrich *never* claimed that there *was* any uniquely or independently "natural" way to represent nature – viz., that the term "'resemblance' or 'likeness' is useless for any definition of pictorial standards" is simply false as well as a non sequitur.[1]

The essential point is this: "natural resemblance" *holds within the terms of representational convention* (*or*, better: *cultural construction*); hence, *realism* (in Gombrich's sense) need not confuse the validity of Brunelleschi's experiments and the acknowledgement of "natural resemblance" in *perspectiva artificialis*.

Gombrich clearly affirms that "iconicity is the basis of the visual image" (1982: 278). This, too, is not entirely perspicuous. What Gombrich should have said is that iconicity is the basis of visual realism, in that sense of "realism" that fits Gombrich's own reading of Constable's landscapes and the difference, for instance, between the "realism" of Picasso's *Woman with Chignon* (a gouache from 1904, which accords with the "realism" of Picasso's blue period and related periods) and a 1927 oil and plaster *Head* (Gombrich offers both pieces as specimens, both in the Chicago Art Institute) – the latter being, apparently, the head of a woman but executed in Picasso's familiar way of deforming the shapes and arrangement of the parts of a familiar representation of a head, so that we begin to make out with a little effort what "must" be the eyes, a mouth full of teeth, "probably" a length of hair, a nose with nostrils, and the like, the ensemble of which is *not*, in the sense intended, "realistic." That there is a "realistic" way of decoding the second is not the point at all; for the point is that, once trained in a run of possible ways of representing perceivable objects in nature, the spontaneous recognition of strong and detailed "resemblances" confirms what Constable achieved and what Gombrich views as realism. *If* Goodman meant to deny that there is any *such* responsiveness (which is not a matter of expertise or quickness in decoding any mode of representation), then he was surely wrong. Resemblance *is* "theory-laden"; but the *theory* of perception explains the sense in which it meets a brute biological limit (a disposition not otherwise specified) that we may guess at by comparison of perceptual tolerances and behavioral responses (themselves burdened in the same way).

Furthermore, Goodman (also Wartofsky) does indeed make extreme claims against this sort of "natural" realism – which, remember, is entirely compatible with the so-called "conventional" (or "arbitrary") nature of pictorial representation. Goodman's mistakes – they are palpable – depend, ultimately, on a confusion between would-be formal or semantic fixities and the testimony of perceptual fluency. Here are two obvious such mistakes:

> unlike representation, resemblance is symmetric: *B* is as much like *A* as *A* is like *B*, but while a painting may represent the Duke of Wellington, the Duke doesn't represent the painting.

> A Constable painting of Marlborough Castle is more like any other picture than it is like the Castle, yet it represents the Castle and not another picture – not even the closest copy. (Goodman 1968: 4, 5)

Goodman's remarks are, of course, hostage to his nominalism; but nominalism is utterly untenable in perceptual terms. For, *if* you concede that *resemblance* can be made determinate to any fluent degree by introducing an ("arbitrary") convention, you will have lost the argument! The extension of the resemblance to new cases will invite an operative sense of "natural" extension; and if you require a fresh convention at every step, you will defeat (before you start) the very point of the original claim. *Relevantly*, in cases of perceptual fluency, you will see the resemblance between a "realist" portrait of Wellington and Wellington as obviously closer than the portrait of Wellington and a representation of Marlborough Castle! Also, of course, the "direction" of the (intended) resemblance *is* a factor in assessing any would-be resemblance. On Goodman's story, we should be baffled by the claim that a picture of Marlborough Castle is "more like any other painting than it is like the Castle," for saying only that ignores the pertinent salience of the intended representations of the specimen paintings in question (see Tormey and Tormey 1979).

This goes some distance toward explaining why J. J. Gibson was so terribly baffled by the failure of all his "ecologically" sensible attempts to decode and retrieve the "information" about the natural world from pictures – information he thought to be (necessarily) embedded in two-dimensional representations: he willingly abandoned the interpretive role of the cognizing subject in natural perception and therefore could not plausibly recover such a function in the perception of paintings. But, of course, that is only to say that the perception of paintings is *not* the recovery of any pre-established harmony of the perceptual powers of animals and their perceivable world (even human animals) within their ecological niche! That is the *reductio* of Gibson's very clever – but obviously misguided – speculation:

> All along I have maintained that a picture is a surface so treated that it makes available a limited optic array of some sort at a point of observation. But an array of what! That was the difficulty. My first answer was, *an array of pencils of light rays*. My second was, *an array of visual solid angles*, which become *nested solid angles* after a little thought. My third answer was, *an array considered as a structure*. And the final answer was, *an arrangement of invariants of structure*. (Gibson 1979: 270; see also pt IV generally)

Of course Gibson could never find such invariances in any depictions that departed from whatever he took to be the informational constants of *natural* perception and perspective – a theory which Gombrich was frank enough to admit he favored (in his theory of realism), that is, combining a respect for the "conventional" styles of representational perspective and the persistence of realism under such variations (the Egyptian, for instance, as well as the Renaissance).

That is, in fact, already the master thesis of Panofsky's famous essay. Perspective in the modern sense – associated, say, with Brunelleschi and Dürer (influenced by Piero del la Francesca) – "translat[es] psychophysiological space into mathematical space; in other words [says Panofsky], an objectification of the subjective" (1991: 66). But, of course, Panofsky means an *artifactual* "objectification" of the "subjective," or visual, as a form of sensory experience; he does not mean the *replacement* – in the representation – of the visual by the "true objectivity" of natural space itself (whatever that may be thought to be). The objectification is made to serve the subjective or visual, but to do so in a way that immensely increases the control and rationality and legibility of the whole of represented space:

Perspective creates distance between human beings and things ("the first in the eye that sees, the second in the object seen, the third in the distance between them," says Dürer after Piero della Francesca); but then in turn it abolishes this distance by, in a sense, drawing this world of things, an autonomous world confronting the individual, into the eye . . . Thus the history of perspective may be understood with equal justice as a triumph of the distancing and objectifying sense of the real, and as a triumph of the distance-denying human struggle for control. It is as much a consolidation of the external world, as an extension of the domain of the self. (Panofsky 1991: 67–8)

## 12.2

If you accept the argument of the foregoing section, you surely see how and why the analysis of the perception of paintings cannot be separated from the analysis of the very nature (or ontology) of such curious objects. This is, of course, *not* to say that all paintings are representations or representations of things found in nature (or fictive extensions of or beyond nature). But paintings (and sculptures) are artifacts possessing intentional structure – "Intentional" structure, I should say (writing the term with a capital "I"), so as to signify that their significative or semiotic or symbolic or representational properties are culturally formed and culturally legible and not merely psychological. Though (or course) what is culturally determinate must correspond (must be "adequated") to what is distinctive in the emergence of selves, their culturally formed powers, and the cultural world they inhabit (see further Margolis 1995).

The peculiarity of artworks, then, lies in this: that, in spite of their lacking psychological standing, their Intentional properties remain ontologically real. This is precisely what the splendid history of perspective makes so clear, what, for instance, Panofsky's account of the "ambivalent method" of perspective confirms (1991: 68).[2] For there is no way to admit the existence of art except as inhabiting a distinctive sector of reality created in some *sui generis* way by human hands and human minds – emergently, Intentionally – by an extension of the very powers by which every human society first transforms its own offspring (its own "specimens" of *Homo sapiens*, so to say) into a second generation of linguistically (and culturally) apt selves, a remarkably dense world easily as close to us and as palpable as anything that is merely physical. My formula for capturing all of this is simply to say that art, like speech, is *uttered* by apt selves, who are themselves not dissimilarly "uttered" (more or less as a by-product of the fluent activities of an ongoing society).

The reason for a bit of caution here is that a crucial conceptual difficulty may be too easily overlooked. Quite recently, for instance, Jerrold Levinson, addressing the question of the nature of visual art and following to some extent Richard Wollheim's well-known conception of paintings as physical objects, neglects to explain just how, precisely, he means to account for expressiveness or representationality (or other "Intentional" structures – those, say, implicating *perspectiva artificialis*) in terms of the actual *nature* of a painting, its ontological standing, so to say. Levinson's treatment is of interest primarily because it is so up to date and so obviously informed by a thorough familiarity with the best-known views in current analytic philosophies of art. Nevertheless, his account is noticeably defective at the point of maximal interest. It is in fact impossible to say (on the evidence) just what Levinson's theory finally comes to. He says for instance:

> Particular physical artworks, such as paintings, typically have subtle aesthetic properties that natural physical objects (e.g., rocks or trees) and nonartwork artifacts (e.g., chairs or pencils) do not, and that is due to both their generally more specific essential patterning and their complicated intentional-historical governing, which brings them into an appreciatively relevant relation to the history of art and art-making. But an intentioned-and-specifically-configured physical object is still, in the important sense, a physical object: it is composed of matter, is at one place at one time, and is subject to a familiar range of causal interactions with other physical objects. (1996: 135–6)

This is an exceedingly slippery and problematic formulation, but it helps to orient us quickly to the principal questions. Notice that Levinson speaks of "an intention*ed*-and-specifically-configur*ed* physical object"; he does not speak of a physical object actually *possessing* or manifesting "intention*al*" (or, as I prefer, "Intentional") properties; paintings, he says, are "configured" – formed, shaped, contrived in the usual craft ways – but it is not clear that *their* being "configured" results in *their* actually possessing, as artworks, say, "stylistic," "genre," or expressively qualified perspectival structures (Intentional structures). Rocks and trees, just as chairs and pencils (unless of course one means, as Levinson does not, an Esherick chair – the one, say, in the Philadelphia Museum of Art!) – *may be* viewed in terms of natural perspective; but ordinary chairs clearly *lack* perspectival properties as part of their own Intentional structure. The "intention*ed*" properties of paintings are "relationally" assigned, it seems, as a result of what is curiously called "their complicated intentional-historical *governing*," which seems to signify either *causal* effects produced *in physical things* or intentional attributions borrowed from the artist's life and justified as a result of a physical object's being involved in a certain kind of craftsmanship and art history. There is no sign in Levinson's account that he could actually examine van Eyck's Arnolfini portrait and *find in it* the Flemish treatment of perspective Panofsky finds. On his own account, it looks as if he could only look at the canvas and paint and, because he *remembers* something of van Eyck's personal history (what he calls "intentional-historical governing"), could validly attribute to the physical object van Eyck's perspectival intentions regarding *it*! Of course, Levinson would never deny that we can directly read or hear one another's words, but he is unwilling to say (in the relevant sense) that we can look at one another's paintings and see them!

Some may not recognize in these somewhat tortured linguistic maneuvers a certain strong adherence to what, following Donald Davidson's lead, is now often called "naturalizing," that is, a philosophical policy on the scope of realism: the policy of restricting the term to the physical, the extensional, the non-intentional (unless heuristic or convenient) characterizations of actual things *explained* entirely (under the best conditions) in causal terms modeled on what is normally offered in the physical sciences (Davidson 1986; Rorty 1986). Roughly, to speak thus is to prefer the idiom (and deliberate limitations) of a lean form of the unity of science program. Something similarly spare plainly attracts Monroe Beardsley, Arthur Danto, Nelson Goodman, and (to a lesser extent) Richard Wollheim. If Levinson's idiom could be shown to be inadequate to our investigative needs, then so too would the idioms of those just mentioned. That would be a windfall.

In any case, Levinson adds that

> a painting or sculpture is not a brute object, on the order of a hunk, mass, or con- glomeration, but rather a specifically articulated one; if, for example, a painting is a piece of canvas and an amount of paint, it is only that canvas and that paint *condi- tioned and configured* in a specific way, and preserving a certain appearance, and not those things *simpliciter*, in any state or arrangement. (1996: 134)

He means, of course, that paintings are interesting hunks; but they are, finally, hunks!

As soon as you consider, however, a connoisseur's appreciation of the very dif- ferent spirit of perspective in Italian and Flemish painting shortly after Brunelleschi's discoveries, you see how impossible it is *not* to attribute directly to *them* "intentioned-and-configured" properties that are Intentional in the fullest and most ramified sense. Surely we can supplement, correct, even check our memory (or research) about the artist's intentions by examining the Arnolfini, say? Here, for instance, is Panofsky's comparison of the Arnolfini portrait and the *Death of St. Ambrose* (already mentioned), the first by a Flemish painter, the second by an Italian – to which is added a brief comparison of van Eyck and Piero della Francesca. (You must bear in mind what has already been said about the dual uses of the new perspective.) "What matters," Panofsky says,

> is that the Italian master conceives of light as a quantitative and isolating rather than a qualitative and connective principle, and that he places us before rather than within the picture space ... [w]here the death chamber of St. Ambrose is a complete and closed unit, entirely contained within the limits of the frame and not communicat- ing with the outside world, the nuptial chamber of the Arnolfini is, in spite of its cozy narrowness, a slice of infinity.

Continuing, he says:

> Millard Meiss has recently pointed out the close connection that exists between Jan van Eyck's *Madonna van der Paele* of 1436 and Piero della Francesca's Brera altar- piece produced for Frederico of Urbino in the early 'seventies ... Yet no two pic- tures so closely related in iconography and composition could be more different in

spirit. Piero's soaring basilica with its unbroken, windowless surfaces is majestic and well-contained, where Jan's small, low, circular church, seen as a "close-up" and communicating with the outdoors by a fenestrated ambulatory, is, like the Arnolfini portrait, both intimate and suggestive of infinity. (1971: 7; see also 1991: section IV)

I put it to you that this kind of comment could hardly have been made without invoking the art-historical experience of the artists of the time (and our own experience of course); and that, assuming that much, some sufficiently ramified Intentional idiom could not possibly be avoided. There is no conceivable argument for admitting the Intentionalized "second nature" of human selves and denying the propriety of applying its distinctions *to what they themselves "utter"* in the way of words and pictures. In fact, *if* the naturalizing idiom has any use at all, it must allow for the paraphrase of analyses like Panofsky's. And, whether or not naturalism's reductive intent could ever be sustained, none of the philosophers just mentioned has ever made a plausible case for it – nor indeed has anyone else. No one has ever shown that there are linguistic and explanatory resources in the "naturalizing" mode that could convincingly compare with the rigor and subtlety and fluency of the Intentional (art-historical) idiom. But if that is so, then it is completely unconvincing to suppose that the objectivity of the latter could be bested by an idiom that *offered no independent way to examine the actual properties of actual paintings*! What possible bearing could a merely general review of the cultural aptitudes of human selves provide that could not validate, perceptually, any objective analysis *of particular paintings* – say, of Panofsky's gauge? It seems a hopeless claim, if it is not merely a dependent paraphrase of the other.

Another argument may be mentioned. The whole point of construing paintings as mere physical objects (in Levinson's way) is to argue that, in principle, the description and explanation of particular paintings (on *their* side) need take into account no more than the purely physical properties of those paintings. That is why Levinson insists on mere canvas and paint (however "configured"): he plainly expects to be able to *supplement* the impoverished vocabulary (thereby allowed) by whatever may be added from the *side* of the artists and informed audiences who are not restricted in the same way in discourse about themselves! It is hard to see, as I say, how remarks restricted to their Intentional lives could possibly be pertinently *applied* in an objective way to any array of admitted paintings. But, in any case, *if* such properties could be imputed *objectively to the paintings*, we should have to explain (first) how Intentional properties *were* rightly ascribed to objects that, on the theory implicated, utterly lack such properties (physical objects).

Levinson nowhere addresses the question. It takes two forms. In one, any theorist would find himself obliged to account for the "*adequation*" of a painting's conceded nature and whatever further objectively ascribable properties it is deemed possible for it to have. In the other, a theorist would wish to provide a theory – an ontology of paintings, say – that fitted our best intuitions about how connoisseurship, prevailing interests, and philosophical puzzles could be met coherently and without paradox. Arthur Danto (1964) has, famously, distinguished between the "is" of identity and the "is" of "artistic identification," precisely because, *on the side of real perceivable objects*, adequation (between physical natures and Intentional attributes) obviously fails (see also Margolis 1998). For the one lacks what the other possesses. Conceptual adequation signifies that a would-be attribute may be claimed to be manifested by a thing of a given kind, *if* attributes of that kind already belonged to that thing's nature or could be rightly ascribed to its nature on the strength of an improved theory. (The standard example holds that it is not simply true or false that a particular stone smiled but that it is conceptually inappropriate to affirm smiling of any stone.)

Danto's attempted resolution treats artworks rhetorically (his own term), *not* in a realist way, so that the attributions are figuratively controlled by our primary grasp of the *artist's* intentional life vis-à-vis "a mere real thing" (*not*, on Danto's reading, "Intentional" in the sense already supplied, since the "intentional" is psychological). I believe every such concoction must fail on internal grounds.[3] Apart, however, from the difficulties already adduced, Danto (or Levinson) would need to show that the individuation and identity of an artwork *can* be managed by individuating and identifying a mere physical object or "mere real thing" – which is profoundly problematic if not plainly false; and he would need to show that the properties rightly ascribed to any artwork can or should be confined (or suitably controlled!) by reference to the original artist's intentions – which, on the hermeneutic evidence, seems much too sanguine.

If you add to these objections the adequation question and the significance of admitting an unrestricted Intentional idiom in discourse about human societies, it looks as if a better case can be made for parity between discourse about selves and discourse about what they "utter" (or what is nominalized from what they utter: their deeds, their speech, their history, their art). For, after all, what is the difference – in terms of conceptual resources – in speaking of persons or selves and of what they say and do and make? To force a disjunction seems to force on us an arbitrary and inexplicable impoverishment. Or, if it is not, then it is a palpable dodge to gain a fashionable form of (philosophical) realism by illicit means. A realism regarding artist's intentions, I should say, entails – does not merely loosely "implicate" – a realism regarding the Intentional properties of artworks themselves. That may be offered as ground zero for all conjoint epistemological and ontological speculations about paintings.

It is quite surprising to discover how widespread a habit it is, among theorists (philosophers) of art, to avoid addressing "the work of art" *as an actual object.* The obvious reason is that it is genuinely difficult to say what it *is* and what its conditions of identity and individuating boundaries are! That must be admitted. But if so, then whatever we affirm about the discipline of *perceiving* a painting will be hostage to our uncertainty here. Levinson and Danto fall back (for purposes of identifying artworks *and* for making criticism hew to the "rules" of objectivity addressed to "actual" objects) to a palpable *division* between the physical ("configured") properties of some physical object or materials that the artist has worked on and what (however generously construed) relevantly occupied his thought and craft.

You see how, inexorably, the argument proceeds. Once we treat paintings as deliberately contrived artifacts, we are bound to distinguish between *perspectiva artificialis* and *perspectiva naturalis*: there will always be an Intentional purpose in pictorial representation that, for one thing, changes with the changing interests of one historical society or another and, for a second, can never (except like the broken clock that tells time correctly twice a day) converge with "natural perspective" (Brunelleschi's trick). But if that is so, then it is more than reasonable to treat the Intentional features of pictorial perspective in terms of the objective perception of paintings themselves. But that requires a theory of paintings (an ontology, if you please) that distinguishes with care between natural (or merely physical) and cultural things.

This makes a tidy collection of findings, though it goes against many strong views in current philosophies of art. To risk a final specimen: Richard Wollheim opens his 1984 Mellon Lectures with the following challenge:

> What . . . is the special feature of the visual arts, something which must be over and above the general way in which all the arts are connected with a tradition, and which has, allegedly, the consequence that if we are to understand painting, or sculpture, or graphic art, we must reach an historical understanding of them? I do not know, and, given the small progress that art-history has made in explaining the visual arts, I am inclined to think that the belief that there is such a feature is itself something that needs historical explanation: it is an historical accident. (1987: 9)

Perhaps, but Wollheim does not venture any supporting arguments in his lectures, and the history of connoisseurship hardly bears him out. Also, you see, of course, that there is no way to explain the perception *of* a painting without bothering to explain what *kind* of "thing" a painting is; and there is no way to explain *that* without bothering to explain whether paintings *and* their perception are (or are not) inherently subject to historical (or historicized) change. Painting's distinction, like that of speech itself (though in its own medium), lies in its being a mode of intentional utterance. But intentional utterance is inherently historicized in its very origin (its cultural generation). There's the answer to Wollheim's challenge: the deeper dread question nearly all fashionable philosophies of art wish to evade. But of course, it cannot be evaded. It is already captive in the argument about perspective.

## Notes

1   Gombrich reports a letter from Goodman supporting this judgment, though, frankly, I find that Goodman backtracks here when he pointedly objects to the view that "the standard rules of perspective embody the one native and easiest way of achieving and

reading a realistic depiction"; cited in Gombrich (1982: 284). See also Gombrich (1961).

2　This explains the import of Panofsky's adopting Cassirer's trope.

3　See, for instance, Danto (1981: ch. 1). In addition to my (1998), Danto has responded to my argument and I to his reply, which may provide a measure of closure on the issue. See Danto (1999); Margolis (2000).

# References

Arnheim, Rudolf (1974). *Art and Visual Perception.* Berkeley: University of California Press.

——(1988). *The Power of the Center: A Study of Composition in the Visual Arts.* Berkeley: University of California Press.

Belting, Hans (1994). *Likeness and Presence: A History of the Image before the Era of Art,* trans. Edmund Jephcott. Chicago: University of Chicago Press.

Damisch, Hubert (1994). *The Origin of Perspective,* trans. John Goodman. Cambridge, MA: MIT Press.

Danto, Arthur C. (1964). "The Artworld." *Journal of Philosophy,* XCI.

——(1981). *The Transfiguration of the Commonplace: A Philosophy of Art.* Cambridge, MA: Harvard University Press.

——(1991). "Description and the Phenomenology of Perception." In Norman Bryson, Michael Ann Holly, and Keith Moxey (eds), *Visual Theory: Painting and Interpretation.* New York: HarperCollins.

——(1999). "Indiscernibility and Perception: A Reply to Joseph Margolis." *British Journal of Aesthetics,* XXXIX.

Davidson, Donald (1986). "A Coherence Theory of Truth and Knowledge." In Ernest Lepore (ed.), *Truth and Interpretation: Perspectives on the Philosophy of Donald Davidson.* Oxford: Blackwell.

Edgerton, Samuel Y., Jr (1975). *The Renaissance Rediscovery of Linear Perspective.* New York: Harper and Row.

Elkins, James (1999). *The Domain of Images.* Ithaca, NY: Cornell University Press.

Foucault, Michel (1970). *The Order of Things: An Archaeology of the Human Sciences,* trans. New York: Vintage.

Gibson, J. J. (1979). *The Ecological Approach to Visual Perception.* Boston: Houghton Mifflin.

Gombrich, E. H. (1961). *Art and Illusion: A Study in the Psychology of Pictorial Representation.* 2nd edn. New York: Pantheon.

——(1972). "The 'What' and the 'How': Perspective Representation and the Phenomenal World." In Richard Rudner and Israel Scheffler (eds), *Logic and Art: Essays in Honor of Nelson Goodman.* Indianapolis: Bobbs-Merrill.

——(1982). "Image and Code: Scope and Limits of Conventionalism in Pictorial Representation." In *The Image and the Eye: Further Studies in the Psychology of Pictorial Representation.* Oxford: Phaidon.

Goodman, Nelson (1968). *Languages of Art: An Approach to a Theory of Symbols.* Indianapolis: Bobbs-Merrill.

Levinson, Jerrold (1996). "The Work of Visual Art." In *The Pleasures of Aesthetics: Philosophical Essays.* Ithaca, NY: Cornell University Press.

Margolis, Joseph (1995). *Historied Thought, Constructed World: A Conceptual Primer for the Turn of the Millennium*. Berkeley: University of California Press.

——(1998). "Farewell to Danto and Goodman." *British Journal of Aesthetics*, XXXVIII.

——(2000). "A Closer Look at Danto's Account of Art and Perception." *British Journal of Philosophy*, XL.

Panofsky, Erwin (1971). *Early Netherlandish Painting: Its Origins and Character*. Vol. 1. New York: Harper and Row.

——(1991). *Perspective as Symbolic Form*, trans. Christopher S. Wood. Cambridge, MA: MIT Press.

Rorty, Richard (1986). "Pragmatism, Davidson, and Truth." In Ernest Lepore (ed.), *Truth and Interpretation: Perspectives on the Philosophy of Donald Davidson*. Oxford: Blackwell.

Steinberg, Leo (1981). "Velasquez' 'Las Meninas'." *October*, 19.

Tormey, Alan and Tormey, Judith Farr (1979). "Seeing, Believing and Picturing." In Calvin F. Nodine and Dennis F. Fisher (eds), *Perception and Pictorial Representation*. New York: Praeger.

Wartofsky, Marx W. (1972). "Pictures, Representation, and the Understanding." In Richard Rudner and Israel Scheffler (eds), *Logic and Art: Essays in Honor of Nelson Goodman*. Indianapolis: Bobbs-Merrill.

——(1979). "Picturing and Representing." In Calvin F. Nodine and Dennis F. Fisher (eds), *Perception and Pictorial Representation*. New York: Praeger.

White, John (1987). *The Birth and Rebirth of Pictorial Space*. 3rd edn. Cambridge, MA: Harvard University Press.

Wollheim, Richard (1987). *Painting as an Art*. Princeton, NJ: Princeton University Press.

# Chapter 13

# The Philosophy of the Movies: Cinematic Narration

*Berys Gaut*

## 13.1  Some Issues in the Philosophy of Film

The philosophy of film is today an established branch of aesthetics, with a well-delineated and ever-growing set of issues with which it is concerned. We shall begin by briefly reviewing some of the more important of these, and then turn to examine one issue, that of the nature of cinematic narration, in some detail.

The first issue concerns the question of film's status as an art form. In the wide sense of the term, "movies" are motion pictures, and this encompasses a variety of media, including video and the emerging digital media, as well as film. Film distinguishes itself from these other kinds of motion pictures by the fact that it is photographically based. It is with film, the historically most influential of the motion picture media, that philosophers and film theorists have traditionally been concerned, and we will conform to this tradition in the present chapter. Because of its photographic basis, the result of a causally generated process which could occur in principle without human intervention, film lays itself open to the charge that it is not a genuine art form, but merely a recording device; at best it might record the artistry displayed by the actors who performed in front of the camera and of the writers who produced the screenplay, but it could never in its own right be a genuine art form. This worry was influential in shaping early film theory (Carroll 1988a) and sparked some of the most insightful writing on film yet produced, including that of Rudolf Arnheim (1957). Arnheim argued that it is the fact that a film deviates significantly from reality, in that the look of a film is saliently different from the look of what it records, which allows an artist to employ it as an expressive and therefore artistic medium. In contrast, Roger Scruton in an important article (1983) argues of photography in general that it is not a genuine, independent art; being a causally generated medium, its images lack the intentional relation to the world that is a necessary condition for their being genuine representations, that is, for photography to constitute a medium for the expression of thoughts about the world. And given film's photographic basis, Scruton believes that the same point applies to film. His article has generated a lot of discussion, and most replies to it have been of a broadly Arnheimian kind, stressing the capacity of photography and film to represent the world in different ways, through the employment of a variety of photographic and cinematic techniques, and so to convey the artists' thoughts about the world (King 1992; Gaut 2002).

A second issue also revolves around the photographically based nature of film: this concerns the claim that film is in some sense a realist medium. There are various senses of "realism" which are in play in this debate. One sense is that in which photographs are realistic in purportedly looking like the objects that they depict. The notion of resemblance between a picture and its object is notoriously suspect (Goodman 1976: ch. 1); but Gregory Currie, in one of the most important recent books about film, has argued that there is a way in which the similarity can be specified: photographs and their objects look similar in virtue of triggering the same recognitional capacities. Mae West and her photograph look similar by virtue of both triggering the Mae-West-recognizing capacity. The relevant kind of similarity on this view is given by contextual and response-dependent factors (Currie 1995: ch. 3).

A different sense of "realism" which has been claimed for photography and film is that of transparency. Something like this view is to be found in the work of the film theorist André Bazin (1967), but it receives its most sophisticated defense in the work of Kendall Walton (1984; see also Scruton 1983). Walton argues that we can literally see through photographs, and therefore photographically based films, to the objects photographed. This is in the same way as we can see an object through a telescope or in a mirror. The object seen in a photograph may no longer exist, but the same may be true of a star which is seen through a telescope. Objects are literally seen through photographs, but not through paintings of them, because as noted above the relation between a photograph and its object is a causal one. So the photographic content is unmediated by beliefs, which is also true of our visual experience, but is not true of the content of a painting (the painter paints what he believes he saw, not what he really saw). Photographs also preserve relevant similarity-relations between an object and its representation, unlike, say, causally generated written descriptions which are not relevantly similar to what they describe. However, Currie queries whether these points are sufficient to establish that we literally see objects through photographs (1995: ch. 2). He notes that all that they may show is that there are two classes of representation: natural ones (such as photographs), which are causally generated, and intentional ones (such as paintings), which stand in intentional relations to their objects. Currie also develops a series of counterexamples to the transparency thesis, the most telling of which is that of two clocks: consider two clocks, A and B, which look just like one other, and where B is controlled by radio signals from A, so that both faces show the same time. Since there is a causal relation between A and B, and they look exactly similar, then on Walton's argument, we would be forced to conclude that when one looks at B, one is also seeing A. But that is plainly false (Currie 1995: ch. 2). Walton has replied that he does not mean to deny that photographs are kinds of representations (natural ones, in Currie's terms), for this is consistent with his claim that one can see through them; and he has also argued that the reason that one does not see clock A through clock B is that not enough of the features of clock B are dependent on those of clock A (Walton 1997). Walton's point about consistency is a fair one; but the reply to the two clocks example is less convincing. One can easily imagine cases where all perceptible features of an object are causally dependent on the perceptible features of another object, but where it is highly implausible to claim that one sees the second object through the first: for instance, one could set up radio-controlled robots which looked identical to real gorillas and all of whose features and movements were controlled by those of the real gorillas, but it would not be true to say that one sees the real gorillas when looking at the robots (Gaut 2003: 637).

A third issue concerns the role, if any, of imagination in audiences' viewing of fiction films. Film theorists sometimes talk of audiences being under an illusion when they watch fiction films. However, if we mean by this that they suffer from a cognitive illusion – for example, that they have false beliefs about being in the presence of fictional characters – then this view is hard to sustain. Had they these beliefs when watching a horror film, for instance, they would be running for the exits screaming, rather than contentedly munching their popcorn. Perceptual illusionism, in contrast, holds that viewers have an experience *as of* actors and fictional characters, but do not have the corresponding false beliefs. A parallel would be to the Müller-Lyer illusion: viewers of the diagram have a visual experience as of the two lines being of different lengths, even though they may correctly believe that the lines are of the same length. In the same way, it has been argued, a viewer may have visual experiences as of Nimoy and as of Spock, but not falsely believe that they are in the presence of either the actor or the fictional character (Lopes 1998). However, even the existence of perceptual illusion in cinema has been denied – Currie notes that in the cinematic case, unlike the visual illusion case, "we do not sit there struggling to maintain our beliefs in the face of a contradictory experience" (Currie 1998: 362).

If no illusion is involved, then a plausible alternative is that audiences exercise their imaginations in viewing fiction films. The proponent of personal imagining, the participation theorist, holds that audiences when they watch films imagine seeing the fictional characters and events depicted; as such, they are fictionally members of the fictional world, observing events from within it from a point determined by the perspective of the image (Walton 1990: ch. 8). The proponent of impersonal imagination, in contrast, holds that viewers perceptually imagine the fictional events, but they do not imagine seeing those events; so they are not fictionally members of the fictional world, observing events from within it. Viewers of cinema are using their visual imaginations, a kind or type of imagination, and do not imagine themselves as visual participants within the fictional world (Currie 1995: ch. 6). We shall return to this issue later and seek its resolution.

A fourth issue concerns whether film can be properly thought of as constituting a language. Many film theorists have argued that it can: Sergei Eisenstein (1999) likened film images to hieroglyphics and pictograms, and Christian Metz (1974) attempted to apply the structure of a language systematically to cinematic form. Analytic philosophers have argued forcefully against such claims (Currie 1995: ch. 4; Harman 1999). Films do not have a vocabulary: the photographs that compose them have a causal, not merely conventional, relation to the world; vocabularies are finite, but photographs can be taken without number; and whereas language has minimal lexical units, the parts of which do not refer, photographs do not have such units, for each part of a photograph of a whole picks out a part of that whole (for instance, whereas the name "Morag" is a minimal lexical unit, and its part "rag" does not refer to anything, a photograph of Morag's head has as its part a photograph of her nose). And because there is nothing like a vocabulary in film, there can be nothing like a syntax in it, that is, there can be nothing like a finite set of rules for combining lexical units recursively to yield a potentially infinite number of meaningful sentences. There are of course conventions for structuring shots together, but to say that a relationship is conventional is not to say that it is grammatical; and there are even conventions for use in communication (such as shaking one's head), which are not syntactic.

A fifth issue concerns whether films can properly be said to have a single author. The existence of an author in this sense need not require one to believe in a language of film, and hence to think of a film as a kind of literary text, since in this context the term "author" is used to cover artists in general, not just those artists who produce literary texts. Auteurist theorists such as Andrew Sarris (1999) have argued that a film can have a single author, and have generally identified this author with the director of the film, though they have disagreed over whether one should think of the director as an actual individual, or as a critical construct, the implied author of the film. Some philosophers have argued against these claims, holding that because mainstream films are produced by large numbers of collaborators, such as writers, actors, directors, composers, cinematographers, etc., single authorship of such films never occurs, and that we should think of them as products of multiple authorship (Gaut 1997). By deploying a Gricean model of communication, others have argued that there is sometimes a single author of collaborative films, a single individual whose communicative intentions are sufficiently identifiable in the film for him to count as the sole author of it (Livingston 1997). Others have defended the claim that detailed critical attention to individual films can reveal that they sometimes have single implied authors (Wilson 1986: 134–9).

These five issues comprise some of the basic issues in the philosophy of film, but they certainly do not exhaust the field. Philosophers have also criticized central tenets of classical and contemporary film theory (Carroll 1988a, 1988b) and of cognitive film theory (Gaut 1995; Wilson 1997a); they have examined whether cinematic meaning is determined by the intentions of filmmakers (Currie 1995: ch. 8); they have addressed the role of music in film (Levinson 1996; Kivy 1997); they have analyzed the phenomenology of cinematic time and space (Sesonske

1974); they have debated whether audiences identify with film characters and what role this might play in audiences' emotional response to films (Carroll 1990: 88–96; Gaut 1999; Neill 1996); and there has also been some sophisticated and interesting work done on the analysis of individual films (notably Wilson 1986).

## 13.2   Film Narration: Symmetry or Asymmetry?

There is one important issue in the philosophy of film which I have not yet mentioned, but which I will now examine in some detail. Put most broadly, the issue concerns the similarities and differences between narration in film and in the other narrative arts. Is there a unique way in which film narrates, which is distinct from those of the other arts? Or are there strong similarities between the narrative powers of film and those of the other arts?

The issue is an interesting one for several reasons. First, almost all films have a narrative and the audience's attention is usually focused on it. This is true not only of fiction films; most documentaries are also narrative films. So in discussing narrative, we discuss a feature of film which is salient in viewers' responses. Second, in addressing the similarities and differences between film's narrative capacities and those of other arts, we can hope to shed light on the nature of film and of how it differs from the other arts. For narrative is a trans-medium property: many works in media besides film narrate. Narrative works include some dances, musical works, and paintings, and almost all comic strips and literature. There has to be some degree of commonality between these different media by virtue of the fact that they can all narrate, but there may also be interesting differences between them in respect of how they narrate, differences which throw light on their different capacities as media. And third, the examination of film narration is closely connected with some other issues in the philosophy of film, such as the role of imagination in responses to films (the third issue mentioned above), and whether there are any media-specific properties which have explanatory weight in film theory.

We will here mainly be concerned with the relation between cinematic narration and literary narration, particularly narration in novels. What we can call the *symmetry thesis* holds that narration in literature and film is identical in respect of the structural features of narration. These include the basic agents and properties of narration, such as narrators, implied authors, mediation, point of view, and the relation between plot and story. Symmetry theorists hold that these structural features are identical in both media, and that merely the mode of communication of the narrative varies – cinema narrates by showing, literature narrates by telling. The *asymmetry thesis* holds in contrast that cinematic narration differs from literary narration in respect of at least one of its basic structural features – for instance, the asymmetry theorist may hold that whereas narrators are ubiquitous in literature, they are hardly ever found in film, or may hold that cinematic narration is not mediated in the way that literary narration is. The explanation for the asymmetry may be provided in terms of the different modes of communication of the two media, so that in contrast to the symmetry view, the asymmetry view holds that the mode of communication does affect structural features of narration.

Though the distinction just mentioned is broader than that which most film theorists and philosophers have explicitly applied to themselves, one can plausibly assign several theorists to one camp or another. This is particularly clear in respect of the structural narrational feature which has been most discussed: that of the relative prevalence of cinematic narrators compared to literary narrators. A proponent of symmetry in this respect is Seymour Chatman (1990), who argues that all narratives, whether cinematic or literary, must have narrators; and that in the case of film there is always a (usually implicit) visual narrator, just as in literature there is always an (often implicit) verbal narrator who tells us the story. The issue of whether the narrative is told or shown is for Chatman a secondary one, which does not affect structural features such as the existence of the narrator, the narrator's mediation and point of view. Bruce Kawin, along with many other contemporary film theorists, also holds that there is always an implicit cinematic narrator through whose eyes we see the action (Kawin 1978). And Jerrold Levinson supports the symmetry view, at least in respect of the existence of cinematic narrators; he argues that there is always a cinematic narrator, however effaced, in a narrative film, and that this narrator's duties may even extend to the music track of a film (1996).

Asymmetry theorists about narrators include Currie (1995: ch. 9.2), Walton (1990: 357–8) and more tentatively Bordwell (1985: 62). All of these theorists hold that narrators are to be found less commonly in film than in literature, though, as we shall see, their grounds for this claim differ.

Something of the complexity of the symmetry issue is evidenced by the fact that some of these writers have come to change their mind on the topic. Chatman initially argued for a lesser role for narrators in film than in literature (1978), but later (1990) came to think that the two domains were symmetric. And Wilson appears to have moved somewhat in the opposite direction, shifting from arguing for only a very restricted view of narrators in film (1986: ch. 7) to a position that at least allows for the possibility of ubiquitous narrators in film (1997b).

I will argue for the correctness of the asymmetry view about narrators; this will be done by arguing for a very restricted role for narrators in film, and then by showing that the same is not true of literature. I will then trace this difference to differences between the media of film and of literature. These differences in the media also explain several other narrative features of film and literature. In this way we will also see the importance of media-specific explanations in film theory.

## 13.3   The A Priori Argument

Some have thought that there is an a priori argument for the existence of narrators whenever there is narration. This view is maintained by Chatman, and seconded by Levinson (1996: 251–2). If this argument is successful, the truth of the symmetry view for narrators is immediately established. Chatman (1990: 115) writes that "I would argue that every narrative is by definition narrated – that is, narratively presented – and that narration, narrative presentation, entails an agent even when that agent bears no signs of human personality." Narration conceptually entails the existence of a narrator, since narration is story-telling, and this requires a teller of the story.

Bordwell has objected to this kind of view, holding that we do not need to appeal to an agent who tells the story, for every property which can be ascribed to an agent can instead be ascribed to the process of narration itself – including properties such as the suppression of information, the restriction of knowledge, and so on (1985: 62). But the problem with this way of talking is that either it is a personification of the process, which is conceptually confused, or it is merely shorthand for saying that an agent is doing these things, since only an agent can perform actions such as suppressing information (see also Currie 1995: 247–9).

If there is narration, we must acknowledge a teller of the story. But it does not follow that this is a narrator. To see this, we need to draw on a familiar distinction in narratology and the philosophy of literature between the actual author, the implied author, and the narrator. The actual author of a text is the real person who composed it. The implied author of a text we will understand here as the author as he manifests himself in his text. These two need not be the same – the real-life personality, say, of Swift, might be quite different from that set of character traits which we would ascribe to him on the basis of reading *Gulliver's Travels*. Neither actual nor implied authors are internal to the world of the story, since they are the actual or implied composers of the story. A narrator in contrast is a fictional entity internal to the story; he is the fictional person, in the world of the story, who reports the events of the story. More precisely, we can define the narrator of a text as a particular fictional character who speaks or writes the words which compose the text (see Walton 1990: 355). For instance, Gulliver is the narrator of *Gulliver's Travels*, because it is fictional that he writes a logbook, the words of which compose the novel. Thus it is make-believe that in reading the novel, we read the text of Gulliver's logbook. Gulliver is distinct from Swift, the implied author of the novel: Gulliver is a hardy seaman faithfully reporting his adventures; the implied author employs these fictional adventures to satirize the beliefs and institutions of eighteenth-century Britain.

With this distinction in mind, we can acknowledge that narration requires a teller of the story, but can see that this is not the narrator. If there is a story, there must be a teller of it; but the teller who figures in this necessity claim is the actual author. For we require there to be an agent who produced a text with communicative intentions if we are to interpret the text as a story, yet that agent cannot be the narrator who is internal to the world of the fiction, for the text is a real object, and cannot be produced by a merely fictional being. So the a priori argument if successful proves the necessity of an actual author, not of a narrator.[1] In many cases, there will be an implied author of the tale as well (that is, the real author as he manifests himself in the work), but again this does not follow of necessity, since it is a contingent matter whether there is a sufficiently distinct set of characteristics manifest in the text for us justifiably to count an implied author as present.

There are further reasons for denying that every narrative requires a narrator. As already noted, not all narratives are fictional: there are historical narratives, for instance. Since the narrator is a fictional character, he should have no place in an historical narrative (Livingston 2001). The teller of the historical tale which is Simon Schama's *Citizens* is Simon Schama, not some fictional entity. Nor does the existence of unreliable narration require the existence of an unreliable narrator. It has been argued that one can analyze such narratives in terms of what the implied author intended (Currie 1995: 269–70).

## 13.4   Three Models of Implicit Cinematic Narrators

Thus one should reject the a priori claim that where there is narration there must be a narrator. But this still leaves it open that one might think on more specific grounds that there are invariably narrators in film. To consider this claim, we need to examine kinds of narrators in more detail.

Some films or film-sequences have explicit narrators – narrators who are explicitly made fictional in the film. A clear instance is the voice-over narrator, a narrator whose voice is heard over the film's images, usually at the start of the film but often at other points in it as well. Another instance is that of a character-narrator: a character who appears in the film and narrates part or the whole of the film. Often voice-over narrators are also character narrators; for instance, in *Murder, My Sweet*, Philip Marlowe narrates in voice-over at several points, but also appears as a character in the film. But there are voice-over narrators of films who do not appear in the film, and thus are not character-narrators: for instance, in *Duel in the Sun* Orson Welles is heard narrating in voice-over at the start of the film, but no character played by him appears in the film. Conversely, some character-narrators do not narrate in voice-over: in *Citizen Kane* several of Kane's friends narrate sequences in flashback about Kane's earlier career, but their sequences are introduced by their talking within the story-world, rather than in voice-over.

Explicit narrators have earned comparatively little attention within film theory, since their existence is uncontroversial. The debate has centered on whether there are *implicit* narrators of films. Such narrators are held to narrate the film as a whole but not to be explicitly present in voice-over or as characters appearing in it. Since they narrate the film as a whole, but their voices are not heard, they are thought of as visual narrators, somehow making sights or images available to us. Believers in such entities usually hold that they are to be found even when there are explicit narrators; the implicit narrator stands behind the explicit narrator, controlling the story in which the latter figures. For instance, Sarah Kozloff writes that the "voice-over narrator is always subsumed by and thus subordinate to a more powerful narrating agent, the image-maker" (Kozloff 1988: 48–9).

Our question about the ubiquity of narrators will focus on implicit cinematic narrators. There are three main models of such narrators. I will examine each in turn, will raise objections to each, and will in the next section consider whether these objections can be answered.

### 13.4.1 *The narrator as invisible observer*

This model of the cinematic narrator is the oldest, drawing as it does on the work of the classical film theorist Lev Pudovkin. It is also probably the most popular model among contemporary film theorists, being maintained amongst others by Bruce Kawin, and by Jean-Pierre Oudart in his suture theory of cinematic narration. According to this model, the cinematic narrator is to be thought of as an invisible observer stationed at the implied point from which a shot is taken, and through whose eyes we see all of the action. The narrator is the visual presenter of the story; each shot is narrated by him from his subjective point of view. The model thus in a way generalizes the "point-of-view" shot in cinema: all shots are held to be taken from the point of view of the narrator. Just as in a literary tale we learn about a fictional world by reading the narrator's words, so in a cinematic tale we learn about a fictional world by seeing it through the narrator's eyes.

If we try to spell out this view more carefully, we encounter difficulties. One option is to say that we are to imagine that we are the narrator, and thus in that sense identify with him, and so fictionally have his experiences. But, apart from anything else, that gets a basic feature of narration wrong, for it is up to the narrator how he chooses to narrate the story, but it isn't up to viewers to choose how the story proceeds. So perhaps we should construe this account in terms of it being fictional that we have the same perceptual experiences as the narrator does, though we are not fictionally identical with him.

However, that version also encounters serious difficulties. It holds that we make-believedly see the fictional events through the narrator's eyes. And here we can return to the third issue mentioned in section 13.1, concerning the role of imagination in viewing films. Even if one agrees with Walton that in films one make-believedly sees the fictional events, then the "narrator as invisible observer" model still fails; for in standard film shots it is fictional that one sees *directly*, not through the eyes of someone else. In viewing such films, it is as if one were looking out through a glass window onto the fictional world (Wilson 1986: 55). Of course, there are some shots (point-of-view shots) in which it is fictional that one is in some sense seeing through a character's eyes, but such shots are almost invariably clearly marked out as such, and are distinct from the general "objective" shots that comprise the majority of shots in most films.

However, there are powerful arguments against the claim that we make-believedly see fictional events in film. On the competing, impersonal-imagination view, the narrator as invisible observer model fails not because we make-believedly see directly, but because we do not make-believedly see at all, whether directly or indirectly. According to Currie, if we make-believedly see the fictional events, then we make-believedly are within the fictional world, stationed at the camera's viewpoint. But that leads to absurd results. Suppose a shot is taken from the ceiling of a room; then, fictionally, I must be attached to the ceiling. How did I get there, and how am I managing to stay there? If a shot is taken from outer space, I must make-believedly be at the point. Am I to imagine that I am wearing a space-suit to keep me alive while floating in outer space? When a sequence changes from a shot of one place to a shot of a completely different place, am I to imagine that I have the power instantaneously to move from one location to the other? And in other cases it seems that I must imagine not absurdities, but downright contradictions: for instance, if a murder in a film is represented as unseen, then I must imagine that I am seeing something which is unseen (Currie 1995: ch. 6). We can add to these problems. How is one to account for the use of different lenses? The image formed by a wide-angle lens (which produces a "fish-bowl" effect) is discernibly different from that produced by a normal lens, and both are perceptibly different from that produced by a telephoto lens (which tends to bring distant objects forward and to flatten space). Are we to imagine that we have eyes which can change their focal length so that they can mimic the effects of such lenses? What other things must be true of us for this to be so? And how do we account within our seeing for the screen-wipe, when one image is gradually replaced by another by a vertical band wiping across the screen? And how do we explain the split screen – can we fictionally somehow see two different scenes simultaneously, with a distinct visual division between their images?

Currie raises his objections against the claim that we make-believedly see fictions (that we are imaginary observers). But if successful, his objections, as well as those just added, work as powerfully against the idea that the narrator is an invisible observer, for this model requires us to make-believedly see through the narrator's eyes, and therefore from within the fictional space. Moreover, the oddity of make-believedly seeing through the narrator's eyes is even greater than make-believedly seeing directly. For how are we to imagine that we can see through the narrator's eyes? Are we to imagine that there is some kind of extraordinary technical device, or magical means, by which the narrator's perceptual experience is presented to us directly? But that is ruled out by the fictional worlds of all those films which are broadly realist – that is, broadly like everyday life, in which these things are impossible. (Indeed, on certain construals of what is at issue, it is conceptually impossible that one should literally be having someone else's perceptual experiences, as opposed to experiences which are qualitatively similar.) So on the impersonal-imagination theory, the narrator as observer should also be firmly rejected.

### 13.4.2   The narrator as guide

A second model of the cinematic narrator avoids some of the difficulties just adumbrated. This model is similar to the first in that it holds that the cinematic narrator is the fictional visual presenter or shower of each scene, but differs from it in that it holds that when we fictionally see, then we see directly through our own eyes, not his. The narrator is, as it were, a perceptual guide to the scenes, showing us the sights and sounds, pointing them out to us, and directing our attention to what is important. This model of the cinematic narrator is defended by Levinson, who believes that it is "the best default assumption" for cinematic narration (1996: 252), and also appears to be the model adopted by Chatman (1990).[2]

In support of this model, Levinson writes that given that we are make-believedly seeing fictional events, we must be able to answer the question of "*how it is* we are seeing what we are seeing . . . Reason . . . demands an answer to how it is that a world is being made visible to us" (1996: 256). And that answer, he thinks, must involve the narrator as a perceptual guide to the sights seen. In support of this, he argues against Wilson's (1986) claim that it is the implied filmmaker that is the agent who performs this perceptual role, rather than the narrator. Levinson correctly points out that if we are to think of the agent as fictionally presenting sights to us, that agent must be internal to the fiction, for the sights are themselves fictional. The implied filmmaker, in contrast, stands outside the fiction, being its author, and thus can make available only *representations* of the fictional events, not the fictional events themselves (Levinson 1996: 255).

The "narrator as guide" model has clear advantages over the first model. It acknowledges that in standard cinematic shots we see directly, not through another's eyes, and thus avoids the extra problems of working out how we fictionally could see through someone else's eyes. But, assuming that the impersonal-imagination view is correct, the second model is also ruled out; for if we are make-believedly shown, we must make-believedly see, the events depicted; hence Currie's objections against make-believe seeing would tell against this kind of narrator too. And the same point applies to Levinson's claims that we must be able to answer the question from within the fictional world of how we are shown the fictional sights. For this is a demand that we must imagine something else to be fictional if we are to imagine seeing something, and this is precisely the kind of demand that leads to the embarrassing questions rehearsed above, which cause such difficulties for the view that we are make-believedly seeing. If reason demands the existence of a narrator, then, it will also demand answers to these kinds of questions. It seems much better to deny the existence of make-believe seeing at all, and then the question of how we are fictionally shown these events simply lapses.

### 13.4.3  The narrator as image-maker

A third model holds that the narrator does not fictionally present events to us, but rather fictionally presents *images* of events to us. It is fictional that we are watching a film about events that actually occurred. The narrator, then, is the maker of that film. The idea seems to have originated with the film theorist Albert Laffay, and was championed by Metz, who talks of each shot being produced by a "*grand imagier*," a great image-maker (Metz 1974: 20–1). A more careful version of the view is championed by Wilson (1997b). He defends what he terms the Fictional Showing Hypothesis in its mediated version: that is, he claims that it is fictional that we are being shown images of actual events. He seems to want to leave it for determination at some future point whether this requires the existence of a narrator; but, for a reason similar to that advanced by Levinson (discussed above) against Wilson's earlier theory, it is hard to see how the image-maker could be the implied filmmaker. For if it is fictional that we are shown images of actual events, then it is fictional that someone made those images of actual events, and that cannot be a role occupied by the implied filmmaker, since he stands outside the fiction, rather than being a character internal to it. So I will take it that Wilson should be committed to the view that the image-maker is indeed the narrator.

This third model is an improvement on both of the earlier ones. It does not claim that we see through the narrator's eyes, and so side-steps the problems which we saw that this claim caused. Moreover, since we are fictionally viewing *images* of real events, rather than those events themselves, we can answer some of the embarrassing questions we rehearsed earlier. There is no need, for instance, to imagine that we have eyes which can mimic wide-angle and telephoto lenses, or which somehow can perform the equivalent of a screen-wipe: since we are make-believedly being shown images, it is make-believe in such cases that the images were shot with various lenses, or edited using wipe techniques; and there is no oddity involved in imagining these things. Moreover, this view yields the closest analog to the literary narrator. The literary narrator, recall, is someone whose words it is fictional that we are reading in reading the novel. The strict parallel would not involve sights and sounds, as the first two models of cinematic narration claim, but the images that it is fictional that the narrator is producing. Hence a strict analog would have the narrator as a documentary-maker of events, and it is fictional that in watching a fiction film we are watching the narrator's documentary.

However, if this is the right way of taking the narrator, then we seem to have some even more absurd things to imagine. Why do the characters in the film not notice that there is a documentary film crew present? How could there be such a crew present in scenes when a character is presented as being alone? Or, as Currie notes, if we are to think of the film as a recreation of something that happened earlier, we have to imagine the narrator as someone who has gone to a vast amount of expense, employing actors and technicians to recreate earlier events, something which becomes particularly odd if the narrator is to be considered as living at a time before the invention of cinema (Currie 1995: 267).

Wilson thinks that these kinds of objection are mistaken. If we assume that it is fictional that we are watching motion-picture shots of actual events, then it may indeed be true by definition that fictionally a camera must be present at the scene. But we need not imagine this; we could imagine that we are watching naturally iconic shots. These are defined as shots, the features of which exhibit natural counterfactual dependence on the scene; which lack a worked surface (unlike a painting); and which are designed to store or transmit visual information (Wilson 1997b: 313). The point of this definition is that it is not conceptually necessary that such shots are produced by a camera; but they are otherwise as like actual photographic images as is possible. It follows that in imagining that I am viewing such shots of actual events, I need not imagine that a camera was present at the scene, so that no absurd consequences need follow.

If we are to imagine that we are seeing naturally iconic shots, then we are to imagine something far removed from what is fictional in the majority of fiction films, the represented worlds of which are overwhelmingly similar to the real world. In the real world, the only way we can produce shots is via the presence of a camera at the scene filmed. So the viewer on this proposal would have to imagine that shots are being taken in a way which is impossible in the world of these fiction films. And it is highly implausible that the proposal captures what viewers imagine, since the concept of a naturally iconic shot is a term of art, one unlikely ever to have occurred to most film viewers, and perhaps not even be understandable by many of them.

However, the main burden of Wilson's reply is that it may be fictionally *indeterminate* what mechanisms cause these shots to be produced and assembled. Indeed, he notes that there are fictions in which this seems to be so – Flash Gordon's view screen seems to give him visual access to what is going on elsewhere, though it doesn't seem to be fictional that a camera is present at the scene, and it is indeterminate how the mechanism operates (1997b: 314–15). The kind of reply that relies on fictional indeterminacy or related notions is open to all of the narratorial models, and we will consider it in the next section. But absent this reply proving satisfactory, we can say that the narrator as image-maker, along with the two other models, should be rejected as a general account of film narration.

## 13.5  Absurd Imaginings and Silly Questions

Several arguments were deployed against the three versions of cinematic narrators, but there was one common objection: that their existence would require us to engage in absurd or even contradictory imaginings. But is that a good objection?

One worry is that the same kind of argument would rule out the existence of explicit narrators too. For how are we to imagine that these manage to narrate when they do so by visual means? We seem to have a choice of one of the three models discussed above, but the objections to them do not depend on the narrator being implicit, so they work equally against explicit narrators. And that suggests that something is wrong with the objection as it stands.

There may seem to be a way to avoid this conclusion. Currie deploys the argument from absurd imaginings against the idea of a *controlling* narrator, who is fictionally the source of the images which we see, and he holds that such a narrator is virtually incoherent. In contrast, he holds that the idea of an *embedded* narrator is coherent: "Where there is an embedded narrator, the text we read tells us of someone's telling, but that teller is not, fictionally, responsible for the text we read. Rather, it is fictional that the text we read *reports* that person's telling" (1995: 266). His examples include those characters who tell what they know of Kane via flashbacks in *Citizen Kane*. However, a similar problem arises with the idea of an embedded narrator. For note that Currie says that it is *fictional* that the text (the sequences we see) reports that character's telling. But since the sequences reporting the telling are within the scope of the fiction operator, how, fictionally, is this accomplished? It isn't fictional that the *character* is showing us images from his past, since the character isn't a controlling narrator, but if fictionally the telling is being reported visually, then we can deploy the same kind of argument from absurd imaginings to conclude that it must be fictional that *somehow* we are being given these images. Is it fictional that there is some other agent within the world of the fiction who is producing a film of the characters' past, or somehow transporting us into the past? Absurd imaginings seem to be required again. So something seems to be wrong with the argument from absurd imaginings.

One can press the point by considering an explicit narrator who seems to be controlling in Currie's sense, that is, to be responsible for the sound and images. *All About Eve* is narrated in voice-over by Addison DeWitt, a theatre critic who introduces us at the start of the film to the characters present at an award ceremony for the actress Eve. DeWitt controls the sound – he says of the aged speaker at the ceremony "it is not important that you hear what he says," and we do not hear the character – until, that is, DeWitt tells us he has decided to let us do so. As he introduces each character, including himself, the camera shows us that person. And memorably at one point there is a freeze-frame on Eve about to receive her award. DeWitt's voice continues over this freeze-frame, teasingly implying that we do not know as much about Eve as we suppose. As Kozloff correctly remarks in discussing this sequence, "The first thing one notices is that the voice here is actually in complete control of the image . . . This narrator is also in charge of the sound track" (Kozloff 1988: 65). The sequence points, then, toward DeWitt's being responsible for the sound and images. But if one tries to imagine how this is possible, one is led to imagine absurdities. DeWitt speaks to us from within the story-world: as he looks knowingly at the camera, we hear his voice saying "it is perhaps necessary to introduce myself. My name is Addison DeWitt." But his lips do not move: somehow we seem directly to hear his thoughts, as he controls what we see and hear. Is this fictionally a case of telepathy? And how can

DeWitt be controlling image and sound while sitting in front of us, himself part of the story? It does not seem to be fictional that the awards ceremony is being filmed, and that his is a voice-over added to that film later. The sense of the sequence is that we are present; indeed, DeWitt tells us that "it is important that you know where you are and why you are here." Yet the fictional world of *All About Eve* is not one filled with magic, but is broadly like the real world; and in the real world this act of narration is impossible. Yet there is no doubt that DeWitt is narrating this sequence, and does so by controlling the sound and images. The argument from absurd imaginings would conclude that DeWitt cannot be the narrator. But he is.

The most powerful response to the argument from absurd imaginings is to hold that it fails since it is an instance of asking *silly questions* about fictions, questions that it is illegitimate to pose and to attempt to answer. How can Othello speak such great verse while holding that he is rude of tongue, and no one notices? Why in Leonardo's *Last Supper* are the disciples all sitting on one side of the table – is it because they are trying to avoid each others' bad breath? Such questions are silly, since there are no answers to them in the fictional world, and we are not supposed to engage in the imaginings which they prompt; the answers to the question lie, rather, outside the fictional worlds, in the need in the first case to enhance the work aesthetically, and in the second to give us epistemic access to what the disciples' faces look like (Walton 1990: ch. 4.5). In the same way, we illegitimately pose silly questions if we query how the implicit narrator could have the powers which he fictionally has. That does not mean he does not exist, any more than posing silly questions about Othello shows that he does not speak great verse.

There are two kinds of move behind this general response. First, one can argue that even when one is prescribed by a fiction to imagine some state of affairs, one is not required to imagine its implications (Walton 1997: 62).[3] So, even if one is required to imagine a narrator, one need not imagine how he is accomplishing his act of narration – that would be to pose silly questions. Since what is fictional is what one is prescribed to imagine, one can put the point this way: it may be fictionally indeterminate what else is the case, when one imagines some state of affairs – this is Wilson's formulation, as noted earlier (Wilson 1997b: 306–9). So though it may be fictional that there is an image-maker narrating, it may be fictionally indeterminate how he is doing so. The second kind of move concerns those cases where one is prescribed to imagine contradictions: for instance, that one is seeing a murder and that the murder is unseen. (In this case, one cannot appeal to the fact that one is not required to imagine the implications of one's imaginings, since here one is directly prescribed to imagine incompatible things.) The response is that this introduces no extra difficulties, since imaginings (for instance, dreams) and fictions sometimes involve incongruities of this kind (Walton 1997: 65).

This reply, if successful, shows that the main argument against implicit narrators fails and thus leaves it open for us to acknowledge their presence. And it also undermines an objection to the related view that we imagine seeing fictions in cinema, rather than impersonally perceptually imagine them (the third issue discussed in section 13.1). But is the reply successful?

Consider the second part of the reply – that fictions and imaginings can involve incoherence and inconsistencies, so that no extra kinds of problem are introduced by positing acts or entities that involve imagining contradictions. It is certainly correct that fictions, such as time-travel stories and many fairy-tales, may involve incoherence. But we can note as a general heuristic principle that when we interpret fictional worlds we should attempt, other things equal, to render them as like the real world as we can. Very many features of fictional worlds are left implicit – we are not usually told that characters have blood in their veins, that they are not robots masquerading as humans, and so on. We assume that these things are so, employing the interpretive principle just mentioned. If we did not assume that fictional worlds were much like the real world, except in those respects in which they explicitly differ, there would be massive indeterminacy as to how correctly to interpret even what is made explicitly fictional. Now this point means that one should seek, other things equal, to minimize incoherence and contradictions in fictional worlds, for the real world does not have incoherence and contradictions in it. Where there are explicit fictional anomalies, such as singing kettles or time-travel, one should obviously accept that these things are fictional. But if the entities are purportedly implicit, such as putative visual narrators, there is reason not to introduce them, unless there are compelling arguments for why we should do so. But we have seen that there are no such arguments: the general a priori argument, and Levinson's argument about what reason demands, both fail. So, insofar as imputing implicit visual narrators to films produces incoherence or inconsistencies, one should reject them.

Now consider the first part of the reply. It may be true that when we are imagining something on our own without fictional guidance, we are not always required to imagine the implications of our imaginings (though this depends in part on the point of our imaginings). But when we appreciate fictions, we generally are required to imagine a wide range of implications of what is explicitly fictional. Comparatively little of a fictional world is made explicit, and we are required to imagine many other states of affairs to interpret correctly what is explicitly fictional. Consider a character's words, reported in a novel: if we seek to understand her motivations, we need to imagine what fictionally are her psychological states which explain her words. So we have to imagine what the implications are of what is explicitly made fictional. In general, we have to imagine the implications of what is explicitly fictional *as part of appreciating a work*. For instance, works can be criticized for having absurd or untenable implications, such as their characters' motivations being implausible, criticisms which may well depend on imagining the implications of what is fictional. So given the general reason to consider the implications of what is explicitly fictional, the argument from absurd imaginings against implicit narrators should stand, given that we have seen no good arguments to show that implicit narrators must be imputed to films. Again, however, if narrators are explicit, we have to admit their existence, and either accept the absurd implications, or background them by refusing to dwell on them.

So the reply fails, and the outcome is that we should acknowledge only explicit narrators in film. We should avoid positing entities which ground silly questions, unless the entities are explicitly fictional. There is another upshot of this discussion. Though it is directly relevant to the issue of narration, Walton's reply is explicitly directed in defense of his view that we make-believedly see fictions, against Currie's view that we impersonally visually imagine them. Since we have argued that the reply fails, we should similarly conclude the default mode in cinema is that we impersonally imagine visual fictions. But, again, the position must allow for what is made explicitly fictional; and in the case of make-believe seeing, it is plausible that in some cases, such as certain point-of-view shots, it is fictional that we make-believedly see what the character sees. The default mode of spectators' engagement with cinema is impersonal visual imagining, but there can be suitably cued episodes of make-believe seeing (Gaut 1998: 336).

## 13.6   Literary Narrators

So far I have argued that we ought to acknowledge only explicit (voice-over or character) narrators in cinema. This supports the asymmetry claim, for matters are apparently different in literature: it is generally held that while there are character-narrators in literature, there are also frequently or invariably implicit narrators as well, however effaced they may be. One reason advanced for this is that in literature, one always has a sense of a "voice" issuing the words of the text. Language is an extremely subtle instrument for expressing nuances and character, so it is natural to think of some personality reflected in the words. One can contrast this with cinema; while a sense of personality may be conveyed by lighting, camera movement, and so on, these devices are crude compared to the subtleties of language. However, while the point about the relative subtlety of language and cinematic technique is correct, the greater sense of a "voice" in deployment of the language does not show that this is a *narratorial* voice. It could be that of the implied author. So the point doesn't prove the ubiquity of narrators in literature.

More promising is the claim that we pervasively employ declarative sentences to report or describe events. The implied author cannot use sentences in a fictional work actually to describe events; these sentences can only be fictionally declarative, so it must be some fictional entity who reports by means of them – and this must be a narrator (Walton 1990: 365–6). Again, we can contrast this with cinema. Since fiction film is the dominant type of cinematic practice, not documentary film, a parallel argument would not show that fiction films are to be thought of as fictional documentaries (which would yield a version of the narrator as image-maker). Now this point is a good one, and gives some grounds for believing that we have more reason to believe in implicit narrators in literature than in film. But how strong are these grounds?

The outcome of our discussion of silly questions was that we should avoid if we can imputing entities to fictions which would ground the asking of such questions of them. Hence I argued that we should avoid imputing implicit narrators to films. But a similar argument would, it seems, yield the same result for literature. For consider the case of purported omniscient narrators, such as that in George Eliot's *Middlemarch*. The omniscient narrator is presumably a human being (the fictional teller is not usually an extraterrestrial or God). How could a mere human being gain access to all this knowledge, often the most intimate thoughts of people which they do not tell to anyone else? Or consider a novel about someone who dies alone, and we read of their dying thoughts; how could the narrator know such things? Clearly, a whole array of silly questions threatens; and a similar argument to that rehearsed against ascribing cinematic narrators should apply to show that implicit narrators are far less common in literature than one might suppose.

I think that this conclusion is correct, and that the role of the narrator is overestimated in literature. Much of the "voice" that we ascribe to a narrator should more properly be ascribed to an implied author. But it isn't correct to conclude that film and literature are exactly alike in this respect. For there is a crucial difference in the epistemic access available to a narrator in film and literature. The easiest way to see this is by considering an example. In *North by Northwest*, Roger Thornhill (Cary Grant) ends up battling on Mount Rushmore, at one point hanging on for his life by one hand from the stony visage of a president, with the heroine, Eve, hanging onto his other hand. The shot is taken apparently from a point in mid-space, down and to the right of Thornhill. Clearly a host of awkward questions could be asked: how, fictionally, can the narrator be suspended in mid-air? Is it fictional that he has wings, and can hover around just out of reach of Thornhill? We've argued that it is best to avoid ascribing entities to fictions that could be the objects of such questions. But imagine that the same scene were told in a novel. There would be no similar set of awkward questions to be asked. For the narrator might have observed the battle safely from the ground through a telescope; or he might have been told of it later by Thornhill; or he might have read about it in one of the participants' diaries; and so on. The crucial difference is that the film image has an intrinsic perspective, from which it is taken; and in anything remotely resembling the real world, it follows that someone or something was observing the scene from that point of space at the time that the scene was occurring. But the same is not true of language. So it is a difference between a *visual* medium and a merely *lexical* medium that explains why certain absurd imaginings are grounded in the first case and not in the second. This point applies not just to the visual but to the *auditory* nature of film too. For we hear Thornhill's and Eve's voices from a point close to them; again, we could ask how, fictionally, the narrator (or the spectator) could be in this position floating in space. But the same point does not apply to a report of the characters' words in a novel: we could have been told later what they said, and so on. So the difference is that in cinema there is the *sound* of the words, in the case of the novel there is merely a lexical report. In short, it is because film is an *auditory-visual* medium, and novels are a *lexical* medium, that there is more grounding for absurd imaginings in the case of the former than the latter.

There are, then, two conclusions. First, there is more reason to believe in implicit narrators in novels than in films; and second, this difference is to be traced to media-specific differences – to the nature of an auditory-visual medium as opposed to a lexical medium.

## 13.7  Medium-Specific Explanations

So far we have concentrated on the question of the existence of narrators in novels and films. Yet the point about medium-grounded asymmetry in respect of narrators generalizes to other aspects of narration too.

First, if, as I have argued, narrators are less common in film than in novels, due to the differences in the media, then that point will also bear on the question of mediation and point of view in film, as distinct from novels. Narrators mediate readers' epistemic access to a fictional world in the sense that it is fictional that the words of a narrated text are the words of the narrator, and hence the reader's knowledge of the world depends on the narrator. In the case of unreliable narrators, the reader must adjust his beliefs about the fictional world in the light of his judgments about whether on various points the narrator is reliable. The narrator, in the way he describes the events which occur, also exhibits an affective point of view on them, reporting them neutrally, favorably, or unfavorably. In the case of those films without narrators, a fortiori access and point of view cannot depend on the narrator. So there is a way in which films without narrators are not mediated, that is, they are more immediate, than literary works with narrators; and this feature depends on properties of the respective media. However, this does not mean that film is completely unmediated: mediation can happen in other ways in film – for instance, the implied filmmaker may mediate access, and as we have noted, Currie has argued that unreliable narration in film can be construed in terms of the implied author.[4]

Second, consider the question of access to characters' subjective states. In literature, we can be given highly specific and detailed descriptions of the nuances of what characters are thinking and feeling. In film, we have to infer characters' inner states from their looks, gestures, and speech – in short, from their behavior. Even if they speak out loud a description which might have figured in a novel about them, the status of this description is different; for in the case of film their speaking the words is itself a part of the behavior which they exhibit, from which we infer their mental states. But a description in the novel would make it directly fictionally true that they were in a certain mental state, without the need for infer-

ence from their behavior on our part. Thus novels can give us direct access to subjective states in a way that films cannot.[5] This is a difference in the narrative powers
of films and novels; and it too is to be traced to media-specific differences. One
can describe people's mental states, their thoughts and feelings. But one cannot
photograph a thought or feeling, nor can one tape-record it; one can only record
the outward manifestations of these things. So there is a simple explanation for
why film and literature differ in respect of subjective access. It is one reason why
Proust's works, with their masterly and extensive nuanced descriptions of inner
states, have been so hard to adapt successfully to film.

Third and relatedly, there is a difference in the range of what films as opposed
to novels make fictionally explicit. It is sometimes said in criticism of films that
they leave less to the imagination than do literary works. For a range of audio and
visual facts, this is true. A film shows very precisely how a character looks and
sounds, whereas a novel may give only a vague, or indeed no, description of how
even an important character looks and sounds. So in respect of the visual and auditory properties of characters and settings, films do leave less to the imagination,
since they make the relevant properties explicitly fictional. But, as we have just
noted, films cannot give direct access to characters' subjective states, so given the
inferences required from behavior, these subjective states are only implicitly fictional, that is, they will require inferences from what is explicitly fictional to establish them. Or, indeed, they may be left fairly indeterminate: it is not uncommon
to have precise knowledge of a film character's looks, yet to be left wondering
about his motivations. So while it is true that in respect of visual and auditory
appearances films typically leave less to the imagination, it is also fairly common
for them to require more imagination in respect of characters' motivations (in the
sense of requiring inferences about them, or leaving them indeterminate). And
again evidently this difference is grounded on a medium-specific difference: as an
audio-visual medium, film must show audio-visual properties of what is in front
of the camera, whereas its access to subjective states is indirect and inferential. In
contrast, novels as a lexical medium have the option of leaving auditory-visual
properties relatively underspecified, but they can directly describe characters' subjective states.[6]

Finally, there is a way in which narrational commentary is more indirect in film
than it is in literature. In his fine study of Jean Renoir's film *Une Partie de cam-
pagne*, an adaptation of Guy de Maupassant's short story of the same name,
Chatman points out that whereas de Maupassant simply describes a young girl as
"pretty," Renoir does not have that option. All he can do is to cast an actress
whom he could hope that many people would find pretty (Chatman 1999: 442).
The point, of course, generalizes: language can be explicitly evaluative; filmed
images cannot be, for one can't photograph a value. So there is a possibility of
explicit evaluative commentary in literature that cannot be achieved by the visual
images of film.

There are evidently other ways in which the nature of the media affects their
narrative capacities – music can contribute narrative information, for instance, in

film, but obviously music cannot be heard at all in novels – but the points just noted should serve to illustrate that there is a rich set of ways in which properties of the media affect narration. And this grounds my final observation, that it is a mistake to think that the issue of media-specificity should play no role in the philosophy of film. Several classical film theorists held a kind of essentialist view, arguing that one could derive general principles of evaluation about films from the nature of the cinematic medium. For instance (to oversimplify greatly), Bazin held that because film is a realist medium, realist films are better than non-realist ones. Carroll has rightly criticized such sweeping essentialist doctrines (Carroll 1988a). But just because media-specific *evaluations* of at least these simple kinds are untenable, it does not follow that media-specific *explanations* should be abandoned as well. In fact, we have just seen that such explanations plausibly figure in an account of cinematic, as compared to novelistic, narration. Of course, the basis of these claims must be specified carefully – medium-specific features should not, for instance, be understood as ones that are necessarily *unique* to a medium, since several explanatorily important features of photographic films are shared with, for instance, digital cinema, and the same is true of properties shared by the novel and, say, the short story and poem. Rather, medium-specific features should be construed not in absolute terms, but rather as being relative to other media, as differential features, that is, as features which differ between one group of media and another specified group. For instance, being audio-visual is a differential feature between film and literature, since the former possesses this property and the latter does not. But being audio-visual is not a feature unique to film, since it is also shared with video and with digital cinema. And this differential feature explains, as we have seen, several important differences between the narrative capacities of film and novels. Medium-specific explanations, in the sense of medium-involving explanations that appeal to differential properties between sets of media, are, then, an important class of explanations. Indeed, if one thought that no explanations of this kind could be found at all, it would be unclear what role, if any, were left for the philosophy of film and for film theory. If all interesting artistic properties and explanations were common to all artistic media, one could still have a general theory and philosophy of art, but the role of the individual arts would be reduced merely to providing illustrations for the general theory. But I have argued that matters do not stand like this with the movies; there is plenty of space for a rich and complex investigation of the philosophy of film.

### Notes

1   The correctness of the a priori argument that narration requires an actual author might be denied. Walton, for instance, thinks that if cracks which seemed to tell a story appeared by natural means in a rock, then they would tell a story, provided that the audience decided to play a game of make-believe with them in which a story was told

(Walton 1990: ch. 1). However, note that even if this were correct, which I would deny, it would still support the weaker claim that narration requires an agent, and would show that the agents could be the audience, rather than an actual author.

2  Though he does not defend this version, this model is what Wilson (1997b) calls the Fictional Showing Hypothesis in the Face-to Face version.

3  To make this claim sufficiently general, I suggest that implications should be understood in a broad sense. Let "$p$" and "$q$" denote states of affairs, and suppose that in the real world, if $p$ were the case, then $q$ would be the case. This might be because $p$ logically entails $q$; or more weakly because $q$ follows from $p$, given some law of nature; or yet more weakly because $p$ makes it probable that $q$. In all such cases we can say that $q$ is an implication of $p$.

4  The immediacy of film may also in part be traced directly to differences in the signs which constitute the media: our visual capacities to understand the world are activated much earlier as children than is our linguistic knowledge, and the capacity to read is gained much later, being a result of an extended learning process. It would be unsurprising if part of our sense of the immediacy of film over novels, then, were derived from films being grounded on a less culturally determined capacity. Communication by visual and auditory means is more immediate than communication by written words.

5  There is one exception: in film a voice-over narrator could make it directly fictionally true that a character is feeling something. But if this device were used as extensively in a film as are descriptions in novels, films would start to approximate literary works being read out, with visuals added to illustrate them.

6  This is not to say, of course, that novels must specify such states with any precision, as some of Hemingway's works illustrate, but only that they can directly specify such states, if they choose, and exploit this ability for striking aesthetic effect.

## References

Arnheim, R. (1957). *Film as Art.* Berkeley: University of California Press.

Bazin, A. (1967). *What is Cinema? Volume I*, trans. Hugh Gray. Berkeley: University of California Press.

Bordwell, D. (1985). *Narration in the Fiction Film.* Madison: University of Wisconsin Press.

Carroll, N. (1988a). *Philosophical Problems of Classical Film Theory.* Princeton, NJ: Princeton University Press.

——(1988b). *Mystifying Movies: Fads and Fallacies in Contemporary Film Theory.* New York: Columbia University Press.

——(1990). *The Philosophy of Horror or Paradoxes of the Heart.* London: Routledge.

Chatman, S. (1978). *Story and Discourse: Narrative Structure in Fiction and Film.* Ithaca, NY: Cornell University Press.

——(1990). *Coming to Terms: The Rhetoric of Narrative in Fiction and Film.* Ithaca, NY: Cornell University Press.

——(1999). "What Novels Can Do that Films Can't (and Vice Versa)." In L. Braudy and M. Cohen (eds), *Film Theory and Criticism: Introductory Readings.* New York: Oxford University Press: 435–51.

Currie, G. (1995). *Image and Mind: Film, Philosophy, and Cognitive Science.* Cambridge: Cambridge University Press.

——(1998). "Reply to My Critics." *Philosophical Studies*, 89: 355–66.

Eisenstein, S. (1999). "Beyond the Shot [The Cinematographic Principle and the Ideogram]." In L. Braudy and M. Cohen (eds), *Film Theory and Criticism: Introductory Readings*. New York: Oxford University Press: 15–25.

Gaut, B. (1995). "Making Sense of Films: Neoformalism and its Limits." *Forum for Modern Language Studies*, 31: 8–23.

——(1997). "Film Authorship and Collaboration." In R. Allen and M. Smith (eds), *Film Theory and Philosophy*. Oxford: Oxford University Press: 149–72.

——(1998). "Imagination, Interpretation and Film." *Philosophical Studies*, 89: 331–41.

——(1999). "Identification and Emotion in Narrative Film." In C. Plantinga and G. Smith (eds), *Passionate Views: Film, Cognition and Emotion*. Baltimore: Johns Hopkins University Press: 200–16.

——(2002). "Cinematic Art." *Journal of Aesthetics and Art Criticism*, 60: 299–312.

——(2003). "Film." In J. Levinson (ed.), *Oxford Handbook of Aesthetics*. New York: Oxford University Press: 627–34.

Goodman, N. (1976). *Languages of Art: An Approach to the Theory of Symbols*. 2nd edn. Indianapolis: Hackett.

Harman, G. (1999). "Semiotics and the Cinema: Metz and Wollen." In L. Braudy and M. Cohen (eds), *Film Theory and Criticism: Introductory Readings*. New York: Oxford University Press: 90–8.

Kawin, B. (1978). *Mindscreen: Bergman, Godard, and First-Person Film*. Princeton, NJ: Princeton University Press.

King, W. (1992). "Scruton and Reasons for Looking at Photographs." *British Journal of Aesthetics*, 32: 258–65.

Kivy, P. (1997). "Music in the Movies: A Philosophical Enquiry." In R. Allen and M. Smith (eds), *Film Theory and Philosophy*. Oxford: Oxford University Press: 308–28.

Kozloff, S. (1988). *Invisible Storytellers: Voice-Over Narration in American Fiction Film*. Berkeley: University of California Press.

Levinson, J. (1996). "Film Music and Narrative Agency." In D. Bordwell and N. Carroll (eds), *Post-Theory: Reconstructing Film Studies*. Madison: University of Wisconsin Press: 248–82.

Livingston, P. (1997). "Cinematic Authorship." In R. Allen and M. Smith (eds), *Film Theory and Philosophy*. Oxford: Oxford University Press: 132–48.

——(2001). "Narrative." In B. Gaut and D. Lopes (eds), *The Routledge Companion to Aesthetics*. London: Routledge: 275–84.

Lopes, D. (1998). "Imagination, Illusion and Experience in Film." *Philosophical Studies*, 89, 343–53.

Metz, C. (1974). *Film Language: A Semiotics of the Cinema*, trans. Michael Taylor. New York: Oxford University Press.

Neill, A. (1996). "Empathy and (Film) Fiction." In D. Bordwell and N. Carroll (eds), *Post-Theory: Reconstructing Film Studies*. Madison: University of Wisconsin Press: 175–94.

Sarris, A. (1999). "Notes on the Auteur Theory in 1962." In L. Braudy and M. Cohen (eds), *Film Theory and Criticism: Introductory Readings*. New York: Oxford University Press: 515–18.

Scruton, R. (1983). "Photography and Representation." In *The Aesthetic Understanding: Essays in the Philosophy of Art and Culture*. London: Methuen: 102–26.

Sesonske, A. (1974). "Aesthetics of Film, or A Funny Thing Happened on the Way to the Movies." *Journal of Aesthetics and Art Criticism*, 33: 51–7.

Walton, K. (1984). "Transparent Pictures: On the Nature of Photographic Realism." *Critical Inquiry*, 11: 246–77.

——(1990). *Mimesis as Make-Believe: On the Foundations of the Representational Arts.* Cambridge, MA: Harvard University Press.

——(1997). "On Pictures and Photographs: Objections Answered." In R. Allen and M. Smith (eds), *Film Theory and Philosophy.* Oxford: Oxford University Press: 60–75.

Wilson, G. (1986). *Narration in Light: Studies in Cinematic Point of View.* Baltimore: Johns Hopkins University Press.

——(1997a). "On Film Narrative and Narrative Meaning." In R. Allen and M. Smith (eds), *Film Theory and Philosophy.* Oxford: Oxford University Press.

——(1997b). "*Le Grand Imagier* Steps Out: The Primitive Basis of Film Narration." *Philosophical Topics*, 25: 295–318.

# Chapter 14

# The Philosophy of Music: Formalism and Beyond
## *Philip Alperson*

Music has long been a subject of philosophical interest, having exercised the philosophical imagination more or less continuously at least since the time of Pythagoras. This interest continues unabated through the present day, when the philosophy of music flourishes as one of the most active, most wide-ranging, and richest subjects within the field of philosophical aesthetics.

Why has music been a source of philosophical wonderment for so long? Several interrelated features help to explain the phenomenon. There is first of all the accessibility of music. To be sure, some music is difficult and inaccessible. Indeed, the familiar distinction between "popular music" and "classical music" is often thought to mark a difference between the music accessible to hoi polloi and a body of music fully understood and appreciated only by a musically educated elite. But even though some music does seem to require a degree of specialized training or acute sensibility, it remains true that there is an enormous amount that is relatively accessible to the untrained listener. In addition – and perhaps even more significantly – some forms of music-making, such as humming, singing, whistling, musical imagining, and so on, are known to virtually everyone by direct acquaintance. These activities – hearing, listening to, and making music – provide a direct and intimate entrée to music for most people from the time they are very young. For most of us music is a familiar part of the furniture of our worlds.

Another reason why music is so intriguing is that it admits of an astonishing variability of means and materials. It is true, of course, that it needs no more in the way of a technical device than the unadulterated human voice. But even here, the variations are, so to speak, breathtaking, as the differences among an operatic aria, a blues holler, Tibetan overtone chanting, and Tuvan throat-singing make clear. The diversity of other varieties of musical instruments is equally impressive. Some, such as the piano, guitar, lute, violin, and sitar, have strings that may be plucked, bowed, or hammered. The sounds of others, such as flutes, horns, and reed instruments, are produced by means of closed columns of air. Instruments such as the gong, triangle, castanets, rattles, and chimes are made of hard elastic materials that emit sounds when struck. In others, including most drums, skins or stretched membranes are sounded by being hit. The sounds of instruments such as the synthesizer, the computer, and the rap turntable are created electronically.

Similarly, the structure and organization of sounds in music are extraordinarily diverse. Western listeners are most familiar with music written in a particular tonal system in which three pitches – a key note (the "tonic"), the pitch five degrees above it (the "dominant"), and the pitch five degrees below (the "subdominant") – determine a cycle of keys and their associated scales that form the basis of the tonal system. Much music in the western tradition is composed with what has been called "loyalty" to the tonic center; but western music may also deviate from this norm. Music may also be polytonal, atonal, or non-tonal. Even within the western tonal tradition, music may be relatively simple or extremely complex and it may exhibit varying degrees of consonance and dissonance. In some musical traditions, melodic and harmonic developments may be featured; in others, rhythmic pulse takes center stage. Music may be instrumental, vocal, or a combination of both. It may be produced by a single soloist or it may involve the combined efforts of hundreds. The variety of musical presentations seems virtually endless.

For most people music also seems a deeply personal affair. It is hard to know why the audible results of these blowings, scratchings, poundings, and vocalizings affect us the way they do. Certainly part of the reason lies in the expressivity of music and its relation to the life of feeling. Music seems capable of moving us in unusually intimate and distinctive ways. We often find ourselves at a loss for words when we try to describe this aspect of our musical experiences, and the gap between the air of deep meaning in music and our seeming inability to describe it adequately only serves to reinforce the idea that musical expressiveness is both profound and mysterious. Perhaps this is what Felix Mendelssohn means when he famously says that music "fills the soul with a thousand things better than words. The thoughts which are expressed to me by music that I love are not too indefinite to be put into words, but on the contrary, too definite" (Mendelssohn 1956: 140).

Music is also remarkable for its ubiquity. We are never very far away from music of one sort or another. One of the reasons for this pervasiveness is the fact that music is easily reproducible. Insofar as it is a performed activity, musical sounds can be repeated at will, given the relevant resources. The possibilities for reproduction are enhanced not only by the existence of musical notation but also by the various means of mechanical and audio-visual reproduction that proliferate in a technological age such as ours. The ubiquity of music is also a result of its great adaptability. Music is an unusually compatible art. It lends itself to presentation in the context of other arts, such as dance, film, theater, and opera, and it is an accompaniment to a vast array of human endeavors and rituals, including religious activities, sporting events, and momentous personal and social occasions such as first dates, weddings, funerals, shopping, television commercials, and on and on. Music, then, has many uses, as it is allied with the myriad institutions and practices of society.

Music of course can also be an object of directed attention in its own right, as an art, in public performances and in recorded forms. People crave listening to musical sounds, seemingly for their own sake, often for long stretches at a time. This fact alone is really quite extraordinary. What is there about music such that it is capable of rewarding sustained attention in this way? Why, one wonders, is there an art of music, rather than none at all? Why are people willing to make such sacrifices for an activity whose practical utility is by no means evident? Leo Tolstoy captures this question acutely in his book, *What is Art?*, where, after a withering description of a brutal and lengthy opera rehearsal in which the singers, musicians, and stage hands are subjected to a series of degradations by an imperious musical director, he writes:

> Raps with the stick, repetitions, placings, corrections of the singers, of the orchestra, of the procession, of the dancers – all seasoned with angry scolding. I heard the words, "asses," "fools," "idiots," "swine," addressed to the musicians and singers at least forty times in the course of one hour. And the unhappy individual to whom the abuse is addressed – flutist, hornblower, or singer – physically and mentally demoralized, does not reply and does what is demanded of him . . . It would be difficult to find a more repulsive sight . . .

> What was being done here? For what, and for whom? . . . What is this art which is considered so important and necessary for humanity that for its sake these sacrifices of labor, of human life, and even of goodness may be made? (Tolstoy 1960: 12–16)

This listing of some of the more intriguing features of music hardly exhausts the subject. But even considering only the combination of musical features we have mentioned – music's accessibility, its ubiquity, its adaptability, its diversity of means and organizational presentations, its expressivity, its personal intimacy, its profundity, its intrinsic interest, and its apparent practical inutility – it is hardly surprising that it has been the object of philosophical wonder for so long.

Contemporary philosophical discussions of music can be thought in a general way to address these features of music. What sort of phenomenon is music? How are we to understand and account for its creation, performance, and appreciation? Of what value is music? In addressing these questions, this chapter will focus on three main questions:

1 What is the meaning of music?
2 What is the nature of the activities and products of music-making?
3 Of what value is music?

We cannot hope in a short chapter to do justice to all the intricacies of contemporary debates in the philosophy of music, or even to present the views of individual philosophers in their completeness. What follows is an account of some of the basic issues as informed by many of the key contributors to contemporary debates, and a consideration of the challenges that face current philosophical thinking on the subject.

## 14.1  Formalism

Contemporary discussions of musical meaning owe a considerable debt to the influential book *Vom Musickalisch-Schönen* (*On the Musically Beautiful*), written in 1854 by the Viennese music critic Eduard Hanslick (1986). The shadow that Hanslick casts over contemporary philosophical discussions of music is so long that his views can be fairly regarded as a template against which contemporary views of music can be situated.

The influence and notoriety of Hanslick's book, which went through 10 editions in his lifetime, rest on at least three things: the particular insights about music that continue to appeal to a broad array of musicians and listeners; the acuity of Hanslick's argumentation; and the notoriety that the book has acquired, in part because of Hanslick's polemical style and in part because of the (mistaken) idea that the book seeks to defend the apparently outlandish claim that music has nothing whatsoever to do with the emotions.

In his book Hanslick seeks to accomplish two main goals. First, he advances a negative claim about the meaning of instrumental music, attacking a widespread view that the primary object of the aesthetics of music and of critical discourse about music can be understood in emotionalist terms. Second, he offers a positive account of musical meaning centering on what he considers to be the proper object of critical and aesthetic attention: "the musically beautiful, as an autonomous species of beauty."

Hanslick offers several arguments to support the negative thesis. When people say that music has essentially "to do with feelings," Hanslick argues, they typically equivocate between two views of the relation between music and emotion, neither of which is defensible. According to the first view, the purpose of music is said to be the arousal of certain sorts of feeling in the listener. According to the second, feeling is said to be the content or subject matter represented in music. Let us refer to these claims as the *causal* and *representational* versions of the emotionalist claim.

Against the causal claim, Hanslick offers four arguments that we may group together as two pairs. The first two arguments derive primarily from Hanslick's view of beauty and the nature of music as an art. These arguments refer, respectively, to objective and subjective aspects of musical understanding:

1   Objectively speaking, beauty in music, considered as a property, inheres in mere form, which can have no purpose beyond itself. The contemplation of the beautiful may produce pleasant feelings but these have nothing to do with musical beauty as such. The causal view falsely supposes that because pleasant feelings may be excited by the beautiful in music, the defining purpose of music is to arouse these feelings.
2   From a subjective point of view, music, as an art, addresses itself to the active imagination as "the activity of pure contemplation" of the sequence of tonal

forms, to which the arousal of feeling is a secondary and peripheral effect. It is true that the beautiful in music pleases – in a specifically musical way – but dwelling on the general emotional effects of music is analogous to trying to get to know the real nature and subtleties of wine by getting drunk.

Hanslick's third and fourth arguments against the causal view center on his account of feeling itself:

3 The causal view confuses "feelings" with "sensations." Sensation – specifically the perception of specific sense qualities such as tones – is prerequisite to the musically beautiful. Definite feelings, such as love, jubilation, and woe, however, involve a specific phenomenological component, an awareness of "our mental state with regard to its furtherance or inhibition, thus of well-being or distress." It does not follow from the fact that music necessarily involves sensations that the purpose of music is to induce specific feelings in the listener.
4 Further, as a matter of empirical fact, there is no strict, constant causal nexus between a piece of music and the specific feelings it might arouse. Musical works affect us differently according to changing musical experiences and impressions, as is evidenced by the different emotional characterizations offered of the same musical works by successive generations of listeners.

It is true, Hanslick concludes, that music may arouse in us intense feelings and moods, as the causal theorists say, but the same may be said of medical reports or our luck in a lottery. We must not be misled into thinking that such feelings have anything to do with the proper understanding of music.

The representationalist version of the emotional claim fares no better. According to this, music is said to be able to represent definite feelings such as love, courage, and piety, much in the way that painting can represent the happiness of a flower girl or the adventurousness of an exploit of Roland. On Hanslick's view, music lacks the resources to achieve this sort of representation. Here his argument is that, from a conceptual point of view, what distinguishes a definite emotion from a merely vague stirring is a particular set of concepts and judgments. A necessary constituent of the feeling of hope, for example, is the idea, however fleeting, of a future happy state with which we compare the present. What music presents is purely *musical* ideas: successions of musical sounds. These musical ideas, it is true, have dynamical qualities in tonal relationship, for example the attribute of motion, speeding up here, slowing down there, rising now, falling now, etc. The mind stands ready to associate these dynamic features of music with definite emotions that may share similar dynamics. But such associations are adventitious. Music can express only the accompanying adjectives, not the substantive: whispering, perhaps, but not the yearning of love. That is the main reason why, while people might agree about the beauty of a piece of music, they cannot agree about the specific emotional content supposedly represented. And if there is no agreement about what is specifically represented, there is no representation. Trying to save the representationalist claim by saying that music represents "indefinite emotions" is gibberish, according to Hanslick, as is the normative claim that the representation of specific emotions is nevertheless an ideal toward which music ought to aspire.

It is important to note three qualifications that Hanslick builds into his anti-representationalist arguments. First, he allows that we may *describe* a piece of music in emotionalist terms as soft, powerful, delicate, arrogant, peevish, yearning, etc. Indeed, Hanslick's own musical criticism is filled with emotive descriptions. He describes the two middle movements of Brahms's Symphony No. 3, for example, as "an invitation to repose . . . , moderate in pace and expression, tender and gracious in sentiment" (Hanslick 1950: 212). And, in a more impassioned and rhetorically charged moment, he writes of the finale of the *Adagio* of Tchaikovsky's Violin Concerto that

> it transfers us to a brutal and wretched jollity of a Russian holiday. We see plainly the savage vulgar faces, we hear curses, we smell vodka. Friedrich Vischer once observed, speaking of obscene pictures, that they stink to the eye. Tchaikovsky's Violin Concerto gives us for the first time the hideous notion that there can be music that stinks to the ear. (Slonimsky 1965: 207)

But, Hanslick insists, in employing affective terminology we only properly refer to the dynamic qualities that the musical ideas and the emotional states share. He acknowledges that music has a limited capability of portraying "external phenomena," to the extent that musical sounds may share dynamic qualities with other audible phenomena (the crowing of a rooster, for example, or the fluttering of birds). In addition, the dynamic qualities of musical sounds have an analogical similarity to the dynamics of sense modalities other than audition. Music can, to an extent, imitate the falling of snow or the flashing of lightning. There is, Hanslick says, "A well-grounded analogy between motion in space and motion in time, between the color, quality, and size of an object and the pitch, timbre, and intensity of a tone." But to think that music can *represent* emotional states associated with such phenomena is to be seriously confused, and to *interpret* music along these lines is to engage in a questionable and arbitrary enterprise.

Second, Hanslick acknowledges that certain individual musical phenomena such as tonalities, chords, and timbres, considered as isolated phenomena, may have individual emotional characters by virtue of an intrinsic "psycho-physiological" connection he calls "symbolic." The nature of this connection is not clear in his discussion, which vacillates between causal and representational explanations. But there is no mistaking his estimation of the artistic relevance of the emotive meanings that may attach themselves to music in this way. They are but fleeting connections that disappear in the flow of music when it is heard as a sequence of musical ideas and events. The content of a musical piece is always most accurately described in terms of the purely musical analysis of melodic, harmonic, rhythmic, and textural events in their myriad interrelationships.

Third, Hanslick accepts that in vocal music words may help to specify a feeling. But this admission cuts both ways, for if it is true that it is the words that help to characterize definite emotions, it remains the case that the underlying music does not play the determining role. That is why, he argues, a particular musical theme (such as the aria *Che faro senza Euridice!* in Gluck's opera *Orpheus*) can be as appropriate to the verbal representation of misery as to happiness and why others (such as certain themes in *Messiah*) may be as fitting for devotional music as for erotic duets. The musical themes of vocal music are like "silhouettes whose originals we cannot recognize without someone giving us a hint as to their identity." Further, even granting that vocal music is capable of representing definite emotions with greater specificity hardly changes the matter with respect to music generally. The aesthetics of music must be driven by what can be said of instrumental music, Hanslick insists. "Of what *instrumental music* cannot do, it ought never to be said that *music* can do it, because only instrumental music is music purely and absolutely . . . the concept of 'music' does not apply strictly to a piece of music composed to a verbal text" (Hanslick 1986: 15). He accordingly deprecates vocal music and opera, calling the union of music and poetry a morganatic marriage in which musical principles are subordinated to literary ones. He holds up the recitative as an example of the dire musical consequences when music is made to be the "handmaiden" to the representation of specific and changing states of mind. The use of music in dance is similarly disparaged.

Hanslick's positive account of musical meaning is as influential as his critique of emotionalist views. The content of music, he says, in what is widely regarded as the classic characterization of the formalist position in music, is "tönend bewegte Formen" – tonally moving forms. In considering this formulation, however, it is important to remember that Hanslick is concerned not simply with any assemblage of tones but rather with what he considers to be musically *beautiful* forms, a "specifically musical kind of beauty." He does not offer a crisp definition of the musically beautiful. Its main characteristics seem to be as follows.

First, musical beauty for Hanslick is a matter of *tones in their relations*, most especially in their melodic, harmonic, and rhythmic relations within the diatonic tonal system. These relations, he asserts, are "determined by natural law," especially the "law" of harmonic progression, instinctively recognized by "every cultivated ear." Neither psychology nor physiology can tell us exactly why musical sounds are heard musically in the way that they are, he asserts, but the proximate causes of the effects of music are always combinations of musical tones heard in the context of a musical system: a particular augmented interval here, short rhythms there, increased chromaticism in this section, and so on. Musical form, especially in the case of larger musical "forms" such as the symphony, overture, and sonata, inheres in the architectonic of the components out of which music is made and which, in accordance with formal laws of beauty, "develops itself in organically distinct gradations, like sumptuous blossoming from a bud" (Hanslick 1986: 81). The works of Beethoven are exemplary in this regard. Music that does not comply with the "laws" of music is capricious at best, ugly at worst.

Second, musical beauty is *autonomous*. Music is an end in itself, on Hanslick's view, not primarily a means for the representation of feelings or indeed of any sort of extra-musical content. He compares musical beauty to the arabesque and, perhaps more aptly, to the kaleidoscope, though, he is quick to say that music manifests itself "on an incomparably higher level of ideality." Indeed, for Hanslick, the beautiful in music is sui generis:

> Where in thought a form does not seem separable from a content, there exists in fact no independent content. But in music we see content and form, material and con-figuration, image and idea, fused in an obscure, inseparable unity. This peculiarity of music, that it possesses form and content inseparably, opposes it absolutely to the lit-erary and visual arts, which can represent the aforementioned thoughts and events in a variety of forms. (Hanslick 1986: 80)

The composer may of course compose under the sway of strong psychological states or with particular worldly events in mind but, Hanslick argues, prefiguring Wimsatt's and Beardsley's famous arguments against the so-called "intentional fallacy" a century later, such matters are of purely historical and biographical inter-est. We cannot tell from the work what these causes and conditions might have been, and even if we could, they would be irrelevant to the meaning and value of the work itself. If the composer thinks these causes are anything more than enabling devices, he or she is deluded. The autonomy of music also puts severe constraints on the familiar analogy between music and language. Music, unlike language, has no semantic function: "The essential difference is that in speech the sound is only a sign, that is, a means to an end which is entirely distinct from that means, while in music the sound is an object, i.e., it appears to us as an end in itself" (Hanslick 1986: 42).

Third, though Hanslick acknowledges that musical styles develop historically, there are at least two senses in which musical beauty is *ahistorical*. First, he wants to insist that the musically beautiful neither refers to nor is it dependent on per-sonal, historical, or political events, affairs, or conditions. This follows from his conception of the autonomy of the musically beautiful. Second, though he acknowledges that what can be heard will be a function in part of what kinds of musical experiences a listener has had, he claims that, in principle anyway, musical beauty can exist in any musical style. This "non-partisan" stance does not prevent him from frequently criticizing music in the Romantic style to the extent that it attempts to adhere to emotional rather than purely musical compositional princi-ples. It is simply the case that some styles are more hospitable to musical beauty than others.

Fourth, musical beauty inheres in musical *works* construed as *ideal objects*. "Philosophically speaking," Hanslick says, "the composed piece, regardless of whether it is performed or not, is the completed artwork" (Hanslick 1986: 48). Composition, then, is the central musical activity, involving the creation of the musical work in a strict sense, insofar as composition individuates the work itself.

Music is a performing art, he allows, but the job of the performer is primarily to externalize the composer's work, making it available to the listener in an audible form. The listener retrieves the musical work from the performance. It is true that performers often take great license in infusing their performances with expressive gestures rather than striving to be faithful to the work, just as it is the case that listeners – especially the technically uninitiated – use music as a means to wallow in the warm bath of emotional reveries. Both habits are to be avoided. Understanding a piece of music is a matter of attending with extreme vigilance to the composer's designs in the composed work, following the composition as it unfolds in the context of what has been heard and of expectations concerning what might yet be heard.

Finally, despite the fact that musical beauty is natural in the sense that its compositional "laws" are in some deep sense rooted in natural laws, there is nevertheless a sense in which it is – with respect to its materials – *artificial*. Strictly speaking, nature produces only material for musical material: the wood for a clarinet that produces the tones. We find in nature neither melody – the music of birds is not scalar – nor harmony and only rudimentary rhythmic patterns. Melody and harmony, says Hanslick, are creations of the human spirit. What we hear in nature is not the musically beautiful but only noise.

## 14.2   Enhanced Formalism

Hanslick's ideas about music are compelling in many ways. One of the main achievements of his view is that it takes the art of music seriously. That is, it seeks to identify what is (arguably) truly musical about music as an art. By isolating tonally moving forms as the object of musical attention, Hanslick speaks to an aspect of music that many musicians and listeners consider to be at the core of musical experience. His account of the musical features that figure into this kind of experience seems to many readers insightful and accurate, and his emphasis on the internal relationships of musical form is congenial to the idea – held by many in the academy – that formal musical analysis of musical structures and relationships is a means to the accurate description of the musical object. His view is applicable to a wide variety of music. Many readers of his book also appreciate his theoretical efforts to curb the more flagrant excesses of emotionalist critical interpretations and responses to music.

At the same time, Hanslick's formalist approach to music seems overly narrow in several regards. In ruling out of court virtually all extra-musical reference, he puts severe constraints not only on the range of musical meaning, but also on the ways in which music might be thought to be connected with the world generally. This isolationist tendency is supported by his ontological account of the musical work, which has the effect of essentially writing the performer out of the story – surely an odd consequence for what is usually considered to be a performing art.

And, in spite of Hanslick's adversions to the pleasures of the imaginative contemplation of musical form, many people regard his account of musical experience as focusing too much on the technical aspects of music, to the exclusion of its affective side.

One strategy to deal with the perceived narrowness of Hanslick's approach while saving his insights about the importance of musical form is to adopt a less constrictive notion of musical form, and to argue for a correspondingly more generous view of the mode of attention appropriate to the appreciation of musical form. We can call such a move "enhanced formalism."[1]

In principle one could apply the view of enhanced formalism to any variety of what Hanslick would have regarded as "extra-musical" meaning, attempting to extend the range of musical form to include events, stories, sounds, philosophical ideas, and so on.[2] Since, however, so many people find the connection between music and the expression of human feeling to be a hallmark of musical experience, it is not surprising that much philosophical attention in the wake of Hanslick's book has focused on the specific problem of expression in music. We shall accordingly concentrate on this aspect of musical meaning. Let us begin then with the question of how an enhanced formalist might deal with the problem of the musical expression of emotion.

Musical expression presents at least two related conceptual difficulties right at the outset. We can call these the *problem of reconciliation* and the *problem of intelligibility*. The problem of reconciliation concerns the twin questions of what we are supposed to pay attention to in listening to and appreciating music, and how the formal and emotive aspects of meaning can be understood to be related. Hanslick clearly thought that a concern with the expressive aspects of music distracted one from a proper concern with musical form; a solution to the problem of reconciliation would show that attention to the formal and the expressive features of music are at least compatible, if not mutually reinforcing.

The problem of intelligibility is a special case of a difficulty that arises with the idea of expressive meaning in works of arts generally, an issue famously articulated by O. K. Bouwsma (1950), but also anticipated by Hanslick. The problem here is that we normally associate the idea of emotional expression with sentient beings (most especially human beings). Since works of art are not sentient beings, the fact that we attribute expressive properties such as sadness or happiness to works of art presents itself as a conceptual puzzle. Surely a piece of music is not sad in the way that a human being might be sad. We might try to explain the sadness of a musical work by locating the sadness in its provenance in the composer: the sad piece of music expresses the sadness of the composer. However, this gambit brings us up against various issues concerning artistic intention, including the plain fact that sad pieces of music may be composed by cheery people. Alternatively, one might parse the emotional expressivity of a work in terms of the emotional states of listeners. (The sad piece of music makes the listener sad.) But this strategy brings us up against, among other things, the challenges to causally based expression theories discussed earlier.

In light of the problems of reconciliation and intelligibility, it is not surprising, then, that two of the most influential contemporary treatments of the topic of expressive meaning in music consider a set of issues that can be grouped under the rubric of what can be called the paradox of feeling and form. Susanne Langer (1953) starts her discussion of expression in her book *Feeling and Form* by acknowledging that the terms "feeling" and "form" are themselves often taken to be antithetical to one another. She argues that if we construe expression in music as the self-expression of the composer, we are faced with the implausible consequence that it is only the composer who could judge the expressive value of the work of art, since only he or she could judge the accuracy of the expression. If we say that expression consists in the evocation of psychological states in the listener, we reduce musical composition to a psychological ploy whose aims are not far removed from those of the advertising agent. We seem to be left with the paradoxical claim that the work itself is expressive of emotion (Langer 1953: chs 2 and 3).

Peter Kivy (1989), in his important book *Sound Sentiment: An Essay on the Musical Emotions*, puts the matter in the context of a typology of musical descriptions. Some descriptions of musical expressivity seem to be biographical rather than musical; they are more about the purported emotional states of the composer than about the music composed. Other descriptions are autobiographical: they refer to the critic's mental states rather than the music itself. Descriptions that seem to predicate expression of the music itself ("emotive descriptions") seem to be both incoherent and unverifiable. Only technical descriptions that point to purely musical formal features such as chordal progressions, voice-leading, tempi changes, and so on seem to be safely about the music itself; but, as Kivy points out, this goal is achieved at the expense of leaving a huge portion of the musical community – those without technical training – out in the cold. Nor is it plausible to suggest that, in describing music in emotive terms, the critic is elliptically redirecting us to the real musical features – such an explanation makes musical criticism into some sort of "elaborate hoax." Kivy sums up the issues of reconciliation and intelligibility by saying that what is needed for an account of musical expression is an "intellectually respectable description of music that is not remote from the humanistic understanding to which music itself has traditionally appealed" (Kivy 1989: 10–11).

Langer attempts to resolve the paradox by elaborating a theory of musical expressiveness in the context of a general theory of art which is in turn explained in terms of how things have significance generally; that is, a theory of signs. She distinguishes two general categories of signs: signals, which refer to matters of fact such as objects and events, and symbols, which refer to ideas. The distinction is crucial because, as we have seen, Langer wants to deny that music functions as a signal, referring to emotions actually had by the composer or actually evoked in the listener. Instead, she argues that music, like all art, functions symbolically to refer to ideas about the life of feeling. She argues further that the individual arts function symbolically by means of the creation of what she calls "semblances" or "illusions" of particular domains of the emotive life. These semblances are emergent qualities that are epiphenomenal on arrangements of given properties such as tones or colors.

Thus, in the case of music, Langer argues that it is a tonal analog of emotive life. More particularly, music functions as a symbol of the particular feeling domain of "transience" – the experience of the passage of time. This music can do because the tonally moving forms of music are iconic with the pattern of time as experienced. That is to say, music functions as a "presentational symbol": its tonally moving forms are a semblance or illusion of the feeling of time. The musical forms and tensions that we hear in music (tensions in tempi, loudness, orchestration, harmony and dissonance, counterpoint, etc.) share the same "logical form" with the moving patterns of physical, emotional, and intellectual tensions by means of which we experience the passage of time. Music, then, presents what Langer calls "musical" or "virtual" time, a directly felt audible illusion or image of "duration," or "psychological" time (Langer 1953: chs 3, 4, and 7).

Langer thus shares with Hanslick the view that there is some similarity between the dynamics of musical form and those of emotional life. She further agrees that musical form cannot be read as a symptom of the actual emotional life of the composer or as an index to the emotional effects stimulated in the listener. And, by identifying the referent of musical expression as the general pattern of a domain of feeling, she avoids the difficulty that Hanslick points out in linking individual musical forms to definite emotions such as love or pity.

The main difference between Langer and Hanslick is in her assessment of the significance of the similarity between music and the emotive life. Hanslick was content to note the formal similarity and to acknowledge its basis in the application of emotive descriptors. Langer, on the other hand, argues that the similarity underwrites a relation of reference by means of which music is able to provide knowledge about the inner life: "It bespeaks [the composer's] imagination of feelings rather than his own emotional state, and expresses what he *knows about* the so-called 'inner life'; and this may exceed his personal case because music is a symbolic form to him through which he may learn as well as utter ideas of human sensibility" (Langer 1953: 28).

Langer's theory has enormous appeal. The theory captures the sense that music has an intimate relation with the emotional life. It promises to offer an intelligible explanation of how this can be, trading on the formal analogy between musical structures and the patterns of sentient life. And, insofar as it is a cognitivist theory, in the sense that it argues that music provides us with knowledge about the inner life, it supports the view that there is something important and profound about music, something that goes beyond the appreciation of mere musical form. The value of music is intimately tied to the human desire for self-knowledge. This last feature has endeared it especially to music educators, in whose hands the theory has been enlisted frequently as a justification of their endeavors. (See for example Reimer 1989.) Langer makes more of the role of emotion in the composition of music than does Hanslick, on whose view the composer's emotional state is at best an initiating but ultimately irrelevant contributing condition to the creation of music. Langer also gives a more plausible account of musical performance than does Hanslick, to whom performance takes on the aura of a necessary evil. This is in part a result of a different account of the ontology of the work of art. Hanslick holds that the work is essentially the composition. Langer, on the other hand, argues, "Once a composition is given to the world it has a status and career as a living work of art." On Langer's view, a piece of music just is "an organically developed illusion of time in audible passage" (Langer 1953: 134), and the performer is someone who makes crucial decisions about the final audible form of the work. The commanding form of the composition falls short of the full realization of the work. The performer completes the work, marshalling not only what Langer calls "sonorous imagination" and the "muscular imagination of tone" but also a qualified sense of "self-expression," the performer's "ardor" for the emotive import conveyed. These are all features of the performer's sense of "utterance" that contribute to the presentation of the illusion begotten by the sounds of the music. These last comments also provide an account of how it is that performers come to have particular repertoires, ranges of music for which the performer is temperamentally suited (Langer 1953: chs 8 and 9).

For all its sensitivities to the particularities of musical composition, performance, and experience, however, Langer's theory is not without its philosophical difficulties. Arguing that music expresses ideas about a general domain of emotion rather than expressing particular emotions is a nice way of getting around some of the problems attached to the view that music expresses definite emotions, but this gain is had at the expense of setting aside the bulk of critical talk about music that *does* employ the language of particular emotions. What are we to make of the fact that so much talk about music is about definite emotions? Or, for that matter, given that the main function of music is supposed to be to "make time audible," why is comparatively little critical discussion of musical works given over to discussion about the idea of time per se? In addition, the theory is underdetermined in one important respect: there is nothing in Langer's account that guarantees that, of all the things with which musical forms *might* be isomorphic, music *must* symbolize the life of feeling or, even more particularly, the sense of transience. Indeed, one wonders whether the life of feeling has a "form" or set of patterns with which musical form might be isomorphic. Additionally, Langer's solution to the problem of reconciliation – the idea that, *in* listening to music, we are in effect being presented with ideas about something else, the life of feeling – has seemed to many not to square with their introspective sense of the matter. Finally, questions have been raised about the notion of an emergent quality of semblance or virtuality, as well as Langer's distinction between musical and psychological time.

Peter Kivy, like Langer, is concerned to offer an account of musical expression that will explain how emotive terms can be intelligibly applied to pieces of music, and to do this in a way that will avoid what he takes to be the errors of a causally based theory. In addition, he endeavors to show how such descriptions of music can be said to be objective, that is, to have standards in virtue of which they can be said to be more or less accurate.

Kivy's argument proceeds on several fronts. First, he sharpens a distinction that Hanslick had gestured toward and that Langer had considered in greater depth, the distinction between something's *expressing* an emotion and something's *being expressive of* an emotion. A person may be said to express an emotion through public behavior, as when my shouting and clenching my fists express my anger. But it is also possible for something to be expressive of an emotion even when we have no call to suppose that an emotion or mood is actually expressed. To take Kivy's now-famous example, the Saint Bernard's face looks sad. The face is expressive of sadness quite independently of the dog's mental state (should it have one) and apart from our speculations about such a state.[3]

Could it be that the sadness in the music is like the sadness of the Saint Bernard's face? Kivy thinks so. He does not want to deny that there are cases where pieces of music are expressions of emotion in the sense of being manifestations of emotions actually had by a composer. We know from biographical research, for example, that Mozart did see himself as expressing his terror of death in his *Requiem* (K626). Kivy's point is rather that the central cases of musical expression can best be understood as instances of being expressive of emotion rather than expressing emotion. Put another way, most emotive descriptions of music are logically independent of the states of minds of the composers of the music.

On Kivy's view, musical expressiveness can be understood in the context of two explanatory theories, which he develops drawing on the work of several seventeenth- and eighteenth-century theorists, including Daniel Webb, Frances Hutcheson, Charles Avison, and Johann Mattheson, and on the music that was the object of their attention. The first of these explanatory theories is what Kivy calls the *contour* theory of expressiveness, which begins with the claim that there are features of music that resemble certain aspects of human expression, a point that both Hanslick and Langer had allowed. Unlike Hanslick and Langer, however, Kivy denies that what music resembles is the phenomenology or the "feel" of human emotion, whether of definite feelings or of general domains of human feeling. The "feel" of the emotions is an imponderable, Kivy says; it is questionable that they possess the sort of structure that a resemblance theory would require (Kivy 1989: 52). Kivy argues instead that music can be iconic with behavioral manifestations of human feeling such as speech, gesture, facial configuration, movement, posture, and so on. Musical expressiveness is therefore parasitic on human expression though logically independent of it.

This analysis serves several purposes at once. First, because musical expressiveness is parasitic on human expressiveness, Kivy's account saves the intuition that music can be expressive of specific emotions. Normal or typical modes of human expression are recognizable in music, much in the way that sadness is recognizable in the Saint Bernard's face. And there are, on Kivy's view, public, objective, and familiar criteria according to which we understand the expression. In the case of the Saint Bernard, for example, we notice the droopiness of the mouth, which is a characteristic of sad human faces. In a similar fashion, the opening oboe solo in the second movement of Bach's first Brandenburg Concerto is, as it were, a "choreography" of expression: "we hear sadness in this complex musical line, we hear it as expressive of sadness, because we hear it as a musical resemblance of the gesture and carriage appropriate to the expression of our sadness. It is a 'sound map' of the human body under the influence of a particular emotion" (Kivy 1989: 53).

How secure is the connection between a piece of music and the emotions of which it is expressive? Kivy responds to Hanslick's claim that there is no general agreement about the expressive meaning of musical works by asking, "How much disagreement is too much disagreement?" Kivy's view is that listeners do generally agree about musical expressiveness, at a relevant level of generality. Critics may disagree about fine distinctions such as whether a piece is expressive of "noble grief" or "abject sorrow," but there is general agreement about gross distinctions, says Kivy, and that is all that is required. As to Langer's contention that there is no "vocabulary" to musical expression, Kivy questions whether the criteria for agreement about musical meaning are most appropriately drawn from the kinds of stricture typically placed on natural language. What is required for the case of musical expressiveness is simply that there be generally agreed-upon public criteria for expressiveness, and that is precisely what the contour theory supplies by means of its recourse to the repertoire of human expressive behavior. In addition, Kivy argues, the expressiveness of music is anchored in a universal psychological human tendency to animate the world. We cannot help but anthropomorphize the world around us, including the music we hear. This psychological condition helps Kivy to avoid the problem that Langer faces in placing so much of the burden of musical expressiveness on formal analogy as such. It is not simply by virtue of resemblance of a musical line to the inflected voice that we hear the weeping in the tenor line in Bach's *Saint Matthew Passion*.

There are, however, some expressive musical features that don't seem to fit easily into the contour model of musical expressiveness. It is hard to say what expressive behavior the expressively sad minor triad, for example, resembles. To handle such examples, Kivy offers a second, complementary theory of musical expressiveness, the *convention* theory, which asserts simply that some musical features have come to be associated with certain emotive meanings, apart from any structural analogy between them. Kivy speculates that certain of these associations may have at one time been heard as resembling expressive behavior or as having contributed to such resemblance. Be that as it may, the main job of the convention part of Kivy's theory is to extend the range of musically expressive features covered by the theory to musical elements, such as the "restless" diminished triad, that contribute to the forming of expressive contours even though they do not in themselves resemble them; those, such as certain chromatic melodic patterns, that may have once been heard as resembling expressive behavior but no longer are so heard; and those, such as the minor triad, that once contributed to resemblance but now function expressively in virtue of convention only.

As we have seen, Kivy's theory can be appreciated as going beyond some of the difficulties facing the theories of Hanslick and Langer. There are other aspects of Kivy's theory that we should mention even if only in passing. Kivy joins Hanslick and Langer in dismissing arousal theories, and he offers what can be considered a "cognitivist" theory in a new sense: it is not, as Langer had it, that music provides or should provide knowledge about the world (the world of sentience) but rather that the mode of attention appropriate to the art of music should be a matter of coming to understand the music alone. In this he is closer to Hanslick than to Langer. Music, for Kivy, is a "decorative" art, albeit one with profound value. Such emotions as are appropriately felt are those related to the way in which we are moved by the beauty or the perfection of music itself. Finally, Kivy has had important things to say about the nature and value of musical performance and the concept of authenticity.[4]

The theories of Hanslick, Langer, and Kivy stand as three landmarks of the philosophical understanding of musical meaning in the formalist tradition, broadly construed. Other philosophers who have been influenced by musical formalism include Monroe Beardsley (1981), Malcolm Budd (1985), and Roger Scruton (1997). (See also Kivy 1993.)

## 14.3   Beyond Formalism

Some philosophers have sought to move away from some of the themes, if not the tenets, of musical formalism, and they have advanced alternative accounts of the meaning and value of music. This has occurred in various and sometimes overlapping ways, many of which pertain to formalist emphases on musical autonomy and the modes of attention thought to be appropriate to musical works of art.

Against the suggestion that keeping large-scale structural relations in mind is fundamental to musical understanding, for example, Jerrold Levinson (1997) argues for a view he calls "qualified concatenationism." Inspired by the work of Edmund Gurney in his 1880 book *The Power of Sound*, Levinson argues the controversial claim that musical understanding consists in the comprehension of relatively short passages of music in their moment-to-moment progression and that musical value is grounded in the appeal of individual passages and the cogency of their succession. He is careful to say that listening will necessarily involve situating a piece in a relevant musico-historical nexus and that this invariably depends on internalizing certain facts about musical structuring, but, on Levinson's view, understanding music requires virtually no intellectual awareness of the architectonics or the large-scale structuring of a piece of music.[5]

Some theorists have advanced the case that, the arguments against musical representation notwithstanding, music may have an important narrative or literary dimension. Edward T. Cone (1974) and Anthony Newcomb (1984), for example, argue that the expressive content of music provides sufficient grounds to anchor psychological patterns or plots. One explanation of how this might occur is provided by Fred Everett Maus (1988), who argues that a musical piece may be understood as presenting a series of actions where the musical events can be described analogically in ways that we might describe human actions: one musical passage may be understood and explained as "a response" to a preceding one. Maus, along with others, including Gregory Karl and Jenefer Robinson (1995), argue that understanding music this way involves a close attention to the formal and expressive unfoldings of the music, often ascribing the psychological development to a musical "persona" or an "indeterminate" musical agent, and involving complex emotions such as hope, nostalgia, and wistfulness. (See also Levinson 1990b.)

There has also been considerable discussion of the dismissal by formalist theorists of arousal theories of musical expression. Some philosophers have argued that musical expressiveness involves the imagination or a consciousness of emotive states, albeit in a way that falls short of full-bodied emotional arousal. Kendall Walton (1988), for example, argues that music evokes imaginary feelings: the listener imagines himself or herself introspecting particular emotions. On Jerrold Levinson's view, musical expression involves an incipient feeling and a cognitively "etiolated" version of the expressed emotion (Levinson 1990c). Stephen Davies goes further in countenancing the arousal of full-bodied emotions. In setting forth a theory of musical expressiveness in some ways similar to Kivy's contour theory of musical expressiveness, Davies does not go so far as to argue that the expression of emotion in music can be explained solely in terms of the evocation of feelings in the listener, but he does allow that such "mirroring" responses are both possible and common features of musical experience, and he suggests that they may be an aspect of the understanding the listener gains from the music. (See Davies 1994: esp. ch. 6.) An explicit theoretical connection between the arousal of feelings by music and our understanding of music and its expressiveness is taken up and developed by Jenefer Robinson (1998), who argues that music can express emotions precisely in virtue of its arousing emotion. (See also Radford 1989; Matravers 1998.)

There has also arisen a critical debate about the general idea of musical autonomy. This discussion has appeared in several guises. Some philosophers have taken issue with the view espoused by Hanslick and Kivy that musical expressiveness is not "about" anything, and particularly not about the emotions. (See for example Davies 1994: ch. 5.) There has also been extensive discussion about ontological matters, especially the ontological status of the notion of a musical "work" and the extent to which understandings of the notion of a musical work must be understood by way of a historicized account. The literature here is vast, but two important works deserve mention. Lydia Goehr (1992, 1998) has argued that the concept of the musical work that has served as a key regulative notion for musical practice and for the philosophy of music derives from the ideals of a particular, relatively recent, historically situated musical tradition – roughly, western classical music of the last 200 years. Philosophical analysis that places undue emphasis on the notion of a musical work, she suggests, will be unable to deal with the complexity of musical phenomena, especially musical practices in which the notion of a work does not have regulative force. Stephen Davies (2001) contends that the philosophy of music has been bedeviled by too narrow a range of musical examples. Davies argues that there are in fact several kinds of musical works that accord with varieties of music-making. He distinguishes six kinds of music – improvisations, live performances of works for live performance, studio performances of works for live performance, works conceived for studio performance, works for playback but not for performance, and purely electronic works for playback – as well as maintaining a distinction between "thinner" works, which determine relatively few details of an accurate performance, and "thicker" works, which specify more detail. He also examines the consequences of this analysis for such topics as the authentic performance, the presentation of understanding of music from other cultures, the question of whether musical works are discovered or created, and music involving the studio and electronic media.[6]

Contemporary philosophy of music has in fact seen an increased interest in the musical and theoretical issues suggested by musical traditions other than those deriving from the so-called common-practice era, the canon of work in the western tradition from roughly 1725 to 1900, which had been the source of many examples in the philosophical literature. Philosophers have been increasingly concerned with such musics as experimental and electronic music, popular music, rock, jazz, and improvised music, and music from non-western cultures. In these cases, there has been of late a renewed interest in questions concerning the performance and interpretation of music and the impact of recording and compositional technologies, and a greater concern with topics bearing on music's social and political context, such as the status of mass art music like rock and hip hop as well as ethico-cultural questions concerning the matter of the appropriation of music within a culture by people outside the culture. (See, for example, Alperson 1984; Gracyk 1996, 2001; Godlovich 1998; Hagberg 2000; Shusterman 2000: chs 7 and 8.)

Finally, there has been a renewed interest among contemporary philosophers in the ancient link between music and morality, a connection featured by writers more or less continuously from Confucius, Plato, and Aristotle through Nietzsche and Adorno. Some philosophers argue that musical works themselves may have a moral dimension, perhaps by way of a connection with the expressive qualities of rhythm, tempo, orchestration, melody, counterpoint, harmony, inflection, and other musical features. (See for example Radford 1991.) Others see the ethical dimension of music issuing from the contribution that aesthetic experience of music is said to be able to make to happiness or Aristotelian *eudemonia*. (See for example Walhout 1995.) Susan McClary (1991) has been influential in introducing discussions of ways in which musical elements and styles may be gender-coded. Kathleen Higgins (1991) takes a more global approach still, discussing the affective character of music and also the symbolic roles that music and musical practices have served in both western and non-western societies, and ways in which music can serve as models for ethical behavior and modes of social organization. The bolder claim – again a suggestion advanced by Plato centuries earlier – that music may serve as a harbinger of social and political organization is advanced with appropriate prophetic nuances by Jacques Attali (1985).

These considerations suggest a rather more radical estimation of the western fine art tradition of composed music in which modern musical formalism arose. It may be that a robust philosophical understanding of music must set the theoretical understanding of the practice of music in the fine art tradition alongside the plurality of functions that music serves. On this note, we may leave the last word to Francis Sparshott, who argues that, in the deeper context of human affairs, the basic concept of music might not be "tone" but "phone," the Aristotelian idea of "voice," sound "that we instantly refer to the meaningful utterance of a living thing" (Sparshott 1994: 47). As Sparshott points out:

> We sit side by side in the same hall listening to the same music as a single audience. We do not know quite how to explain that, but the inexplicability is not disturbing because it is the basic condition of human social existence: strangers from different backgrounds understand and misunderstand each other, and we cannot articulate or hope to unravel this fact because it comprises the entire substance of our knowledge of social reality and is therefore not to be reduced to anything simpler (and therefore less substantial). (1994: 85–6)

The challenges of such a deepened notion of philosophy of music remain before us.

## Notes

1  The notion of enhanced formalism is set out in greater length in Alperson (1991).
2  On the topic of musical representation, see Peter Kivy (1984), Walton (1998), and Davies (1994: ch. 2).
3  The distinction between expressing and being expressive of is set out in Tormey (1971).
4  On these points see Kivy (1990, 1995).
5  For further discussions on the connection between musical perception and understanding, see Raffman (1993) and DeBellis (1995).
6  See also Jerrold Levinson (1990a), especially "What a Musical Work Is" (originally published in *Journal of Philosophy*, 77 [1980]: 5–28) and "What a Musical Work Is, Again."

## References

Alperson, P. (1984). "On Musical Improvisation." *Journal of Aesthetics and Art Criticism*, 63: 17–30.

——(1991). "What Should One Expect from a Philosophy of Music Education?" *Journal of Aesthetic Education*, 25: 215–42.

——, ed. (1994). *What is Music? An Introduction to the Philosophy of Music*. University Park, PA: Pennsylvania State University Press.

——, ed. (1998). *Musical Worlds: New Directions in the Philosophy of Music*. University Park, PA: Pennsylvania State University Press. (Many of the essays were originally published in *Journal of Aesthetics and Art Criticism* [1994] 52.)

Attali, J. (1985). *Noise: The Political Economy of Music*, trans. B. Massumi. Minneapolis: University of Minnesota Press. (Original work pub. 1977.)

Beardsley, M. (1981). "On Understanding Music." In K. Price (ed.), *On Criticizing Music: Five Philosophical Perspectives*. Baltimore: Johns Hopkins Press.

Bouwsma, O. K. (1950). "The Expression Theory of Art." In Max Black (ed.), *Philosophical Analysis*. Ithaca, NY: Cornell University Press: 75–101.

Budd, M. (1985). *Music and the Emotions*. London: Routledge and Kegan Paul.

Cone, E. T. (1974). *The Composer's Voice*. Berkeley: University of California Press.

Davies, S. (1994). *Musical Meaning and Expression*. Ithaca, NY: Cornell University Press.

——(2001). *Musical Works and Performances: A Philosophical Exploration*. Oxford: Oxford University Press.

DeBellis, M. (1995). *Music and Conceptualization*. Cambridge: Cambridge University Press.

Godlovich, S. (1998). *Musical Performance: A Philosophical Study*. London: Routledge.

Goehr, L. (1992). *The Imaginary Museum of Musical Works: An Essay in the Philosophy of Music*. Oxford: Oxford University Press.

——(1998). "Political Music and the Politics of Music." In P. Alperson (ed.), *Musical Worlds: New Directions in the Philosophy of Music*. University Park, PA: Pennsylvania State University Press: 131–44.

Gracyk, T. (1996). *Rhythm and Noise: An Aesthetics of Rock*. Durham, NC: Duke University Press.

——(2001). *I Wanna Be Me: Rock Music and the Politics of Identity*. Philadelphia: Temple University Press.

Hagberg, G., ed. (2000). Special issue on improvisation. *Journal of Aesthetics and Art Criticism*, 58.

Hanslick, E. (1950). *Music Criticisms 1846–99*, ed. and trans. H. Pleasants. Harmondsworth: Penguin.

——(1986). *On the Musically Beautiful*, trans. G. Payzant. 8th edn. Indianapolis: Hackett. (1st edn. 1891.)

Higgins, K. M. (1991). *The Music of Our Lives*. Philadelphia: Temple University Press.

Karl, G. and Robinson, J. (1995). "Shostakovich's Tenth Symphony and the Musical Expression of Cognitively Complex Emotion." *Journal of Aesthetics and Art Criticism*, 53: 401–15.

Kivy, P. (1984). *Sound and Semblance: Reflections on Musical Representation*. Princeton, NJ: Princeton University Press.

——(1989). *Sound Sentiment: An Essay on the Musical Emotions*. Philadelphia: Temple University Press. (Expanded version of *The Corded Shell: Reflections on Musical Expression*. Princeton, NJ: Princeton University Press, 1980.)

——(1990). *Music Alone: Philosophical Reflections on the Purely Musical Experience*. Ithaca, NY: Cornell University Press.

——(1993). *The Fine Art of Repetition: Essays on the Philosophy of Music*. Cambridge: Cambridge University Press.

——(1995). *Authenticities: Philosophical Reflections on Musical Performance*. Ithaca, NY: Cornell University Press.

Langer, S. K. (1953). *Feeling and Form.* New York: Charles Scribner's Sons.

Levinson, J. (1990a). *Music, Art, and Metaphysics.* Ithaca, NY: Cornell University Press.

——(1990b). "Hope in *The Hebrides.*" In *Music, Art, and Metaphysics.* Ithaca, NY: Cornell University Press: 336–75.

——(1990c). "Music and Negative Emotions." In *Music, Art, and Metaphysics.* Ithaca, NY: Cornell University Press: 306–35. (Earlier version in *Pacific Philosophical Quarterly* (1982) 63: 327–46.)

——(1997). *Music in the Moment.* Ithaca, NY: Cornell University Press.

Matravers, D. (1998). *Art and Emotion.* Oxford: Oxford University Press.

Maus, F. E. (1988). "Music as Drama." *Music Theory Spectrum,* 10: 56–73.

McClary, S. (1991). *Feminine Endings: Music, Gender, and Sexuality.* Minneapolis: University of Minnesota Press.

Mendelssohn, F. (1956). Letter to Marc-André Souchay. In S. Morgenstern (ed.), *Composers on Music: An Anthology of Composers' Writings from Palestrina to Copland.* New York: Pantheon Books: 140. (Original letter 1842.)

Newcomb, A. (1984). "Sound and Feeling." *Critical Inquiry,* 10: 614–43.

Radford, C. (1989). "Emotions and Music: A Reply to the Cognitivists." *Journal of Aesthetics and Art Criticism,* 47: 69–76.

——(1991). "How Can Music be Moral?" In Peter French, Theodore E. Uehling, Jr, and Howard K. Wettstein (eds), *Midwest Studies in Philosophy. Volume XVI.* Notre Dame: University of Notre Dame Press: 421–38.

Raffman, D. (1993). *Language, Music, and Mind.* Cambridge, MA: MIT Press.

Reimer, B. (1989). *A Philosophy of Music Education.* 2nd edn. Englewood Cliffs, NJ: Prentice-Hall.

Robinson, J. (1998). "The Expression and Arousal of Emotion in Music." In P. Alperson (ed.), *Musical Worlds: New Directions in the Philosophy of Music.* University Park, PA: Pennsylvania State University Press: 13–22. (Earlier version in *Journal of Aesthetics and Art Criticism* (1994) 52: 13–22.)

Scruton, R. (1997). *The Aesthetics of Music.* Oxford: Oxford University Press.

Shusterman, R. (2000). *Pragmatist Aesthetics: Living Beauty, Rethinking Art.* 2nd edn. Lanham: Rowman and Littlefield.

Slonimsky, N. (1965). *Lexicon of Musical Invective: Critical Assaults on Composers since Beethoven's Time.* Seattle: University of Washington Press.

Sparshott, F. (1994). "Aesthetics of Music – Limits and Grounds." In P. Alperson (ed.), *What is Music? An Introduction to the Philosophy of Music.* University Park, PA: Pennsylvania State University Press: 33–98.

Tolstoy, L. (1960). *What is Art?,* trans. A. Maude. Indianapolis: Bobbs-Merrill. (Original work pub. 1896.)

Tormey, A. (1971). *The Concept of Expression: A Study in Philosophical Psychology and Aesthetics.* Princeton, NJ: Princeton University Press.

Walhout, D. (1995). "Music and Moral Goodness." *Journal of Aesthetic Education,* 29: 5–16.

Walton, K. (1988). "What is Abstract About the Art of Music?" *Journal of Aesthetics and Art Criticism,* 46: 351–64.

——(1998). "Listening with Imagination: Is Music Representational?" In P. Alperson (ed.), *Musical Worlds: New Directions in the Philosophy of Music.* University Park, PA: Pennsylvania State University Press: 47–62. (Originally pub. in *Journal of Aesthetics and Art Criticism* (1994) 52: 47–61.)

## Further reading

Addis, L. (1999). *Of Mind and Music*. Ithaca, NY: Cornell University Press.

Cook, N. (1990). *Music, Imagination, and Culture*. Oxford: Oxford University Press.

——(1998). *Music: A Very Short Introduction*. Oxford: Oxford University Press.

Kerman, J. (1985). *Contemplating Music: Challenges to Musicology*. Cambridge, MA: Harvard University Press.

Krausz, M., ed. (1993). *The Interpretation of Music*. Cambridge: Cambridge University Press.

Levinson, J. (1996). *The Pleasures of Aesthetics*. Ithaca, NY: Cornell University Press.

Meyer, L. B. (1956). *Emotion and Meaning in Music*. Chicago: University of Chicago Press.

——(1967). *Music, the Arts, and Ideas: Patterns and Predictions in Twentieth-Century Culture*. Chicago: University of Chicago Press.

Nettl, B. (1983). *The Study of Ethnomusicology: Twenty-Nine Issues and Concepts*. Urbana: University of Illinois Press.

Sharpe, R. A. (2000). *Music and Humanism: An Essay in the Aesthetics of Music*. Oxford: Oxford University Press.

# Chapter 15

# The Philosophy of Dance: Bodies in Motion, Bodies at Rest

*Francis Sparshott*

The center of dance aesthetics is the apparent fact that human movement in all its forms and contexts can be read and appreciated, just because it is human; and, in counterpoise to that, the worldwide practice of devising special ways of moving (dances, traditions) to be read and appreciated in ways that can be systematically articulated, explored, and developed. The substance of dance aesthetics is the establishing of determinable aspects of how this comes about. The challenge to dance aesthetics is to make coherent sense of it all. The scandal or paradox of dance aesthetics is that this topic is persistently ignored by students of aesthetics and their journals.

Discussions of the philosophy of dance commonly start by commenting on the scarcity of treatments of the topic, and the fact that general discussions of aesthetics and the philosophy of art seldom take their examples and illustrations from dance. Because dancing is traditionally held to be among the major forms of artistic activity, the reasons for its near absence from the everyday concerns of academic aesthetics remain a central topic for the philosophy of dance itself. Could the explanation be no more than a self-perpetuating absence of a tradition of debate, or some form of moral or intellectual snobbery? Does the unscripted and transitory aspect of dance performance deprive theorists and teachers of an accessible canon of familiar masterpieces to which arguments may be anchored? Is it simply that most students of aesthetics do not think of dance as deserving to be taken seriously, or even that dance proves on inspection not to be worth discussing? Perhaps. But it may be that there is something in dance that resists the preferred methods of aesthetics and of philosophy generally. If so, the philosophy of art needs to consider what that might be.

If artistic dancing does not lend itself to the preferred topics and procedures of aesthetics, that could be because it belongs to some different domain. In recent decades, meaningful recreational, communicative, and expressive modes of behavior have fallen within the purview of certain inchoate fields of discourse: semiotics, which examines the overall field of meaningful behavior and meaning generally;

critical theory (or simply "theory"), which extends the methods and stances of literary criticism and interpretation to recognizable forms in the human world generally; and, most recently, "cultural studies," which borrows recent approaches from anthropology and uses them to articulate the cultural scene. The development of these studies reflects a widespread conviction that the electronic means of communication currently being developed are reshaping the ways their users see themselves and their world, and it may be in this context that dance phenomena call most stridently for attention. At present, it is not easy to link such studies with aesthetics as a philosophical discipline, because they still function at a level of observation and suggestion rather than argument.

The philosophy of dance does have a history. The present scope of philosophy in general consists largely of what has survived from its long tradition, beginning with ancient Greece. Philosophical debates about the fine arts drew strength from wider areas of rational concern that seemed to involve them: music from mathematical cosmology and psychological order, painting from the cognitive orders of representation and spatiality, poetry from the boundaries and dimensions of veracity and imagination, architecture from civic ceremony. What about dance? Dance has traditionally been tied in to ideas of individuality and community, of creative force ("the dance of life"), of grace and order in human societies and the starry heavens; but these ideas have worked themselves out in imaginative suggestion rather than in prosaic contention. People start to use this metaphor of dance when their topic is the mutual adjustment of intricate systems which have their own evident orderliness but defy reduction to formal integration. One possible reason why theorists have found little to say about dance could be that people resort to dancing and gesturing when the meaning they wish to convey cannot or must not be put into words.

The philosophical tradition of philosophy affords some materials for assigning cognitive or moral significance to dance. Although treatments of Plato's views on art usually emphasize the handling of poetry in his *Republic*, his most emphatic notice of artistic behavior is in the *Laws*, according to which ceremonies embodying and symbolizing the ordering principles of the civic constitution are to be danced out, counterpoised by countercultural forms of ecstatic dance (Lonsdale 1993): it is through participation in dance that social relationships are to be brought to consciousness. The order thus danced out was commonly thought of as derived from the planetary "dance" of the heavens (Miller 1986). Official dance forms such as the Italian and French court ballets of early modern times were designed to be read along these lines. This way of thinking was vastly influential until the demise of monarchic ideology in the eighteenth century. Interpreters and theorists of modern and postmodern dance forms habitually replace this way of thought by working out ways in which danced relationships embody and symbolize democratic forms.

An important variant of Plato's employment of dance form as exemplar of social order is Plotinus' use of the dancing body, thought of as forming a spontaneous unity of integrally intelligible articulations, as a model of the way in which the variety of the physical universe manifests a unified intelligence. Such reflection on the kind of intelligibly unified order a dancing body spontaneously displays has been a recurrent theme in dance philosophy.

Aristotle's systematic listing of forms of representation (*mimesis*) in the opening chapter of his *Poetics* included one sentence on dance. The significance assigned to the *Poetics* in the Renaissance earned this sentence an emphasis disproportionate to its brevity. Representation, to Aristotle, is a central mode of human cognition, and representations are distinguished by their objects, their methods, and their materials: dance represents actions, emotions, and states of character by patterned movements of the body. When the notion of the fine arts was formalized in the eighteenth century, Aristotle's example was followed in giving pride of place among artistic dances to those in which gestural significance was paramount. The resulting tension between formal and mimetic dance persists, and its cognitive complexities remain a standard topic for the philosophy of dance.

In the eighteenth-century period in which aesthetics and the philosophy of art became a recognized discipline, a place was sought for dance as a mimetic art alongside the "sister arts" of painting and poetry (Noverre 1760). Meanwhile, however, speculations on the origins of human language were postulating a prelinguistic phase in which undifferentiated sounds and movements were used for spontaneous expression, later to be developed into the specialized forms of speech, music, and the graphic arts. This way of thinking assigned dance to a subcivilized, pre-artistic level of behavior; Hegel, especially, found no distinctive cognitive function for dance in his system of the fine arts. The fact that artistic dance everywhere takes on determinate forms does not suffice to earn it a place among the artistic manifestations of *Geist*. Hegel's influence here has proved decisive. S. K. Langer's system, which assigned to dance the function of symbolizing psychological forces, was found suggestive rather than persuasive (Langer 1953).

So much for background. What of the philosophy of dance itself? Roughly, a dance form is categorized as "art" according to whatever theory or theories of art and the aesthetic one may be using, and an art form is categorized as dance if its principal medium is the unspeaking human body in motion and at rest. The key concept is that of *body*: the significance of human embodiedness is invoked to overcome Hegel's disdain. Although every actual dance form disposes of a more or less elaborate and restricted system of poses and movements, by which it is characterized and which may require specialized training, the fact remains that it is with our bodies that we humans do everything we do. Virtually all of us necessarily have inexhaustible capacity for dexterity and versatility in body movement. This unspecialized virtuosity has three apparent consequences. First, it seems easy to downgrade the arts of dance by saying that dancing is something everyone spontaneously does when moved to express feeling, and that expressive dance quality is unreflectively manifested in the movement patterns of all sorts of people whose lives call for sensitive mobility. Second, it was equally easy for avant-garde exponents of dance to say, in the countercultural 1960s, that dance could be discerned or practiced wherever the quality of any human movement was attended to "as dance" – that is, without regard for the practicality of whatever the moving person was engaged in. And third, the range of significant movement that can be developed in dance traditions is practically inexhaustible.

There is, then, a way in which any human movement can become dance and can be seen as dance. But the philosophy of dance still faces the question of what sorts of movement quality actually repay attention and cultivation as dance. General art theory at once suggests three likely candidates: expressiveness; "beauty" and other formal properties; mimetic force. The aesthetics of dance has traditionally explored the specific possibilities of these three, their relative importance in artistic dance, and the ways they interact. In particular, the nature and significance of the formal properties significantly sought in human movement were traditionally much discussed, especially in relation to the long-standing use of "dancing lessons" to improve social deportment: grace, elegance, dignity, and athletic prowess. A complicating factor is that humans as such are language users, eloquently voluble; this volubility has a counterpart in gestural behavior, "body language," systematically produced and interpreted in ways variously related to the articulate speech that may or may not accompany it. How this sort of behavior is to be identified and classified, the methods and limits of its interpretation, and its place among the resources of artistic dance are questions prominent in the aesthetics of dance and importantly relevant to the study of human rationality in general. In the classical dance of India, and in a rudimentary form in European ballet, and elsewhere, formal vocabularies of gesture are developed; how such vocabularies are to be used and integrated into the affective and formal meanings of dances is a matter for study. In the absence of such a vocabulary, the recognized gestures current in society at large (kiss, goose, handshake, bow) afford a resource posing the same questions of significant modification and integration (Humphrey 1962; Shawn 1953).

The previous paragraph sufficiently shows that the meaning to be assigned to a human movement depends on the vocabulary or symbol set taken to be available, the set supposed to be actually in use, the way the mover is taken to be using the set of options, the context taken to be relevantly operative, and an indefinitely large number of variables answering to the open flexibility necessary to human communication. If the movement in question belongs (or is construed as belonging) to artistic dance, or to a specific dance or kind of dance, one supposes that specific values are to be assigned to some or all of these variables, or at least that limits are to be placed on the variability; otherwise the assignment to dance, or to a specific dance or kind of dance, becomes vacuous. But it is not easy to see what this supposition buys one, for the following reason.

The arts of dance are the arts of the human body visibly in motion. What is the human body? Dancers, whether displaying a previously choreographed sequence, or creating a dance, or improvising a sequence within technically developed parameters, or expressing themselves, or simply *moving*, are in all cases human beings doing things humanly. If their dancing is an exercising of their dancing art, they are presumably doing what they do so *as to be seen* – for a real or possible audience, if only for God. But what do spectators see when they see a dancer's body moving in dance? Those two words "in dance" do not impose a restriction on what is visible to spectators. The body they see must surely include most of the following – how to compile and order the best list is a topic for philosophical consideration. First is the "flesh," the actual material stuff in motion. Next is the articulated mechanical system of the body moving as its members, joints, and muscles permit. Next is the organic body, moving as a living thing controlled by its nervous system. Next is the gesturing human, its movements not merely vital but essentially meaningful as expressions of a conscious, perceptive, motivated being. Next is a corporeal person of definite age and gender in essential relation with other such persons for whom or with whom he or she is dancing. Next is the social body, clothed and endowed like all other human bodies with a social reality that is what we immediately see when we see *somebody*. Next is, or may be, the emblematically equipped body in a determinate ceremonial setting – for many artistic dances are realized only in such settings, and mimetic dances have often taken advantage of this fact to organize their presentations. And perhaps we should add the body taken up into ritual that endows its owner with an extra symbolic significance. What matters is that a dancer is a person who cannot assume these layers of visible order otherwise than by being, in the first instance, a human being, whose behavior and reality can be taken in only if we recognize (without having to acknowledge it explicitly) that they are grounded in the most elementary levels of corporeality. Some people get round this by saying that "the body is the dancer's instrument," but others rejoin that "I do not *use* my body, I *am* my body" – I am present in my dance. It is of crucial importance that what dancers know of their dancing selves has a density and complexity no less than, and quite different from, those that the spectators see in them (so that dancers in practice are, as it were, haunted by virtual mirrors even when not surrounded by actual mirrors, as they habitually are). All the arts encounter comparable entanglements when they try to disengage the artist from the art, but it is only in dance that they threaten the very core of what the art is as an art.

Artistic dance as a profession, teachable and learnable and subject to technical criticism, focuses on dance "as such," phenomena in the middle of our range of movements of the body: organic movements with cultivated animal and human intelligence, meaningful in their own terms rather than on physiological and social levels. Such dancing is in many traditions broken down into danceable units, "steps," which can be practiced and perfected. Often, perfectibility has been related to such specific dance qualities as those mentioned above; in particular, the proper analysis of "grace," as the form of beauty most characteristic of the movements admired in animals as well as dancers, used to be a favorite topic among theorists (for example Bayer 1933).

The tendency of teachable dance movement to admit of analysis into steps has invited teachers and choreographers to attempt codification of the movements recognizably recurring and relevant to the structuring and perfecting of dance, so that a variety of dance notations has been developed in which the repeatable structures of dances have been recorded. Two systems in particular are widely used in professional art dance today, based on widely different principles: the Benes notation for ballet, and Labanotation for all human movements. The success of the latter encouraged Nelson Goodman (1968) to speculate that dance might itself become a "notational art" – that is, one in which a dance performance could be produced by following a written score, a relevantly identical score prepared by observing and transcribing the performance, and so ad infinitum. The precision and elegance of Goodman's formulations were on an intellectual level seldom reached in aesthetics, and attracted wide attention. He notes that if dance did become a notational art it would be very different from dance as we know it. Given the multiple ambiguity that I have pointed out in the "body" of which the motions are perceived and appreciated in the dance, any dance notation inevitably privileges some relations over others, which in practice is going to mean (just because it is designed to be a *dance* notation) that it will fasten on the middle range of movements and interpretations that belong to "dance as dance," professionally learnable techniques. But an essential feature of artistic dance is that these movements are not all we see and appreciate in dancing; if dance were a notational art it would presumably be by these and only these movements that a dance would be defined, and hence perceived and evaluated. Be that as it may, consideration of the construction and use of dance notations, and the constraints on their applicability, is a fruitful source for reflection on how intelligence is used in the structuring, identification, and recognition of dances.

Dance notations tend to treat the dancing body as an articulated system, showing how the recognizable functioning body parts move, where they go and when and how. But speculative choreographers and anthropological analysts have emphasized that the way body movement has meaning is not relevantly reducible to those terms, so that dance cannot be quite like that either. Our eyes, like other animal eyes, are part of a visual system that responds differently to different sorts of animal movement, particularly in our conspecifics. We read human faces with extraordinarily fine discrimination: faces are expressive and are seen as such. Legs, arms, torsos, hands, fingers have different masses and rhythms, have different functions in the organism, and are bearers of different meanings. Traditional discussion of dancing has often dwelt on the difference between dances centered on leaping legs and those emphasizing gesturing hands (with the rougher and cruder distinction between what is above and what is below the waist). Such differentiations are not theoretical constructs but a cultural (perhaps psychological) heritage with which theory has to cope as it can. Just because dancers are people dancing, these discriminations are built into the way we make and see dances. Are they data, or aspects of how we process data? Either way, the result is that dance inevitably has an indeterminately vast range of affective meanings, exploited in extending the possibilities of human experience in ways comparable to those developed in such other arts as music, painting, poetry. This is how *mimesis* should be understood: not as a repertory of ways of depicting and narrating, but as the development of new fields and capacities for our original ways of perceiving and feeling.

The general designation of the arts of dance as those of which human bodies in motion are the focus of attention opens up two choices of interpretation that have sometimes divided critics. First, the emphasis may be either on the body, or on the motion. On the former view, the center of appreciation is the physical body of which the mass and weight, the yielding and resistance, are affirmed or denied; the glory and pathos of dance depend on its being a human body that is moving and being moved. On the latter view, it is the system of energies generated by the dancer that constitutes the dance, so that it is after all not altogether out of place to say that the body is the dancer's instrument. Some people write as if it were the use of point shoes in the Romantic ballet that chiefly promoted this way of envisaging dance; others point to the late nineteenth-century proliferation of "skirt dances" and forms in which the visual effect depends on the manipulation of veils, scarves, and fabrics generally, in ways made possible by the development of sophisticated stage lighting and epitomized by the productions of Loie Fuller. The latter were ridiculed by some critics as mere displays, not really dance at all, but they could be and were also seen as emanating from and representing the living energies of the performer.

The other choice of interpretation opened up by the ambiguities of the dancing human body is that the skilled dancer can be seen either as an expert performer absorbed in the practice of a demanding art (as we could never be, unless we are also trained dancers) or as a person coping (like all the rest of us) with the exigencies of the human condition. Dancers are both, can be seen as either or as both, and can variously make this double predicament the subject of their mimesis. This ambiguity is ubiquitous in the arts, where the artist practicing his or her profession is also a person whose art is embedded in his or her life; but it is especially in dance, where the whole of the dancing person is directly before us, that the ambiguity is continuously there to be exploited. Perennially prominent among the resources of dance is to make the labor, effort, commitment, and fatigue of making a dance with one's body into the very substance of one's dance, or to make a stylized show of doing so. Dance necessarily shows the dancing person, and can make a point of doing so: a topic of dance, as Aristotle said, is human states of mind, and these may or may not formally and practically coincide with the dancer's thought and feeling. The dancer's personal presence accordingly makes it possible for the whole course of a human life and the practical wisdom of the body to be made seemingly visible. Some dance forms and traditions specialize in doing this sort of thing; just what sort of thing it is, and how it does what it does, await phenomenological analysis – or demystification and debunking. It would seem to be the kind of thing that can only be done, if it is done at all, within the understanding of a reflective civilization in which thinking about the shapes of human life is sufficiently cultivated that it can be made visually available to a public.

Nothing is apparently easier and more familiar than to distinguish the dance a dancer is performing, together with the dancer as the performer of the dance, from the person who is dancing and the whole activity of that person. And yet the attempt to isolate the dance tends to break down, because a dance as such can normally only be seen in one way or another as the specifically human movements of a human body, hence of a human person; the human person remains present in the dance. This sort of reflection repeatedly leads people who are trying to think philosophically about dancing to look for a kind of phenomenological epistemology that will relate experience not to the origin of visual and auditory systems as such but to the perceptive person embodied within the (seen, heard, touched) world that is experienced. The writings of Maurice Merleau-Ponty have been mined for this purpose. A more recent demarche cites a pragmatic rather than a phenomenology ancestry: Richard Shusterman (1999) argues that a more patient reading of Baumgarten's *Ästhetik* than most of us achieve bases aesthetics on the immediate qualities of an embodied perceiver. It may be that the future of the philosophy of dance lies in this direction.

Another line of phenomenological thought argues that, since a dance as such is a movement sequence cut off from practical concerns or abstracting from their practicality, the inner meaning of any dance has to be the basic way in which the dancers put themselves in motion in the environment that sustains them, and thus implicitly realize and present for themselves and others the fundamental ways in which a human being (or the basic kind of human being they are, whatever that may be) exists in the world. Just how "the world" is to be construed here is itself a topic for investigation. Phenomenology is a broad and nowadays little cultivated territory, and the suggestions mooted here are not so much results of the philosophy of dance as domains for a future philosophy of dance to set in order or reveal as illusory.

The preceding material may suggest that a theater dance presented by sophisticated performers to a suitably sensitive audience is likely, unless strictly contained by ad hoc semiotic parameters, to suffer from severe semiological overload. A dance may come across as disorganized or chaotic, not because its meanings are indeterminate, but because there is nothing in the performance to show from moment to moment on which level of meaning the attention is to be focused. This often seems to happen in our postmodern age, when dancers instructed in a variety of methods and schools come together in collaborative companies, though a spectator whose selective experience answers to the indiscriminate preparation of the dancers might be able to decode the shower of symbols.

The foregoing remarks have been couched in suitably universal terms; the assumption has to be that such relations as person and technician, culture and nature, will take on determinate forms in specific historical/cultural settings. It is these forms that make up the substance of what "we" "know" as "dance." There is such a thing as dance in general to the extent that human physiology, ethology, and psychology, in their cultural malleability, afford a common material that takes form throughout geography and history as dance traditions. These traditions themselves are realized in systems of dance events. These events differ from culture to culture, and those involved need not group them together in a single category as "dance" – the culture may well not have any generic term like "dance" to group them together under, and may not make much use of it if it has one. Readers of this chapter, however, who have the concept of a dance and may (because of the way things are done in our culture) well have thought about the scope of that concept, can use it as a blanket term to apply cross-culturally to all sorts of behavior. Representatives of other cultures who dispose of analogously flexible blanket terms can apply them in analogous ways.

How does this cross-cultural application work? Like this: if I recognize a foreign practice (ritual, or whatever) as dance, that means that what I already knew and thought of as dance included in some way this foreign practice as a possible extension. On reflection, I should be able to tell just how it is recognized and included. That this sort of thing keeps happening is an important and increasingly recognized fact about dance worldwide.

If cultures are to be recognizably human cultures, they must be superimposed as variants on basic human repertoires of behavioral elements and systems of organization, whatever those may be. This consideration partly justifies the old notion, mentioned above, that dance is (or was) originally a freely elaborate and expressive use of the body's resources to communicate or celebrate what will later develop into language and art, and it is in and from this resource that the formally elaborated movement and posture systems that form the basis of actual dances in specific cultures are grounded and developed. In the same spirit, it used often to be said that the basic human dance is analogous to dance-like behavior in animals, spontaneous free use of the body's capacities in naturally expressive forms. After all, we do all have the neural and muscular equipment to perform and perfect an indefinite range of movements; why should not dance at the most basic level be a free use of this freedom? The freedom in question, however, is probably chimerical. The occasions on which spontaneously expressive movements were performed, and what forms they would take, would most likely be determined for a person by the culture within which his or her capacities and sensibilities had taken shape.

In our civilization, the one within which the architectonic of the intellectual disciplines has been articulated, the philosophy of any art is usually centered on classical traditions of artistic practice. Other traditions, and the traditions of other cultures, are in practice treated as peripheral to these. In the philosophy of dance, the traditions of ballet and of "modern" dance and its successors take this central place. But they do so with less assurance and apparent success. Since specific dance traditions and dance skills are developed by systematization of the undifferentiated and unlimited potential virtuosity that human bodies must have for culture to be possible (for survival value must accrue to indefinite adaptability and an unrestricted aptitude for specialized development), the cultural privilege accorded to any specific dance tradition must be arbitrary. David Best (1978) argues that no dance tradition counts as "art" unless it has the potentiality of relating to important life issues; but this, even if we agree with it, is nugatory, since what counts as an important life issue must itself depend on cultural choices and on the development of what turn out to be viable means of expression.

The phrase "the art of dance" falsely implies a unified system of practice within which one may be a practitioner. One should perhaps avoid that phrase and speak rather of "arts of dance" separately cultivated in different cultures and belonging to separate "dance worlds" between which there is no meaningful communication. That may be an exaggeration, since in today's world of global intercommunication mutual recognition and comprehension are becoming institutionalized; but just what it is that is happening, and what the scope and limits of this comprehension are, are questions that call for the attention of philosophers and social scientists. Meanwhile, the concept of "art," theory-laden and prone to rhetorical hijacking as it is, may be ill suited to the philosophical exploration of the sorts of meaning that dance has. It has been suggested that the concept of a "practice" could be developed as affording a useful basic framework (Sparshott 1988: 113–S40), but that remains to be seen. In any case, the singular place of the phenomena of dance in human behavior demands a more strategic role in the philosophy of art than they have usually been allowed.

Dance as a performance art, in which professional dancers put on a show for an audience, may differ from other arts in the way its meanings are embedded in systems of meaning other than its own. Not only are dances performed professionally as parts of other performances (a topic to which we return in a moment), but the forms and values of performance dance are continuous with or overlap those of dance activity in other contexts. The virtuosic dance components of the French and Italian court ballets, from which today's ballets descend, were integral to ceremonies in which less exacting dance movements had emblematic and formal meaning; much of the world's dancing forms part of sacred rituals; the various forms of social dancing practiced in our civilization are aesthetically formed practices that have meaning as constituting or exemplifying special states of existence to which anthropologists and sociologists have drawn attention – if we dismiss them as mere recreation, the effect of our dismissal vanishes when we inquire into the significance of recreation itself.

In any society, if an occasion is to be marked as special, one of the few basic ways of doing so is by the performance of special movements (things not usually done for practical reasons, or done in non-practical ways). And the ways of doing this are going to be continuous with and significantly akin to things that performing dancers do in performance. The object for philosophical reflection here is the way in which dance meanings are embedded in course-of-life meanings. Comparable questions arise in the philosophy of other arts (such as poetry and song) of which generalized repertories of skill form the basic material; what seems distinctive of dance is the way its artistic meanings are embedded in other systems of meaning.

We have noted that to dance is usually to dance *a* dance, and at least always to dance a *kind* of dance, and that dances are generally articulated or susceptible of articulation into steps, poses, figures, sequences, and other like segments, but that nonetheless the dancer is an active person in motion and is seen as such. Dancing is something the person is doing, and the dancer's body-in-motion is necessarily perceived as that of a person incarnated in all possible modes. To this we must now add that a dancer whose body configuration and habits of motion have been formed by training and practice within a specific dance tradition, as must usually be the case, can (and often does) learn to perform the dances of another tradition. The outcome of this superimposition is likely to be some sort of more-or-less idiosyncratic amalgam or compromise. Such phenomena are themselves a resource of dance that may be unselfconsciously realized or deliberately cultivated. In addition, someone who has learned a dance or a dance style has, in doing so, learned to dance, in that he or she now knows from experience what it is to learn a dance and a way of dancing. Such a person's movements in any dance are likely to be in importantly recognizable ways the movements *of a dancer*. This familiar fact has to be set alongside two no less familiar facts: first, a non-dancing person who is performing some non-dance movements with special attention to their movement qualities may be seen "as dancing"; and second, in a weaker sense, any person whatever, moving or still, can be seen "as dancing" by anyone whose perceptual range includes actual dances and who superimposes on what is seen the relevant skills of analysis, interpretation, and appreciation – simply looking at what is done *as one would look at a dance*, whatever that may come to in the given case. If I say that someone can be seen as dancing, or looks as if they were dancing, I am saying only that there is some analytic, interpretive, or qualitative filter that is relevantly applicable to the perception of what the person is doing.

Dances are characteristically meant to be seen. They are performed for spectators, or as if for spectators. In fact, art dances in our civilization are characteristically theater arts, the dancers performing on a stage for an audience. (The "stage" need not be a physically demarcated area, though it often is, provided that the division between those looking and those being looked at is somehow observed.) This is a broad topic; the relations between dancing for oneself, dancing for others, and dancing as a member of a group and finding satisfaction in that membership raise large questions about perception and self-knowledge. The immediate point to be made here is that, though dances are performed on stages, not everything performed on a stage is or purports to be a dance.

The theatrical stage is a very powerful institution. Let us say that a stage is a recognized public place where people come to be seen performing – all sorts of people: dramatic actors, musicians, jugglers, gymnasts, exponents of any recognized genre of performer, including "performance artists" and off-beat individuals known only for doing what they are known by name to do. All share the same stage; there is a standing possibility for genres to blend or to contaminate each other in the context of what early twentieth-century Russian practitioners conceptualized as "theater."[1] If the theatrical stage becomes the locus for the presentation of artistic dance, dancers who confine themselves to pure dance as they conceive it share a context of presentation with performers who acknowledge no such purism and whose audiences may not impose any such defining or restricting context of expectation. The dancers are inescapably present on the stage both as the people they are and as "performers," in a setting where whatever they do can be accepted as performance within the embracing and shaping experience of "theater" in whatever way it operates then and there. There is a constant tendency for dance performances (centrally defined as organized body movement intended to reward being looked at and scrutinized for meaning) to incorporate within themselves anything available that can be expected to reward attention of the same general sort – "the same sort" being defined pragmatically as what will be accepted without jarring. And again, just because what the special skills and gifts of dance exploit are all the underlying capacities of human mobility, whatever dancers do in a performance situation in a theater context can take on directly all the dimensions of interpretation and appreciation for which the theater has prepared its audiences. One more thing should be borne in mind: just because the stage is essentially the potential bearer of all these multifarious meanings and delights, an important component of experience *in* the theater is always experience *of* the theater.[2]

One thing the stage does is celebrate and enforce separation between artists and spectators. Such separations may be variously significant. Some feminists urge that in theater dance, typically, female bodies are subjected to the male gaze; to others, what matters is that lower-class performers are being put on show for upper-class flaneurs, or that young and handsome bodies are displayed for their decrepit elders.

Even if dance as an art is publicly realized in theatrical and processional displays, dance is learned and developed in studios. Some artistic purists feel that their art loses its integrity when it goes public and a necessarily ignorant and imperceptive audience tacitly claims that its crass demands are what the devoted endeavors of art exist to fulfill. This tension is in various forms common to all the arts, where the public at large is oblivious to what every artist knows. In dance, however, the tension may be especially poignant, if the invention of a dance on one's own body amounts to a self-transformation among companions engaged in the same exacting process, but the performance of that dance comes down to putting on a show for people who know and care nothing for all that. Whether that is the case or not, there must in principle be a gulf between the massive organization of an opera house and the individual dancer personally present on a particular night. One outcome of this gulf may be an extended articulation of the design process. At one extreme is the impresario, providing opportunities and making demands to fill out a performing season feasible for the means at hand. Then there is the scenarist, who formulates the shape of a dance performance, perhaps the outline of a narrative to be danced or the idea of a danceable emotional scheme. Next is the dance designer, who articulates the outline or scheme in terms of dance numbers having a certain shape, requiring a certain number of dancers, taking a given length of time, and being assigned a certain prominence within the whole. Then comes the choreographer, who fleshes out the articulation with actual movements and relations for the dancers to perform, working these out with the actual performers. After that, if the dance is planned on a large scale or has to be revived after interruption, there will have to be regisseurs or coaches, who act as brokers between the design as choreographed and what will actually be done on a given occasion by specific dancers with different shapes and capacities. Last of all will be the actual dancers, each of whom in the end is creator of his or her own performance because, however loyal to what is taken to be the choreographer's invention and instruction, it is in the end only he or she who is the person doing the dancing. Even here, there is an important division between the repeatable dance or role (*her* Giselle, say) which is learned, worked up, perfected, and polished as a design to be exemplified over and over again, and the actual performance as danced on a given night, which is all the actual audience on that night will see. (At every stage there is likely to be a corresponding stage in the invention and performance of the music to which the dance will be done, if any; the relations between music and dance, so differently structured, provide the philosophy of dance with a topic of immense complexity.) These linked stages in creation need not be carried out separately, but they may be, for they are functionally distinct. The hierarchy, however, is not necessarily worked out in a series of artistic dependencies. Artistic innovation and aesthetic significance may be centered on any point, and any such focal point may become what a given named dance is known by. As a whole, such articulation is as integral to the form of theater dance as the corresponding organization is to the art of cinema.

What, then, are the conditions of identity of a dance? What makes a dance recognizably "the same as" another dance, or suitably given the same name? The considerations raised here mean that there can be no determinate answer. If a company announces a new production of *Swan Lake*, there is no telling what it will do, except that it will bear some relation to something in a complex and intricate history with some of which people in the dance world will be intimately but unequally familiar. It is a history that all are aware of but nobody knows. What *Swan Lake* is determines and is determined by the relationships that dance-makers, critics, and audiences can detect and accept as justifying their procedures and identifications (Cohen 1982). In discussing these phenomena, people often invoke the Wittgensteinian notion of "family relations" in concept formation, but that notion misses something essential: the dynamic of historical awareness in the formation and validation of traditions of practice.

If anyone wants to do the philosophy of dance, it is easy in principle. All one has to do is take some general theory of art or the aesthetic and examine in detail how it applies to dance phenomena which one knows about or takes an interest in (for example Redfern 1983). My own work has been propaedeutic: to assemble from extant writing on the subject, and arrange in some semblance of order, the topics and thoughts that anyone who was going to think seriously about the philosophy of dance would need to know about and come to terms with. Such an enterprise raises questions. Are these the right topics? Are these the right thoughts? Are they arranged in the most illuminating sequence? But I have not the least idea whether these questions are worth answering. It is no doubt better that we all do what we all do: say what seems to us to need saying.

## Notes

1 Charles Batteux in 1746 already thought in terms of generic stage spectacles that would be identified as drama, as music, or as dance, depending on where the creative center and the focus of interest were. (For Batteux, see Sparshott 1988: 70.)
2 The artistic place of the onstage dancer has much in common with that of the dramatic actor, which has long been extensively discussed – see especially Huston (1992).

## References

Bayer, Raymond (1933). *L'Esthétique de la grâce*. Paris: Felix Alcan.
Best, David (1978). *Philosophy and Human Movement*. London: Unwin.
Cohen, S. J. (1982). *Next Week, Swan Lake*. Middletown: Wesleyan University Press.
Goodman, Nelson (1968). *Languages of Art*. Indianapolis: Bobbs-Merrill.
Humphrey, Doris (1962). *The Art of Making Dances*. New York: Grove Press.
Huston, Hollis (1992). *The Actor's Instrument: Body, Theory, Stage*. Ann Arbor: University of Michigan Press.
Langer, S. K. (1953). *Feeling and Form*. New York: Scribners.
Lonsdale, S. H. (1993). *Dance and Ritual Play in Greek Religion*. Baltimore: Johns Hopkins University Press.
Miller, James (1986). *Measures of Wisdom: The Cosmic Dance in Classical and Christian Antiquity*. Toronto: University of Toronto Press.
Noverre, J.-G. (1760). *Letters on Dancing and Ballets*, trans. Cyril W. Beaumont. London: Beaumont.
Redfern, Betty (1983). *Dance, Art and Aesthetics*. London: Dance Books.
Shawn, Ted (1953). *Every Little Movement: A Book about Delsarte*. Reprint New York: Dance Horizons, 1968.
Shusterman, Richard (1999). "Somaesthetics: A Disciplinary Proposal." *Journal of Aesthetics and Art Criticism*, 57: 299–313.
Sparshott, Francis (1988). *Off the Ground: First Steps to a Philosophical Consideration of the Dance*. Princeton, NJ: Princeton University Press.

## Further reading

Armelagos, Adina and Sirridge, Mary (1978). "The Identity Crisis in Dance." *Journal of Aesthetics and Art Criticism*, 37: 129–39.
Bose, Mandrakanta (1991). *Movement and Mimesis: The Idea of Dance in the Sanskrit Tradition*. Dordrecht: Kluwer.
Carroll, Noël and Banes, Sally (1989). "Working and Dancing: A Response to Monroe Beardsley's 'What's Going On in a Dance?'" In G. Dickie, R. J. Sclafani and R. Roblin (eds), *Aesthetics: A Critical Anthology*. 2nd edn. New York: St Martin's Press: 645–50.
Copeland, Roger and Cohen, Marshall, eds (1983). *What is Dance?* New York: Oxford University Press.

Fancher, Gordon and Myers, Gerald, eds (1981). *Philosophical Essays on Dance*. Brooklyn: Dance Horizons.

Foster, Susan Leigh (1986). *Reading Dancing: Bodies and Subjects in Contemporary American Dance*. Berkeley: University of California Press.

Fraleigh, Sondra Horton (1987). *Dance and the Lived Body: A Descriptive Aesthetics*. Pittsburgh: University of Pittsburgh Press.

Hanna, Judith Lynne (1979). *To Dance is Human: A Theory of Non-Verbal Communication*. Austin: University of Texas Press.

Kaeppler, Adrienne L. (1972). "Method and Theory in Analyzing Dance Structure with an Analysis of Tongan Dance." *Ethnomusicology*, 16: 173–215.

McFee, Graham (1992). *Understanding Dance*. London: Routledge.

Novack, Cynthia J. (1990). *Sharing the Dance: Contact Improvisation and American Culture*. Madison: University of Wisconsin Press.

Royce, Anya Peterson (1984). *Movement and Meaning: Creativity and Interpretation in Ballet and Mime*. Bloomington: Indiana University Press.

Sheets, Maxine (1966). *The Phenomenology of Dance*. Madison: University of Wisconsin Press.

Sheets-Johnstone, Maxine, ed. (1984). *Illuminating Dance*. Lewisberg: Bucknell University Press.

Souriau, Paul (1983). *The Aesthetics of Movement*. (Manon Souriau, trans.). Amherst: University of Massachusetts Press. (Original work pub. 1889.)

Sparshott, Francis (1995). *A Measured Pace: Toward a Philosophical Understanding of the Arts of Dance*. Toronto: University of Toronto Press.

Thomas, Helen, ed. (1993). *Dance, Gender and Culture*. Basingstoke: Macmillan.

Van Camp, Julie (1982). "Philosophical Problems of Dance Criticism." PhD dissertation, Temple University. Ann Arbor: University Microfilms International.

Williams, Drid (1991). *Ten Lectures on Theories of the Dance*. Metuchen, NJ, and London: Scarecrow Press.

# Chapter 16

# Tragedy

*Susan Feagin*

*Count no man happy until he dies.*

Greek proverb

The history of tragedy, both in theory and in practice, is usefully seen as a series of footnotes to Aristotle, who, for good reason, continues to be the touchstone against which new ideas about tragedy are tested. Philosophically, however, differences of opinion persist over the most crucial aspects of Aristotle's account, such as what he takes tragedy's end or *telos* to be, what he takes catharsis and mimesis to be, and why the combination of pity and fear is so important. After Aristotle, Shakespeare, Hume, Corneille and Racine, Kant, Hegel, Nietzsche and Schiller figure among the most important dramatists and theorists to reconceive tragedy in ways that were appropriate to their own times. Recurrent debate exists over the centrality of certain types of plots to tragedy, that is, between how a good person may knowingly choose to do harm because compelled to choose between conflicting goods, and how a person may do harm unknowingly. Recurrent themes are the relevance of both pleasure and pain in response to tragedy, and the myriad ways of accounting for the apparently paradoxical pleasures that humans experience in response to what is unpleasant or painful. Tragedy is thought to have enduring significance because, broadly speaking, its subject matter is no less than the nature of a good, happy, or meaningful life – something of concern to all human beings – and the ways such a life may be threatened. In the twentieth century, however, many theorists proclaimed the concept of tragedy to be sufficiently alien to the beliefs and concerns of modern life that attempts to adapt it to them no longer made sense. In opposition to this claim, I discuss three twentieth-century American films, two of which, I shall argue, have plots that qualify as tragic in the full-blooded Aristotelian sense, and the third of which, a late twentieth-century comedy, demonstrates the relevance of the tragic to contemporary life by showing how one can maintain one's happiness and therein avoid tragedy.

## 16.1 Aristotle

At least from the time of Homer, poets were seen as teachers of what is good, and hence of how to live a good life (Thayer 1975). The sophist Gorgias, a generation prior to Plato, challenged this commonplace and claimed that poetry is, in its very nature, a trick, fraud, or deception (*apate*). Plato countered that poetry is not inherently deception, but instead, imitation (*mimesis*). Furthermore, Plato held that poets and their dramatic interpreters such as Ion, in the dialogue carrying his name, imitate persons, not ideas or events, and therefore that they present ideas and events from only one point of view. (See Pappas 1992, against Halliwell 1986.) Notoriously, Plato drew the conclusion that a poem is no better as a source of knowledge than a painting, which presents only one point of view on the objects it depicts. As Pappas puts it, "a poetic imitation does not even attempt to give a general account of its object" (1992: 92), a deficiency also manifested by numerous characters in Plato's dialogues who can't even understand what it is to seek the truth or how one would go about doing so. In early works, such as the *Ion*, Plato presents the view, associated with Socrates, that a poet's power to move an audience comes from the gods through inspiration. In later works, notably book X of the *Republic*, he tenders an alternative, psychological, explanation of a poet's powers, that is, that they practice various tricks and gimmicks until they know them by rote (*tribe*). Poets thus obscure their artifice and use language that seems natural, believable, and persuasive, as if communicating something true. Most importantly, neither poets nor interpreters need to depend on knowing the truth about what they imitate in order to imitate it effectively.

Aristotle's *Poetics* is a systematic exposition of the nature and end of tragedy that is at the same time a response to Plato's attacks on it. Writing a good tragedy, Aristotle maintains, is a skill or *techne*, the exercise of which does require knowledge, specifically, of its nature (*phusis*) and end (*telos*) or function. Pity and fear clearly play a key role in tragedy's *telos*; suffering is mentioned as well. Tragedy's "true nature" (1449a16) provides the rationale for identifying it as a type of drama having this particular cluster of attributes. This much can be taken for granted, but there is surprisingly wide disagreement over the details of Aristotle's position on the *telos* of tragedy, how he and Plato differ with respect to the elusive concept of mimesis, whether mimesis can ever be a source of knowledge, and how the combination of pity and fear relates to catharsis.

Aristotle says repeatedly that the single most important thing about a tragedy is its plot (*muthos*). Plots are constructions. They are not found in the world and copied – they are made, or deliberately selected, by the poet. Therefore, writing tragedy is not merely mimesis but *techne*, usually translated as "art," whose Indo-European root means to put things together. Aristotle's treatise on tragedy is called the *Poetics* partly because the tragedies he wrote about are written in verse, a practice that continued, more or less, to the eighteenth century. Verses are constructed and not merely imitations of everyday spoken language, reflecting the fact that tragedy is about issues of universal applicability and does not merely present a single point of view. Aristotle similarly defends tragedy as superior to lyric poetry since the latter imitates the perspectives and feelings of individuals. He also defends tragedy as more philosophical than history because of the universality of its plots, *types* of actions, as opposed to what actual individuals have done.

One goes to see a tragedy but its importance lies in what one hears. That is, the manner of presentation for tragedy is visual (*opsis*), but its means is auditory, through language (*lexis*) and song (*melopoieia*). The average fifth-century BCE Greek had access to the language, and hence the ideas expressed, by attending performances, much as today we watch films rather than read their scripts. The visual experience can help to hold the audience's attention, and increase its dramatic impact, but in the best tragedies, the meaning is conveyed through words. *Opsis* is unfortunately often translated as "spectacle," which in English has the connotation of something showy and even glitzy, but which in the Greek is simply the look or appearance of something. Aristotle identifies *opsis* as one of the ways unity or wholeness can be achieved, though inferior to unity created through plot. In a good tragedy, he says, one is able to experience the pity and fear through language alone (1453b2).

Aristotle is generally credited with developing the first cognitive theory of emotions in his *Rhetoric* and is referenced explicitly in the *Poetics*. On his view, pity is felt toward people one judges to be basically good, but who suffer through no fault of their own. Fear is felt for oneself in perceiving a situation to be potentially dangerous to oneself. Members of the audience are expected to connect these two emotions, cognitively and affectively, in recognizing that they, too, are vulnerable to suffering in the same way as the tragic figure in the play or as a result of that individual's actions. That is, we may work responsibly and diligently, only to find out later that our efforts brought about precisely what we were trying to avoid. Martha Nussbaum (1986) elegantly identifies this feature of the human condition as "the fragility of goodness." The ultimate significance of this fragility is acknowledged in the Greek proverb that acts as this chapter's epigraph, "Count no man happy until he dies."

Nussbaum also argues that the suffering of the tragic figure results from a conflict of values, such that one cannot fulfill one without transgressing the other. For example, Agamemnon is commanded to sacrifice his daughter, Iphigenia. He has a choice: either disobey the gods, which will result in even greater suffering, or kill his daughter. One would ordinarily prefer a broader range of options. Clearly, though, Agamemnon should choose the latter. Nussbaum claims that Agamemnon is able at least to acknowledge, emotionally, the horror of his action as he carries out the sacrifice. Aaron Ridley cautions that such acknowledgment will not be possible in all cases. Some actions a tragic figure might be required to perform, what he calls "committed" actions, require "a highly concentrated state of mind" that does not allow for "the luxury of affective moral rectitude" (1993: 241). Eteocles, for example, presented with the dilemma of either taking up arms against his brother or allowing the citizens of Thebes to become enslaved by him, correctly decides that the former is the lesser of the two evils. In fighting his brother, however, Eteocles must summon his skills and concentration if he is to have any chance of winning. He must *try* to defeat his brother; his success is not assured. In such cases, the agent "must choose . . . to become evil for whatever length of time his action takes – to become a person who is called by the worst names" (Ridley 1993: 244). This point is central also to the defense of Shakespeare's *The Merchant of Venice* against charges that it is anti-Semitic. Under this interpretation, Shylock is a tragic figure because the society in which he lives has not allowed him any options for making a good living other than demeaning ones, and then scorns him for choosing a demeaning vocation.

The view that a tragic figure's character flaws, such as hubris, are to blame for his acting in ways that bring about suffering faces at least two objections. On linguistic grounds, according to Gerald Else (1986), *hamartia*, the Greek word sometimes taken as referring to a character flaw, actually refers to a mistake or acci-dent, a way of doing wrong or causing harm uncontrollably or unknowingly. On conceptual grounds, if the tragic figure's suffering is brought about by a charac-ter flaw, the suffering would not be undeserved, and hence the agent would not be an appropriate object of pity. This conceptual objection, however, is tempered by the fact that an agent, even if morally deficient, might suffer a great deal more than such a character flaw warrants, and others may suffer because of his hubris.

There has long been controversy over what Aristotle takes to be the *telos*, end or "final cause," of tragedy. Candidates include having a certain kind of plot, evoking pity and fear in the audience, effecting a catharsis, or producing pleasure by these or other means. One problem with taking catharsis to be a serious can-didate for the end of tragedy is that, in the *Poetics*, Aristotle mentions it only once and provides no account of what he takes catharsis to be. His explanation of cathar-sis may be in a passage that is lost, but another plausible train of thought takes the absence of such an explanation at face value, that is, as indicating that Aristo-tle does not take catharsis to be a defining condition of tragedy, even though it may be implicated in the value of tragedy in some way. Indeed, any account of the *telos* of tragedy in terms of its actual effects on an audience is suspect. Surely, all the tragedian could be held responsible for is to write a work to which pity and fear are *appropriate* responses, and, as Aristotle emphasizes, this will be to write a work that has a certain type of plot.

In the *Nicomachean Ethics*, Aristotle makes the point that "like activities produce like dispositions" (1103b21). In the case of tragedy, responding with pity and fear to appropriate objects in appropriate circumstances, as represented in a tragedy, would help to reinforce one's dispositions to have such feelings in rele-vantly similar actual situations. The cognitive content of pity and fear, whether in response to fictional or to actual situations, would be the same. Thus, in attend-ing performances of tragedies, one has an opportunity to reinforce one's disposi-tions to feel as one should and to do what is right. In Aristotle's day, the primary medical sense of catharsis was homeopathic, which fits well with the idea that appropriate emotional responses to tragedies help to establish the habit of responding with appropriate feelings to the appropriate degree, to the appropriate types of objects in the appropriate circumstances. That is, it helps to maintain and restore moral virtue, even in those extremely difficult situations where the right action entails one's own demise, as is so often the case in tragedies.

Another candidate for the end of tragedy might be to impart knowledge, especially moral knowledge, about how to act. Aristotle distinguishes sharply between moral virtue and intellectual virtue. Moral virtue is acquired through habit, but intellectual virtue is acquired by being taught. Unlike habits, knowledge can be communicated through descriptive discourse. Tragedies do not employ descriptive discourse, except for the chorus, which sometimes "sums up" the moral lesson to be learned, but which more often expresses commonplace views within the community. Even so, it is unlikely that the moral lesson will be something that audience members do not already know. One might say that tragedy enables us to "internalize" moral knowledge rather than to expand it, but this view obscures the particular contributions that tragedy appropriately makes to living a good life that cannot be made by descriptive discourse. What is internalized is not knowledge but a disposition to feel in appropriate ways to appropriate objects under appropriate circumstances.

## 16.2   After Aristotle

Extant classic Greek tragedies were written for competitions governed by explicit rules to serve particular political and social functions that were in many respects unique to their own time (Buxton 1998). For example, they were written as trilogies for annual competitions. The top three would be performed, followed by a satyr play, as part of the annual civic celebrations, where a few ordinary citizens were chosen to decide on the winner. Tragedies were performed only once and in this highly specialized context. The authors, unlike virtually all subsequent playwrights, did not have to worry about whether potential members of the audience might choose to attend some other play on Saturday night at an amphitheater down the road. They certainly didn't have to worry about repeat business. Shakespeare, though not totally unconcerned with political favor, had to pay much more attention to commercial viability.[1] He enjoyed the freedom to incorporate comedy and lewdness into the tragedy itself, which were both enjoyable and provided relief from the intensity and suffering in the play. And though he is known for defying the purity of the genre, it should be remembered that the Greeks also sent audiences home laughing, after the satyr play, and not directly after the tragedy itself.

The tension between happiness and suffering has been a persistent theme in theorizing about tragedy, its value and appropriate role in human life. In "Of Tragedy," Hume seeks to explain, psychologically, why audiences enjoy tragedies. He agrees with Dubos that something painful and disagreeable is often preferred to boredom and ennui, and with Fontenelle that sorrows can be made "agreeable" by the audience member's knowledge that the story or narrative is a fiction. Hume's own account is downright Aristotelian in its appeal to the way authors put together just the right words, exercising their rhetorical skills to produce, for example, surprise and suspense. How to explain, or explain away, the so-called paradox of tragedy – how it is possible to experience pleasure in response to suffering or pain – has turned out to be one of the most frequently discussed philosophical issues at the beginning of the twenty-first century. The resurgent interest in cognitive theories of emotion and other work in philosophical psychology fuels this interest, no doubt, to a degree. In addition, the issue is not confined to tragedy, but has implications for almost any individual work of art, including the comic, that deals with conflicting emotions.

Some versions of rationalism maintain that everything in the world can be understood and appreciated by a properly functioning human mind, so that any mental conflict that remains is a symptom of its improper functioning, to be exposed and corrected. The seventeenth-century French theorists and playwrights Corneille and Racine were in thrall to Cartesian rationalism, and focused their attention on the logic of tragedy as a genre rather than on what others have seen as the paradoxical emotional power of a play. Particularly rigid sets of rules for tragedies came to be in vogue, rules that were much more stringent than anything Aristotle advocated: no humor, no subplots, no change of scene, and action must take place within a span of twenty-four hours. Some even stipulate that, in true tragedy, the performance time of the play must be of the same duration as its fictional content. Such constraints manifest a recurring felt need for the seriousness and refinement that tragedy can provide for the theater; the trade-off is that intellectualizing it to such an extent alienates it from audience members' day-to-day lives.

In the first part of his Third Critique, the *Critique of Aesthetic Judgment* (1790), Immanuel Kant cites tragedy as the source of experiences of the sublime. The ground of the sublime is in ourselves rather than in the world; it is a type of experience, according to Kant, that involves both pleasure and pain (*unlust*). The mathematical sublime is implicated in one's experience of "the starry heavens above" inasmuch as it brings the idea of infinity along with it, even though the infinite is not presented to us in that experience. The dynamical sublime is implicated in one's experience of "the moral law within" inasmuch as it brings the idea of being morally responsible for one's actions with it, even though the metaphysical basis for moral responsibility is not presented to us in experience. In tragedy, the inevitability of the tragic events is handled by the determinism of nature, yet one also has a sense of moral responsibility that is so deep and strong that one accepts responsibility for one's actions even when one performed them unknowingly or involuntarily. In the world of tragedy "ought" does not imply "can" and "ought not have" does not imply "could have not." Certainly, as Kant puts it, the world is presented to us, but not as for us. The potential for pleasure afforded by the realization that we are not dependent on nature for all of our ideas may be minimal compared with the realization that one has been cosmically screwed, but Kant never let pleasure play much of a role in his moral theory anyway. The sense that one is doing the right thing, taking responsibility for one's own actions even when it means one's own demise, may well have some positive affective potential, even if not for full-fledged pleasure.

Gotthold Ephraim Lessing explained his early thoughts about drama in his *Hamburg Dramaturgy*, which, for the most part, accepted it as a formal rule-governed domain as theorized by Johann Gottsched, who emulated the French rationalists. At a later date, heavily influenced by Kant, Lessing began the text we know as the *Laocoön*, where he defended, on a priori grounds, different standards for evaluating the visual arts, on the one hand, and for non-dramatic poetry, on the other. Unfortunately, one task left undone in the unfinished *Laocoön* is to explain how to apply these ideas to drama in general and to tragedy in particular. His dramatic works, however, provide some insights into how his thoughts changed. *Miss Sara Sampson* is often called the first modern tragedy, because it contains fictional characters from the lower levels of the aristocracy rather than from those prominent in history or myth and because it is not written in verse. Ironically, the type is sometimes referred to as "domestic tragedy" because home and family are the source of the tragic action, as if they weren't involved in the tragedies of Oedipus and Creon and Agamemnon! One of the challenges in adapting the concept of tragedy to new cultural environments is to articulate how different the political role of family had become by the eighteenth century, and how its importance continues to recede in political systems where wealth and power depend less on accidents of birth. The family, once freed from its political obligations, may then exercise its potential as an emotional torture chamber for the psyches of the children, for example, along the lines described much later by Sigmund Freud.[2]

Hegel reconceived tragedy as due to conflicts between two goods that are incompatible with each other in the sense that achieving, or even pursuing, one entails destroying another. If one takes this type of conflict to be the essence of tragedy, a tragic figure may do wrong knowingly. If Oedipus had known who his parents were, he would not have done what he did; but, of course, he couldn't have known. Agamemnon and Eteocles, in contrast, do know the horrific nature of what they must do. Knowledge can neither serve to prevent tragedy nor rescue one from it. Aristotle's idea that the highest type of tragedy begins with a clouded awareness that something is wrong, which in turn leads to a discovery that what is wrong is within oneself, and concludes with the protagonist's tragically having to make things right, fits surprisingly well with Hegel's view of history as the process of Spirit coming to know itself as both subject and object, as knower and known, as agent and patient.[3]

Internal, psychological conflict is at the core of the work of Nietzsche, whose early essay *The Birth of Tragedy* rivals Aristotle's *Poetics* as the most discussed text on the topic. *The Birth of Tragedy* appears to endorse an Apollonian approach to life's difficulties, emphasizing control and reason to the extent that they can be applied in a given situation. In his later writings, however, Nietzsche favors a

Dionysian course of intoxication and indulgence – at least for himself. Far from seeing knowledge as at the core of a meaningful human life, he revives the Greek fascination with the irrational and lauds the courage it takes to embrace it without apologies or excuses. The rift within the self, alienation from oneself, and the insufficiency of the self alone are all themes that have become heavily entrenched in western civilization and the arts, from Plato to Freud, and from Aristotle to cognitive science.

Friedrich Schiller, a near contemporary of Hegel's, touted tragedy as a source of experiences of the sublime (*das Erhabene*) in which "our sensuous nature feels its limitations, but our rational nature feels its superiority, its freedom" (quoted in Norton 1991: 8). Thus, tragedy "must elevate us to an intuition of our own inner freedom to obey the promptings of duty" (ibid.). Needless to say, protagonists in Schillerean tragedy are fully aware of the conflict of goods, and their suffering is embedded in their struggles to do what they know they should do and their failure to do it. They are therefore, according to Schiller, appropriate objects of pity, which he defines as analogous emotional suffering (*mitleid*), perhaps better understood as sympathy (ibid.: 7).

Schiller also defended tragedy as having a moral purpose through catharsis in a way that Aristotle might have endorsed. Catharsis was a homeopathic, medical cleansing or purgation in which a small amount of a substance that is destructive in larger amounts is dispensed, often in multiple doses, to protect, restore, strengthen or otherwise benefit the patient. Schiller extends the medical metaphor to describe the beneficial effects of suffering: "Pathos is an inoculation of inexorable fate, whereby it is robbed of its malignity." The benefits are achieved through and sustained by the "*reiterated* experience of the sublime" to make the "execution of duty . . . the stronger side of man" (quoted in Norton 1991: 9).

## 16.3   Tragedy in the Twentieth Century

The American literary zeitgeist through much of the twentieth century questioned the viability of tragedy as a form of dramatic literature. If Greek tragedy of the fifth century BCE is founded on the fragility of goodness, the alleged irrelevance of tragedy in the twentieth is predicated on the ultimate impossibility of goodness. A cultural environment may provide panaceas – from religious faith to the Cartesian *Cogito* – but not solutions. Joseph Wood Krutch (1929) writes passionately about the pathetic insignificance of individual human actions and choice. Unamuno (1924), more positively, replaces the concept of tragedy with a "tragic sense of life," seeing humans *as* tragic heroes performing noble acts of self-sacrifice for the good of others, paradigmatically, when there is no hope left for themselves. A counterpoint to the tragic sense of life is the existentialist idea of absurd freedom. In Sartre's only novel, *Nausea* (1964, originally 1938), he expresses the view that life, like art, is a construction and one *makes* one's life have value by endorsing it as such. On this view, audience members become the poets: they put things together; they do things. They make their lives works of art.

It is always dangerous to make simplistic generalizations about complicated cultural environments over an arbitrarily defined period of time, especially one as lengthy as a hundred years. The fact is, however, that tragedy was not a living genre for drama, narrative, or poetry during the twentieth century. As a genre, it is archaic, a relic of the past, and ipso facto a handicap to being taken seriously. Nevertheless, classic tragedy, including not only the Greek plays but also works by Shakespeare, Ibsen, and even occasionally Corneille and Racine, continue to be read and performed. Theatrical conventions allow for staging plays in anachronistic ways, encouraging us to *make* the message of a work relevant to contemporary life. Though the genre is no longer alive, various types of plots are similar enough to those described by Aristotle as the best types of tragedy mutatis mutandis, to make it reasonable to consider works having such plots to be tragedies to that degree. Such plots cut across numerous commonly recognized contemporary genres, such as science fiction, horror stories, and political thrillers. Even comedy can represent the importance of tragedy to us by showing how it can be avoided.

As has often been noted, movies stand in well as a contemporary analogue for what Plato condemned in drama, and they serve equally well as a medium for the presentation of plots characteristic of tragedy. Music is virtually always involved, though more as background than as counterpoint to dialogue. Dialogue is virtually never in verse, but there are other ways to indicate that the movie strives to present something of universal human importance and not just a particular point of view, such as shooting a film in black and white once color has become the norm. Such technical details should not dissuade us from recognizing what is most central to tragedy, the plot. Let us suppose, then, that the potential for tragedy exists where it always has, at the nexus of family, culture, religion, and the actions of an individual person attempting to live a good life. We should look for plots in which people suffer undeservedly, where someone brings about that suffering unknowingly, so that pity and fear are appropriate responses to such situations in the ways Aristotle describes.

A more serious challenge concerns the role of mythology, religion, and fate, which used to provide a context for seeing events as inevitable and beyond human control, but which are no longer part of the common consciousness. Nietzsche's proclamation that God is dead is often seen as a turning point after which theological explanations – even in terms of parables or allegories – can no longer be seriously entertained. Yet what is inevitable and beyond human control can easily be reconceived as within the domain of the sciences: the natural sciences, the social sciences, as well as the self-described sciences of the mind. By the 1950s, popularized versions of Freudian psychology and psychoanalysis, on the one hand, competed with behaviorism and empirical psychology in general, on the other, as intellectual frameworks for thinking about human beings as ultimately determined by forces beyond their – our – control. Toward the end of the century, the cognitive sciences, the Genome Project, the possibility of animal and human cloning, neurological knowledge, artificial intelligence, and robotics continued to provide new avenues for attempts to understand the nature of the mind, personhood, and personal identity. Questions about the nature of the self reach their apogee in noumenalism, the view that the human mind is not capable of understanding its own nature, and hence as inaccessible to science, though grounded, ironically, in psychological universals, whatever they may be.

Consider first some possibilities within the genre of science fiction. A common type of plot within the genre has scientists inventing or discovering something that, unforeseeably, causes a great deal of suffering. Science fiction overlaps with horror when scientists create monsters, which Noël Carroll (1990) proposes as essential to the genre. In the science fiction "creature feature" *A Monster on Campus* (1958), the protagonist is an anthropologist, a sensitive and responsible scientist who is respected and reasonably well liked within his campus community. (Though he is no megalomaniac, he does have a penchant for making expensive, long-distance phone calls without prior approval from his dean.) His research is designed to find "the missing link" between *Homo sapiens* and our evolutionary ancestors. Our scientist has invented a potion that he believes would make it possible to find out what such proto-humans were like. In the world of the movie, the genes of species from which humans evolved continue to exist within each individual human being. The potion temporarily silences our "civilized" genes and thus allows the more "primitive" ones to control our behavior. Though not encumbered by the myriad regulations governing research on human subjects today, the scientist is unwilling to risk others' lives and resolves to drink the potion himself. He grows larger, stronger, distinctively apelike and compulsively violent. He kills. When the effects of the potion wear off, he remembers nothing. He eventually correlates the times of the killings with the times he was under the influence of the potion and realizes that *he* is the monster on campus. Knowing *what* he is and what he has done, he cannot bear to live. Suicide, however, is not the solution. The *monster* must be killed, and it must be *killed* and not merely fail to reappear. Therefore, he leads friends and co-workers into a situation where they are attacked by the monster, which they then kill in self-defense. In doing so, they restore the community to its proper state, effecting a kind of catharsis.

According to Carroll, monsters are both threatening, and hence cause fear, and impure or "interstitial," in that they cross the categories of accepted science in some way. The monster on campus is not the traditional "missing link," a member of a distinct biological category, but biologically impure, infecting the identity of later species. We pity the scientist for having to suffer because, unknowingly, he upset the balance of different aspects of our biological nature. Another avenue for fear is opened up by recognizing that every person is partly this lower form of life, and hence vulnerable in the same way as the scientist. The movie sends the message that we cannot help being what we are, so it is better to leave well enough alone: it is better not to know.

*The Manchurian Candidate* (1962, dir. John Frankenheimer, co-written and co-produced with George Axelrod) is a political thriller and a tragedy, successful to a large degree on both counts, though possibly more as the latter than as the former. The basic plot concerns a scheming wife's participation in a communist conspiracy to take over the world, in part by making her dimwitted (second) husband president of the United States. The tragic figure is her son from her first marriage. He despises them both, but, unknowingly, assists their conspiracy. When he realizes what he has done, he knowingly commits an act that is, morally speaking, even more heinous than what he did unknowingly, and then kills himself.

The movie begins with a flashback to the Korean War in 1952. Raymond Shaw, the tragic figure, and nine members of his unit are captured and taken to the Pavlov Institute in Manchuria, "the foremost institute for Conditioned Reflex Therapy in the world." All are "brainwashed" to forget everything that happens during their captivity. Shaw alone is programmed to be controlled through post-hypnotic suggestion and not to remember what he does. He is thus made free from what the director of the institute describes as two uniquely American attributes, guilt and fear. Guilt bears an interesting relationship to pity: it is pity's first-person counterpart. Both emotions have the cognitive component that a person has done something grievously wrong. For guilt, it is a belief about oneself; for pity, it is a belief about someone else. By robbing Shaw of guilt, the institute robs him of his personhood, his agency, his moral responsibility, his freedom. It makes him less than human, a state symbolized by his robot-like behavior when obeying orders delivered through post-hypnotic suggestion. We pity him for this undeserved misfortune, for, whatever Shaw's unlikability, and it is substantial, he is brutally honest about himself, which was about the only thing remaining for which he could take responsibility.

Aristotle points out in the *Nicomachean Ethics* that some acts are involuntary because compelled by an outside force. Typically such acts are voluntary to some degree, making it difficult to sort out the patterns of responsibility. Other acts are involuntary because performed out of ignorance. The moral distinctions among acts of this type depend on whether subsequent knowledge of what one did causes pain and regret. Both Oedipus' and Shaw's actions are of this latter type, which is why the two cannot know the nature of what they are doing when they do it. The director of the Pavlov Institute reassures us on this point, saying that the commonplace view that a person cannot be made to do anything under hypnosis that he wouldn't have been able to do otherwise is false. What remains unsaid is that a person might come to be able to do something horrific as a result of a deliberate process of conditioning when one would not have come to be able to do it otherwise. As with Shylock, Shaw is made to be a worse person than he would otherwise have been. In this sense, both are victims of the conditioning process. Deliberately and with full knowledge of what he is doing, though in the semizombie mode of behavior he displays when under the effects of post-hypnotic suggestion, Shaw shoots his step-father. Waiting a second or two for his mother to realize who killed him, he shoots, and kills, his own mother. Hating the person he has become, he kills himself, and the story ends.

Operant conditioning and Freudian psychology make strange bedfellows, but in this film, they comfortably cohabit because each affords an explanation for how one can perform certain actions quite deliberately yet unknowingly. Hypocrisy rises to the level of a subtheme within the film, most deliciously in the character of Mrs Iselin. By day, she is a rabid anti-Communist; by night, she wears Chinese dressing gowns and gives parties where appetizers sport images of the American flag made out of Russian caviar. She was instrumental in developing the plan to brainwash and program a soldier to carry out the assassinations, yet vows revenge on the Manchurians for selecting her son to be the one. The Iselins deliberately destroy other people's lives for their own political advantage, as when the senator claims to have the names of government workers who are members of the Communist party. An ingenious twist inoculates the filmmakers against assault by lingering McCarthy sympathizers, since, in the film, those who attack others as being Communists turn out to be Communists themselves.

The plot clearly conforms to the requirements of tragedy to a high degree. There is cosmic significance in the form of a global conspiracy. There are innocent people who suffer. There is fear. There is pity – and guilt, to boot. There is an explanation for how a person can go out and deliberately shoot to kill four people, and strangle another, and yet do so involuntarily. There is a chorus member (Janet Leigh's character) expressing popular, romantic ideas about love at first sight. Along the way, the movie is loaded with references to the genre of tragedy and its history: an aside about Orestes and Clytemnestra, a costume party, puns, and possibly a joke about catharsis (when Shaw is described as not only brainwashed but also dry-cleaned). Indeed, the double-edged nature of humor is also a subtheme, from the villainous director of the therapy center, who laughs at everything, to Mrs Iselin, who laughs at nothing, to Shaw, who joyously discovers that he indeed does have the ability to make a joke. There is even a reference to the encyclion, a circular platform that could be moved forward on the Greek stage for the enactment of background events that led up to the tragedy. Toward the beginning of the film, the director of the Pavlov Institute is presenting his latest "achievement," the brain-washed American soldiers, prized examples of what "conditioning therapy" can do. The camera continuously pans the circular auditorium from center stage, displaying a montage of hypnotic suggestion and actual fact. This reversal of the perspective of the encyclion produces a confusing barrage of images of the sort experienced by Shaw and the other soldiers, a growing curiosity about which initiates the action of the tragedy itself. But most of all, there are ambiguities about personal identity, both seen and unseen, a theme that is endemic in tragedy.[4]

A Greek chorus introduces *Mighty Aphrodite* (1995, dir. Woody Allen) with a text straight out of Sophocles, but soon lapses into a contemporary mode of speech, shamelessly exploiting the comic potential of masked and draped chorus members uttering stilted translations from the Greek side by-side with colloquialisms and classic Woody Allen one-liners. The plot follows Lenny Weinrib's desire to know the identity of his adopted son's parents. Once he conceives the idea of doing so, he is a man obsessed. The chorus mocks the foreboding atmosphere of tragedy: "Oh, cursed fate! Some thoughts are better left unthunk." Allusions to classical tragedy and theorizing about it are, as in *The Manchurian Candidate*, sprinkled throughout the movie. There is a lot about whether words are fitting to what is in the world, the meanings of names, and the relationship of one's name to one's personal and professional identity. This is all in the spirit of tragedy, but not of contemporary views of language that hold that proper names, as such, do not have meanings. Lenny chides a chorus member who advises him not to proceed: "That's why *you'll* always be a chorus member. I act. I make things happen." Finally, Linda and Lenny have sex. She becomes pregnant without his knowing it and bears his child, though married by then to someone else. In the penultimate scene, two years later, Lenny and Linda, each with the other's child, unexpectedly meet in a toy store. They are delighted to see each other, glad the other is doing well, and continue happily along their separate ways. The chorus is astounded. "But they have each other's child, and they don't know," to which the response is given, "Yes, yes. Isn't life ironic?" By the final scene, the chorus has become transfigured into an upbeat, jazzy choral and dance ensemble. *That* is one way tragedy is avoided. Unlike a tragedy, when the movie is over, this story does not end.

By the end of the sixth century BCE, tragedy had become a deeply institutionalized genre of theatrical presentation which integrated personal, familial, religious, and political aspects of Athenian life. Dramatic forms similar to the Greek and deriving from it have been written and recognized as such through much of western civilization, enduring major revisions in the process. By the time of Shakespeare, tragedies were sources of popular entertainment, laced with humor and lust, but without deep, formal ties to politics or religion. A recurrent challenge faced by tragedy that lacks the imprimatur of a religious or other overtly official, ceremonial context or function has been to maintain its high-mindedness and claim to veritably cosmic significance without appearing to take itself too seriously. So-called "domestic tragedy" rejected plots embedded in religious myth and mythologized history and hence faced the concordant problem of disposing its audiences to take it seriously enough.

The biological sciences continue to provide us with knowledge about our biological selves far beyond anything envisioned by the ancient Greeks and to a degree to which the self-proclaimed sciences of the mind aspire. Yet it is likely that no science, properly so called, can help us understand who we are as persons and as moral agents. Tragic plots presuppose that individual persons can make a difference. The moral imperative to be self-conscious about what cultural and intellectual traditions one chooses, or refuses, to participate in is a late twentieth-century realization of the Socratic admonition to "know thyself." Aristotle made peace with the poets by seeing their works as intellectual resources for contemplating the true nature of truth, beauty, and justice. In our own time, such reflection is abetted by deliberate references within tragic and some other types of plots to the history of philosophical thought and literary tradition with respect to the nature and importance of tragedy.

## Notes

1   Robert Altman's *The Player* provides a lighthearted yet ultimately cynical perspective on "what sells." Mel Brooks' *The Producers* takes a more slapstick approach.

2   In John Frankenheimer's *The Manchurian Candidate*, discussed in more detail below, the tragic hero is born into an American family that qualifies as "the lower levels of aristocracy."

3   When put into a context of the everyday rather than of cosmic significance, a subject's becoming the object of its own thought is exemplified in John Perry's (1979) account of a *de re* belief coming to be replaced by a *de se* belief. In his example, a grocery shopper follows a trail of sugar to alert the shopper who is leaving the trail, only to discover that *he* is that shopper.

4   It is also endemic within Frankenheimer's films. The darkly pessimistic *Seconds* (1966) includes an extraordinary performance by Rock Hudson and shares, with *The Manchurian Candidate*, a "gray eminence" of unacknowledged sexualities often labeled as "unnatural." Slightly more positive possibilities emerge in *Ronin* (1997), though it is less satisfactory as a movie.

## References

Aristotle (1941). *Nicomachean Ethics*, trans. W. D. Ross. *Poetics*, trans. I. Bywater. *Rhetoric*, trans. W. R. Roberts. In R. McKeon (ed.), *The Basic Works of Aristotle*. New York: Random House: 935–1112, 1455–87, 1325–1451.

Buxton, R. (1998). Tragedy: Greek tragedy. In M. Kelly (ed.), *Encyclopedia of Aesthetics*. New York: Oxford University Press: IV, 396–99.

Carroll, N. (1990). *The Philosophy of Horror, or, Paradoxes of the Heart*. New York: Routledge.

Else, G. (1986). *Plato and Aristotle on Poetry*. Chapel Hill: University of North Carolina Press.

Halliwell, S. (1986). *Aristotle's Poetics*. London: Duckworth.

Hume, D. (1970). Of tragedy. In *Four Dissertations*. (Original work pub. 1757). New York: Garland: 3–24.

Kant, I. (1951). *The Critique of Judgment*, trans. J. H. Bernard. New York: Hafner. (Original work pub. 1790.)

Krutch, J. W. (1929). *The Modern Temper: A Study and a Confession*. New York: Harcourt, Brace.

Lessing, G. (1957). *Laocoön: An Essay upon the Limits of Painting and Poetry*, trans. Ellen Frothingham. New York: Noonday Press.

——(1962). *Hamburg Dramaturgy*, trans. Victor Lange. New York: Dover.

Nietzsche, F. (1967). *The Birth of Tragedy and the Case of Wagner*, trans. Walter Kaufmann. New York: Vintage.

Norton, R. E. (1991). "The Aesthetic Education of Humanity: George Eliot's *Romola* and Schiller's Theory of Tragedy." *Journal of Aesthetic Education*, 25: 3–20.

Nussbaum, M. C. (1986). *The Fragility of Goodness*. Cambridge: Cambridge University Press.

Pappas, N. (1992). "The 'Poetics' argument against Plato." *Southern Journal of Philosophy*, 30: 83–100.

Perry, J. (1979). "The Problem of the Essential Indexical." *Nous*, 13: 3–21.

Plato (1961). *Ion*, trans. L. Cooper. (Originally pub. 1938.) *Republic*, trans. P. Shorey. In E. Hamilton and H. Cairns (eds), *The Collected Dialogues of Plato*. Princeton, NJ: Princeton University Press: 216–28, 576–84.

Ridley, A. (1993). "Tragedy and the Tender-Hearted." *Philosophy and Literature*, 17: 234–45.

Sartre, J.-P. (1964). *Nausea*, trans. Lloyd Alexander. New York: New Directions. (Original work pub. 1938.)

Schiller, F. (1965). *On the Aesthetic Education of Man, in a Series of Letters*, trans. Reginald Snell. New York: Ungar.

Thayer, H. S. (1975). "Plato's Quarrel with Poetry: Simonides." *Journal of the History of Ideas*, 36: 3–26.

Unamuno, M. (1924). *The Tragic Sense of Life*, trans. J. E. Crawford Flitch. New York: Dover. (Original work pub. 1913.)

## Further reading

Bassi, Karen (1998). *Acting like Men: Gender, Drama, and Nostalgia in Ancient Greece*. Ann Arbor: University of Michigan Press.

Hegel, G. W. F. (1975). *Aesthetics: Lectures on Fine Art*, trans. T. M. Knox. 2 vols. Oxford: Clarendon Press.

Lamport, F. J. (1981). *Lessing and the Drama*. Oxford: Clarendon Press.

Lattimore, R. (1967). *Story Patterns in Greek Tragedy*. Ann Arbor: University of Michigan Press.

Orr, J. (1981). *Tragic Drama and Modern Society: Studies in the Social and Literary Theory of Drama from 1870 to the Present*. London: Macmillan.

Schwarz, A. (1978). *From Buchner to Beckett: Dramatic Theory and the Modes of Tragic Drama*. Athens, OH: Ohio University Press.

Vernant, J.-P. (1981). *Tragedy and Myth in Ancient Greece*, trans. J. Lloyd. Atlantic Highlands, NJ: Humanities Press. (Original work pub. 1972.)

# Chapter 17

# The Aesthetics of Nature and the Environment

## Donald W. Crawford

What is it about nature and natural objects that we find aesthetically interesting or pleasing? Do we respond to beautiful animals, seashells, flowers, and scenery simply because of their color, texture, and design characteristics, or is our response guided by scientific knowledge? What part do our biological and social needs and interests play in the aesthetic appreciation of nature? How is the aesthetics of nature related to the aesthetics of fine art? Do we find nature beautiful because it resembles art, or is art beautiful because it resembles nature? How do aesthetic values form a part of contemporary environmental and ecological concerns? From a philosophical perspective, the aesthetic appreciation of nature raises many challenging questions.

## 17.1 The Aesthetic

The concept of the *aesthetic* as a mode of awareness or a way of framing one's attention has a history going back at least to Kant's discussion of disinterestedness in his *Critique of Judgment* (§§2–5) and Schopenhauer's insistence on a pure will-less contemplation as necessary to appreciating the beautiful and the sublime. But the twentieth-century version that gave rise to the debate about the aesthetic attitude originates in Edward Bullough's introduction of the concept of psychical distance in 1912–13. Significantly, Bullough introduced "psychical distance" not in an artistic context but through the example of experiencing the aesthetic features of a fog at sea "by putting the phenomenon, so to speak, out of gear with our practical, actual self; by allowing it to stand outside the context of our personal needs and ends – in short, by looking at it 'objectively'" (1912–13, as reprinted in Townsend 1996: 303). But exponents of the aesthetic attitude, such as Jerome Stolnitz, Eliseo Vivas, and Virgil Aldrich, as well as critics such as George Dickie, have largely ignored whether it is a viable concept in the aesthetics of nature.[1] A noted exception is Arnold Berleant, who in a series of books (1991, 1992, 1997) has argued for a model of aesthetic appreciation of nature characterized by engagement – a participatory rather than contemplative aesthetics.

Malcolm Budd has correctly observed that "a theory of the aesthetic appreciation of nature will be well-founded only if it is based on a conception of what it is for appreciation to be aesthetic." (1998: 1). In a recent special issue of the *Journal of Aesthetic and Art Criticism* titled "Environmental Aesthetics" (Carlson and Berleant 1998), many of the authors seem to be in tune with Budd's dictum. By focusing on two models of the aesthetic appreciation of nature – cognitive and imaginative – they are attempting to analyze the concept of the aesthetic. The debate centers on whether the aesthetic appreciation of nature must be directed by knowledge about it, especially that provided by scientific understandings of the workings of nature (such as ecology), or whether it should instead or in addition include emotion, bodily engagement with nature, meditative and imaginative experiences and responses. This is an area of fruitful contemporary discussion.

## 17.1.1 Aesthetic nature

Budd's dictum is surely right. But the corollary to his claim is an equally important but relatively neglected thesis, namely: "A theory of the aesthetic appreciation of nature will be well-founded only if it is based on a conception of what it is for aesthetic appreciation to be *of nature*." Analogous to the philosophy of art, attempts to clarify the aesthetic valuing of nature must recognize that our attitudes toward the aesthetic quality of natural objects and environments are informed by complex intellectual and philosophical histories going back at least to the late seventeenth century. And just as the philosophy of art requires a careful examination of the concept of *art*, so the aesthetics of nature requires clarification of the concepts of *nature* and the *natural* within the context of aesthetic appreciation. After concluding the present discussion of the major issues in the aesthetics of nature and the environment, I explore this issue in depth in the subsequent sections of this chapter.

## 17.1.2 The beautiful, sublime, and picturesque in nature

A common approach to these issues would be to examine traditional aesthetic theories for their relevance to appreciating nature. For example, the classical conception of beauty, as that which is pleasing to the eye or ear because of the harmony and proportion of its parts, would apply equally to art and to nature. Beauty is formal – almost logical or mathematical – and the object of rational contemplation. Applying this to nature, one can appreciate the symmetry and design found in natural organisms and structures. Indeed, this is one way in which art is often said to imitate nature, by presenting a unified whole embodying a rational design.

When art modifies nature in this way, the result is a formally designed artifact, displaying balance, proportion, and unity of design (as in a formal garden) – a result consistent with classical beauty.

Some would claim that nature is more aesthetically appealing when there is complexity due to subtle integration of various parts rather than in a rigidly formal, geometrical design, however intricate. Variety also pleases, not only in and of itself, but as integrated into larger complexes. Many eighteenth-century aesthetic theories make use of the principle of unity amidst variety, which takes different forms ranging from Francis Hutcheson's "uniformity amidst variety" to Kant's "purposiveness without a purpose." Similar concepts continue into the twentieth century in many writers, and into the twenty-first, and they are easily applied to nature.

In these conceptions, however, the experience of nature is focused on organized, rational structures. But nature also pleases in its wildness, vastness, and brute power. Seemingly unbounded oceans and deserts, or the starry heavens, can give rise to positive feelings of awe and astonishment that traditionally have been incorporated into aesthetics. Violent thunder and lightning storms, powerful waterfalls, even hurricanes and earthquakes, can be fascinating experiences if one feels safe from real danger. Philosophical theories of the sublime in nature developed in the eighteenth century and have been important especially for those who relate our experience of nature to underlying metaphysical realities.[2]

Depending on etymology, "picturesque" means either "like what is found in a picture" or "like the vision of a painter." In either case, the picturesque in nature relates to what can be viewed as an artistic composition. And this need not be symmetric design or order. The theories of the picturesque that developed in the late eighteenth century were based on aesthetic principles still applicable to much of our common aesthetic perception of nature. Our conception of what constitutes a beautiful scene, as represented in a postcard or a photograph, is little different from earlier conceptions of the picturesque.[3]

## 17.1.3 Nature and art

The picturesque, in particular, raises the issue of the similarities and differences between the aesthetics of nature and art. Historically, landscape painting seems to have provided the model for appreciating actual landscapes and for modifying them through the art of landscape gardening. Recent theories of architecture emphasize the interaction between a building and its natural site in creating an aesthetic totality. Photography has also informed our appreciation of natural scenery. Contemporary earth works and environmental art sometimes appear to be in conflict with nature, but other times to create an appealing harmony between nature and art.[4]

### 17.1.4    The aesthetics of nature as social norm

The aesthetic appreciation of nature as art links nature to social and cultural values. This link has been achieved more directly in several ways, two of which are worth investigating. First, the natural setting can be seen as a retreat from society, in which the aesthetic qualities of nature provide a context for a pastoral life of self-sufficiency, peace, and tranquility, as well as nurturing individual moral virtues. "Back to nature" movements have been influential several times in history. Second, aesthetic and social values grounded the establishment of public parks and nature preserves, both urban and rural, with the goal of providing recreational opportunities to rejuvenate the spirit away from the workplace (Chadwick 1966; Fitch 1961).

### 17.1.5    Wilderness aesthetics

Since biblical times, the wilderness has held a double significance for us. On the one hand, as nature primeval, it is wild and untamed, filled with many actual and many more imagined threats to life and civilization. On the other hand, as nature in contrast with society and culture, it is perceived as a place of redemption, which should be respected and maintained as a spiritual sanctuary. In western culture particularly, the aesthetics of the wilderness is a central aspect of a positive but not altogether univocal relationship with nature.[5]

### 17.1.6    Environmental aesthetics

Somewhat related to this, there is the issue of what aesthetic values are found in natural environments such as ecosystems. When considered as an environment or ecosystem, nature is no longer appreciated as a mere perceptual object, phenomenon, or scene; nor is it a natural setting whose aesthetic value results from its positive contributions to a cultural nexus. Appreciation of nature (or an aspect of nature) as environment requires knowledge or at least very strong beliefs, either metaphysical or scientific, that there are natural forces deserving of our appreciation and warranting our respect in the form of minimal interference. The important philosophical question is the extent to which such appreciation is still aesthetic in any meaningful sense of that term. Have we moved from an aesthetic to an ethical perspective on nature? If so, is that shift justified? Are there important links between aesthetics and ethics?[6]

### 17.1.7    Evaluative judgments

Finally, there are two important issues of aesthetic evaluation. Can there be meaningful comparative aesthetic judgments about natural beauty and environments?

Do evaluative judgements about natural beauty have degrees? Does it make sense on purely aesthetic grounds, for example, to declare that a swan is more beautiful than a cockroach? An even more fundamental question is whether there are any negative aesthetic values in nature. The view that every aspect of the natural world is beautiful – referred to as "positive aesthetics" – has been hotly debated.[7]

## 17.2   Appreciating Nature

Let's begin with the obvious. Nature, natural beauty, and the natural environment are concepts that today evoke positive feelings together with a concern for their preservation and protection. Our natural parks, wilderness areas, and nature preserves exist to protect the beauties of nature from human destruction and to make them available to present and future generations. Nature writing abounds in local book shops and libraries, and nature documentaries continue to be popular on television. Education programs in schools and universities have joined the more specialized nature programs in parks and nature areas in offering diverse courses, lectures, and guided tours designed to develop an awareness of natural organisms, ecological habitats, and environments. Some focus on learning how to identify species and varieties of flora and fauna, while others emphasize a holistic approach to objects and organisms in their natural settings. Not infrequently, such programs also attempt to develop a richer appreciation of the aesthetically pleasing dimensions of nature. Attention to natural beauty, of course, is nothing new. People long have cultivated, arranged, and displayed flowers and plants in their gardens and homes, and in recent decades collected and displayed natural objects such as sea shells, driftwood, and rocks because of their aesthetically interesting features. And for several centuries scenic travel has been a recreational pastime. All of these activities are self-consciously planned and carried out, however much they are dependent upon cultural norms. And they remain deeply rewarding. Nature as an object of aesthetic appreciation is an important part of our cultural heritage and values.

An older, less culturally developed, and more childlike fascination with nature nonetheless remains, and also claims a place within the realm of the aesthetic as a value found immediately in perceptual experience. Some find it when strolling along a beach, looking at shells or pebbles. It captures others each spring when the first shoots and bulbs emerge from the cold, damp earth. Some are struck by nature's charms in the visible beauty of sunsets, passing cloud formations, or the sound and smell of fresh rain. And there are the simple pleasures of throwing a stone into a still pond and watching the concentric ripples spread out from the center, of having pure sand run through one's fingers, of watching waves crest and break along a shore. These simple aesthetic fascinations often seem to occur spontaneously, somewhat distinct from cultural practices, and not guided by the more intellectual concerns of ecology and the environment. This pre-reflective, childlike fascination with nature nonetheless forms an important part of the aesthetic appreciation of natural objects, events, and phenomena and exists alongside cultural, scientific, and ecological modes of appreciation.

Historically, theories of natural beauty have focused on four aspects of nature – the human body, natural organisms and objects, natural phenomena, and scenery. Traditional discussions of the natural beauty of the human body treat the beauty of the human form as expressive of intellectual or physical powers (virtues). Thomas Reid, for example, analyzed the beauty of the human body as due to the proportion of its parts as indicating "delicacy and softness in the fair sex, and in the male either strength or agility" (1785, reprinted 1967: I, 506). But in more recent times, theories of natural beauty have focused almost entirely on nature in the narrower sense in which nature is contrasted with human beings, their artifacts and cultural creations. Whether this should be the case is still debated (see for example Eaton 1998: 150).

The second category of natural beauty is that of non-human natural objects. It is a very extensive category, including plants and animals, their parts, their products, as well as inorganic complexes that exhibit orderly structures or intensive qualities. A list of examples illustrates some of these many subdivisions: a swan (organism), a cedar tree (plant), a tulip blossom (part of a plant), a bird's plumage (part of an animal), a bird's nest (product of an animal), a pine cone (product of a plant), a snowflake (orderly inorganic structure), a sapphire (inorganic orderly structure with an intensive quality).

A third focus in the appreciation of nature consists of natural events and phenomena – rainbows, cloud formations, sunsets, the sun or moon shining through the clouds, waves breaking against the shore. What is surprising about this category is that it seems to involve the point of view of a spectator; that is, these are aspects of nature developing in time as viewed from a human location. Their beauty is in the eye of the beholder – not necessarily in the sense that their beauty is subjective, but in that the perception of their beauty depends on a human vantage point.

A fourth type of natural beauty in the literature also requires a human perspective. This is the category of scenic beauty, as most clearly represented in the concept of a landscape, and is the area of nature aesthetics most closely connected to the aesthetics of fine art (as exemplified in landscape painting).

A fifth and more recent interest in the aesthetic appreciation of nature focuses on natural environments and ecosystems, which involves appreciating nature in light of our knowledge provided by the natural sciences, especially the environmental sciences such as geology, biology, and ecology. Ecological communities, like human communities, do not always evolve simply. Sometimes, indeed perhaps most frequently, their development is based on phases of co-operation and conflict. For example, think of the successive stages of development of a glacial lake to a meadow, then to a softwood forest, then to a hardwood forest, followed by a forest fire, then followed by regrowth through the establishment of entirely different plant communities – and the non-duplicative cycle continues.

In short, nature in these various forms is an aesthetically relevant concept. The major challenge to incorporating nature into a philosophically based aesthetic theory has been in explaining the aesthetic *significance* of our basic aesthetic responses toward nature, and how these responses are similar to or different from our aesthetic appreciation of art. Only a few major theorists, such as Kant, have made the attempt. And even Kant was content with very simple examples of nature appreciation and barely hints at the relevance of his more theoretical model of nature as a cosmic system to his discussion of the significance of appreciating nature aesthetically.

## 17.3 Skepticism Regarding Aesthetic Nature

The importance of appreciating nature aesthetically may seem obvious to us today. Few if any would consider themselves unresponsive to the beauties of nature, and the topic has a contemporary urgency about it. But it has not always been so. Denials of the significance if not the very existence of natural beauty can be found in western cultural history in two main forms, theological and philosophical.

The first consists of a partial repudiation of aesthetic nature on the basis of theological doctrines concerning the unworthiness of human beings to inherit the earth after the Fall. According to this line of thought, many of the most striking land formations are the products of God's wrath and hence are not suitable objects for aesthetic appreciation. The soil resists efforts to produce bountiful harvests; the forces of nature bring forth floods and natural disasters; and much of the surface of the earth is unsuitable for habitation. Mountains, in particular, were taken as evidence of God's displeasure, now made to deviate from the smooth, fertile plains of the Garden of Eden. This theologically inspired view can be found well into the eighteenth century, as exemplified in Charles Jennens' 1741 libretto for Handel's *Messiah*, which renders the Old Testament's Book of Isaiah literally, glorifying in anticipation the time when:

> Every valley shall be exalted, and every mountain and hill shall
> be made low: and the crooked shall be made straight, and the
> rough places plain.
>
> (Isaiah: 40: 4)

Various forms of philosophical idealism provide a second type of impugnment of aesthetic nature. If value is placed exclusively in the spiritual, then material nature is precluded from being the repository of true beauty simply because of its lack of spirituality. In *Republic* V (476d) Plato writes disparagingly of those who are mere "lovers of sights and sounds" and do not reflect on the underlying, unchanging reality. Although he seems to be criticizing those enthralled by dramatic and musical performances, a Platonist might equally well cast aspersions on those who enthuse about the beauties of nature rather than intelligible beauty. Shaftesbury, following the neo-Platonic tradition, characterized the beauties of nature as "superficial beauties" and claimed that "whatever in nature is beautiful or charming is only the faint shadow of that first beauty" (1709, as given in 1900: II, 130, 126). The philosophical denial of natural beauty reached its peak in nineteenth-century post-Kantian idealism. Friedrich Schelling acknowledged it only insofar as natural forms such as crystals reveal themselves as products of creative spirit (1800: pt VI, sec.2). Karl Solger (1829) found beauty only in the explicit manifestation of spirit in art, thereby completely rejecting the concept of natural beauty. And although Hegel, the most famous post-Kantian idealist, did not repudiate natural beauty completely, he relegated it to the lowest point on his scale of beauty as expressive of spirit (1823: intro., ch. II).

Skepticism concerning natural beauty is by no means universal during this period. Other strands of nineteenth-century thought elevated the aesthetics of nature to the realm of spiritual enlightenment. In poetry and painting, and even to some extent in music, the Romantics did not neglect natural and scenic beauty. Kant's emphasis on natural beauty found continued life in the writings of Schopenhauer, Wordsworth, and Coleridge, and through them was then passed on to American transcendentalists such as Ralph Waldo Emerson and Henry David Thoreau. In fact, strains of American transcendentalism inform a continuing current of the multi-dimensional American fascination with nature.

## 17.4   Aesthetics and the Concept of Nature

The multiple meanings of the term "nature" are legend,[8] but one major meaning seems unrelated to the use of "nature" in aesthetic contexts, namely the sense in which each kind of thing is said to have its own nature. In this sense, the nature of something is its essential or characteristic properties, that which makes it the kind of thing it is. This sense of "nature" appears to be the root meaning of both the Latin *natura* and the Greek *phusis*, and its use persists both in philosophical and in ordinary discourse, as in speaking of the nature of a problem, the nature of the soil, the nature of a discovery, or even human nature. This meaning does not seem to relate in any obvious way to what we mean by "nature" when we speak of aesthetically appreciating nature. For the Presocratics, and Plato as well, the concept of nature seems to occur only in the context of the *nature of* something, or a thing's nature – its essential character. So nature in this sense is not an existential domain but a property; it is what some but not all things *have*. Nature in the sense of whatever exists – the physical universe and all of its parts, organic and inorganic – is not a concept clearly found in early Greek thought, although it is prevalent today. We can call this concept *unrestricted nature*. In this sense everything is a part of nature, whether beast or human, physical or mental, object

or force, event or place. Curiously, the *Oxford English Dictionary's* earliest cita-
tion for "nature" in this sense dates from 1862.[9] This view of nature as unlimited
and all-encompassing, which makes no distinction between nature and human
beings, or nature and art, could well go back to the Stoic view that everything
existing is part of the cosmos, which is a rational, complex, and dynamic system.
And thus every product of human skill, even the highest form of art, would still
be part of nature in this unrestricted sense. Neo-Platonists also tended toward the
view that everything is a part of a single, rational order, although from our limited
viewpoint we are unable to see the interdependency of all things. The *Oxford Dictionary of English Etymology* claims that the use of "nature" in the sense of "the
material world" goes back only to the seventeenth century (Onions 1966: 606).
And *Webster's Third New International Dictionary of the English Language* gives
the following relevant entries for "nature":

a) (1) the created world in its entirety.
   (2) the totality of physical reality exclusive of things mental.
b) the total system of spatio-temporal phenomena and events that can be explained
   by other occurrences in the same system. (1961: 1508, entry 10)

However, it is doubtful that the concept of unrestricted nature maps very well
onto our contemporary concept of nature in aesthetic contexts, which almost
everyone agrees relies on some distinction between nature and art. But as a limiting or polar concept it marks a conception that can prove useful in explicating
more viable, less extreme conceptions of aesthetic nature.

### 17.4.1 Aristotelian nature

Aristotle's discussion of the different uses of the term *phusis* includes his major
means of distinguishing nature from art or, as he puts it, things which exist *by
nature* from things which exist *by art*. Things which exist by nature have something products of art do not have, namely a principle of movement and stability
– a principle of change within themselves and an innate tendency to *persist* in their
natural state of completeness, once it is attained. Acorns turn into oaks, kittens
become cats, and even apples fall to the ground as the result of principles of change
internal to them (they are of the earth, and so to earth will they return). Such
things, on Aristotle's view, *exist by nature*. Of course oak trees can also become
ships, and pieces of marble can be changed into sculptures, but in these transfor-
mations the artistic product – at least its form – does not result from the operation of any *internal* principle of change. Instead, external causation is required for
wood to become a ship or for a chunk of marble to become a piece of sculpture.
Empirically, Aristotle reminds us, we become aware of this important distinction
by noting recurrent patterns of events. As it happens, trees do not invariably turn
into ships of their own accord. In a rare humorous moment, Aristotle reports

Antiphon's observation that if you were to plant a wooden bed and it sent up a shoot, the shoot would be a young plant, not a young bed. The humor of the example reveals a philosophical or conceptual truth, according to Aristotle. He says it shows "that the arrangement in accordance with the rules of art is merely an incidental attribute" and not an essential, persisting one (*Physics*, II, 193a).[10] "For those things are natural which, by a continuous movement originated from an internal principle, arrive at some completion" (*Physics*, II, 199b).

Of course products of art may change without being acted upon from without. Thus a wooden ship will eventually rot if not maintained, but it rots not because it is a ship (a product of art) but because it is (made out of) wood. Aristotle thus implies that the very same entity (formed matter) could be either a natural thing or a product of art, depending on its etiology. It is a natural thing if it got to be the way that it is, so to speak, *on its own*, and for Aristotle this is the key meaning of "naturally" or "by nature."

The examples discussed so far contrast things existing by nature with those existing (or coming into being) by art. But art is not the only non-natural mode of being, according to Aristotle. There are two other alternatives to existing by nature. First, there is the Prime Mover – that which exists in and of itself. It is eternally unchanging; having no principle of change, it is not a natural thing. Second, there are things which happen simply by chance. They exist neither by nature nor by art, and – unlike the Prime Mover – they do undergo and result from change, but the change here is not due to a principle internal to them. Chance occurrences and events come about when two or more chains of natural events collide. If you are walking along and step on an apple that has fallen off a tree, the squashed apple does not result from any principle of change internal to either it or you.

To be textually accurate it must be noted that Aristotle never explicitly provides a characterization of nature in the generic sense, even though he states several times that he has said what nature is. But it is reasonable to conclude that nature, for Aristotle, is the totality of things existing *by nature* (as opposed to the supernatural, art, accidents, and perhaps mathematics). Nature consists of all those things whose principles of change are internal. Aristotle even begins to enumerate them: "Animals and their organs, plants, and the elementary substances – earth, fire, air, water – these and their likes we say exist by nature" (*Physics*, II, 192b). Clearly, this Aristotelian view is a major part of the conceptual heritage to our aesthetics of nature.

### 17.4.2 *Aesthetic nature and unrestricted nature*

Thus Aristotle's concept of nature in the generic sense is *not* that of *unrestricted* nature; Aristotle's concept of nature is more limited. And so is *our* concept of nature as an object of aesthetic appreciation, that which I am calling "aesthetic nature." That is not to say we do not have the concept of unrestricted nature.

Indeed we do. We still employ the concept of nature in the sense of unrestricted nature and consider ourselves to be a part of it, whether that concept is interpreted as the totality of spatial-temporal particulars and complexes or as a unity of diverse systems.

But aesthetic nature is not equivalent to unrestricted nature, being more limited than it. When we speak of aesthetically appreciating nature today, we generally have in mind the physical world, usually the out-of-doors, as perceived directly with our own sense organs, and the emphasis is on what is visible. Aesthetic nature includes living things in their native environments, but ordinarily excludes human beings, their activities, institutions, and artifacts. This concept shares with Aristotle's the exclusion of products of art in the broad sense used by the Greeks.

But our concept differs from Aristotle's conception in two important ways. *First,* it almost always excludes human beings and what they do by nature (breathing, eating, drinking, defecating, and procreating). *Second,* our concept of aesthetic nature includes non-human things that arise, in Aristotle's sense, by accident. For example, aesthetic nature includes the effects of glaciation on a valley such as Yosemite, a spectacular sunset, and the form of a prehistoric organism captured in a fossil. These must be excluded from Aristotle's conception of nature, for they happen not in the course of an internal principle changing something toward a state of completion, but merely "by chance" in his sense – the unforeseen meeting of two or more chains of rigorous causation not derivable from any principle of change internal to any of the individuals involved (W. D. Ross 1959: 80). Our concept of aesthetic nature encompasses some such "accidents" and "chance occurrences" that are in no way attributable to human efforts. Thus, nature in our concept of aesthetic nature is broader than Aristotle's conception of nature because it includes some processes and products of two or more accidentally interacting forces in nature; and it is narrower than Aristotle's because it almost always excludes human beings and their activities, however "natural" they may be.

### 17.4.3   Aesthetic nature and limited nature

At this point one might question the fruitfulness of any attempt to characterize aesthetic nature by means of placing limitations on the concept of unrestricted nature. After all, why not adopt a more open conceptual scheme? There is always a certain philosophical attractiveness to a cosmic perspective. The penguin's evolutionary development, resulting in marked deviation from its winged ancestors, may differ insignificantly from the border collie's evolution from the wolf, even though the latter was helped along by human agency through selective breeding. From the cosmic perspective, the temporal succession of plant and animal communities in a given location is a fact of nature, regardless of the influence of human action or inaction. And unrestricted nature might seem to be the most relevant concept if one is inclined toward the view that the aesthetic is essentially an attitude or mode of perception that can be adopted toward any object of awareness whatsoever (see for example Stolnitz 1960: 35; Sparshott 1982: 111–12). White marigolds, seedless grapes, farm fields and square tomatoes are all part of unrestricted nature and they are potential objects of aesthetic appreciation. But, unfortunately for tidy theorists, so are wax bananas, silk flowers, and football games. The problem with embracing all the phenomena equally with open arms, sticking simply with the concept of unrestricted nature, is that it fails to allow for a distinction between an aesthetics of nature and an aesthetics of art. So some limitation on the concept of unrestricted nature seems necessary to make sense of the field of inquiry, at least as historically constituted.

Various possible qualifications of unrestricted nature suggest themselves in keeping with historical and current conceptions of nature per se. One is reflected in the contrast we sometimes make or imply between nature on the one hand and the heavens or cosmos on the other hand. The limitation of nature to the sublunary was prominent in the Middle Ages, and it can be traced to Aristotle's distinction between the sublunary and the translunary (*De Mundo*, 292a). The restriction is also implicit in Aristotle's remark that both the heavens and the world of nature depend upon the Prime Mover (*Metaphysics*, XII, 1072b). But twentieth-century developments require us to part with Aristotle. For aesthetic purposes, limiting the concept of nature to the earth and its atmosphere, or even to the sublunary or planetary realm, does not seem useful. Aesthetic nature must range wide enough to incorporate discoveries in unknown parts of the universe, whether at the macroscopic or microscopic level.

### 17.4.4  Pure nature

Perhaps the simplest aesthetically relevant limitation of the concept of nature is to conceive of nature as it would be without the existence or influence of human beings. This conception we shall label *pure nature*. It is the idea of nature as pure wilderness, nature primeval – nature as it exists apart from any human intervention. No doubt this is an idealization, but pure nature is easy enough to conceive and should not be summarily dismissed. The problem with pure nature is not in its conception but in its realization. True wilderness has almost ceased to exist, and thus the concept of pure nature may be too limited to be very useful. Still, the concept may be operative in some cases. The discovery of previously unknown forms of life in areas of active hydrothermal vents many thousands of feet below sea level has revealed amazing new subspecies of organisms which utilize a non-solar energy source. Part of our wonder at and aesthetic fascination with these organisms is perhaps due to their being examples of pure nature – completely undisturbed (until now) by human beings. A large anthill in the African wild brings with it a similar fascination in encountering a complex biological unit existing seemingly independently of humans.

The contrast between pure and unrestricted nature may be summarized as follows:

*Pure nature:* completely unmodified and unaffected by human beings. For example: native stands of conifers in a primeval setting (unaffected by proximity of humans, their paths, vehicles, pollution, etc.); the Galapagos rift ecosystem; the interior of an ant colony.

*Unrestricted nature:* everything in the universe, individual and general, object or power, above and below, on and within and beyond the earth, sun and moon, however individuated and whatever its origin. Thus, not only is the native stand of conifers listed above part of unrestricted nature, so is a planted Christmas tree, or even an artificial one.

To use "nature" in the sense of "pure nature" is to disallow any part of nature that has been affected by human modification, alteration or even the slightest disturbance to count as aesthetic nature. Pure nature completely excludes artifacts and human modifications of nature, but it also excludes all aspects of nature that have been affected by human beings. This creates tremendous problems for a workable theory of the aesthetics of nature. It seems far too austere to make the concept useful except as an ideal or a boundary.

But what are the alternatives? As we have seen, on the other hand "nature" in the sense of "unrestricted nature" includes human beings, their artifacts, their modifications of nature in any way, shape, or form. And this does not fit well either with our use of "nature" in aesthetic contexts.

The conclusion is inevitable. *Neither of these polar concepts – pure or unrestricted nature – adequately maps aesthetic nature.* In other words, the concept of *pure nature* does not allow for any human alteration of nature, however slight, to occur without the object ceasing to be natural, while *unrestricted nature* countenances any and all such changes. Pure nature is too scarce, and unrestricted nature is too abundant. Thus, we seem forced to look elsewhere to clarify the concept of aesthetic nature, and the most likely place is in the old dichotomy between the natural on the one hand and the artificial or artifactual on the other.

## 17.4.5  The natural versus the artifactual

Our concept of aesthetic nature seems to relate directly to the long-standing opposition between the natural and the artifactual, and to side with an idealized conception of the state of the empirical world as it subsists and evolves more or less independently of human activity. Aesthetic nature is thus consonant with the traditional division of aesthetics into two species, the natural and the artistic (or artifactual). But any attempt to draw a hard-and-fast line between these two is destined to encounter serious obstacles. A little reflection will reveal the tip of the iceberg that is a major obstacle to aesthetic theory in this area.

To begin with, one might worry that our initial rough characterization of aesthetic nature is too limited. Have we not excluded that large portion of the biological world whose existence is dependent upon human civilization? The domestication of animals consists in the human domination of a species to the point that its members are brought into the human domain and altered genetically by selective breeding. As a result, most of them are now almost totally dependent upon us for their survival (Tuan 1984: 99–109). Are they a part of aesthetic nature? However this question is answered, the problem runs even deeper. There are many varieties of plants and animals that are not simply dependent upon humans for their *continued* existence, but whose *coming into* existence and whose essential characteristics themselves (their "natures") are the result of calculated human effort and skill. Most domesticated animals, fruits, grains, vegetables, and flowers raised in the agriculturally advanced parts of the world today are products of our conscious manipulation of biological resources. And this is true without even considering contemporary genetic engineering. The natural environment has been and continues to be so modified by human intervention that Aristotle's criterion of what exists "by nature" may well be obsolete in practice.

Nor is the concept of *artifactuality* itself any longer clear enough to provide a negative necessary condition for aesthetic nature. Square tomatoes have been developed to reduced damage in shipment. It is not an artificial (or artifactual) tomato. But it still is something that human beings have produced from the earth's natural resources. Difficult examples abound if one tries to make the concept of aesthetic nature coincide with nature in its pure, pristine state. What are we to say about restored prairies and wilderness, tangelos, beefalos (a cross between a buffalo and cattle), and the more common results of controlled breeding such as domestic cats and dogs? The ability to reproduce true without human intervention might seem an appropriate criterion, eliminating introduced hybrids, but counterexamples are easy to find. There are, after all, naturally occurring hybrids – perhaps nothing quite so dramatic as a seedless grape or a tangelo, but certainly there is that old standby and Aristotle's nemesis, the mule (*Generation of Animals*, II, 747a). So-called "freaks of nature" are nonetheless part of unrestricted nature and may become part of aesthetic nature, quite independently of human intervention.

### 17.4.6 Altered and disturbed nature

Perhaps there is a less direct way to make use of the concept of artifactuality to clarify the concept of aesthetic nature. Let's take pure nature and artifactuality as poles on a continuum:

*Pure nature . . . . . . . . . . . . . Artifact*

This allows for the recognition of a wide range of intermediary concepts whose content will be a function of the manner or extent of human incursion or modification. Whether useful points exist on this continuum will depend in part upon our specific interests. But it will also depend upon the empirical data – whether the important examples form clusters. In other words, it may be that certain kinds of human modifications of nature still allow (or even promote) the appreciation of something as nature. One might try to indicate a few of the relevant parameters for such nodes. As one moves along the continuum away from pure nature, degrees or types of human modification begin to creep into what is still considered nature. At some point one reaches the realm where we cease to call things or events nature (or natural) but consider them artifacts. There is no reason to think there is a clear boundary here.

But there is an important complication. For our purposes, the single-dimensional continuum is not very helpful, because two major *types* of modification of pure nature must be noted: those that are done for aesthetic reasons and those that are not. That is, sometimes we alter nature for aesthetic purposes and sometimes we modify (or simply disturb) it for other reasons or completely unintentionally. This provides a two-dimensional continuum:

With aesthetic intent

*Pure nature* . . . . . . . . . . . . . . *Artifact*

Without aesthetic intent

Looking first at the aesthetic dimension, we can distinguish several relevantly different modifications of nature:

1  Close to pure nature are cases in which nature is altered but we still want the result to be appreciated as nature. For example, we might polish a stone to better display its colors and striations, or remove a piece of driftwood or a sea shell from the beach and place it on a shelf in the house. Or we might observe birds bathing in a bird bath. Nature was modified – the birds were drawn to the water by something someone did – but our interest is in the natural activity of the birds in the water.
2  Further toward artifactuality is a restored native ecosystem, such as a prairie, which still can be appreciated as a natural ecosystem and not merely as a restoration.
3  Zoological gardens, botanical gardens, aquariums and aviaries all involve intensive modification of nature but still present specimens to be appreciated as nature, some even in their natural environments.

So there are many degrees of modification of nature before one reaches the point where the product of the alteration can *only* be considered as an artifact. Even a bonsai tree can be appreciated as nature.

The lower branch of the continuum is itself multidimensional, branching between unintentional and intentional non-aesthetic modifications of nature. Smog results from intentional activities without being itself intended. It might be characterized as *disturbed* rather than *altered* or *modified* nature. Of course, the line between disturbed and altered nature is not sharp; there is no reason to think that it can be drawn precisely.[11]

## 17.4.7 *The concept of aesthetic nature*

What, then, is the relevant sense of nature when nature is considered in relation to aesthetic appreciation? In terms of its usefulness for philosophical analysis, I believe one must be fairly liberal, opting in the direction of the polar concept of unrestricted nature and resisting the temptation to limit the concept to something close to pure nature. From my own personal perspective, I think that plants can be fertilized and watered, maintained in rows or in pots or even transplanted, that animals can be moved to new locations or prevented from ranging over their natural habitat, without my being unable to appreciate them *as nature*. We do indeed disturb biological nature, whether intentionally or not, by modifying the behavior, growth, and mobility traits of organisms. An example of disturbed, but not altered nature (in terms of the above scheme) is a roadside plant community. Which species are present and flourish, and even some of the characteristics of the individual plants such as height, color, and type of foliation, are partially determined by human modifications of pure nature. Similarly, an aquarium provides an artificially controlled natural environment in which marine life can exist in a more or less natural state. Of course the extent to which this is achieved depends upon the characteristics of the individual aquarium; but no aquarium is the same as pure nature.

To set out the necessary and sufficient conditions for the above concepts is not essential for our present purposes, and in any event it is doubtful whether they could be given without excessively artificial stipulation. Borderline cases will always arise, given the parameters of the continuum. The importance of the above sketch, however, is simply this: the aesthetic appreciation of nature cannot be identified with the relatively clear concept of *unrestricted* nature or with that of *pure* nature. The moral to be drawn is that when considering nature as an aesthetic norm, one should be wary of attempts to restrict the aesthetically relevant categories either to the concept of pure nature or to that of unrestricted nature.

An additional set of cautions is in order. None of the above categories can be delimited merely in terms of monadic properties of individuals. Whether something is pure, altered, or disturbed nature need not depend simply upon qualities it has independently of its relationships with other things. Consequently the application of any of these concepts to individual cases is not always clear cut. Many instances of aesthetic appreciation of nature are directed to *collections* of individuals (for example, a kindle of kittens, a gaggle of geese, a school of fish), or to *parts* of individuals (such as feathers, flowers, leaves), or to *products* of individuals (shells, webs, tracks, nests). Other instances focus on phenomena or events rather than individual objects, collections, parts, or products. Some of these are almost momentary (such as a streak of lightning or a shooting star); others are short-term (a sunset, a halo around the moon); still others are long-term (erosion); and many are continuing or recurrent (for example, waterfalls, seasonal changes, tides). Another important category of natural objects of aesthetic appreciation consists of relationships of diverse objects to each other in more or less accidental ways (a sunset over the sea, cloud formations over the mountain tops). These constitute radical departures from the living organism as the paradigm of natural beauty, since they directly introduce the issue of the relevance of human perspective and subjectivity to the aesthetics of nature. The aesthetic appeal of land and water forms (mountains, lakes) and their interfaces (such as a shoreline) is tied to their properties as visually revealed from a given human perspective. They are beautiful prospects, enchanting vistas, lovely scenes. In short, our aesthetic enjoyment of them is relative, quite literally, to the *point of view* of the perceiver. Nonetheless, these are among the most common examples of aesthetic nature, as represented in the concept of a landscape, which is perhaps the most central concept in the historical development of our modern aesthetic sensitivity to nature.[12]

I believe there are several conclusions that can be drawn from this brief inquiry into our conceptualizing of nature. The first can be formulated as a simple moral: from the perspective of philosophical aesthetics, it is unlikely that a single, much less a pure and simple, concept of nature will be adequate to deal with the complexity of the various modes of our aesthetic appreciation of nature. And consequently, aesthetic nature and art, as well as other forms of human modification of nature's raw materials, are likely to be more closely related to each other than our intuitions, or even the history of our subject, would lead us to believe.

## Notes

1 George Dickie provides a useful, succinct discussion of the aesthetic attitude in the twentieth century in his (1997: 28–37).

2 Many important eighteenth-century texts are included in Ashfield and de Bolla (1996). Full discussions of these views can be found in Monk (1935); Hipple (1957).

3 Established works on this topic include Hussey (1927); Pevsner (1944). For more recent discussions, see S. Ross (1987); Andrews (1989).

4 For a discussion of some of these complex relationships between art and nature, see Crawford (1983); Carlson (2000: chs 8, 10, 11, and 12). For the aesthetics of gardens, see Miller (1993); S. Ross (1998).

5 For the history of wilderness aesthetics, see Nicolson (1959); Nash (1967); Graber (1970).

6 A number of these issues are addressed in articles in a special issue on environmental aesthetics in the *Journal of Aesthetics and Art Criticism* (Carlson and Berleant 1998, and in Carlson (2000: chs 4, 5, and 7).

7 For a careful analysis and defense of this view, see Carlson (1984).

8 Arthur Lovejoy began his now classic paper, "'Nature' as Aesthetic Norm" (1927), with a remark Friedrich Nicolai made over 200 years ago that remains an appropriate epigram for any inquiry into the concept of nature: "Der Begriff und das Word 'Natur' ist ein wahrer Scherwenzel" ("The concept and the word 'nature' is a real jack-of-all-trades"). Lovejoy (1927: 444, reprinted 1948: 69).

9 "'Nature' is being used in the narrow sense of physical nature . . . But these selves of ours do belong to 'Nature'" (citing *Edinburgh Review*, CXVI, p. 381). This is followed by an 1873 entry: "Holding nature to represent the whole cosmos, and to

include both the physical and the spiritual" (citing Dawson, *Earth & Man*, XIV, p. 343).

10 Quotations are from *The Basic Works of Aristotle* (1941).

11 Stephanie Ross (n.d.) has written the following: "Maybe we could formulate some sort of complicated recursive definition [of nature] along the following lines: nature consists of (i) areas of unexplored wilderness (the original 'given'), (ii) areas that were wilderness, have been entered, but haven't been developed, (iii) areas that have been entered, have been affected by humankind, yet remain noticeably wilder than other areas in specifiable respects, (iv) areas that have been entered, developed, but then returned to a more natural state through careful management."

12 Francis Sparshott outlines an alternative conceptual mapping of non-artistic beauty in (1982: 111 and 555, notes 20 and 21).

# References

Andrews, M. (1989). *The Search for the Picturesque*. Stanford: Stanford University Press.

Aristotle (1941). *The Basic Works of Aristotle*, ed. Richard McKeon. New York: Random House.

Ashfield, A. and de Bolla, P., eds. (1996). *The Sublime: A Reader in British Eighteenth-Century Theory*. Cambridge: Cambridge University Press.

Berleant, A. (1991). *Art and Engagement*. Philadelphia: Temple University Press.

——(1992). *The Aesthetics of the Environment*. Philadelphia: Temple University Press.

——(1997). *Living in the Landscape: Toward an Aesthetics of Environment*. Lawrence, KS: University Press of Kansas.

Budd, M. (1998). "Delight in the Natural World: Kant on the Aesthetic Appreciation of Nature. Part I: Natural Beauty." *British Journal of Aesthetics*, 38(1): 1–18.

Bullough, E. (1912–13). "'Psychical Distance' as a Factor in Art and as an Aesthetic Principle." *British Journal of Psychology*, V: 87–118. (Widely reprinted in anthologies.)

Carlson, A. (1984). "Nature and Positive Aesthetics." *Environmental Ethics*, 6: 5–34. (Reproduced in *Aesthetics and the Environment: The Appreciation of Nature, Art and Architecture*. London and New York: Routledge, 2000: 72–101.)

——(2000). *Aesthetics and the Environment: The Appreciation of Nature, Art and Architecture*. London and New York: Routledge.

Carlson, A. and Berleant, A. (eds) (1998). *Journal of Aesthetics and Art Criticism*, special issue, 56(2).

Chadwick, G. F. (1996). *The Park and the Town: Public Landscape in the 19th and 20th Centuries*. London: Architectural Press; New York: Praeger.

Crawford, D. (1983). "Nature and Art: Some Dialectical Relationships." *Journal of Aesthetics and Art Criticism*, 42: 49–58.

Dickie, G. (1997). *Introduction to Aesthetics: An Analytic Approach*. Oxford and New York: Oxford University Press.

Eaton, M. M. (1998). "Fact and Fiction in the Aesthetic Appreciation of Nature." *Journal of Aesthetics and Art Criticism*, 56(2): 150–6.

Fitch, J. M. (1961). "American Pleasure Gardens." In *Architecture and the Aesthetics of Plenty*. New York: Columbia University Press: 173–87.

Graber, L. H. (1970). *Wilderness as Sacred Space*. Monograph Series No. 8. Washington, DC: Association of American Geographers.

Hegel, G. W. F. (1823). *Vorlesungen über die Philosophie der Kunst.* (Trans. T. M. Knox (1988) as *Aesthetics: Lectures on the Fine Arts.* Oxford: Clarendon Press.)

Hipple, W. J. Jr (1957). *The Beautiful, the Sublime, and the Picturesque in Eighteenth-Century British Aesthetic Theory.* Carbondale, IL: Southern Illinois University Press.

Hussey, C. (1927). *The Picturesque: Studies in a Point of View.* London: G. P. Putnam's Sons. (Reprinted, London: Frank Cass, 1967.)

Lovejoy, A. O. (1927). "'Nature' as Aesthetic Norm." *Modern Language Notes,* 47. (Reprinted in *Essays in the History of Ideas.* Baltimore: Johns Hopkins University Press, 1948.)

Miller, M. (1993). *The Garden as an Art.* Albany, NY: State University of New York Press.

Monk, S. H. (1935). *The Sublime: A Study of Critical Theories in 18th Century England.* New York: Language Association. (Reprinted Ann Arbor: University of Michigan Press, 1970.)

Nash, R. (1967). *Wilderness and the American Mind.* New Haven, CT: Yale University Press. (Revised edn 1973.)

Nicolson, M. H. (1959). *Mountain Gloom and Mountain Glory: The Development of the Aesthetics of the Infinite.* Ithaca, NY: Cornell University Press. (Reprinted New York: Norton, 1963.)

Onions, C. T., ed. (1966). *Oxford Dictionary of English Etymology.* Oxford: Clarendon Press.

Pevsner, N. (1944). "The Genesis of the Picturesque." *Architectural Review,* 96: 139–46. (Included in Pevsner, *Studies in Art, Architecture and Design.* New York: Walker, 1968: 78–101.)

Reid, T. (1785). "Of Taste." In *Essays on the Intellectual Powers of Man.* Edinburgh. (Also in *The Philosophical Works of Thomas Reid,* ed. William Hamilton. 8th edn, 2 vols. Edinburgh: James Thin, 1895. Reprinted as *Thomas Reid: Philosophical Works.* 2 vols. Hildesheim: Georg Olms, 1967: I, 506.)

Ross, S. (1987). "The Picturesque: An Eighteenth-Century Debate." *Journal of Aesthetics and Art Criticism,* 46(2): 271–9.

——(1998). *What Gardens Mean.* Chicago and London: University of Chicago Press.

——(n.d.). "Ecofeminism: A Misguided Marriage." Unpublished manuscript.

Ross, W. D. (1959). *Aristotle.* New York: Barnes & Noble.

Schelling, F. W. J. (1800). *System des Transcendentalen Idealismus.* (Trans. Peter Heath (1978) as *System of Transcendental Idealism.* Charlottesville: University Press of Virginia.)

Shaftesbury, Anthony Ashley Cooper, third Earl of, *The Moralists: A Philosophical Rhapsody* (1709). (Ed. John M. Robertson. London, 1900.)

Solger, K. W. F. (1829). *Vorlesungen über Ästhetik* [*Lectures on Aesthetics*]. Leipzig: Brockhaus. (Delivered 1819.)

Sparshott, F. (1982). *The Theory of the Arts.* Princeton, NJ: Princeton University Press.

Stolnitz, J. (1960). *Aesthetics and Philosophy of Art Criticism.* Boston: Houghton Mifflin.

Townsend, D., ed. (1996). *Aesthetics: Classical Readings from the Western Tradition.* Sudbury, MA: Jones and Bartlett.

Tuan, Y.-F. (1984). *Dominance and Affection: The Making of Pets.* New Haven, CT: Yale University Press.

*Webster's Third New International Dictionary of the English Language* (1961). Unabridged edn. Springfield, MA: G. & C. Merriam Co.

# Chapter 18

# Art and the Aesthetic: The Religious Dimension
## Nicholas Wolterstorff

### 18.1

A standard part of the canon used for introducing students to aesthetic theory of the twentieth century is the first section, titled "The Aesthetic Hypothesis," of the opening chapter of Clive Bell's *Art* (Bell 1914); one finds this section reproduced in almost all the standard anthologies. What is never reproduced is the third section, "The Metaphysical Hypothesis," or the opening section of the second chapter, "Art and Religion." As good a way as any into our topic is to consider what Bell says in these two sections. We have to begin, though, with the opening section.

Bell begins his line of thought in the essay by ringingly affirming that there is an aesthetic emotion: "All sensitive people agree," he says, "that there is a peculiar emotion provoked by works of art." He does not mean, he adds, "that all works provoke the same emotion. On the contrary, every work produces a different emotion. But all these emotions are recognisably the same in kind; so far, at any rate, the best opinion is on my side" (Bell 1914: 17). As he proceeds, it becomes clear that the emotion Bell has in mind is a species of joy – or as he rather often calls it, "ecstasy." Likewise it becomes clear that one experiences the aesthetic emotion when one's mode of engagement with a work of art is contemplation.

The question Bell asks in the opening section of the book is, then, what it is in works of art that evokes, upon contemplation, that joy which is the aesthetic emotion. Answering this question, so he says, is "the central problem" of aesthetics. Furthermore, if we can find what it is that evokes the aesthetic emotion, we will also "have discovered the essential quality in a work of art, the quality that distinguishes works of art from all other classes of objects" (Bell 1914: 17). The answer to the central problem of aesthetics will be at the same time the answer to the fundamental question in theory of art.

Bell's well-known answer to his question is that *form* is what evokes the aesthetic emotion. Sometimes he calls it *significant* form. But by the adjective "significant" he just means form that evokes the aesthetic emotion in qualified percipients. So his thesis is simply that it's the form of a work of art that evokes, upon contemplation, that particular species of joy which is the aesthetic emotion.

Content of whatever type – representation, symbol, expressiveness – is irrelevant to the aesthetic emotion. There's nothing wrong with content; Bell is not arguing that only abstract art is truly art. "Let no one imagine that representation is bad in itself; a realistic form may be as significant, in its place as part of the design, as an abstract. But if a representative form has value, it is as form, not as representation" (Bell 1914: 27). Nor is there anything wrong with enjoying the content, or enjoying such reveries as may be evoked by attending to content – or indeed, by attending to form. To do so, however, is to "have tumbled from the superb peaks of aesthetic exaltation to the snug foothills of warm humanity. It is a jolly country. No one need be ashamed of enjoying himself there." But "let no one imagine, because he has made merry in the warm tilth and quaint nooks of romance, that he can even guess at the austere and thrilling raptures of those who have climbed the cold, white peaks of art" (Bell 1914: 31).

That last passage makes clear Bell's evaluation of the worth of aesthetic emotion. It is, he says, one of "the most valuable things in the world" – "a gift beyond all price." So "valuable, indeed, that in my giddier moments I have been tempted to believe that art might prove the world's salvation" (Bell 1914: 32). What accounts for this high value is that attention to form puts us in touch with a "world" that transcends the ordinary practical concerns of human beings. "Art transports us from the world of man's activity to a world of aesthetic exaltation. For a moment we are shut off from human interests, our anticipations and memories are arrested; we are lifted above the stream of life" (Bell 1914: 27). We "inhabit a world with an intense and peculiar significance of its own; that significance is unrelated to the significance of life. In this world the emotions of life find no place. It is a world with emotions of its own" (Bell 1914: 28).

The language Bell here uses to develop his "aesthetic hypothesis" carries unmistakable echoes of religious language; indeed, it *is* religious language. "A gift beyond all price." "The world's salvation." "Lifted above the stream of life." "Out of life into ecstasy." A world "whose significance is unrelated to the significance of life." The thought that lies behind the religious language comes to the surface in those other two sections of *Art* that I mentioned, "The Metaphysical Hypothesis" and "Art and Religion."

Bell opens the former of these two sections by posing what he calls "the metaphysical question": why do certain arrangements and combinations of form move us so strangely? Form moves us, so he begins his suggestion, "because it expresses the emotion of its creator" (Bell 1914: 43). And what sort of emotion is that? Very often, it's the emotion the artist felt upon contemplating certain natural objects as *pure forms*. The emotion the artist expresses is of the same sort as that which we feel upon contemplating his work. "The emotion that the artist felt in his moment of inspiration he did not feel for objects seen as means, but for objects seen as pure forms – that is, as ends in themselves . . . [I]n the moment of aesthetic vision he sees objects, not as means shrouded in associations, but as pure forms" (Bell 1914: 44–5).

To see objects "as pure forms is to see them as ends in themselves" (Bell 1914: 45). So the question becomes, in turn, what "is the significance of anything as an end in itself? What is that which is left when we have stripped a thing of all its associations, of all its significance as a means" (Bell 1914: 45)? Bell professes to be somewhat shy about offering his answer; but his hypothesis is that what's left is "that which philosophers used to call 'the thing in itself' and now call 'ultimate reality'" (Bell 1914: 45).

> If an object considered as an end in itself moves us more profoundly (*i.e.* has greater significance) than the same object considered as a means to practical ends or as a thing related to human interests – and this undoubtedly is the case – we can only suppose that when we consider anything as an end in itself we become aware of that in it which is of greater moment than any qualities it may have acquired from keeping company with human beings. Instead of recognising its accidental and conditioned importance, we become aware of its essential reality, of the God in everything, of the universal in the particular, of the all-pervading rhythm. Call it by what name you will, the thing that I am talking about is that which lies behind the appearance of all things – that which gives to all things their individual significance, the thing in itself, the ultimate reality. (Bell 1914: 54)

So back to the question: why are we so profoundly moved by contemplation of form? Because, says Bell, we are responding to an artist's expression in form of an emotion felt for that ultimate reality which reveals itself through form. Significant form is

> form behind which we catch a sense of ultimate reality . . . [T]he emotion which artists feel in their moments of inspiration, that others feel in the rare moments when they see objects artistically, and that many of us feel when we contemplate works of art, are the same in kind. All [are] emotions felt for reality revealing itself through pure form. (Bell 1914: 46)

That art is "a means to a state of exaltation is unanimously agreed, and that it comes from the spiritual depths of man's nature is hardly contested . . . Art is, in fact, a necessity to and a product of the spiritual life, . . . to which it gives and from which . . . it takes" (Bell 1914: 59). It is for this reason that, for some, anyway, art "makes life worth living" (Bell 1914: 59).

Art is thus kin to religion. The physical universe for the mystic, as for the artist, is

> a means to ecstasy. The mystic feels things as 'ends' instead of seeing them as 'means.' He seeks within all things that ultimate reality which provokes emotional exaltation;

and if he does not come at it through pure form, there are . . . more roads than one to that country. Religion, as I understand it, is an expression of the individual's sense of the emotional significance of the universe. (Bell 1914: 62)

Both art and religion "have the power of transporting men to superhuman ecstasies; both are means to unearthly states of mind. Art and religion belong to the same world . . . The kingdom of neither is of this world" (Bell 1914: 63).

"Between aesthetic and religious rapture there is [thus] a family alliance." "Art and Religion are . . . two roads by which men escape from circumstance to ecstasy" (Bell 1914: 68), twin manifestations of man's "religious sense" – provided we mean by this, man's sense of ultimate reality (Bell 1914: 69). Art is not the expression or manifestation of any particular religion. To think thus would be "to confuse the religious spirit with the channels in which it has been made to flow" (Bell 1914: 69). To be sure, "many descriptive paintings are manifestos and expositions of religious dogmas"; there's nothing wrong with that. "But in so far as a picture is a work of art, it has no more to do with dogmas or doctrines, facts or theories, than with the interests and emotions of daily life" (Bell 1914: 69). Art is related rather to "that universal emotion that has found a corrupt and stuttering expression in a thousand different creeds" (Bell 1914: 69). The mystic and the art lover represent "twin manifestations of the spirit" (Bell 1914: 63).

## 18.2

A number of the particularities of Bell's discussion mark him as very much a theorist of the modern period. I will shortly be taking note of some of those particularities. But before I do so, let me call attention to the fact that there's a long lineage behind Bell's suggestion that what ultimately accounts for the character of aesthetic joy is that in experiencing such joy we are in touch with ultimate reality. We are all acquainted with Kant's thoroughly secular account of aesthetic delight. The source of aesthetic delight – or pleasure in beauty, as Kant describes it – is the delight one gets from the free play of one's cognitive faculties. Nothing of the transcendent here! But behind Kant there was an older tradition; and it was this older tradition that Bell was carrying on in his own way – whether wittingly or not, I do not know.

The topic of *Enneads* I.6 of Plotinus is beauty. The account as a whole is very much reminiscent of Plato's discussion in the *Symposium*. Rather than beginning at the top, as it were, Plotinus begins, as did Plato, at the bottom, with physical manifestations of beauty. What is it, he asks, "that attracts the gaze of those who look at something, and turns and draws them to it and makes them enjoy the sight? If we find this perhaps we can use it as a stepping-stone and get a sight of the rest" (I.6.1). Beauty is that which, by definition, gives delight in the contemplating. If we can discover what it is that gives delight in the contemplating, we will thereby have discovered the nature of beauty. The similarity of Bell's question to this of Plotinus is striking!

The answer of the Pythagorean-Platonic tradition to this opening question was that beauty consists in due proportion of parts. Plotinus dissents. Among the things that are beautiful are some in which there are no perceptually discriminable parts related to each other in some proportioned way – colors, for example, and the light of the sun, gold, stars, lightning in the night. All of these are, or can be, beautiful, the proof of which is that they give us delight in the contemplating; yet there's no due proportion of perceptually discriminable parts. And when it comes to non-perceptual things, like beautiful ways of life, beautiful characters, beautiful modes of thought, beautifully developed laws, the concept of *proportion of parts* just seems to have no application – no *literal* application, at any rate.

With the Pythagorean-Platonic account out of the way, Plotinus again poses his question: what constitutes beauty in bodies? We know that it's "something which we become aware of even at the first glance; the soul speaks of it as if it understood it, recognizes and welcomes it and as it were adapts itself to it." Accordingly, the explanation he will develop, says Plotinus, is "that the soul, since it is by nature what it is and is related to the higher kind of reality in the realm of being, when it sees something akin to it or a trace of its kindred reality, is delighted and thrilled and returns to itself and remembers itself and its own possessions" (I.6.2).

What then is that "higher kind of reality" of which beauty in bodies is a "trace," that trace evoking in us a delight and thrill because it reminds us of what truly belongs to us? *Form*, says Plotinus; "the things in this world are beautiful by participating in form." More specifically, *unity*. "Beauty rests upon the material things when it has been brought into unity" – be it the unity of a complex or the unity of a simple.

Having begun with beauties present to the senses, Plotinus proceeds along the path of a classic Platonic ascent to beauties revealed only to the intellect – until, going beyond even the Forms, we arrive finally at the One, God, "the good which every soul desires" (I.6.7). What we discover along the way is the beauty of a unified self, and wherein lies that beauty. As with everything else, "the soul's becoming something good and beautiful is its being made like to God, because from Him [comes] beauty" (I.6.6). A beautiful unified self is perforce a moral self; hence ethics is revealed to be a subdivision of aesthetics. At the same time it's revealed to be a condition of aesthetic ascent; for what we discover is that we cannot advance far up the scale of beauty without ourselves becoming beautiful. If anyone comes

blear-eyed with wickedness, and unpurified, or weak and by his cowardice unable to look at what is very bright, he sees nothing, even if someone shows him what is there and possible to see. For one must come to the sight with a seeing power made akin and like to what is seen. No eye ever saw the sun without becoming sun-like, nor can a soul see beauty without becoming beautiful. You must become first all godlike and all beautiful if you intend to see God and beauty. (I.6.9)

As one ascends this scale of beauty, the joy one experiences in the contemplation of beauty becomes ever more intense. Plotinus' language is rhapsodic even when speaking of our enjoyment of the beauty of sensed objects. "Whenever there is contact with any sort of beautiful things, wonder and a shock of delight and longing and passion and a happy excitement" are the consequence, he says (I.6.4). But when contemplating beauty in things that cannot be sensed but only known intellectually, we are not just delighted and excited but "overwhelmed" (I.6.4). And when finally we arrive at the One, if we ever do, what we experience is a "shock of delight" and a desire for union. "The man who has not seen it may desire it as good, but he who has seen it glories in its beauty and is full of wonder and delight, enduring a shock which causes no hurt, loving with true passion and piercing longing" (I.6.7).

## 18.3

I have skipped over many of the details of Plotinus' exposition – for example, his contention that in one way God (the One) is paradigmatically beautiful whereas, in another way, God is beyond beauty – because my purpose on this occasion is not to engage in Plotinus exegesis but to indicate that Clive Bell represents in the contemporary world a long tradition in the West of regarding beauty (or aesthetic excellence) as in one way or another related to "the Transcendent," and of regarding the delight we experience in our contemplation of something beautiful (or aesthetically excellent) as grounded in some sort of intimation of this Transcendent.

Many of us, when listening to some piece of music, looking at some painting or sculpture, experiencing some work of architecture, have had a strange, mysterious feeling of exaltation. It's that experience that those who appropriate and participate in this tradition of transcendental accounts of beauty begin with; they are convinced that purely secular accounts, such as that which Kant offers, are inadequate. How they proceed from that beginning depends very much on their particular metaphysic and theology. Plotinus was working with a generally Platonic picture, according to which things in this world are beautiful on account of their resemblance to, and participation in, the paradigmatically beautiful being – viz., the form Beauty, and behind that, the divine One. Bell, by contrast, was operating with a pantheistic picture, according to which God, or Ultimate Reality, is manifested in form. And these are but two of many.

One's evaluation of a particular transcendental account of beauty will depend very much then on one's evaluation of the theology. My own theology is closer, in the relevant respects, to Plotinus than to Bell: I regard God as the paradigmatically excellent being, and I hold that what accounts for some entity other than God being excellent in some respect is that it stands in some excellence-transmitting relation to that paradigmatically excellent being. The contemporary fashion of trying to account for excellence in terms of counterfactual desire-satisfaction seems to me a dead end. But I am not persuaded that this metaphysical account of excellence – God alone is intrinsically excellent, everything else is extrinsically excellent, having its excellence transmitted to it by virtue of its relation to the intrinsically excellent being – has much of anything to do with our experience of excellence in entities other than God. This work of music that I'm listening to is excellent, more specifically, beautiful; though its excellence has been transmitted to it from something intrinsically excellent, nonetheless it is now itself excellent. How does the metaphysical fact that its excellence is extrinsic explain the exaltation I feel in listening to it? How does that metaphysical fact intrude itself, as it were, into the experience, so that in some inchoate way it's God – the paradigmatically and intrinsically excellent being – that I'm delighting in? I fail to see that it does. Yet I too feel that secular accounts don't explain my feeling of exaltation. The suggestion that I'm just enjoying the harmonious working of my faculties strikes me as a non-starter!

## 18.4

We saw that in his discussion of art and religion, Bell dismisses with a wave of the hand any consideration of the relation between art and *actual* religions. When we're dealing with actual religions we're dealing with "doctrines and dogmas," creeds, claims to historical fact, "metaphysical fancies" – that sort of thing. Often art does have such things as its content. But content has nothing to do with the aesthetic emotion, and nothing to do with the essence of art. It's Bell's formalism that steers him away from consideration of how art and religion do actually engage each other.

Bell's approach is, in this regard, like that of a good many of those theologians of the contemporary period who have systematically discussed the relation of art to religion. Let me cite the two that seem to me the most significant, Gerardus Vander Leeuw and Paul Tillich.

Vander Leeuw was an extraordinary Dutch polymath who spent the first third of his career as an anthropologist of religion, the next third of his career as a theologian and aesthetician, and the last third as a theorist of liturgy. The great, endlessly fascinating, book from his middle career, in which he probes the relation between art and religion – or as he puts it, the beautiful and the holy – is *Sacred and Profane Beauty: The Holy in Art*. Like Bell, Vander Leeuw acknowledges all sorts of "external connections," as he calls them, between the beautiful and the holy. None of those is of any interest to him, however. What he's after is "the essential continuity." To get at that we must "protect ourselves against the external continuity which forces itself upon us. Nine-tenths of the 'religious works of art' which we know evidence no inner, essential continuity between holiness and beauty, having only a purely external connection, which admittedly can be very refined, violating neither art nor religion, but not proclaiming their unity" (Vander Leeuw 1963: 230). What grips Vander Leeuw's interest is not the aesthetic emotion and its religious significance, however, but rather those cases in which a work of art is intrinsically *expressive* of the holy. Whether Bell would be sympathetic to this approach is not clear, since it's not apparent from his discussion whether he regards expressiveness as a feature of form.

Paul Tillich was an eminent German theologian who emigrated to the United States shortly before World War II. Alongside his systematic theology he developed a theology of culture; it was within this that he discussed the relation of religion to art. In Tillich's case it was more his understanding of religion than his commitment to artistic formalism that led to his lack of interest in the actualities of the engagement between religion and art.

Religion, he says, can be understood as "activities within a group of human beings who have a set of symbols and rites, related to divine powers." But it can also be understood as "the state of ultimate concern about something ultimate" (Tillich 1987: 172). If it's religion in the first of these senses that we have in mind, "then the religious dimension of art could only mean the use by art of the symbolic material provided by a historical religion. In this way, the arts have used as subject matter the story of the Christ, the legends of the saints, the mythical symbols of creation, salvation, consummation," and so forth.

As a theologian of culture, this sort of art is not of concern to him, says Tillich. In the contemporary world it comes to very little. Given the decline of religion thus understood in the face of the heavily secularized character of our contemporary "encounter with reality," religion in this sense "provided an astonishingly small amount of content for the visual arts" in the twentieth century (Tillich 1987: 172). We must not assume, however, that the emergence of contemporary secularism means the disappearance of religion in that other, broader sense. Quite to the contrary. Secularism

> does not deny the question of the ultimate meaning of life. With respect to the larger concept of religion, secularism is indirectly religious. Just as religion in the narrow sense has many forms, so secularism exhibits many forms in which the question of the meaning of life is asked, not only intellectually, but with a total concern and an infinite seriousness. (Tillich 1987: 173)

Accordingly, when looking at art of the twentieth century – and indeed, art of any century – it will be with the religious dimension *thus understood* that he will be concerned, says Tillich, his thesis being that all creative art, including then the art that emerged from the secular culture of the twentieth century, "is an expression of an encounter . . . with 'ultimate reality.' [All art] contains an answer to the question of meaning" (Tillich 1987: 173). It was Tillich's view that what's determinative of the subject matter of art is *style*, and what's inherent to art is *expressiveness*. Hence it's to the religion of which the style is expressive that Tillich proposes to attend; it's through the expressiveness of style that "the religious dimension is manifested."

## 18.5

There's something very strange about the approach of the thinkers I have cited – and they are only a sampling – to the issue of art and religion. Surely the way in which icons function in the religious practices of eastern Orthodoxy, the way in which chant functions in the religious practices of Judaism, and the way in which congregational hymns function in the religious practices of Protestantism – to mention only a few examples – represent to the people involved in these practices an extraordinarily important engagement of religion with art. Yet all such modes of engagement are dismissed by these thinkers as not worthy of their attention. The reasons offered are in each case slightly different; but the result is the same. The only mode of engagement that's of interest to them is *contemplation*; such alternative modes of engagement as veneration of icons and congregational singing of hymns falls outside their purview. Furthermore, whereas the representational content of the painting hanging in the church is of great concern to the Orthodox worshipper, as are the words sung by the cantor in the synagogue and by the congregation in the Protestant church, this too is of no interest to these thinkers. What's of interest is only the formal features of the artwork and its expressiveness.

What is it that accounts for this strange lack of interest in the actualities of the way in which religious people engage the arts, and in the representational and symbolic content of the works they engage? As already remarked, the reasons given for the dismissal of representational and symbolic content vary a bit from thinker to thinker. What's striking, however, is that none of them offers any reason at all for focusing entirely on the contemplative mode of engagement. The propriety of this is simply taken for granted. I suggest that what this indicates is that all of them accept without question the grand narrative concerning the place of the arts in human existence that emerged in the eighteenth century and has remained the dominant narrative in the West ever since.

Here, on this occasion, I must content myself with stripping down the story line to its essentials. It goes like this. Once upon a time the arts were in service to all sorts of interests extraneous to the arts themselves: to ecclesiastical interests, to political interests, to the interests of the aristocracy, to commercial interests, even to magical interests. Then in the eighteenth century the arts began to be, to a significant extent, liberated from these extraneous interests and allowed to come into their own. Artists were freed to follow out the internal dynamics of the art in question, rather than being in the service of princes, bishops, entrepreneurs, and so forth; the arts became autonomous, self-normed. And we the public were likewise freed to treat works of art *as* works of art rather than as means to worshipping God, evoking rain, or whatever. We were freed to treat works of art as ends in themselves. To treat them thus is to concern ourselves with their internal qualities and relationships, rather than concerning ourselves with how they relate to one thing and another outside themselves. Our concern is now with their "internal rationality."

That's the heart of the grand narrative. I submit that it's because they accept the narrative without question that Bell, Vander Leeuw, Tillich, and their cohorts focus exclusively on the contemplative mode of engagement with art in their discussion of art and religion, without even bothering to give a reason for such exclusivity. What to their mind is worth considering is only whether, when we're concerned with the religious dimension of art for contemplation, we should attend to such representational and symbolic content as may be present or should concern ourselves exclusively with form and its inherent expressiveness.

There's much that's strange about the story, taken for granted though it usually is. Let me take note of just one oddity. Works of art, like chairs and shovels, are human artifacts, produced with some purpose in mind – that purpose normally being some intended use. Chairs are made for sitting on; they "come into their own" when thus used. They can be put to other uses, or to no use. They can be displayed in art museums or stored in attics without ever being used. But in such a case, the chair isn't "coming into its own." And as for the sort of art on which the grand narrative has its eye: such art is made for contemplation. It can be used for other purposes; a sculpture made for contemplation can be used as a door stop. But when thus used, the sculpture isn't "coming into its own." It's "coming into its own" when people engage it as an object of contemplation.

Now consider the Orthodox icons. They come into their own not when they're hung in an Orthodox church and venerated, not when they're displayed in some art museum and engaged as objects of contemplation. They can function in this latter way; many of them do so function. But when so functioning, they aren't "coming into their own." So too with the Jewish chant and the Protestant hymns: they come into their own when they function liturgically, not when Joshua Cohen and his Boston Camerata record them on a CD disk.

The moral should be clear: if it's with art "come into its own" that we are concerned, then, when considering the relations between art and religion, we will have to look beyond art meant for aesthetic contemplation. The point is not that there's nothing of interest to be said about the religious significance of museum paintings, concert-hall music, and reading-room poetry; the point is that those who have focused exclusively on that have neglected the thing of first importance, namely, the actual ways in which the religions of humanity have engaged the arts.

## 18.6

Suppose we embrace the broader perspective. What will we then take note of? We will take note of the fact that for the religious person poetry is often not so much contemplated as interiorized, so that the words of the poet become words the person uses to express her own feelings, convictions, apprehensions, and so forth. We will take note of the fact that for the religious person stories often function not as objects of aesthetic delight but as narratives into which one's own life and that of others are fitted. We will take note of the fact that for the religious person music often functions to enhance one's praise of God rather than as an object of contemplation, be it for aesthetic or other purposes. We will take note of the fact that symbols regularly function for the religious person as *reminders*; remembering is fundamental to most religions. And so forth, on and on. And having taken note of this diversity of ways in which religious people engage the arts, we will try to understand them theoretically.

Of course, once one notices the diversity of ways in which art functions in religious practice, the thought quickly comes to mind that many of these have their close analogues outside of religion as well. Attending to the ways in which art and religion engage each other can be of service to theory of art in general by freeing us from the narrowness of vision induced by the grand narrative. Contemplation, and in particular, contemplation for the purpose of aesthetic delight, is just one of a multiplicity of ways of engaging the arts – just one of a multiplicity of *worthwhile* ways.

It is of visual images that Bell, Vander Leeuw, and Tillich were especially dismissive in their discussions of art and religion. So let me take the bait, descend from the high level of generality of the preceding paragraph, and say something about the role of images in religion. To understand that role we need a far richer understanding of how images function than the constricted view one typically finds in modern and contemporary theories of art; that richer understanding, once acquired, will prove in turn to open our eyes to things we overlooked in the role of images outside of religion.

To prevent my discussion from becoming too diffuse I'll have to focus on just one of the ways in which images function in religion, and on just one religion. The religion I will focus on will be the one I know best, namely, Christianity; the reader will easily be able to generalize to other religions. (An excellent historical introduction to the role of images that I will be discussing is Hans Belting's *Likeness and Presence: A History of the Image before the Era of Art* [1994].)

Fundamental to what it is that makes the Christian tradition distinct is that those who identify with the tradition tell a story of God's dealings with human beings – a story that begins with narratives contained in the Christian scriptures and then continues from there up to the present. As one would expect, the story told by one individual and by one subcommunity is somewhat different from that told by another; strictly speaking, then, we should speak not of *the* Christian story but of the *family* of Christian stories. But for my purposes here there will be no harm in speaking as if there were just one Christian story.

With the fact firmly in mind that the Christian tradition has a Christian story, suppose one looks at the representational visual art produced over the centuries by and for members of the Christian community. What then strikes us is that a great deal of this art, if not most of it, represents important individuals and incidents from the Christian story.

How should we understand this? I suggest that the function of such art is understood as what I will call *memorial* art. Let me explain. Fundamental to the lives of human beings in general is *commemoration*. All sorts of things are done by us in commemoration, and all sorts of things are produced as commemorations: coins are struck, stamps are issued, fireworks are shot off, speeches are given, trees are planted, cities are founded, academic conferences are held, etc. Evidently something deep in us comes to expression in our surrounding ourselves with commemorative objects and in our repetitively engaging in commemorative activities.

What is that? Well, for each of us there are certain persons and events that we regard it as important for us and our community to remember. In fact, however, we find ourselves and our community often forgetting what we think it's important to remember; or if we don't actually forget, we find that we fail to keep those things clearly in mind. Commemorations serve the function of keeping alive the memory of someone or something that we want not to forget. Commemorations enhance memory.

And why do we find it important to enhance memory? No doubt for many reasons. But especially prominent among our reasons for wishing to enhance memory is the desire to praise or honor: we issue a coin in commemoration of Susan B. Anthony not just to remember her but to honor her. Indeed, I am inclined to think that if we look closely enough at commemorations, we will always discern some element of honoring – though that's not always what first catches the eye.

A great deal more could be said about commemorations. But let me restrain myself and move to the application: among the sorts of things produced as commemorations, works of visual representational art are prominent. Upon the retirement of its president, the university commissions a portrait so as to commemorate him; the United States commissioned the Lincoln Memorial, with its imposing sculpture, so as to commemorate the Great Emancipator. Both of these are cases of memorial art, of commemorative art. Yes, one can contemplate them so as to discern, evaluate, and perhaps revel in their aesthetic qualities. But that's not why we have them, nor is that how they function for most viewers.

Very much of the visual representational art produced by and for the Christian community is memorial art – as, for example, is a great deal of the visual art produced by and for the Buddhist community. It became common in western medieval Christianity to say that the point of the images in the church was to instruct the illiterate. That seems to me not so much false as incomplete. The sort of instruction that the images performed was that of *reminding* the faithful of important persons and incidents in the Christian story. But they did more than merely remind; they commemorated. And their commemorative function was as relevant to the literate as to the non-literate.

Art has often stirred up controversy, and does so yet today. However, no controversy over art has ever matched the length and ferocity of the Byzantine iconoclast controversy, lasting for roughly a century and a quarter from its beginnings around 725. Late in the controversy, an empress who found herself on the opposite side of the issue from her son had his eyes gouged out; our contemporary controversies pale before that.

The controversy was over memorial art; in fact, rather often the defenders of the icons spoke of them as "memorials" of holy persons. There were several distinct flash-points of controversy. The opponents of the icons, the so-called "iconoclasts," had their doubts about the worth of composing images of Christ and the saints; they argued that it was far more important to image the saints in one's soul and life than on wooden boards. And they accused the defenders, the "iconodules," of implicit heresy in the icons of Christ. But one of the main points of controversy concerned the proper mode of engagement with these iconic memorials. The iconodules insisted that they should be venerated by means of such gestures as kissing them, kneeling and lighting candles before them, and so forth. The iconoclasts insisted that nothing of the sort should be done; veneration was tantamount to idolatry.

As part of their argument in defense of veneration, the iconodules developed theories of the iconic image according to which in looking at an image of a person one sees the person – provided the image has been produced as a rendering of the person. And since surely it would be appropriate to offer gestures of veneration if one were looking at a saint in the flesh before one, how could it be wrong to offer such gestures when one was seeing the saint by way of looking at an icon of him or her?

This raises fascinating and complicated questions. I dare say that most of us would be reluctant to say, when looking at a portrait of the current president of the United States, that we were seeing the president; yet it would come naturally to us to say that we saw the president on TV. Well, if we can see him on TV, how about seeing him in a photograph? And if in a photograph, why not in a painting?

Be all that as it may, however, what I want to highlight is that act of veneration around which the controversy swirled. If we've been seduced by the modern grand narrative of the arts into thinking exclusively of contemplation as the way of engaging the arts, veneration will seem like a by-gone piece of magic. But not so. Most of us would be reluctant to stomp on a picture of our mother – unless we hated her. Why is that? And the feeling of horror that we would experience if we saw a Rembrandt being slashed – how exactly is that different from what an iconodule would feel if someone spat at an icon? There is, indeed, one crucial difference between these last two examples: in the case of the Rembrandt, it's the painter that we venerate; his subject is pretty much indifferent to us. In the case of the icon, it was the subject that the iconodule venerated; he seldom even knew who had painted it. But veneration has by no means disappeared from our engagement with works of art.

18.7

Let me close by suggesting, without on this occasion exploring, yet a third approach to our topic of "Art and the Aesthetic: The Religious Dimension."

According to the modern grand narrative of art that I briefly discussed earlier, art in the eighteenth century finally freed itself from service to religion. What strikes anyone who follows out the various tellings of the narrative, however, is how often this liberated art is described in religious terms, and how often religious hopes and expectations are lodged in it. I described Bell, in his transcendental account of beauty, as continuing in his own way a long tradition that goes back to Plotinus, and back behind that to Plato. At the same time, however, Bell is thoroughly modern. The modern narrative of art was caught up by the Romantics into their even grander narrative of modernity, according to which modernity in the polity, in the academy, in the economy, in institutional religion, represents the fragmentation of what was once-upon-a-time unified. Art, however, provided it's liberated art, art produced purely for contemplation, represents the great social exception: here we still find unity. Perhaps, just perhaps, the unity that we still find in art will prove salvific.

In his excellent article, "Art-as-Such: The Sociology of Modern Aesthetics," the literary theorist M. H. Abrams first takes note of some formulations of the Augustinian tradition of "the selfless and gratuitous contemplation of the ultimate beauty of God" (Abrams 1989: 156), and then notes how much of the language used in that tradition both for the act and for the object of contemplation was borrowed by art theorists in the latter part of the eighteenth century and the first part of the nineteenth century to articulate their defense of the priority of engaging the arts contemplatively. Here, for example, is a passage that Abrams quotes from Karl Philipp Moritz, writing in 1785, that is redolent of Augustinian language:

> While the beautiful draws our attention exclusively to itself . . . we seem to lose ourselves in the beautiful object; and precisely this loss, this forgetfulness of self, is the highest degree of pure and disinterested pleasure that beauty grants us. In that moment we sacrifice our individual confined being to a kind of higher being . . . Beauty in a work of art is not pure . . . until I contemplate it as something that has been brought forth entirely for its own sake, in order that it should be something complete in itself. (Abrams 1989:156)

An exploration of this eminently modern religious understanding of art and its powers would take us into such nineteenth-century figures as Schiller, Schopenhauer, and Matthew Arnold, and into such twentieth-century figures as Heidegger, Marcuse, and Adorno.

## References

Abrams, M. H. (1971). *Natural Supernaturalism*. New York: W. W. Norton.
——(1989). *Doing Things with Texts: Essays in Criticism and Critical Theory*, ed. Michael Fischer. New York: W. W. Norton. (See esp. "Art-as-Such: The Sociology of Modern

Aesthetics" [135–58] and "From Addison to Kant: Modern Aesthetics and the Exemplary Art" [159–85].)

Adorno, T. W. (1984). *Aesthetic Theory*, trans. C. Lenhardt. London: Routledge and Kegan Paul.

Bell, C. (1914). *Art*. London: Chatto & Windus.

Belting, H. (1994). *Likeness and Presence: A History of the Image before the Era of Art*. Chicago: University of Chicago Press.

Brown, F. B. (1989). *Religious Aesthetics: A Theological Study of Making and Meaning*. Princeton, NJ: Princeton University Press.

Heidegger, M. (1971). *Poetry, Language, Thought*, trans. and intro. Albert Hofstadter. New York: Harper Colophon.

John of Damascus (1980). *On the Divine Images*, trans. David Anderson. Crestwood, NY: St Vladimir's Press.

Marcuse, H. (1978) *The Aesthetic Dimension: Toward a Critique of Marxist Aesthetics*. Boston: Beacon Press.

Plotinus (1966). *Enneads*, trans. M. H. Armstrong. Cambridge, MA: Harvard University Press.

Schiller, F. (1967). *On the Aesthetic Education of Man*, trans. E. Wilkinson and L. Willoughby. Oxford: Oxford University Press.

Schopenhauer, A. (1969). *The World as Will and Representation*, Vol. I, trans. E. F. J. Payne. New York: Dover Press.

Theodore of Studios (1980). *On the Holy Icons*, trans. Catharine Roth. Crestwood, NY: St Vladimir's Press.

Tillich, P. (1987). *On Art and Architecture*, eds John and Jane Dillenberger. New York: Crossroad. (See esp. "Existentialist Aspects of Modern Art" [89–101] and "Religious Dimensions of Contemporary Art" [171–87].)

Vander Leeuw, G. (1963). *Sacred and Profane Beauty: The Holy in Art*, trans. David C. Green, pref. Mircea Eliade. New York: Holt, Rinehart & Winston.

Wolterstorff, N. (1980). *Art in Action*. Grand Rapids: Eerdmans.

# Index

aboutness 58, 206

Abrams, M. H. 16, 196, 197, 338

abstract kinds/entities/types 79, 82, 83, 86, 90, 130–1, 182, 183, 189

absurd imaginings 242–6

action-type hypothesis 83

Addison, Joseph 18, 29, 37, 39, 42, 160; *Spectator* essays 16, 30, 31, 32, 33, 34–5, 153

adequation 225, 226

Adorno, Theodor 338

aesthetic concepts 164

"Aesthetic" movement 174

aesthetic objects 63, 67, 69, 71–6 *passim*, 143; require imaginative acts of consciousness 81

aesthetic values 68, 69, 99, 106, 107, 142, 152, 156, 157, 162; in nature 310

aesthetics 1–4, 63–77, 142–6; interpretation in 109–25; modern, origins of 15–44; musical 254, 257, 260; nature and environment 10–11, 66, 67, 306–24; properties and principles 96–8; remapping 152–66

affects 36, 37, 98

Agamemnon 293, 297

Albers, Josef 180–1

Alberti, L. B. 216, 218

Aldrich, Virgil 306

alienation 182

*All About Eve* (Mankiewicz) 243–4

allegories 299

allusion 89, 303

Alperson, Philip 9, 271

ambiguity 86, 207, 208, 217, 282, 302; moral 105; multiple 281

American transcendentalism 313

analogy 50, 181, 259, 261, 265, 268

analytical philosophy 204, 205, 223, 233

Andersen, Hans Christian 120

anthropology 3, 175, 277, 285, 331

anti-intentionalism 110, 115, 116, 123

anti-rationalism 199

anxiety 182, 188, 190

appearance 38

appreciation 65, 93, 104, 106, 115, 119, 245, 287; aesthetic 66, 67, 72, 75, 76, 306–24; artistic 72, 98; characterizing 154; cognitive aspects of 206; design 71; formalism and 207–8; literary 203–11 *passim*; musical 102, 256; nature 66, 76, 310–12; paradigms for 101; poetry 153; precondition for 205–6; tragedy 103

approval 101

Aquinas, St Thomas 153, 157

architecture 18, 39, 80, 83, 189, 308, 330

arguments 29, 85, 257–8, 261; a priori 235–7, 245; aesthetic 127, 142–6; anti-representationalist 259; cognitive 127; empirical 24; epistemic 127, 128, 129–40; inductive 24; moralizing claims leading to 116; ontological 127, 140–1; transcendental 170

Aristotle 5, 10, 48, 104, 132, 153, 172–3, 174, 184–5, 186, 271, 291, 295, 297, 298, 299, 316; *De Mundo* 317; *Generations of Animals* 319; *Metaphysics* 317; *Nicomachean Ethics* 294, 301; *Physics* 314–15; *Poetics* 196, 206, 278, 292, 294; *Rhetoric* 293

Arnheim, Rudolf 218, 230

LaVergne, TN USA
07 September 2010
196142LV00003B/2/A